Contents

Get Hooked is printed on environmentally friendly paper 

Published by Diamond Publications
PO Box 59, Bideford, Devon EX39 4YN.
Tel: 01271 860183 Fax: 01271 860064
Email: info@gethooked.co.uk Web Site: www.gethooked.co.uk

Editor: Graham Sleeman 01566 785754
Distribution: Jane Diamond 01271 860183
Advertising: Jane 01271 860183
Printed by Broglia Press 01202 621621

Cover Pictures: Chris Yates (Tench), Mike Weaver (Trout), Henry Gilbey (Wrasse).

Special thanks to the team at the Environment Agency, annually understanding partners and children, Mitch for the web, Mandy for 'databasing', Gavin for loads. IT'S A MONSTER!

ISBN 0-9527547-7-0

Welcome...

To the 10th annual edition of the Get Hooked Guide to Angling in South West England published in association with the Environment Agency.

Once again we have contacted EVERY fishery and association, known to us or the Environment Agency, throughout the area. Everyone who has responded is detailed in our directory, which has increased in size yet again and has over 800 entries, re-affirming our position as THE DEFINITIVE guide to angling throughout the South West of England.

May we take this annual opportunity to ask those who we don't know of to contact us for insertion in next year's issue, a directory entry, in the guide, and on the web site, costs you nothing. If you have access to the internet you can use the on line form to send us your details for inclusion on the web site database, or next year's guide as well as notifying us of any changes throughout the coming year. The website database will be updated on a regular basis. If technology has not caught up with you yet we find the phone or fax still works perfectly!

Within our editorials this year we have the regular Environment Agency section, covering all the latest byelaws and licensing details and we have contributions from charitable groups and many organisations dedicated to improving and supporting the sport. Please take the time to read them. I know everybody just looks at the pictures on the first browse, but all of these organisations need our support. Our tuition feature also makes a welcome return.

Talking to people throughout the preparation of this year's guide I got a real feeling of optimism. There are lots of initiatives to bring new people into fishing and although there are still a lot of questions over major issues throughout the sport, many seem are being addressed.

Our yearly thanks go out to all the advertisers and contributors who help us make this publication what it is. We know the advertising is successful and hope the new advertisers will benefit as much as those who have been with us from our first edition. An big thank you is due to all the tackle shops who have helped enormously in finding previously unknown (to us) fisheries and clubs, enabling us to make the directory so comprehensive. Our sea fishing section has, historically, been hard work but we are comitted to improving it and are pleased to see it almost double in size this year.

Thanks to everyone who made the effort and sent in pictures this year and apologies for not being able to get them all in. We would like to reiterate that most of the pictures are supplied by anglers and fishery owners, not professional photographers, so don't be too critical if some of them aren't pin sharp! All photos of catches from fisheries covered by guide are welcome.

Our Web Site 'Fish Finder' contains all the information published in our directory in a fully searchable format. There is no quicker way of finding fishing in the South West. If you feel advertising on our site may benefit your business please contact us.

Point your browser at:
www.gethooked.co.uk
Or Email us at: info@gethooked.co.uk

Ten years of Get Hooked and every issue has been able to provide more information than the last. We are very proud of what we do but please keep talking to us, we appreciate your comments and we strive to continue improving the guide.

From some of the best sea fishing to a huge, and ever increasing, variety of coarse fishing plus quality game fishing, on stillwaters and rivers, to equal anywhere in the country. The South West has a huge amount to offer anglers from all branches of the sport.

Enjoy your fishing

Graham Sleeman - Editor.

ENVIRONMENT AGENCY

The Environment Agency is the leading public body for protecting and enhancing the environment in England and Wales.

Our vision is a healthy, rich and diverse environment for present and future generations.

We contribute to sustainable development through the integrated management of air, land and water. Sustainable development is about ensuring a better quality of life for everyone, now and for generations to come.

Specific responsibilities for the Agency are fisheries, conservation, recreation, water resources, pollution prevention and control, waste management, flood defence and navigation.

Visit our website at:
www.environment-agency.gov.uk to find out more about the work of the Agency and your local environment.

A key element in our vision for the South West is looking after the region's important fisheries.

Fish are one of the best indicators of the state of rivers and lakes. Healthy and abundant freshwater fish stocks and populations will demonstrate the Agency's success in contributing towards sustainable development.

The work of the Agency helps fisheries in many ways. Some good examples are pollution-prevention, dealing with low river flows and habitat improvements.

In addition, the Agency's fisheries staff carry out a number of vital tasks.
These include:

- Controlling the pressure on fisheries through issuing licences and making byelaws

- Preventing damage to fish and fish stocks by effective enforcement of fishery laws
- Ensuring the health and abundance of fish stocks through regular fisheries surveys
- Rescuing fish when pollution incidents occur and minimising damage to fish stocks
- Carrying out habitat improvements
- Constructing fish passes
- Monitoring of fish stocks i.e. catch returns, juvenile surveys and fish counters
- Carrying out fisheries research to allow future improvements and developments
- Stocking fish to restore and improve fisheries.

Fisheries operations in South West Region are organised by staff based in the Agency's four areas.

They can be contacted as follows:

Cornwall:
Environment Agency
Sir John Moore House
Victoria Square
BODMIN PL31 1EB
Tel: 01208 78301
Fax: 01208 78321

Devon:
Environment Agency
Exminster House
Miller Way
EXMINSTER EX6 8AS
Tel: 01392 444000
Fax: 01392 316016

North Wessex:
Environment Agency
Rivers House
East Quay
BRIDGWATER TA6 4YS
Tel: 01278 457333
Fax: 01278 452985

South Wessex:
Environment Agency
Rivers House
Sunrise Business Park
Higher Shaftesbury Road
BLANDFORD DT11 8ST
Tel: 01258 456080
Fax: 01258 455998

Regional policy and planning issues are co-ordinated by the Strategic Environment Planning staff at the Regional Office (Manley House, Exeter Tel: 01392 444000).

The Region is advised by the South West Regional Fisheries, Ecology and Recreation Advisory Committee. The Committee usually sits four times a year and its meetings are open to the public and the media. A local fisheries group, known as a Fisheries Forum also meets in each of the four areas.

AGENCY REORGANISATION

During 2002, the Environment Agency underwent a national reorganisation - BRITE - Better Regulation Improving The Environment. The purpose of this is to enable the Agency to deliver improved environmental outcomes by operating more efficiently, regulating more effectively and consistently, whilst influencing and advising its customers.

The result of this reorganisation has brought some significant changes to the way the Agency works. However, the four area offices have remained as the main contact points for customers.

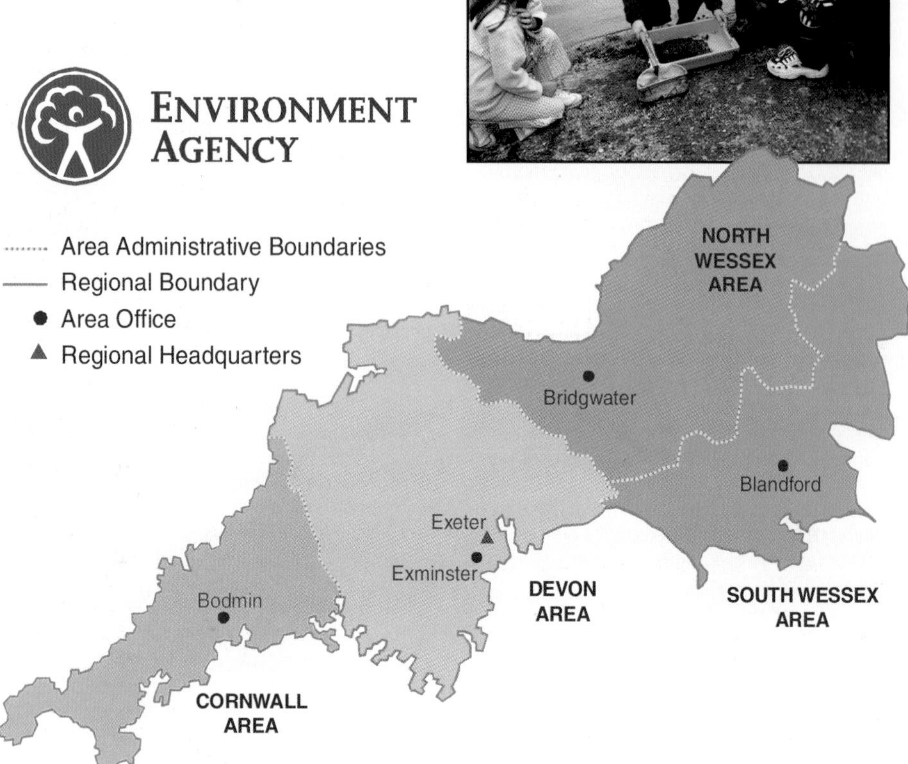

TEACHING PEOPLE TO FISH

Last year saw the introduction of a new three-year scheme to promote angling, particularly for juniors and disabled people. The project is a joint venture with SPORTLOT to increase the number of anglers and involves working with national angling bodies and professional angling coaches.

New wheelchair access path at St. Ives

Our target in the South West for 2002 was to train 1200 new anglers and establish/refurbish a major urban fishery for junior anglers and disabled people. This was achieved and the target exceeded.

Special events were organised last year to encourage young and disabled people to take up angling. Extremely successful events were held at Devizes, Newton Abbot, Ringwood and Bodmin Moor. We are also carrying out projects to improve access to angling for young and disabled anglers at St Ives, Bridgwater, Bristol, Bath, Bideford and Plymouth.

The events provide the opportunity for youngsters to try angling, catch their first fish and 'get hooked' on fishing for life. Participants also have the chance to discover more about what lives in the fishing lakes and how to protect wildlife. Following the huge success of the 2002 events, Cornwall Area will be funding another series of angling 'taster' events throughout Cornwall in 2003. Details are available from Gary Champion on 01872 863551. For details of events in the other areas, contact the local Area office.

A group of disabled people and their helpers from the Churchtown Farm Activity Centre attended a special session near Bodmin and thoroughly enjoyed the day. Some good sized fish were caught at the events and, at a recent event near Hayle, one of the youngsters was amazed and thrilled to catch a ten pound trout as his first fish!

New junior anglers 'get hooked'

In 2003, we will continue to train new anglers and establish/refurbish major urban fisheries for junior anglers and disabled people.

National Rod Licences

Before fishing for salmon, sea trout, trout, freshwater fish or eels in any* water in England and Wales, it is necessary to have both a current Agency rod fishing licence and permission to fish from the owner of the fishery.

*Except in waters where a general licence is in force - please check with the owner of the fishery in advance.

The area where a rod licence is required for fishing for salmon, sea trout, trout, and freshwater fish includes estuaries and the sea out to six miles from the shore.

In most cases in tidal waters, a rod licence is not required to fish for freshwater eels, although there are exceptions. Before fishing for eels in tidal waters, please check with your local Area Environment Agency Office.

The Agency has a national rod fishing licence. This means that fishing in all regions is covered by one licence. It does not cover you to fish in Scotland.

Licences are available for coarse fish and non-migratory trout or for all-inclusive fishing, including the above species in addition to salmon and sea trout.

The licence structure is aimed at raising approximately £16 million for essential fisheries work.

Coarse fish and non-trout

The price of the full annual licence (2003/2004) for coarse fish and non-migratory trout is £22 (£11 concessions [disabled anglers in receipt of invalidity benefit or severe disability allowance, and anyone aged 65 years and over]).

A short-term coarse fish and non-migratory trout licence covers a period of eight consecutive days, giving anglers the benefit of being able to fish over two weekends. This costs £7 (no concessions). A one-day licence, aimed at beginners and casual anglers costs £2.75 (no concessions).

Junior Licence - Children under 12 years of age do not require a licence. A full annual junior licence is available for coarse fish and non-migratory trout priced £5. Junior licences are available to anyone less than 17 years old.

Salmon and sea trout

The price of the full annual licence (2003/2004) for salmon and sea trout (also including coarse fish, eels and non-migratory trout) is £61 (concessions £30.50 - including juniors). An 8-day licence costs £18 and a 1-day licence is £6. There are no concessions on the 8- or 1-day licence.

Licences are available from every Post Office in England and Wales or from a range of local distributors. A list of these local distributors is available from the Agency offices. If necessary, you may obtain your licence by post. A form to do this is available from Agency offices.

Alternatively a 'telesales' service operates from 8am to 8pm, 7 days a week, except bank holidays, for full, junior and concessionary licences. The number to ring is 0870 166 2662.

It is also now possible to obtain full licences, 8- and 1-day and the new full junior licence - through the Agency's 'on-line licensing system'. Details are available on the fisheries web site: www.environment-agency.gov.uk/fish

Payment by credit/debit card for 'telesales' and 'online': the licence will be immediately valid as the purchaser will be provided with a reference number to quote if challenged when fishing. Proof of identity will also be needed until the full licence has been received.

The 2003/2004 licences will be valid until 31 March 2004. Licences are issued on a 12-month basis and are subject to price reviews.

The licence has the following benefits:

- You can use a rod and line anywhere in England and Wales.
- You can use up to two rods per licence, subject to the National Byelaws included in this Guide and subject to any local rules.

Your rod licence will help the Agency continue to improve the vital work it carries out, including:

- Management of fish stocks.
- Improvements in fisheries and the fish's environment.
- Protection of stocks through enforcement activities, including anti-poaching patrols.

- Rescue of fish which would otherwise be lost through drought, pollution or other causes.
- Surveys, essential for picking up changes and problems.
- Advice on fishing and management issues.
- Fish rearing and stocking of rivers.

Please note that:

1. The licence gives you the right to use a fishing rod and line but does not give you the right to fish. You must always check that you have the permission of the owner or tenant of the fishing rights before starting to fish.

2. Your licence is valuable - if it should be lost, a duplicate can be issued from PO Box 432, National Rod Licence Administration, Environment Agency, Richard Fairclough House, Knutsford Road, Warrington, WA4 1HH. A charge of £5 will be made.

Please make a note of the Licence Stamp Number before going fishing.

3. The licence is yours alone; it cannot be used by anyone else. Please make sure that you sign the licence before you go fishing.

4. Your licence must be produced on demand to an enforcement officer of the Agency who produces his or her warrant, a police officer or to any other licence holder who produces his or her licence. Failure to do so is an offence and may make you liable to prosecution (maximum fine £2,500).

5. The licence is only valid if the correct name, address and date of birth of the holder, and the date and time of issue are shown without amendments, a stamp of the correct duty is attached and the licence is signed by the holder and the issuing agent.

6. A national rod licence is not required where a General Licence is in force. Please check with the owner in advance.

7. The catch return form attached to the salmon and sea trout licence is very important. This information is required by law and you should send in the return form, even if you recorded a 'nil' catch. Please fill in and return the form in an envelope when your licence expires, using the FREEPOST address.

8. Details of local rod fishing byelaws and angling information can be obtained from Agency offices. Fishery byelaws may vary between different Agency Regions - if in doubt, check first before going fishing.

Details of the main byelaws applying to the Agency in the South West can be found on pages 9 to 14.

Salmon and sea trout kelts

Salmon and sea trout which are about to spawn, or have recently spawned but have not recovered, are known as unclean. The law says that fish in either condition, if caught, must be returned to the water with as little damage as possible. Fish about to spawn are identifiable by the ease with which eggs or milt can be extruded from the vent.

Those having recently spawned are called kelts and can be identified from clean fish by using the comparison given below.

KELT

1. Line of back and belly parallel
2. Gill maggots almost invariably present (salmon only)
3. Distinct 'corner' or change of direction in profile of body at back of skull
4. Fins invariably frayed
5. Vent suffused red and easily extruded by pressure
6. Belly normally blackened

CLEAN

1. Back and belly convex in relation to each other
2. Gill maggots only present in previous spawners or fish which have been some time in the river
3. Head tapers into body without a break
4. Fins entire; rarely frayed
5. Vent firm and compact
6. Belly normally pale

Smolts and parr

Young salmon known as parr look very similar to brown trout and are often caught by trout anglers. These parr are destined to run the rivers in a few years as adult salmon after feeding at sea. It is an offence knowingly to take, kill or injure these parr, and any which are caught by mistake must be returned to the water.

Salmon parr can be identified from trout by using the comparison given on the next page. In March, April and May, salmon and sea trout parr begin to migrate to the sea. The spots and finger marks disappear and the body becomes silvery in colour. They are then called smolts and must be returned to the water if caught.

SALMON PARR

1. Body slightly built and torpedo-shaped
2. Tail distinctly forked
3. A perpendicular line from the back of the eye will not touch the maxillary bone
4. Eight to twelve finger marks, even in width, well-defined and regularly placed along the sides
5. No white line on leading edge of fins
6. No red colour on adipose fin

TROUT

1. Body thicker and clumsier looking
2. Tail with shallow fork
3. A perpendicular line from the back of the eye will pass through or touch the maxillary bone
4. Finger marks less numerous, uneven in width, less defined, irregularly placed along the sides
5. Normally white line on leading edge of fins
6. Adipose fin generally coloured with orange or red.

ROD FISHING SEASONS

The "Open Seasons", i.e. the periods when it is permitted to fish, are set out in the table opposite.

★ There is no statutory close season for coarse fish and eels in stillwaters, but some clubs and fishery owners may impose their own close seasons.

Fisheries patrol on the River Tamar

FISHERY DISTRICT	MAJOR RIVERS WITHIN DISTRICT	ROD & LINE OPEN SEASON (dates inclusive)	
SALMON		**Starts**	**Ends**
Avon (Devon)	Avon (Devon)	15 Apr	30 Nov
	Erme	15 Mar	31 Oct
Axe (Devon)	Axe, Otter, Sid	15 Mar	31 Oct
	Lim	1 Mar	30 Sept
Camel	Camel	1 Apr	15 Dec
Dart	Dart	1 Feb	30 Sept
Exe	Exe	14 Feb	30 Sept
Fowey	Fowey, Looe, Seaton	1 Apr	15 Dec
Tamar & Plym	Tamar, Tavy, Lynher,	1 Mar	14 Oct
	Plym, Yealm	1 Apr	15 Dec
Taw & Torridge	Taw, Torridge	1 Mar	30 Sept
	Lyn	1 Feb	31 Oct
Teign	Teign	1 Feb	30 Sept
Frome (Dorset) & Piddle		1 Mar	31 Aug
	All other rivers in North & South Wessex Areas	1 Feb	31 Aug
MIGRATORY TROUT			
Avon (Devon)	Avon (Devon)	15 Apr	30 Sept
	Erme	15 Mar	30 Sept
Axe (Devon)	Axe, Otter, Sid	15 Apr	31 Oct
	Lim	16 Apr	31 Oct
Camel	Camel, Gannel, Menalhyl Valency	1 Apr	30 Sept
Dart	Dart	15 Mar	30 Sept
Exe	Exe	15 Mar	30 Sept
Fowey	Fowey, Looe, Seaton, Tresillian	1 Apr	30 Sept
Tamar & Plym	Tamar, Lynher, Plym, Tavy, Yealm	3 Mar	30 Sept
Taw & Torridge	Taw, Torridge, Lyn	15 Mar	30 Sept
Teign	Teign	15 Mar	30 Sept
	All rivers in North & South Wessex Areas	15 Apr	31 Oct
BROWN TROUT			
	Camel	1 Apr	30 Sept
	Other rivers in Devon & Cornwall Areas	15 Mar	30 Sept
	All rivers in North & South Wessex Areas	1 Apr	15 Oct
	All other water in Devon & Cornwall Areas	15 Mar	12 Oct
	All other waters in North & South Wessex Areas	17 Mar	14 Oct
RAINBOW TROUT			
	Camel & Fowey	1 Apr	30 Sept
	Other rivers in Devon & Cornwall Areas	15 Mar	30 Sept
	All rivers in North & South Wessex Areas	1 Apr	15 Oct
	Reservoirs, Lakes & Ponds	★ No statutory close season	
GRAYLING, COARSE FISH & EELS			
	Rivers, Streams and Drains including the Glastonbury Canal	16 Jun	14 Mar
	Enclosed waters - Ponds, Lakes & Reservoirs All other Canals	★ No statutory close season	

NATIONAL BYELAWS TO PROTECT SALMON STOCKS

National byelaws to protect spring salmon were introduced in April 1999.

A summary of the byelaws is as follows:

Mandatory catch and release of all salmon for all rivers before 16 June.

Fly and spinner only (where not already limited by existing byelaws) before June 16 for salmon fishing.

These measures replace some of the existing measures already in place.

Catch and release of salmon is mandatory to 16 June, removing the earlier bag limit of two salmon before 1 June on the Taw and Torridge. It also supersedes any early season voluntary bag limits.

Anglers are still encouraged to fish catch and release after 16 June and especially to return any large red fish late in the season which may be 'springers'. The 70 cm limit in August/ September on the Taw and Torridge still applies.

Permitted baits are restricted to artificial fly and artificial lure until 16 June. Exceptions where other restrictions remain include the Taw and Torridge (fly only from April 1) and North and South Wessex (fly only before 15 May).

These national byelaws are designed as a baseline and are considered to be the lowest common denominator across the country addressing the national problem of a decline in early-run large salmon.

Measures to address other local stock problems will continue to follow a river-by-river approach based on the programme of individual Salmon Action Plans being developed by the Agency with local fisheries interests.

PERMITTED BAITS

The use of particular baits for fishing is regulated by byelaws and in some cases additional restrictions are imposed by the fishing association or riparian owner. The byelaw restrictions are shown in the table below:

★*This restriction only applies to water where a statutory coarse fish close season is applicable. It does not apply to stillwaters. See also section on rod fishing seasons and the note on canal close seasons (page 13).*

★★ *All references to 'Trout' include migratory trout and non-migratory trout.*

★★★ *This is a change introduced in 1998.*

No spinning for trout in waters included within the Dartmoor National Park, the Exe above Exebridge, Otter above Langford Bridge, Torridge above Woodford Bridge, Bray above Newton Bridge, Mole above Alswear Bridge, Little Dart above Affeton Bridge, and the whole

PERMITTED BAITS

FISHERY DISTRICT	SPECIES	BAITS (REAL OR IMITATION)
South West Region	Salmon	Artificial fly and artificial lure ONLY before 16 June
Avon (Devon)	Salmon & Trout ★★	No worm or maggot.
Axe (Devon)	Salmon & Trout	No shrimp, prawn, worm or maggot. Fly only after 31 July below Axbridge, Colyford.
Dart	Salmon	No worm or maggot. No shrimp or prawn except below Staverton Bridge. No spinning above Holne Bridge.
	Trout	Fly only.
Exe	Salmon & Trout	No worm or maggot.
Barnstaple Yeo (tidal)	All species (inc. sea fish)	No fishing
Taw & Torridge (except Lyn)	Salmon & Trout	No shrimp, prawn, worm or maggot. No spinning after 31 March. ★★★
Lyn	Trout	No worm or maggot before 1 June.
Teign	Trout	No worm or maggot before 1 June.
Camel & Fowey	Salmon	No byelaw restrictions on bait after 16 June
	Trout	No byelaw restrictions on bait
Tamar	Salmon & Migratory Trout	No worm, maggot, shrimp or prawn after 31 August.
North Wessex & South Wessex Areas	Salmon & Migratory Trout	Artificial fly only before 15 May.
North Wessex & South Wessex Areas	All species in rivers, drains and canals	No maggot (or pupae), processed product, cereal or other vegetable matter during the coarse fish close season. ★

of the Okement, Lyn and Barnstaple Yeo.

Artificial baits which spin: When fishing for salmon or trout in the Avon (Devon), Axe (Devon), Exe, Dart, Taw and Torridge and Teign districts, use of any artificial bait which spins is restricted to those with only a single, double or treble hook. The width of the hook must not be greater than the spread of the vanes of the bait.

SIZE LIMITS

Length to be measured from tip of the snout to the fork or cleft of the tail.

The size limits, below which fish must be returned, imposed by byelaws are set out in the table below. Riparian owners and fishing associations may impose further restrictions which anglers should familiarize themselves with before fishing.

These size restrictions do not apply to:

(a) Any person who takes any undersized fish unintentionally if he/she at once returns it to the water with as little injury as possible.

(b) Non-migratory trout in any waters included within the Dartmoor National Park, the Exe above Exebridge, the Otter above Langford Bridge, the Torridge above Woodford Bridge, the Mole above Alswear Bridge, the Little Dart above Affeton Bridge and the whole of the Rivers Okement, Lyn and Barnstaple Yeo.

MANDATORY BAG LIMITS

See section on National Byelaws to protect salmon stocks (page 9).

North Wessex Area. The bag limits set out in the table below are imposed by the byelaws, however, some riparian owners or angling associations obtain dispensation to increase their bag limits. Anglers should familiarize themselves with bag limits before fishing. Once a bag limit has been taken, the angler may continue fishing for the same species, provided that any fish caught are returned without injury. Freshwater fish other than grayling, pike and eels may not be permanently removed from the water.

TAW & TORRIDGE

The original size limit and bag limit byelaws, introduced following a public inquiry in 1997, expired in September 2001. The Department for Environment, Food and Rural Affairs (DEFRA) has renewed these byelaws which remain in place until 2008.

NOTE: Since 1 April 1999, with the introduction of national salmon byelaws, the bag limits apply after 16 June.

MANDATORY BAG LIMITS

RIVER OR AREA	SPECIES	PERIOD		
		24 HOURS	7 DAYS	SEASON
North Wessex	Non-migratory Trout	2	N/A	N/A
	Grayling	2	N/A	N/A
Taw	Salmon	2	3	10
	Migratory Trout	5	15	40
Torridge	Salmon	2	2	7
	Migratory Trout	2	5	20

SIZE LIMITS

AREA, DISTRICT OR CATCHMENT	MIGRATORY TROUT	NON-MIGRATORY TROUT	GRAYLING
Camel, Fowey, Tamar and Plym	18 centimetres	18 centimetres	N/A
Avon (Devon), Axe (Devon), Dart, Exe, Taw & Torridge, Teign	25 centimetres	25 centimetres	N/A
River Lim	N/A	22 centimetres	N/A
North Wessex (except By Brook)	35 centimetres	25 centimetres	25 centimetres
By Brook & tributaries	35 centimetres	20 centimetres	25 centimetres
South Wessex	35 centimetres	25 centimetres	N/A

VOLUNTARY BAG LIMITS

See section on National Byelaws to protect salmon stocks (page 9).

Spring salmon

In addition to the national byelaws, the Agency is encouraging salmon anglers to return any larger salmon, particularly red ones caught later in the season, as these are likely to be multi-sea-winter fish and valuable to the spawning stock. On many rivers a variety of voluntary measures have been adopted to protect fish stocks. All anglers should familiarize themselves with these rules before fishing. Details are provided below.

Rivers Camel/Fowey/Lynher (Cornish limit)

For the above combined Cornish rivers, a maximum of: Salmon – 2 per day, 4 per week and 10 per season. Sea trout – 4 per day. These numbers apply cumulatively to you as an individual and not as a limit from each river, i.e. on any particular day, you should not take more than 2 salmon in total, regardless of how many Cornish rivers you fish. Please check with your club or Association as more stringent rules apply on certain waters.

River Fowey
- Fowey River Association

Salmon 1/day, 2/week, 5/season.
Sea trout 4/day or night. All sea trout to be returned in September.

River Camel
– Camel River Association

Same as Cornish limit above.
No fishing in April. All sea trout to be returned in September.

River Tamar
– Tamar & Tributaries Fisheries Association

Salmon 1 per day followed by catch/release. All fish over 10 pounds returned from 1 September onwards. Return red/unseasonable fish.

River Tavy
– Tavy Walkham & Plym Fishing Club

Salmon 1 per day. Return of all hen fish, and alternate cockfish. Limited fishing methods.

Rivers Plym, Tavy
- Plymouth and Dist. Freshwater Angling Association

Salmon 1 per day, 3/season;
Sea trout 3 per day or night.

River Exe
- River Exe and Tributaries Association

After 16 August, salmon of 27.5" or over (8 pounds) to be returned unless injured, in which event, the next salmon caught **under** size limit to be returned. Red or coloured fish to be returned, no fishing by prawn or shrimp in September.

River Teign
- Lower Teign Fishing Association

Sea trout 4 per 24 hours.

River Otter

Salmon All salmon to be returned.
Sea trout 1 mature and two school peal/season.

River Axe
- Axe Fly Fishers

Salmon Catch and release only for salmon. Fly only.

River Avon (Hants)
- Avon and Stour Riparian Owners and Wessex Salmon Rivers Trust.

Salmon Catch and release only for salmon. No worm fishing.

Some river associations will not have held their AGM prior to going to print. Please check with local club secretary for any voluntary measures that may have been agreed for other rivers before fishing.

CATCH AND RELEASE

With stocks of salmon under increasing pressure, the Environment Agency is seeking to do everything possible to protect the species for the future.

Catch and release is now becoming an established management technique for increasing spawning escapement, particularly where stocks are low. Salmon anglers are encouraged to consider this approach as a means of safeguarding salmon stocks in our rivers.

If you do decide to practice catch and release, the following guidelines may be useful to give your catch the best chance of surviving after you have returned it to the river:

Hooks - single hooks inflict less damage than doubles or trebles, barbless hooks are best. Flatten the barbs on your hooks with pliers.

Playing Fish - fish are best landed before complete exhaustion and therefore all elements of tackle should be strong enough to allow them to be played firmly.

Landing Fish - Fish should be netted and unhooked in the water, if possible. Use knotless nets - not a tailer or gaff.

Handling and Unhooking - Make every effort to keep the fish in the water. Wet your hands. Carefully support the fish out of water. Do not hold the fish up by the tail, this may cause kidney damage. Remove the hook gently - if necessary, cut the line if deeply hooked. Take extra care with spring fish, as they are more susceptible to damage and fungal infection.

Do not under any circumstances keep out of the water for more than 30 seconds a fish which is to be returned. Changes in the fish's body affect survival within one minute.

Reviving the Fish - Support an exhausted fish underwater in an upright position facing the current. Estimate weight and length in the water. Avoid weighing. Handle the fish as little as possible. Be patient and give it time to recover and swim away on its own.

TESCO SWAP A SALMON SCHEME

An arrangement, originally negotiated with Tesco for the Hampshire Avon, by Wessex Salmon Rivers Trust, entitles an angler catching and returning a salmon after 16 June to a voucher to be exchanged for a farmed salmon. This scheme now applies to other rivers as follows: Frome, Dart, Teign, Camel, Fowey, Tavy, Lynher, Plym, Otter and Fal. Contact your local fisheries office for further details.

WILD TROUT SOCIETY

Anglers are asked to return all brown trout caught on the East Dart above Postbridge, on the Cherry Brook and the Blackbrook; while on the West Dart between Blackbrook and Swincombe they are to return fish between 10" and 16" long.

USE OF OTHER TACKLE

Use of float. The use of a float when fishing for salmon or trout in any waters within the Avon (Devon), Axe (Devon), Dart, Exe, Taw and Torridge, and Teign districts is prohibited.

Use of gaff is prohibited. See section on national byelaws Phase 1

Limit on number of rods in use. See section on national byelaws Phase 1.

Prohibition of use of lead weights. No person shall use any instrument on which is attached directly or indirectly any lead weight (except a weight of 0.06 grams or less, or one of more than 28.35 grams) for the purpose of taking salmon, trout, freshwater fish or eels in any waters within the Agency's region.

Prohibited Fishing Area - Kilbury Weir. It is illegal to take, or attempt to take by any means, any fish in any waters within 50 yards below the crest of Kilbury Weir on the River Dart.

LANDING NETS, KEEPNETS AND KEEPSACKS

A new national byelaw was introduced on 1 April 1998 making it illegal to use landing nets with knotted meshes or meshes of metallic material.

Similarly, keepnets should not be constructed of such materials or have holes in the mesh larger than 25mm internal circumference; or be less than 2.0 metres in length. Supporting rings or frames should not be greater than 40cm apart (excluding the distance from the top frame to the first supporting ring or frame) or less than 120cm in circumference.

Keepsacks should be constructed of a soft, dark coloured, non-abrasive, water permeable fabric and should not have dimensions less than 120cm by 90cm if rectangular, or 150cm by 30cm by 40cm if used with a frame or designed with the intention that a frame be used. It is an offence to retain more than one fish in a single keepsack at any time.

The retention of salmonids (adults or juveniles) in keepnets is illegal except when specially approved by the Agency for collecting broodstock.

THEFT ACT

The Theft Act 1968, Schedule 1, makes it an offence for anyone to take or attempt to take fish in private waters or in a private fishery without the consent of the owner.

The Agency may bring a prosecution under this Act on its own fisheries. It cannot do so on behalf of an individual, and any fishery owner who wishes such a prosecution to be brought should consult the police or a solicitor.

ATTENTION

SALMON AND SEA TROUT ANGLERS

Your catch return is needed by 1 January each year. Nil returns are also required. Send returns to:

Environment Agency, FREEPOST, P.O. Box 60, Patchway, Bristol, BS12 4YY.

Failure to submit a return is an offence.

NATIONAL BYELAWS

A number of national byelaws are now in place. These replace or modify regional byelaws that existed before.

A summary of the national byelaws is given below.

Phase I

1. The annual close season for fishing for rainbow trout by rod and line in all reservoirs, lakes and ponds has been dispensed with.
2. A close season for brown trout is to be retained on all waters.
3. Use of the gaff is prohibited at all times when fishing for salmon, trout and freshwater fish or freshwater eels.
4. The number of rods that may be used at any time is as follows:
    a. One rod when fishing for salmonids in rivers, streams, drains and canals.
    b. Two rods when fishing for salmonids in reservoirs, lakes and ponds (subject to local rules).
    c. Up to four rods when fishing for coarse fish and eels (subject to local rules).

When fishing with multiple rods and lines, rods shall not be left unattended and shall be placed such that the distance between the butts of the end rods does not exceed three metres.

5. Catch returns for salmon and migratory trout should be submitted no later than 1 January in the following year.
6. See separate section on landing nets, keepnets and keepsacks.

Phase II

1. Crayfish of any species whether alive or dead, or parts thereof may not be used as bait for salmon, trout, freshwater fish or eels.
2. Livebait may only be retained and used at the water they were taken from.
3. All salmon, migratory trout or trout, hooked other than in the mouth or throat, shall be returned immediately to any river, stream, drain or canal.
4. The byelaw limiting the length of a rod to not less than 1.5 metres (that may be used in North or South Wessex) has been revoked.
5. A rod and line with its bait or hook in the water must not be left unattended or so the licence holder is unable at any time to take or exercise sufficient control over the rod and line.

COARSE FISH CLOSE SEASON ON CANALS

In March 2000 a new National byelaw removed the close season for coarse fish on canals within the region, with the exception of the Glastonbury Canal which is an open system with the South Drain.

FISH WITH ADIPOSE FINS REMOVED

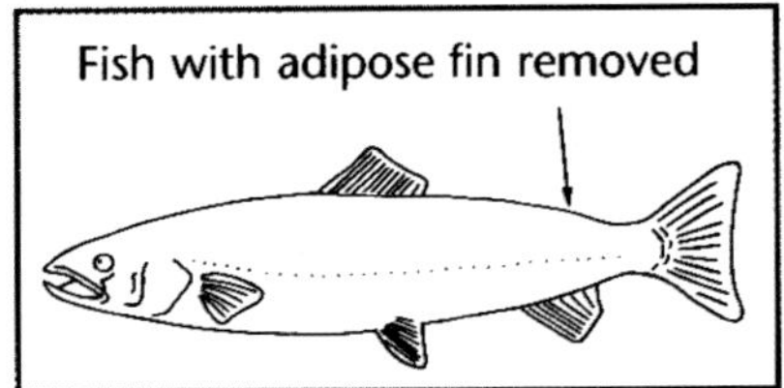

As indicated on your rod licence, you may catch a fish from which the adipose fin has been completely removed. These fish may carry a micro tag implanted within their nose - invisible to you. If this occurs, you should contact your local Environment Agency office.

Any fish caught before 16 June without an adipose fin should be returned to the water and reported to your local Environment Agency office.

* Tell us your name, address and telephone number.

* Record details of your catch (where, when, size and species of fish).
* If the fish is caught after 16 June, you may keep the fish (or just the head) frozen if necessary and we will contact you to make arrangements for it to be inspected.

If caught after 16 June we will pay you a reward of £5 if it carries a micro tag and, of course, you keep the fish.

Details should be sent to the appropriate Area Fisheries Office.

PURCHASE AND RELEASE OF SALMON FROM LICENSED NETS

In recent years, the Wessex Salmon Rivers Trust has purchased salmon from the Mudeford nets for release to the Hampshire Avon as extra spawners to help boost stock recovery rates. Arrangements for the 2003 season are still under consideration.

Similar schemes have also operated on the rivers Tamar, Tavy, Lynher, Fowey and Camel, funded by a variety of sponsors including South West Water, the Maristow Estate, fishery owners and European funding under the Habitats Directive.

STOCKING FISH - *BUYER BEWARE*

The Environment Agency has produced a free leaflet entitled 'Buyer Beware - Your guide to stocking fish'. The leaflet explains the Agency rules on fish introduction (Section 30, Salmon and Freshwater Fisheries Act 1975) and the commonsense things which fishery owners can do to protect themselves and their fisheries when buying/stocking fish.

Before introducing (stocking) any fish (or fish spawn) into inland waters, you must obtain written consent of the Agency. Failure to meet this obligation is a criminal offence and could lead to prosecution, with a fine of up to £2,500. In addition, the stocking of non-native species such as Wels Catfish or Grass Carp requires DEFRA approval under the Import of Live Fish Act - Prohibition of Keeping or Release of Live Fish Order 1998.

Mandatory health checks will be required where fish are to be moved into rivers, streams, drains or canals, or where the risk to other fisheries is high.

Health checks will not normally be required in waters where the risk of fish escape is minimal (e.g. enclosed waters). However, there may be occasions where the Agency will still insist on a health examination.

Regardless of the Agency's requirement for health checks, it should be stressed that establishing the health of fish is essential before any stocking takes place. The Agency encourages everyone to follow the Agency's 'Buyer Beware' code. Copies of the leaflet can be obtained from any of the Agency's Fisheries Offices.

LOOK OUT! - LOOK UP!

ADVICE ON SAFE FISHING NEAR OVERHEAD ELECTRIC POWER LINES

Several people have died and others have been seriously injured whilst using fishing rods and poles near overhead electric power lines. The following advice is designed to prevent these events recurring:

i Because rods and poles conduct electricity, they are particularly dangerous when used near overhead electric power lines. Remember that electricity can jump gaps and a rod does not even have to touch an electric line to cause a lethal current to flow.

ii Many overhead electric power lines are supported by wood poles which can be and are mistaken for telegraph poles. These overhead lines may carry electricity up to 132,000 volts, and have been involved in many of the accidents that have occurred.

iii The height of high voltage overhead electric power lines can be as low as 5.2 metres and they are therefore within easy reach of a rod or pole. Remember that overhead lines may not be readily visible from the ground. They may be concealed by hedges or by a dark background. Make sure you **'Look Out'** and **'Look Up'** to check for overhead lines before you tackle up and begin fishing.

iv In general, the minimum safe fishing distance from an overhead electric power line is 30 metres from the overhead line (measured along the ground).

v When pegging out for matches or competitions, organisers and competitors should, in general, ensure that no peg is nearer to an overhead electric power line than 30 metres (measured along the ground).

vi For further advice on safe fishing at specific locations, contact your local Electricity Company.

vii Finally, remember that it is dangerous for any object to get too close to overhead electric power lines, particularly if the object is an electrical conductor, e.g. lead cored fishing line, damp fishing line, rod or pole.

ENVIRONMENT AGENCY AREAS

Devon Area
Fishery Districts (Rivers in brackets):
Avon (Avon, Erme); Axe (Axe, Sid, Otter); Dart (Dart); Exe (Exe); Taw and Torridge (Taw, Torridge, Lyn); Teign (Teign). The River Lim is included in the Devon Area.

Cornwall Area
Fishery Districts (Rivers in brackets):
Camel (Camel, other streams flowing into the sea on the North coast between Marshland Mouth and Lands End); Fowey (Fowey, East and West Looe, Seaton, Tresillian, other streams flowing into the sea on the South coast between Lands End and Rame Head); Tamar and Plym (Tamar, Lynher, Plym, Tavy and Yealm).

North Wessex Area
River Catchments:
Bristol Avon (including all tributaries), Axe (Somerset), Brue, Parrett, Tone, Yeo and all other rivers, drains and streams flowing into the Bristol Channel between Avonmouth and Foreland Point.

South Wessex Area
River Catchments:
Hampshire Avon (including all tributaries), Stour (including all tributaries), Dorset Frome, Piddle, Wey, Brit and Char and all other streams flowing into the sea between Christchurch Harbour and Charmouth.

ROD LICENCE

IN ORDER TO FISH FOR SALMON, TROUT (INCLUDING MIGRATORY TROUT), FRESHWATER FISH AND EELS IN ANY* WATERS IN THE SOUTH WEST REGION, ANGLERS WILL NEED AN ENVIRONMENT AGENCY NATIONAL ROD LICENCE AND PERMISSION FROM THE OWNER OF THE FISHERY.

ANGLERS MUST CARRY THEIR ROD LICENCES WITH THEM AT ALL TIMES WHILE FISHING.

** Except in waters where a General Licence is in force - please check with the owner of the fishery in advance.*

DISCARDED
TACKLE
KILLS
Please do not leave litter, hooks, nylon or other items dangerous to wildlife

Game

Going Wild

Fly fishing on a tiny Exmoor Stream

Mike Weaver goes in search of wild trout on tiny streams

There is something a bit special about tiny streams, especially for the wild trout fisherman. Our native wild brown trout is ideally suited to thrive on the smallest rivers and fortunately the south west has more than its share of these exciting waters, whether high on Dartmoor, Exmoor or Bodmin Moor, among the meadows of the rolling country of mid Devon or on the silky little chalk streams of Wessex.

The great advantage of these tiny waters, many of which you could almost jump across, is that they usually give up their secrets readily, and the hot spots can be identified with an ease rarely possible on larger rivers. So the first trip to a new piece of fishing can often produce as good a catch as anything experienced on later visits.

Success on small rivers, like anywhere else, is all about using the right tackle and techniques, and that means scaling things down. You will certainly need a short fly rod, but not one of those ghastly implements that used to be called "brook rods". They were almost always far too sloppy, making it impossible to cast the tight loop that is essential in a confined space. What you want is a rod of no more that seven feet with a stiffish action that will punch a narrow loop under the canopy of leafy branches that spans so many of these little rivers. Leaders should also be kept fairly short - I normally use four or five feet of braided butt attached to a couple of feet of 5X nylon and finally a point of three feet of 6X or 7X. The secret weapon on many small streams with heavily bushed banks is body waders, without which much of the water will be unavailable, and a wading staff can avoid those stumbles that can send the trout heading for cover.

Throughout the south west there are countless opportunities for getting a day's fishing on these tiny trout streams and usually at a modest cost - as reference to the directory section of this guide will readily demonstrate. And there are many more waters where the farmer will often let you cast a fly for a nominal charge. So let's go to the river and look at some of the tiny trout streams that have given me some great days in recent seasons.

Two of the most reliable little trout streams that I know are the Yeo and Creedy at Crediton, and that is where I start the season year after year. When the water is still cold and the fish a bit lethargic it is best to stick to the waters that you know well - exploring new waters is best left until things start hotting up in late May. The water here is controlled by the Crediton Fly Fishing Club and can fish well at any time in the season, with plenty of wild trout up to around 14 inches.

Around mid May in 2002 I went exploring new waters, particularly on the upper Torridge and its tributaries, where several stretches are available through the Angling 2000 scheme

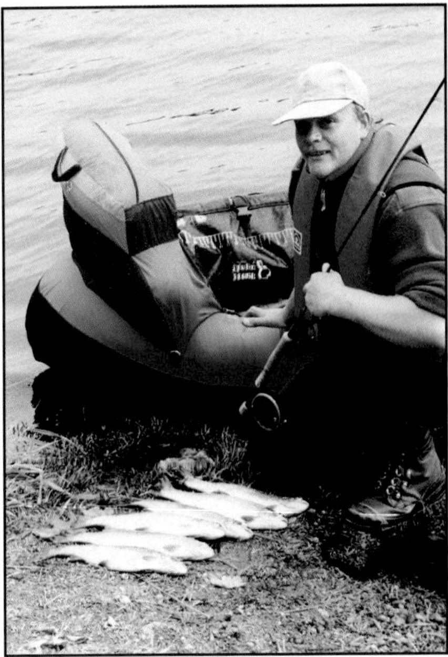

A successful float tubing session.
South West Lakes Trust

Westcountry Fly Fishing
Guided Saltwater & Freshwater
Fly Fishing for Bass, Mullet & Trout
Fully Insured Experienced Professional Guide
Cornwall, Devon and Southwest Ireland
Tel: 01209 831539 Mob: 07971 167414
www.westcountryflyfishing.com

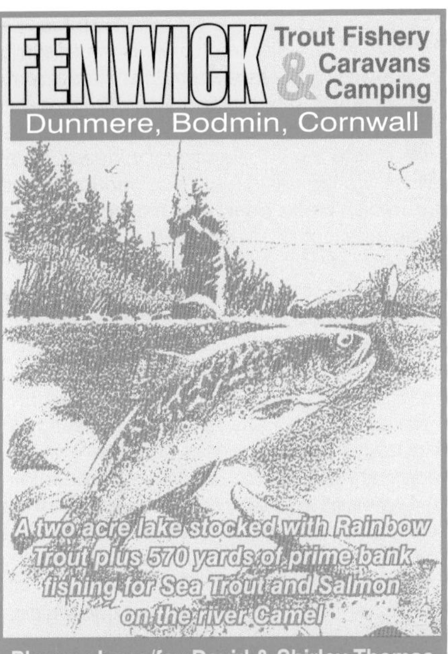
FENWICK Trout Fishery & Caravans Camping
Dunmere, Bodmin, Cornwall
A two acre lake stocked with Rainbow Trout plus 570 yards of prime bank fishing for Sea Trout and Salmon on the river Camel
Please phone/fax David & Shirley Thomas on 01208 78296 for more detail.

Bake
Fishing Lakes
Open 365 Days a Year
8am to Dusk
TACKLE
BAKE
TWO FLY LAKES
LAKES
FLIES
ROD HIRE
E.A. ROD LICENCES AVAILABLE
Catch and release for Rainbows & Browns to 15lb
Contact Tony Lister
Trerulefoot, Saltash, Cornwall.
Tel 01752 849027 & 0498 583836
Email: tony.lister@bakelakes.co.uk.
www.bakelakes.co.uk

Game

operated by the West Country Rivers Trust. With the black gnats swarming over the streams I found plenty of free-rising wild trout on the Torridge at Woodford Bridge, the Walden at Henscott and the Lew at Rutleigh.

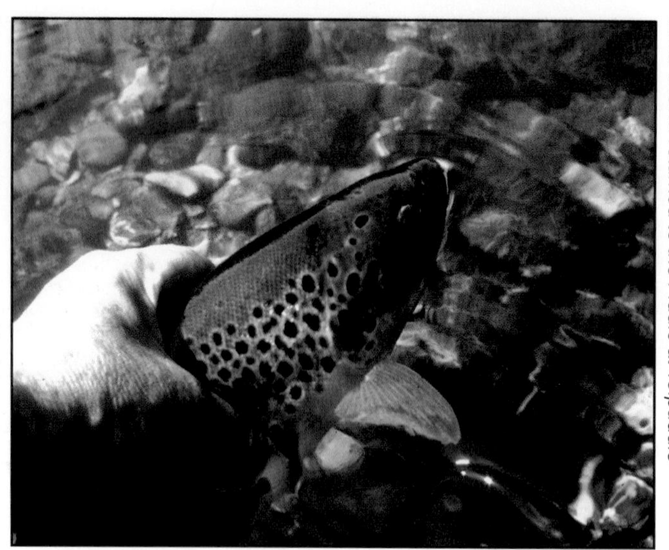
A 2lb Brown returned to the Piddle at Tolpuddle

Early last season I came upon a little gem in the shape of the Little Dart at Witheridge, where a lengthy stretch of this Taw tributary can be fished with an Angling 2000 permit. It was a dull afternoon in early June, which looked far from promising, but as soon as I slipped into the water I realised that there was a steady hatch of blue winged olives and that the trout were rising steadily. Over the next two hours I waded upstream for over half-a-mile with rising fish always within casting range and my reward was over 30 wild browns up to just short of 12 inches.

In the border country between Devon and Cornwall, the Arundell Arms at Lifton offers around twenty miles of trout stream for the fly fisherman to explore. Although this fishery includes the Tamar and Lyd, it is to the tiny tributaries that I turn for the most enjoyable trout fishing. The most westerly and easterly of the hotel's beats - on the Ottery and Lew respectively - are two of my favourites, especially in late May or early June when the Mayflies are hatching. Both of these prolific little rivers can produce big catches in such conditions.

When I first came to the south west over 30 years ago, it was to the tumbling streams of Dartmoor and Exmoor that I turned for wild trout fishing and the three rivers that have provided many great days over the years are the upper Dart and its tributaries, the upper Teign and the East Lyn. Although the East Lyn produced some good fishing in 2002, the Dartmoor rivers were distinctly below par, so I shall be hoping for a return to form by these streams in 2003.

My 2002 season ended with a couple of wonderful days in October on the Piddle, a delightful little chalk stream in Dorset. As closing day approached, many fly fishermen had put away their rods, so I had the Piddle beats operated by Richard Slocock of Wesex Fly Fishing virtually to myself. It was classic autumn weather with a clear sky, warm but not too hot and, best of all, not a breath of wind. I was fishing at Culeaze and the mile or so downstream and, although there was no great hatch of fly, the trout were high in the water looking out for the few duns that trickled down on the surface. There can be few moments more exciting than when you wade round a bend on a tiny chalk stream to find a trout of 17 or 18 inches steadily sipping in insects - except possibly the moment when it takes your fly and heads for cover. Those two days produced that experience on several occasions, as well as plenty of smaller trout, bringing the 2002 season to splendid climax.

For the exploring fly fisherman in search of wild trout there always seems to be another stream around the corner. As I completed this article, I heard from the Westcountry Rivers Trust that they had added fishing on two little rivers in West Cornwall to their Angling 2000 collection, so as soon as the 2003 season gets going I shall be heading west in search of new experiences with wild trout.

Rainbow from Tavistock Trout

Protecting and Enhancing the Stocks of Wild Trout in the rivers of the South West.

If you wish to find out more about the Wild Trout Trust, send for details to

The Wild Trout Trust, PO Box 120, Waterlooville PO8 0DG

Tel: 023 9257 0985 Email: office@wildtrout.org

www.wildtrout.org

INNIS INN & FLY FISHERY

Innis Moor, Penwithick, St Austell.

Open all year, 8am to Dusk, 7days a week

Three lakes totalling 15 acres

- TACKLE SHOP -

Public House - Hotel - B&B, Full or half board

Caravan & Camping Site

25 pitch site with toilet & shower block.

Telephone 01726 851162

www.innisfishery.com

Just 1.25 miles from THE EDEN PROJECT

The Arundell Arms

Lifton, Devon PL16 0AA.

England's premier sporting hotel offers the perfect fishing holiday

Twenty miles of exclusive Salmon, Sea Trout and Brown Trout fishing on the river Tamar and tributaries and a 3 acre stocked lake

Famous fly fishing school with casting champions.

Award Winning Restaurant with three AA Rosettes

For details ring the proprietor Anne Voss-Bark, herself a fisherman, on 01566 784666

Email: reservations@arundellarms.com www.arundellarms.com

Game

Westcountry Rivers Trust

Cornwall Rivers Project & Angling 2000 Reel in New Angling Opportunities in the Duchy!

The Cornwall Rivers Project programme of river catchment based farm plans and fishery improvement works is racing ahead with new farmers and river owners joining the project every week. The Westcountry Rivers Trust led Cornwall Rivers Project is a partnership Objective One funded initiative spanning ten of Cornwall's most important river catchments, creating major benefits for anglers. The project provides opportunities for farmers and river owners to save money, diversify and improve their rivers.

Cornwall Rivers Project offers:

- Free & confidential practical advice and grant assistance for farmers and river owners (including clubs) on land, rivers and streams
- Free Integrated River Basin Resource Management Plans identifying opportunities for economic and environmental benefit
- Free fisheries management and tourism diversification advice
- Grants for environmental and water quality improvements including fencing along watercourses
- Grant search and filter to other schemes who may be able to provide assistance
- Angling 2000, an angling marketing network scheme for anglers benefiting farmers and river/stream owners

Ten Cornish rivers...

The project area covers most of Cornwall but specifically the land areas that form the catchments or river basins of the rivers:

Ottery, Inny, Neet & Strat, Lynher & Tiddy, Seaton, East & West Looe, Fowey & Lerryn, Camel & Allen, Fal & Tresillian, Cober and Loe Pool.

Key project outputs include...

- 700 management plans for farmers and river managers covering some 40,000 hectares- (around 200 plans have already been completed)
- 100 kilometres of grant aided fencing on farms to protect watercourses- (over 25 kms have already been contracted)
- 7 demonstration sites including education, farming "Best Practice", water, fisheries and waste management issues
- Colour newsletters with project information, updates, case studies and useful contacts
- Development and support of the Angling 2000 scheme in Cornwall to open up new angling opportunities and assist farmers and river owners with fishery development and marketing
- 5000 copies of an education pack which will go the every school in the Duchy
- Informative river walks led by Trust Officers and scientists
- Scientific and community presentations to local groups
- Improved access for anglers, particularly the disabled and new entrants to angling initiatives

A partnership...

Project partners and liaison include the Environment Agency, Royal Holloway Institute for Environmental Research (RHIER), BDB Associates, Imery's, SWW and the Pennon Group who have generously assisted with the cashflow of the project. Forty percent of the project funds are provided by the EU under the Objective One secretariat, these are matched

Bob Whittaker with a fresh run 11lb Salmon.
Half Moon Inn

Before and after - WCRT Habitat improvement

by DEFRA, with the remaining money coming from the Trust and private sector. The Trust will be fundraising in Cornwall over the next few years to provide matching funds to draw down the all important European grant to deliver this ambitious project. So please help by joining the Trust as a Supporter, or why not consider running an event yourself to raise funds.

If you would like further information on the Cornwall Rivers Project, or you are a farmer or landowner who would like to be involved, please do not hesitate to contact the Trust on 01566 784488.

Elsewhere in the Westcountry, the Rivers Trust's Department of Fish & Wildlife is expanding its research work on salmonid genetics and factors limiting juvenile recruitment. Project Officers are still working on the Tamar, Taw & Torridge catchments with a major programme of works recently completed on the River Tale, a tributary of the Otter, in partnership with the Tale Valley Trust. Survey and scoping work is taking place on the rivers Dart & Exe, while on the River Axe in East Devon the Rivers Trust is working in a partnership with the Environment Agency, English Nature and others on a large project based on the river's candidate, Special Area of Conservation (cSAC) status.

Angling 2000-
great prospects for 2003!

Angling 2000, the Rivers Trust's immensely successful flexible angling day permit scheme expands further into Cornwall for 2003 with a new choice of hitherto un-fished beats. The scheme is now well established and for 2003 it branches out to include coarse fishing for the first time. After last years excellent results, the rods and participating farmers are eagerly looking forward to this season. The number of beats in the scheme for 2003 has increased to 20, with 8 new beats included.

The beats range from Tiverton to Truro and offer a massive variety of fishing, from the streams of Dartmoor and Bodmin Moor, that clear quickly after rain, to the languid upper Tamar and Torridge, with their excellent dry-fly fishing for wild trout. This year the range of fishing in the scheme has expanded with particularly exciting new beats on two rivers in Cornwall, that despite their small size have heavy runs of sea trout and, two previously un-fished carp and tench pools with carp to 20lb seen during reconnoitres last autumn.

The trout fishing is generally good on all the beats although the lowland rivers have a larger stamp of fish with 15"+ fish not being uncommon. The highlights of the 2002 season included a marvellous catch of 50+ trout to 14" in an afternoon on the upper Torridge and the lucky rod that landed two sea-liced spring salmon in a day in late May on the Okement.

The best of the seatrout fishing is on the middle Torridge, Okement, Inny and Lyd with the main run of larger fish in May and June and the schoolies in July and August. Ottery and Torridge sea trout rise readily to a dry fly during the day and have surprised many a trout angler when a small dimple rise takes off with a "reel screaming" run. The Lerryn, Tressillian and Fal down west are unknown quantities but have

Ten year old Eve Coburn with a personal best! Bake Lakes

good runs of sea trout to over 6lbs. Simon Evans the Trust's, Head of Fisheries has high hopes this season that the new beats on these rivers will fish very well. As these are spate rivers, the salmon fishing is dependent on adequate water. The Torridge and Okement have a spring run with beats offering the best chance of a fish from March to June. Fish were present in the Okement beats by the middle of April this year. The best of the backend fishing is on the Okement, Inny and Lyd.

The Tamar tributaries have a good population of grayling with some large fish over 2.5lbs. The season is extended until the end of October on selected beats to allow autumn fishing for this species.

How the Angling 2000 scheme works...

As well as offering angling access to some wonderful natural stretches of river it has also provides a welcome boost to farm incomes and a number of farm B&B's in each area adding value and extending the season. Anglers can buy books of ticket tokens from the Rivers Trust or from local tackle shops and then using the Angling 2000 booklet select a beat to fish for salmon, sea trout or grayling.

Once at their chosen location the angler leaves the appropriate number of tokens in the collection box next to the parking area and proceeds to fish the waters. The income from the scheme goes mainly to the farmers or beat owners with a small amount retained by the trust to contribute to printing and marketing expenses.

Angling 2000 allows farmers and riparian owners to get a modest income from their river beats and helps provide a return for the effort they have put into on farm river restoration and fisheries improvement. Angling 2000 also provides local opportunities for youngsters and others to fish in their parish through the controlled access offered by the scheme as well as valuable diversification opportunities for on farm and other local farm based tourism enterprises.

For details of the Angling 2000 scheme and beats for 2003 contact: Simon Evans (Head of Fisheries) on 01566 784488

The Westcountry Rivers Trust is working for you...

To continue its important work improving fisheries and helping rivers, wildlife and communities in the region, the Trust needs your help. You can join the Westcountry Rivers Trust as a "Supporter" for £50 a year (less that £1 per week). In return the Trust will send you its Newsletter and invitations to its events, river walks and other activities including "Angling 2000". Please ring or write for your free information pack.

You can also find out more about the work of the Trust and talk to our Scientific Team at the Westcountry Rivers Trust stand at the Devon County Show and Royal Cornwall Show in the Countryside Area, we look forward to seeing you there!

For further information please contact:
Westcountry Rivers Trust,
Fore Street, Lifton,
Devon, PL16 0AA

Telephone: 01566 784488
Fax: 01566 784404

Web address: www.wrt.org.uk
E-mail: wrt@wrt.org.uk

Game

The S&TA in its Centenary year

"100 years of service to game anglers and the environment"

It is incredible to think that the Salmon & Trout Association has now been working for one hundred years to safeguard the salmon and trout fisheries of the UK. It was in 1903 that a small group of men met in Fishmongers' Hall to resolve that "in view of the decadence of many salmon rivers, an Association be formed called the Salmon and Trout Association, the principle objects of which shall be to improve the Salmon & Trout Fisheries of the United Kingdom..."

The threats to our salmon and trout fisheries are far more complex today than back in 1903: abstraction, drift netting, aquaculture, the antis and predation to name but a few. But the Association has responded to these changes and from an initial membership of less than 100 of the privileged few, this has now grown to more than 100,000, open to all, with 42 county Branches. The Association now also has professional staff based in London and Scotland and a permanent lobbying representative in Brussels. Our views have become respected and sought by Government and its agencies. The Association also takes the promotion of its sport very seriously and, through our beginner courses, we introduce more than 2,000 anglers of all ages to fly fishing each year.

We have taken the opportunity in our centenary year to focus our activities on the promotion of integrated catchment management for our rivers, especially in light of the recent Habitats and Water Framework Directives. The whole ecosystem of a river relies upon the quality of its upper catchment, and it is likely that if things are right at the top, they will remain so throughout its length, notwithstanding the effects of flood defence schemes, pollution from industry or large-scale agriculture. Alas, too many upper catchments have been affected by lesser-recognised agricultural problems, such as overgrazing and land drainage, both of which result from the CAP paying farmers to over-produce on a ludicrous scale.

In Cornwall, the Warleggan rises on Bodmin Moor and flows south to feed the Fowey. It is an important spawning stream for salmon, sea trout and brown trout, but has the misfortune to flow through an upper catchment heavily grazed by livestock, which is controlled by farmers paid under CAP on a headage basis. In other words, the more animals that graze up on Bodmin, the more money gets paid to farmers under European agricultural policy.

Of course, we do not blame the hard-pressed farmers for this, but the results are desperate for the aquatic system. Overgrazing means that little vegetation is left to retain rainfall, and ground compaction from too many hoof movements adds to the ease with which water flows off the moor into the nursery streams to create spates, and a lack of any storage within the catchment to feed the system during dryer conditions. The ground is unstable from the effects of foraging livestock and so heavy rainfall takes soil into the streams, silting up redds and juvenile habitat in the process. Add bank erosion from livestock poaching and one is left with an untenable situation for most of the wildlife dependent upon upland streams, and the habitat for spawning and juvenile fish is especially affected.

Fortunately, there are already people doing terrific remedial work, most notably the various Rivers Trusts and Associations and some of the more visionary individual fishery owners. However, their task would be made so much easier if it was supported by legislation under an agricultural policy which protected sensitive upland habitats, without robbing farmers of their income from what is still the least-forgiving environment in which they try to eke out a living.

Farmers are paid to set-aside land each year to counter over-production. Is it too simplistic to ask that, wherever feasible, such land should be made into permanent buffer zones to protect aquatic habitat, and that our upland catchments be returned to their natural state? Not only would the environment benefit; flooding might also magically decrease as a perennial national problem, allowing some of that flood defence budget to be spent more sensibly elsewhere.

Success on Clatworthy Reservoir.
Nick Hart Fly Fishing

Europe is providing the glimmer of an opportunity for member governments to produce some intelligent, coordinated policies for the management of the aquatic environment. In this our Centenary year, and beyond, S&TA will be lobbying in the UK and Brussels to try and ensure some consistency appears across European and national legislation concerning the Water Framework and Habitats Directives, and that CAP is reformed to enable it to dovetail with them. Long-term thinking is required, so let us hope that we can help convince politicians to show some vision in these vital areas of environmental rehabilitation and conservation, and some commitment to provide funding to help carry out the work.

Local Contact details:

Bristol & West

Mr JS Tennant
Littlefield, The Village, Burrington, Bristol
BS40 7AD
Tel: 01761 462947 (h) 01275 852143 (w)

Wessex

Mr P McLeod
61 Collingworth Rise, Park Gates,
Southampton, SO31 1DD
Tel: 01489 564225

Somerset

Mr S Tolley
7 Lambpark Court, Churchinford, Taunton,
Somerset, TA3 7PL
Tel: 01823 601355

North Devon

Lt Col D Michie
The Round House, Webber Hill Farm,
Sampford Courtnay, Okehampton, Devon
EX20 2RU
Tel: 01837 54698

South & East Devon & Tamar

Mr C Hall
Higher Sticklepath Farm, Belstone,
Okehampton, Devon, EX20 1RD
Tel: 01837 840420

Cornwall

Mr A Hawken
5 Meadow Close, St Stephen, St Austell,
Cornwall, PL26 7PE
Tel: 01726 822343
Fax: 01726 824175

For further information please telephone: 020 7283 5838. www.salmon-trout.org

Recipe

Silverstream Gravadlax

Ingredients:

1 Sea Trout or Salmon 4-6 lb.
1 heaped Tablespoon Coarse Sea Salt
1 rounded tablespoon granulated Sugar
1 tea spoon crushed black pepper corns
2 rounded tablespoons fresh dill or 1 tablespoon of dried dill

Method:

1. Gut and fillet the fish but leave skin on
2. Mix all the rest of the ingredients together
3. Spread 1/3 of mixed dry ingredients on bottom of flat dish (dish should be as near to the size of the fish as possible)
4. Lay the fillet skin side down on top of mixture
5. Sprinkle over 1/3 of the mixture
6. Lay second fillet flesh side down on top
7. Sprinkle remaining mixture on top
8. Cover fish with Clingfilm
9. Weigh down with evenly distributed heavy weights (i.e. a brick in a poly' bag)
10. Place into fridge
11. Turn daily for 3-5 days pouring off the excess liquid each day
12. Serve sliced as for smoked salmon and accompanied with dill sauce

If your fish has been frozen do not freeze the Gravadlax but you can do so with a fresh fish.

Recipe supplied by Angi Stoop www.Silverstreamukfishing.com

Irish Netting Must be Curbed

The South West River Association and the fight to save our salmon

by SWRA Secretary Michael Charleston

Twelve months ago I hailed the decision of the Irish Fishery Minister, Frank Fahey, to impose a severe limit on Ireland's enormous salmon drift net catch. Sadly, my rejoicing proved to be premature. But I am glad to report that in recent weeks my optimism has returned.

Last year Mr Fahey was advised by his scientists to reduce the drift net catch to 117,000 salmon. That would have reduced the slaughter to a third or less of the fish taken legally and illegally over recent years. But he caved in to protests and the driftnets were legally allowed to kill 230,000 salmon, well above the average declared catch of the previous five years. Illegal catches and sales will have pushed that figure to well over 300,000. Some scientists think that is half of all the wild salmon that struggle to survive in the North Atlantic.

It is an unfortunate fact of life that when our salmon leave their sea feeding grounds off Greenland and Iceland and head for their home rivers in Cornwall, Devon, Dorset and Hampshire, their long journey eventually takes them down the west coast of Ireland. And there, barring their path, are some 700 legal drift nets. Each net may be a kilometre in length.

If you think this gives the salmon little chance I'm afraid it gets worse. Unmarked and just below the surface, a good many illegal nets lie in wait, too. It's not just our salmon stocks that suffer. Many of the fish are trying to reach Irish rivers and the nets also take salmon heading for Wales, Spain, France and Germany. These countries and their anglers - particularly the Irish rodsmen - have been getting increasingly angry about it.

So much for the bad news. Here's our latest intelligence from Ireland where the signs of a change of heart in Dublin are much more hopeful. I hesitate to shout too loudly after last year's experience of Mr Fahey's extraordinary behaviour. But Fahey is gone, there's a new fishery minister and there are indications from several different quarters that at long last the Irish Government is planning some kind of netting buyout.

In November I was a member of an international delegation to Dublin led by the SWRA's Patron, Orri Vigfusson, international chairman of the North Atlantic Salmon Fund. There, John O'Connor, Chief Executive of the Central Fishery Board, revealed that by the end of December he had to give the new Fishery Minister a wide-ranging report on what a buyout would involve. Since then European diplomatic sources have reported that the Irish Government intends to act on the report.

I do not think it is a coincidence that this sudden surge of activity follows a brilliant move by a member of our SWRA Council. Brian Marshall, Chairman of the Wessex Salmon and Rivers Trust, uncovered a clause in EC legislation which suggests that in ignoring the effects of its netting on other countries the Irish Government is in breach of the EC Habitats Directive. The European Commission is now investigating his complaint. We can be sure of one thing. Having gained so much from EC funds Ireland will not wish to upset the Commission.

As a result of Orri Vigfusson's tireless work and travels on both sides of the Atlantic the Dublin authorities are under considerable pressure from Irish anglers and from governments and organisations in other countries. If the new hopes of a buyout are realised, the support and practical assistance Orri gets from the SWRA will have been an important factor. But at the time of writing it is still too early to know if we have finally won.

At home the SWRA's less dramatic work continues apace. As the only regional organisation of river associations in the country we are official consultees for both the Environment Agency and DEFRA. It is a position we have steadily developed and expanded and we have taken part in several consultations on

swlakestrust

www.swlakestrust.org.uk

Trout Fishing

PREMIER RAINBOW FISHERIES

KENNICK - Nr Christow, Devon.
Permits: Self Service Kiosk
Season: 22 March - 31 October
Best Flies: Black Gnat/Montana/Damsel Nymph
Biggest Fish 1997: 10lb 14oz Rainbow.
Information: (01647) 277587

WIMBLEBALL LAKE - Nr Dulverton, Somerset.
Permits: Self Service at Hill Farm Barn
Season: 22 March - 31 October
Best Flies: Montana/Soldier Palmer/Buzzer.
Biggest Fish: 10lb 12oz Rainbow.
Information: Office hours (01398) 371372

SIBLYBACK LAKE - Nr Liskeard, Cornwall.
Permits: Self Service Kiosk at Watersports Centre
Season: 22 March - 31 October
Best Flies: Viva/Black & Peacock/Montana
Information: Ranger (01579) 342366

PREMIER BROWN TROUT FISHERY

ROADFORD - Nr Okehampton, Devon.
Permits: Angling and Watersports Centre at Lower Goodacre.
Season: 22 March - 12 October
Biggest Fish: 8lb 4oz Brown.
Information: (01409) 211507

INTERMEDIATE RAINBOW TROUT

STITHIANS - Nr Redruth, Cornwall.
Permits:
Stithians Watersports Centre (01209) 860301.
Sandy's Store, 7 Penryn St, Redruth (01209) 214877
Season: 15 March - 12 October
Information: Ranger (01579) 342366

WISTLANDPOUND - Nr Sth Molton, Devon.
Permits:
Post Office in Challacombe (01598) 763229.
The Kingfisher, Barnstaple (01271) 344919.
Lyndale News, Combe Martin (01271) 883283.
Variety Sports, Ilfracombe (01271) 862039.
Season: 15 March - 12 October
Information: Ranger (01288) 321262

LOW COST RAINBOW & BROWN

BURRATOR - Nr Yelverton, Devon.
Permits: Esso Garage, Yelverton.
Season: 15 March - 12 October
Information: (01837) 871565

COLLIFORD LAKE - Nr Bodmin, Cornwall.
Permits: Colliford Tavern.
Season: 15 March - 12 October
Information: Ranger (01579) 342366

FERNWORTHY LAKE - Nr Chagford, Devon.
Permits: Self Service Kiosk
Season: 1 April - 12 October
Best Flies: Black Gnat/Invicta/G&H Sedge
Information: (01837) 871565

FREE TROUT FISHING

MELDON - Nr Okehampton, Devon.
Free to holders of a valid E.A. Rod Licence and is zoned into spinning, bait and fly.
Season: 15 March - 12 October

AVON DAM - South Brent, Devon.
Angling by spinning, fly or bait and is free to valid E.A. licence holders.
Season: 15 March - 12 October

VENFORD - Nr Ashburton, Devon.
Free to holders of valid E.A. Rod Licence and can be fished by spinning, bubble float and bait.
Season: 15 March - 12 October.

CROWDY RESERVOIR - Nr Camelford, Cornwall.
Free to holders of valid E.A. Rod Licence.
Season: 15 March - 12 October.

EC, DEFRA and Environment Agency policies. Some of these will be vital to the future of both game and coarse fish stocks because they set out new strategies for abstraction and discharges.

We have several other important matters in hand. On the face of it the recent Agency reorganisation seems to have relegated fisheries to a very small place in Agency affairs. Yet the top regional officials insist that fisheries will gain from the changes. The SWRA is reserving judgement but we are carefully watching developments.

The SWRA has been offered the opportunity to launch a Fisheries Action Plan Group. This could be a far-reaching development. It would enable anglers and riparian owners to help the Agency to decide in practical terms on the management and improvement of the rivers they fish and own. This project is still under discussion so I cannot yet tell you what form the FAP will take in Devon.

If you wish to know more about our work, why not read the quarterly SWRA Newsletters? You can get copies by phoning me at 01822 853293 or e-mailing mwcharl@aol.com. You will also be invited to our annual general meetings at which an important national angling figure is always the main speaker.

A brace of 'doubles' for Gordon Tyson.
Tree Meadow

Wainsford Egg–Box Project River Fowey

Paul Eliot

The project was set up in 2000 as an attempt to sustain salmon stocks pending habitat and other improvements on the river. It followed a long term decline in numbers of salmon returning from the sea, very much in common with other salmon rivers throughout the British Isles. It was inspired by trials carried out by the Westcountry Rivers Trust in 1999 on the river Tamar. These trials were more experimental than intended to be an ongoing management tool.

The underlying concept of the project is that wild stocks are struggling to produce adequate juvenile numbers, due to degradation of the River Fowey by massive drainage works carried out by farmers high on the Bodmin Moor headwaters. These works were carried out to drain wetlands thus enabling more cattle to be ranched and more Government (DEFRA) subsidy claimed. Thousands of tons of sand now migrate down the river each year, smothering salmon spawning sites. The damage to the Moor is in many ways irreparable with peat bogs lost and increased flooding downstream a common feature, but we can only try to deal with the impacts on the fish population.

The egg box is a simple device which forces water upwards through gravel where the eggs are placed and the "upwelling" water keeps the eggs oxygenated and alive until hatching.

Our first consideration was obtaining salmon as brood stock. A strong desire not to deplete the natural stock was satisfied by using rod-caught fish only, they would otherwise have been served up as dinner! Local anglers took to the idea , along with visitors to the area on holiday and this year we held 28 adult fish in tanks until ripe for spawning. This took from one to three months and the eggs were then stripped from the females , fertilised and placed in the egg boxes for incubation. 70,000 were seeded from Fowey stock plus another 50,000 from the River Camel. All the latter eggs have been returned to that river.

With the first fry now hatching, we are planning release of the fry into the river system. It is important to spend time managing and improving the "in-river" habitat to support the increased numbers of fish. There is little point in placing fish where the food supply is inadequate. We therefore coppice trees to allow more light to the river. This enables plant life to flourish and invertebrate populations to sustain the little fish through the first feeding months. Light also promotes plant growth which stabilises river banks and reduces the sediment inputs which so damage spawning. Our farmer friends fence river banks keeping damaging cattle away from the spawning fish and a general "upwards" spiral of the whole system is created.

Why is this important? Forgetting for a moment the environmental issues, we begin to exploit a huge advantage that Cornwall enjoys in terms of revenue generated through Angling. We have the latest season for salmon in the country (season closes 15th December) and also the last real stronghold of migratory fish in England. Sea trout and salmon are in catastrophic decline throughout the rest of the country.

Healthy Smolt

A Cornish 'winter' Salmon.
Liskeard and District Angling Association

Game

What we now need to do is awaken the local authorities to the tourist potential of our two main rivers – the Fowey and the Camel. For so long they have been used as drains by the Highways people and as a source of Cornwall's drinking water (The Fowey) with no real concern, awareness or frankly even basic understanding of the potential value of the resource to the local economy. We will change all that once fish numbers are increased to a fraction of what they were just a few years ago and Cornwall takes its share of the £ multi-billion angling industry that exists worldwide.

The Hatchery at Wainsford has been financed by the Fowey River Association , supported by the Environment Agency and local riparian owners. With ongoing success we desperately need help from local business and visitor anglers to maintain the momentum into the future.

LET'S ALL PULL TOGETHER in restoring the bountiful wildlife of Devon & Cornwall's rivers! – the last stronghold of migratory fish in England.

Healthy fish re-stocking our rivers

Tom Bacon with a 6lb 9oz Rainbow.
Amherst Lodge

Game

The Experience Factor ...

By Nick Hart

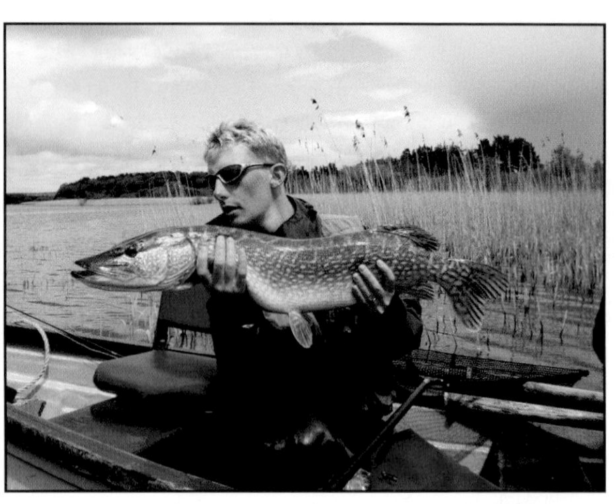

Nick with a 12lb Pike

The fish rises again, the angler tenses, makes final adjustments to tackle and fires an artful cast upstream towards the unsuspecting Brown Trout. The fly line lands cleanly behind the fish, hardly making an impression on the waters surface as the carefully prepared tapered leader turns over positioning the fly perfectly above the quarry. Now the river current takes over, seconds later the anglers artificial is within the Trout's window of vision, totally fooled the fish gently sips in the rogue offering. Stunned that this fly has actually bitten back the little spotty takes to the air in a rage tussling all the way to the anglers moistened hand, within moments the barbless hook is gently released and the fish swims back to it's territory, just a little wiser. Makes your mouth water, doesn't it?

So what caught that fish? Was it the expensive carbon fibre rod? Well that helped. What about the computer designed and profiled fly line? Again it is certainly important. Ah, then it must have been the loving crafted dry fly. Well, actually no, this fish would probably have taken almost anything that was the right size and colour. No the answer to this question is ... experience.

The problem with experience is that it cannot be purchased like a rod or whipped together like our little dry flies, no, this valuable asset has to be earned through many hours of trials and tribulations on the river bank. I suppose that this very fact is what keeps the hooked angler coming back for more; it is the constant learning curve and search for a new challenge that sees millions of us stringing up our rods each week. All very well but many of us have families, work commitments and all the other stresses and strains of modern day life to think about which doesn't always leave us much time to become piscatorial masters. Enter the Fly Fishing Guide.

This new breed of Ghillie has started to grow in popularity across the U.K. and especially in the West Country. Now for a fee you can hire your own personal tackle box of experience. A Guide can set up beats for you, organise accommodation if required and most importantly be right there to advise you just before you make that important cast. Guides will have an intimate knowledge of their venue, the flies required, which angle to approach the fish from, the best times of day, and indeed most will (and should) posses a casting qualification. So, if you are in a situation where you need to make a single handed Spey cast, perhaps a specialised mend or avoid a variety of obstacles, professional help is right there by your side. Of course many people will immediately shun the idea because they like to fish in solitude, don't we all! But, hiring a guide at the beginning of a trip can give you that extra edge. Now the casting is in tiptop shape, you have all the local fly patterns in your box and you know exactly how to go about catching that big old Trout under a root. This surely increases the enjoyment factor immensely and after all isn't that why we go fishing in the first place?

Not convinced that a Guide can help you? Perhaps you fancy trying for a new species on fly? Don't know where to start? Guides are available to catch not just Trout, Salmon or Sea Trout. Now there are stunning fish such as the Bass on offer, hard fighting Pollack or Mackerel

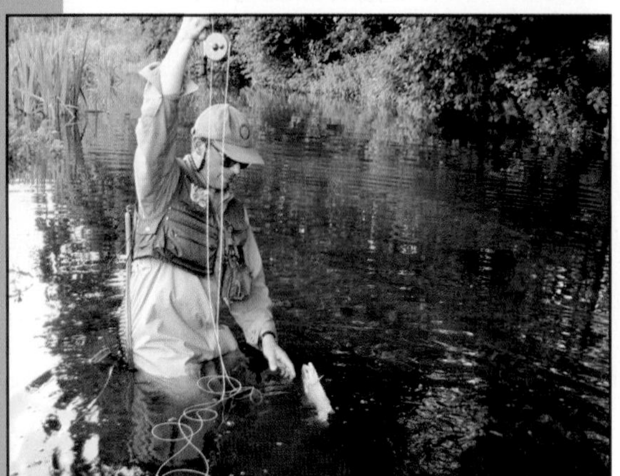
A more traditional quarry - Brown Trout

and in some cases even Wrasse. When tackling saltwater species such as this and with such a vast expanse of water to cover a Guide is invaluable. But the list doesn't end there with Fly Fishing Guides diversifying into Coarse fish such as the awesome Pike or crafty Carp. So how do you go about finding a Guide?

Hiring guides is easy enough, for a start just take a look at "Get Hooked!". Other places to enquire at are Hotels with fishing rights, local tourist boards and indeed many venues nowadays have a "resident professional" Guidance is most often purchased by the half or full day and no it won't always be cheap. However with that extra experience under your belt you can return to a venue with an edge, which could have only been achieved by spending many years, fishing it. We Brits do tend to be a bit of a D.I.Y. bunch but just think about it for a moment, hours of frustration trying to find the right fly, or a few extra tenners and a memorable fishing holiday?

So fly anglers seeking that extra bit of help with their fishing are well catered for but what do you do if you have never cast a fly before? Often providing the services detailed above Fly Fishing Instructors go one step further and offer regular courses which teach the skills required to become a proficient fly angler. This interesting experience doe's not only centre on fly casting but also the whole process of finding fish, choosing the right fly through matching the hatch and finally hooking, playing and landing your prize. Many people say that you can teach yourself but look at it this way, how many golfers purchase a set of clubs and then go hacking their way through the nearest course!? Full time Fly Fishing Instructors are professionals and will have all the gear required to hand, plus suitable venues and often a set of notes which can be referred to at a later date. Most importantly they should also come complete with a qualification such as that set by the Advanced Professional Game Angling Instructors (APGAI).

This network of Instructors and Guides has opened Fly Fishing to the masses. No longer is it the preserve of the rich dressed in traditional attire, these days you are more likely to see a Fly Fisher sporting a Baseball Cap and Jeans rather than an old-fashioned tweed number. With this barrier gone it has made way for Fly Fishing to become a multi cultural sport not dominated by males but enjoyed by women and children also. Indeed in my experience as an instructor I often find that women and children listen more intently and learn faster (sorry chaps!) than most men!

This season I urge you to look up a guide or instructor and make use of one of their exciting services, I assure you that the results can be fantastic and even on the more difficult days at least there is someone on hand to sort out those annoying tangles! Yes, a day out with a Fly Fishing Guide can certainly be an experience to remember. I wish you all tightlines, screaming reels and dry waders ....

Fly caught Bass

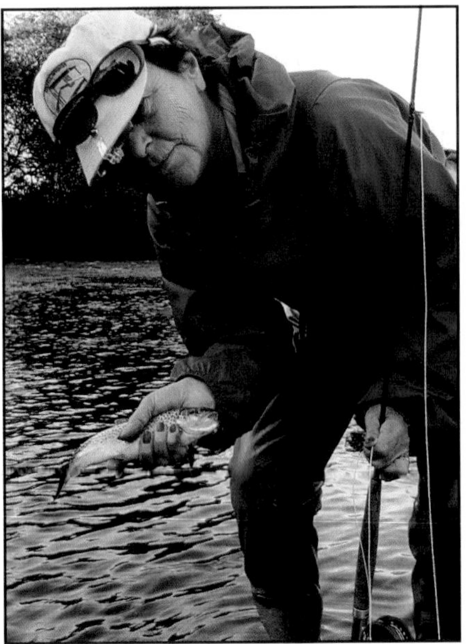

Classic Westcountry Brown Trout
Nick Hart Fly Fishing

Game

CHEW VALLEY LAKE
BLAGDON LAKE
THE BARROWS
LITTON

Catch rates were again very high at our fisheries in 2002 with nearly 60,000 hard fighting rainbow and brown trout landed over the season leading to an awful lot of enjoyable visits and a huge number of happy anglers!

Woodford Lodge is now firmly established as a very popular venue. Rebuilt in 2000, the lodge provides excellent facilities for anglers such as the full scale tackle shop, as well as a comfortable lounge and restaurant serving breakfasts, lunches and evening meals and a bar.

We continue to offer a friendly and helpful fishery service to all from the Lodge even though it is now open to the public as well as to anglers. Those seeking a quieter venue can still visit Blagdon which still caters only for anglers.

Disabled anglers may fish from a special wheely boat at Blagdon and we have priority bank fishing spots, suitable for those with limited walking ability, marked out at Chew and Blagdon. Our Lodges are all accessible to wheelchair users.

CHEW

at 1200 acres, is our largest lake and it lies some seven miles due south of Bristol. It is most renowned for loch style boat fishing and has a fleet of 32 motor boats, each equipped with an outboard motor. There is plenty of room on the lake for expert and pleasure angler alike and the scenery and bird life are a real bonus for those with time to look around. May and June are usually, but not always, the best months and are the time of year when a variety of buzzers hatch and bring the trout to the surface. Casting to rising fish and hooking and playing our superb, home-grown rainbows, which average well over 2lbs, is the pinnacle of stillwater fly fishing.

Bank fishing can also be very good at Chew, particularly early in April, through May and June and then again in September and October. There are many miles of uncrowded lake margins to choose from and though the main season ends in mid October we continue for winter fishing up until the end of November.

BLAGDON

is 440 acres in area and has 18 rowing boats for which anglers are welcome to use their own electric outboards. With no noisy petrol engines the fishery is a peaceful and beautiful place to fish. In recent seasons there have been less buzzers than at Chew but more sedges and damsel flies and the nature of the fishing is thus slightly different.

The banks provide very good sport and there

Woodford Lodge at Chew

12lb Rainbow caught by Roger Cannock during the Heart Foundation Charity final. Tavistock Trout

are numerous hot-spots from where you will find ample space to cast a line. The surrounding meadows support cowslips and native orchids and overhead you will often see buzzards riding the thermals and swallows and martins competing with the trout to take the flies; fishing at Blagdon is about more than just catching fish!

THE BARROWS

are three reservoirs of 60, 40, and 25 acres lying close to Bristol on either side of the A38 some three miles out of the city. They are bank only fisheries. All the lakes contain a mixture of brown & rainbow trout. We stock slightly smaller fish, so permit prices cost less, but the Barrows perhaps provide the most reliable bank sport of all our fisheries. The evening rise can be a very profitable time with buzzer and sedge hatches giving great sport to rising fish.

LITTON

gives fishermen the chance to have exclusive use of a fishery for a day's fishing. There are two lakes; the lower is 8 acres and is the main fishery stocked with rainbows and browns, while the upper is 11 acres but reduces in size through the summer and is stocked mostly with brown trout. There is a rowing boat on each lake and a permit will allow you to fish at both. The limit is 5 trout per person. The fishery is available on Thursdays, Fridays, Saturdays and Sundays and bookings are made at Wooford Lodge.

PERMITS.

The centre for bookings, enquiries and tackle Sales is Woodford Lodge at Chew. All kinds of permit are issued here. At Blagdon our half-timbered lodge offers a lesser range of facilities but is still a comfortable place to eat your lunch or warm up in front of a log fire and the building is staffed during the morning for permits, enquiries, small tackle sales and advice. At the Barrows there is a self-service kiosk for permits and separate lavatories and shelters.

SPECIAL OFFERS.

This year we offer the following special deals:

1 Any experienced angler can take a junior angler fishing on his day bank permit at no extra cost. (limit bag is shared).

2 In August all bank permits will entitle the permit holder to a free bank permit to be taken during August.

3 In August if you purchase two days boat fishing you will be entitled to a third day FREE OF CHARGE!

TUITION.

We are keen to encourage all ages to take up fly fishing and offer a range of lessons backed up by half price permits for your first few visits after a lesson. Casting lessons are held on most Saturday mornings and cost just £10.00, (tackle can be provided). Following one of these you can have 2 bank permits at half price to get you going. Many beginners will also want a full fishing lesson, (normally held once a month on a Saturday) in order to move on from casting to actual fishing and these cost £20 and entitle you to 2 half price bank permits.

Our tutors hold the Stanic qualification and we will continue to give advice and help on subsequent visits for as long as it takes you to feel confident about your fishing. We can also put you in touch with private tutors and particularly recommend Mike Gleave for tuition at our lakes or elsewhere and England International John Horsey who offers a coaching service for boat fishing at Chew or Blagdon.

We run popular Beginners Days on most Saturday afternoons during the season for all ages. These combine basic teaching with you having a go at bank and boat fishing at only £10 per person. Booking is essential.

YOUTH COMPETITION.

On the 27th May we will hold our annual Youth Fishing Competition. Open to all anglers between 12 and 19 years, this is a boat competition at Chew with a local expert as a boat partner, and a top prize of a tackle voucher for £200. The entrance fee of £15 includes permits and an evening buffet. Details and booking forms from Woodford Lodge.

ENQUIRIES AND BOOKINGS.

Phone or write to Bristol Water Fisheries, Woodford Lodge, Chew Stoke, Bristol. BS40 8XH. Telephone or fax: 01275 332339 for a free brochure, for all enquiries and for bookings.

You can e-mail us at:
bob.handford@bristolwater.co.uk
or visit our web site for regular updates on the fishing at, www.bristolwater.co.uk.

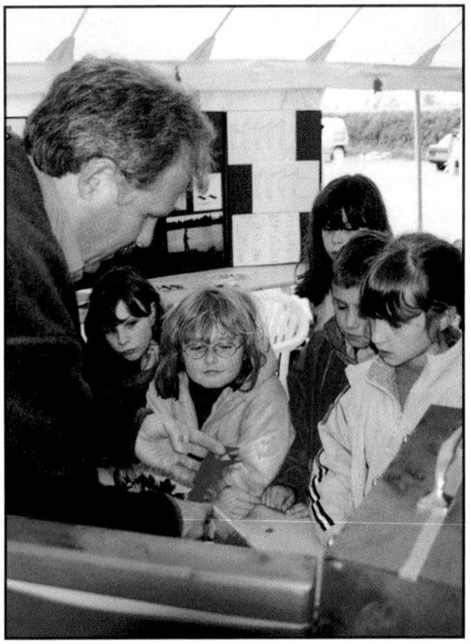

Gary Champion demonstrating fly tying.
South West Lakes Trust

Go fishing with Wessex Water

Whether you are a keen angler or just enjoy an occasional day out fishing, Wessex Water's reservoirs provide the perfect setting.

Anglers can enjoy their favourite sport at our Somerset fisheries at Clatworthy, Hawkridge and Sutton Bingham. Durleigh Reservoir, just south of Bridgwater, offers coarse anglers a similar opportunity.

Clatworthy:

Season: 19 March - 12 October 2003

Situated in the Brendon Hills on the edge of the Exmoor National Park in west Somerset, Clatworthy Reservoir impounds the head waters of the River Tone.

Anglers can enjoy fishing for rainbow and brown trout from the banks of this 130 acre reservoir or from a boat, which anglers are recommended to book in advance.

Clatworthy offers good top of the water fishing with nymphs or dry flies or at the deep areas with sinking lines and flashing lures.

For further information about fishing at Clatworthy, contact the ranger Dave Pursey on 01984 624658.

Hawkridge:

Season: 19 March - 12 October 2003

This upland reservoir, seven miles west of Bridgwater, nestles in a small valley on the Quantock Hills in an Area of Outstanding Natural Beauty.

The 32 acre reservoir provides fishing facilities for brown or rainbow trout from the bank or a boat, which anglers are recommended to book in advance.

An updated fishing report as well as information on the latest flies, tactics and catch rate can be found in the lodge.

For further details about fishing at Hawkridge, please contact the ranger Gary Howe on 01278 671840.

Sutton Bingham:

Season from 19 March - 12 October 2003

Situated some four miles south of Yeovil, Sutton Bingham reservoir is a 142 acre lowland fishery, set in the gently rolling hills of the Somerset and Dorset border.

The reservoir offers excellent fly fishing for rainbow and brown trout, either from the bank or a boat. A " wheelie " boat is available for wheelchair users. It is recommended to book boats in advance.

Because Sutton Bingham is a lowland reservoir, the water is not deep and the most popular method of fishing is with a floating line and mainly small lures and nymphs.

For more details about fishing at Sutton Bingham, contact ranger Ivan Tinsley on 01935 872389.

Otterhead Lakes:

Season from 1 April - 30 September 2003

The two lakes at Otterhead once formed part of a landscaped estate. The surroundings have now run wild and provide a beautiful setting for fishing.

It is now a nature reserve managed by the Somerset Wildlife Trust on behalf of Wessex Water.

The lakes are situated on the Blackdown Hills, south of Taunton and one mile north of the village of Churchingford.

For further information contact club secretary Mike Woolen on 01460 65977.

Durleigh:

Open every day except 25 & 26 December and 1 January

One of the oldest in the Wessex Water region, Durleigh reservoir is the only Wessex Water reservoir dedicated to public coarse fishing.

Anglers can fish over 80 acres which provide an abundance of coarse fish for matches or the casual angler.

Trout Fishing in the South Wessex Area

By Matt Carter

Rivers

The South Wessex Area encompasses many 'chalk streams' which are nationally famous for fly-fishing for trout. These include the Upper Avon at Salisbury and associated tributaries, the Rivers Frome, Piddle and River Allen a tributary of the River Stour.

Fishing access to these waters is generally controlled by local owners, estates, syndicates and in a limited way by local angling clubs.

Many of these waters are currently stocked with brown trout, however several fisheries are now turning away from this to catch and release, promoting natural production and 'wilder' fish populations. Further details regarding access are given in this guide.

Stillwaters

There are several stillwater 'put and take' fisheries spread across this area. These are generally stocked with rainbow trout although a few specialise in brown trout.

In the north of the area good stillwater fly fishing can be found at Steeple Langford Fisheries near Salisbury. In the West of the area good fly fishing can be found at the Wessex Chalk streams Ltd site near Tolpuddle.

Other notable fisheries can be found at Damerham and Rockford near Ringwood.

This lowland reservoir contains carp, roach, bream, perch, tench and specimen size pike.

For further details about fishing or matches, contact the ranger Paul Martin on 01278 424786.

Blashford Lakes

Blashford Lakes are a series of former gravel pits set in the River Avon Valley on the Dorset and Hampshire borders.

Blashford, Spinnaker Lake offers coarse fishing to members of the Christchurch Angling Club during the coarse fishing season.

For further information, contact the club secretary Mr C Harrison, 19 Victoria Gardens, Ringwood, Hampshire BH24 1FD or telephone 07885 761 381.

Tucking Mill:

Season from 16 June 2003 to 14 March 2004

Set in a secluded wood, Tucking Mill is located in the attractive Midford Valley, south of Bath.

Wessex Water offers free coarse fishing for disabled anglers at this small lake which is stocked with roach, chub, tench and large carp.

There are six specially designed wheelchair platforms with space for two wheelchairs each plus further platforms for the more mobile anglers.

Each disabled angler may bring along one able-bodied person who may also fish but has to use the same site.

For more information: General enquiries on fishing, a request for our free brochure on fishing and recreation or season tickets should be made through Wessex Water customer services on 0845 600 4 600.

Alternatively you can view our fishing brochure on-line at:

www.wessexwater.co.uk

Day or evening tickets for fishing and boat hire are available on a self serve basis from the public fisheries at each lodge.

The South West Federation of Fly Fishers

The South West Federation of Fly Fishers belongs to the Confederation of English Fly Fishers. The Confederation is, amongst other things, responsible for running National and International Fly Fishing Teams and Competitions. The grassroots of all the National and International Competitions are the Regional Eliminators run by Federations all over the Country.

The South West Federation runs Eliminators at Chew Valley Lake. This years dates are as follows

FIRST ELIMINATOR: SUN 27 APRIL
SECOND ELIMINATOR: SUN 25 MAY
FINAL ELIMINATOR: SUN 22 JUNE

Competitors can ONLY enter ONE of the first two eliminators and if successful would qualify for the Final Eliminator. Thirty competitors compete in the Final Eliminator. In 2002 there were fourteen places available for the Loch Style National, and we would hope for a similar number in 2003.

The Loch Style National in 2003 is at GRAFHAM WATER on SAT SEPT 27th.

ELIGIBILITY

Anyone can enter provided that they are over 18 years of age, and have been domiciled in ENGLAND for 3 years.

Competitors can ONLY enter eliminators in ONE Region in any one year. Anyone who has previously fished at International Level for another Country is NOT eligible to fish.

If you are interested in competitive Fly Fishing, with the chance to fish for England, write to me at the address below or give me a ring.

J.A. Loud,
153/155 East Street,
Bedminster,
BRISTOL BS3 4EJ
Tel (Daytime) 0117 9872050
Tel (Evenings) 0117 9232166

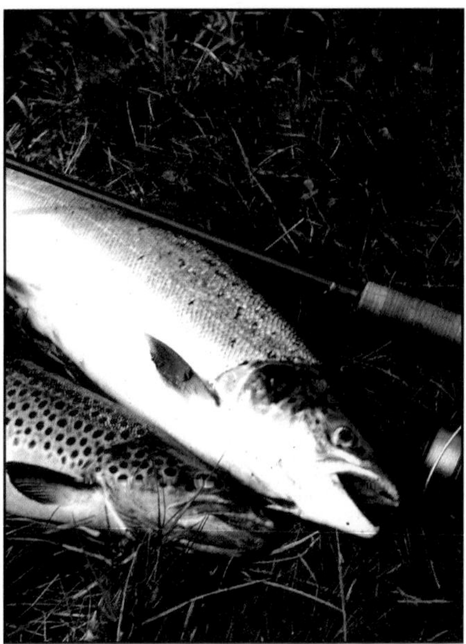

7lb Salmon and 4lb Sea Trout from the Teign. Picture - Mike Weaver

Six Superb Spring Fed Lakes

plus a half mile of chalkstream

Corporate Hospitality a Speciality

Email: rockbourne@talk21.com
Website: www.rockbournetroutfishery.co.uk
Rockbourne Road, Sandleheath, Fordingbridge, Hampshire SP6 1QG. **Tel 01725 518603**

Wiltshire's Best Kept Secret

Open All Year

- Four acre Trout Lake fed by the Hampshire Avon situated near Upavon in the heart of Pewsey Vale
- Quality Fly-Fishing for hard fighting Rainbows
- Tickets, Food and Accommodation from the Woodridge Inn adjacent to the fishery on the A345

Phone for details and directions

Manningford Trout Farm and Fly Fishery

Tel: 01980 630033

www.trout4u.co.uk

The Hampshire Avon

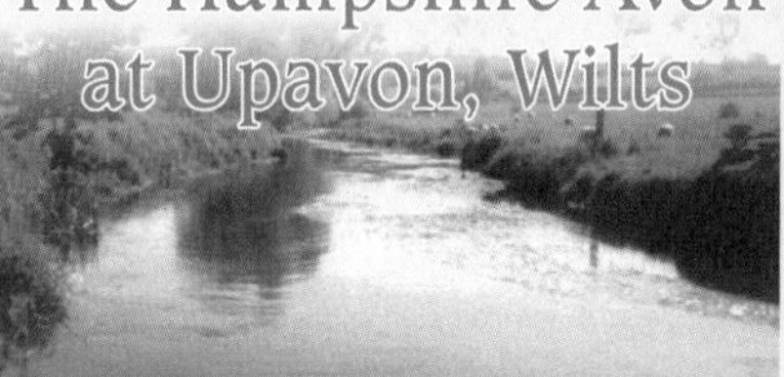

This is a select chalk stream renowned for it's wild Brown Trout and Grayling fishing. We offer a 3/4 mile stretch which is open to both day and season ticket holders.

The river is ideally suited to a 8.5ft rod (max river width 40ft, min 20ft). Waist waders are advisable with depths between 18 inches and 3ft. Average fish are 1 to 1.5lb. Last season's largest fish was a 2lb 10oz brown. Access to the river by car is no problem.

Season tickets are £450 and day tickets are £45

BED & BREAKFAST AVAILABLE

Tel 01980 630008

Mobile: 07770 922 544

Email: chris.young16@btopenworld.com.

Who needs to be a Millionaire!

Chris with the late Bernard Venables

Chris Tarrant

I still remember my first fish as vividly as if I had caught it this morning. It was a perch of probably no more than 3 or 4oz. The greedy little creature had somehow managed to pull a very large homemade cork float, attached to a hook baited with a huge worm, under the surface of the river Thames just downstream of Reading. I caught two or three more that afternoon, fishing with my gran dfather, and that was me literally hooked for life.

I have never, ever looked back. I have never regretted a single second's fishing. In good times, in bad times, in busy times, and in recent years there have been plenty of those, I have always enjoyed my fishing and, perhaps more importantly, appreciated the opportunity to fish clean, pure waters for healthy fish.

These days my angling tends to consist of grabbing a few hours anyhow anywhere I can - but perhaps this makes me appreciate these occasions even more.

Many kids these days coming into the sport start with carp. Entirely understandable as the carp is probably the most common and, at smaller sizes one of the most eager of all our coarse fish. These budding anglers get hold of all the latest all-singing all-dancing carp rods, reels, rigs, buzzers, baits and bivvies and sadly, all too often, have lost all interest in the sport inside three or four years. Perhaps they are starting a little two far 'up the ladder'. The angling press is awash with pictures of massive carp but these leviathans are frequently only landed by the specialist.

There is no real substance to their fishing. They have missed out on the precious learning curve. They have missed out, through no fault of their own, on experiences such as the wonderful summer's afternoons I spent catching perch and bleak with my grandad.

Learning to appreciate the value of catching any fish, regardless of size or species is vital. Of course we all like to catch specimen fish and we all have our own tales to tell of monsters from the deep that disdainfully smashed our tackle, but any fish is a good fish.

In my youth the bleak shoals in the Thames were absolutely huge. They teemed in every swim. They were lightening fast biters, but if you missed one there'd be another one along in seconds. Sadly, they have more or less completely disappeared from my childhood stretches. I haven't caught or even seen a bleak for many years.

The perch are not there in the numbers they were either. Those wonderful hours spent watching a float bob, bob, bobbing as a small perch tried to somehow engulf a huge lobworm don't really seem to happen anymore.

These days if you are fortunate enough to catch a perch in my local stretches of the Thames it'll probably be a two-pounder or bigger, more often it's huge chub. Small fish don't seem to exist in the Thames near me at all these days, I haven't caught a gudgeon in years, and while it's great to catch these bigger fish it does make me concerned for the future when the big old fish die.

James Underwood from Plymouth with a nice summer Carp.
Picture from Manadon Angling Supplies

The fate of all our waterways is always in the balance. Never mind the damage caused by careless, mindless polluters, the damage done by cormorants in my area is unspeakable. The silverfish population is virtually non-existent and it's not just the small stuff. Only last winter, I watched a cormorant flying away from a small river in Oxfordshire that used to be packed with big roach, carrying a beautiful specimen of well over two pounds in its beak.

Not surprisingly the big roach population in this particular river, like so many others, is now down to just a handful of fish. In spite of absurd successive surveys, it is a fact that cormorants are a very real threat to our sport. These voracious birds have come inland en masse in recent years and many countrymen will bear witness to the cormorant's massive appetite for fish of all species and sizes. I cannot imagine who these surveys ask for their information - but it certainly does not seem to be the people who actually live and work on the waterways of this country.

So things are tough enough without idiots who in a few seconds thoughtlessness or utter carelessness drop something into our waterways that can kill everything downstream and take ten or twenty years to rebuild. In many cases the waterways simply never recover or, at best, are a pale echo of their former selves.

I can still vividly remember the first pollution that I ever witnessed. I was probably only 10 or 11 years old and fishing on a very easy local pond that had been getting progressively more difficult for weeks. It was also starting to smell, and then the first dead fish started to show up. Bream at first, then perch in their hundreds, some huge fish too. Looking back some of those fish were well over 3 lbs. Finally the lake disgorged the bloated corpses of a few enormous carp, well enormous to us, those poor defenceless bodies were probably the remains of magnificent 7 or 8 pounders!

That lake that had provided pleasure to thousands of anglers, including my dad, my grandad and even his grandad, over generations, died in less than a fortnight. It lingered on for a few years but it smelt of death and there were virtually no fish. No local clubs would risk re-stocking it and, as far as I know, it is now somewhere underneath junction 9 of the M4 motorway! There cannot surely be a more inglorious end for a water that had brought so much pleasure to so many for probably two or three hundred years.

This is why I was delighted to be asked to become president of the A.C.A. Without their tireless work in recent years I seriously wonder how much sport worth the mention would be left for anglers in this country. Their results, working on a shoestring for years, are absolutely magnificent but still only a handful of anglers actually get involved. If every angler in this country paid only £1 a year towards the future of his or her sport, it would amount to a huge sum of money, a massive fighting fund and the future for our anglers, our fish and our waterways in this country could be safeguarded for a thousand years!

It is through publications such as Get Hooked that we can spread our message, make anglers aware of what the A.C.A. do and recruit new members. Full membership costs just £15 per year with junior membership at only £3. That really is very little, how much did you spend on your last fishing trip? Bait, petrol, permits? If there is anything at all that I can do in my role as president of the A.C.A to make that happen, then it would be my life's proudest achievement.

Go on, join today, and when you have joined get your mates to join, get your club to join. It will be for your benefit in the long run

A.C.A., Eastwood House,
6 Rainbow Street, Leominster,
Herefordshire HR6 8DQ.

Contact details:

Telephone: 01568 620447
Fax: 01568 614236
E-mail: admin@a-c-a.org
Website: www.a-c-a.org

Disabled Angling Association Land Big Fish

More than nine million disabled people may soon have more opportunities to go fishing after the English Federation of Disability Sport recently decided to officially endorse the work of the British Disabled Angling Association (BDAA).

The EFDS decision to join forces with the BDAA is a positive move which both charities hope will proactively and sustainably change and develop the future of angling for disabled people in England.

One of the first tasks for the EFDS is help the BDAA provide disabled people with information on where to go, and the equipment to use as they prepare to cast a line. Added Peter Thompson, "I'm sure that the co-operation of the EFDS and BDAA will make life easier for those searching for a start in fishing and feel that the future is in our hands. We have to ensure that we make significant and lasting changes that are so desperately needed in this field of angling."

The BDAA was formed 6 years ago and is the leading European organisation dedicated to the promotion of Coarse, Sea, Carp, Game and Cat Fishing for disabled people. With a growing membership, the BDAA are striving to widen and improve facilities at fishing venues and raise awareness amongst and support from the non-disabled community.

The partnership has been welcomed by BDAA Director Peter Thompson who, in his appreciation of the EFDS endorsement, praised the work of BDAA secretary Terry Moseley for achieving the latest recognition. 'Terry Moseley has worked tirelessly in ensuring people with disabilities have the same opportunities to go fishing as non-disabled people. As an Association we look forward to a long and fruitful working relationship with EFDS"

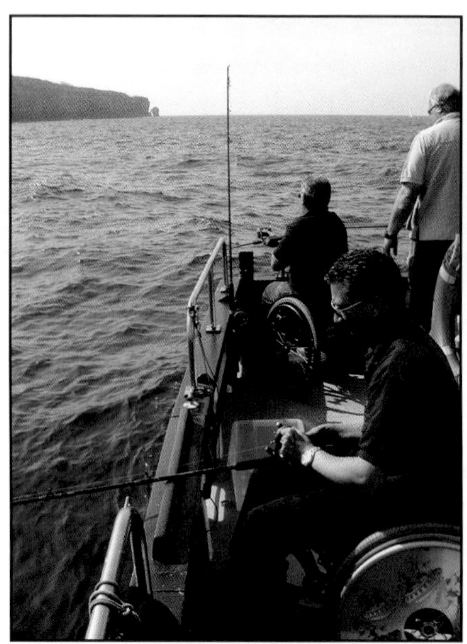

Sea fishing off Weymouth

EFDS Chief Executive Colin Chaytors highlighted, "There are almost 9 million disabled people in this country and we know that over 60,000 of these already go fishing on a regular basis. By working closely with the BDAA and other key organisations such as the Environment Agency, we can help to ensure that these and many other people with disabilities, can become more involved in fishing either as participants, coaches and administrators."

The British Disabled Angling Association (BDAA) is a registered charity established to develop and promote angling opportunities for disabled people in the UK.

With help from celebrity patrons, parent bodies of angling, disability groups and individuals, the BDAA aims to ensure that any disabled person, be they beginner or expert, can have the opportunity to cast a line.

It is FREE to join the BDAA and members receive:

- Online access to information on all aspects of disability angling and the work of the BDAA
- Answers to questions and/or requests via e-mail or through the BDAA website are provided within 24 hours

Carl Okill with a Bream caught on a Tightline Tours expedition.

MELLONWATTS MILL

Pensagillas Farm, Grampound, Truro

2 acre lake, stocked with Carp (Common & Mirror) Roach, Tench and Golden Rudd

CAMPING & TOURING CARAVANS
(electric hook up)

SELF-CATERING CABIN

Day Tickets £5 - Seasons Tickets available
Night fishing by arrangement

For Further Details Tel: 01872 530808
Email: pensagillas@farming.co.uk

Summercourt, Nr Newquay

3.5 acre Lake stocked with Carp, Tench, Rudd, Bream, Perch, Roach and Crucians

OPEN ALL YEAR ROUND DAWN TO DUSK

Night Fishing by arrangement.

Day Tickets - pay kiosk - Adults £4 (2 rods), Junior/OAP/Disabled £3 (2 rods). Barbless Hooks only, No Tiger or Peanuts. No Carp to be kept in keepnets. All nets to be dipped on site.

Enquiries to Brian & Sandra Hiscock, 89 Pydar Close, Newquay. Tel: 01637 871275
Email: oakside.fishery@btopenworld.com

In one of our six self catering cottages sleeping from 2 to 10

Plenty for the whole family to enjoy while the anglers enjoy the 1 acre lake stocked with Carp to 15lb Roach, Tench and Rudd

DAY TICKETS £4. WEEK £16

FREE Facilities include - Tennis, Putting Green, Games Room. Lounge Bar, Children's Play Area, Animal Paddock & Barbecue.

All linen and electricity included in price

3 miles from Sea Fishing & Beaches at Looe

Joyce & Robert Brown, Badham Farm
St Keyne, Liskeard, Cornwall PL14 4RW
Tel:Fax: 01579 343572 for a Brochure
www.looedirectory.co.uk/badhamcottages.htm

- Access to a telephone information hotline on all aspects of disability angling
- Information about disability angling events around the UK
- Information about access to angling worldwide
- Advice on a range of specially adapted I angling equipment only currently available through the BDAA

The work carried out by the BDAA in the past year includes:

Shore fishing event

BDAA have successfully entered into the promotion of Sea fishing for anglers with disabilities by organising an annual shore event at Otterspool, Liverpool where 100 anglers from around the UK attend the event.

Boat fishing

Through television production the BDAA have set up sea fishing boats in Weymouth and Brighton whereby disabled anglers now have the opportunity of trying boat fishing as a new experience afloat on adapted vessels.

Coarse Fishing

The BDAA successfully organised its 5th National event for anglers with disabilities attracting over 300 participants nation-wide in this now recognised event.

HAT and BDAA

A working relationship has been set up with the Handicapped Anglers Trust (who provide wheelyboats for use by people with disabilities) to create a unity in the sport. As a result BDAA/ HAT are now to provide access via wheelyboats to areas that at one time were only available to able bodied anglers.

Salmon Fishing

The BDAA have obtained life fishing rights on the famous River Doon, Ayrshire, and this new venture will see anglers with disabilities try salmon fishing on and accessible and professionally designed salmon river in Scotland.

Organisations requests

The number of requests for help and introduction of angling from multi-disability organisations has risen dramatically and seen a major improvement whereby requests for theory and practical hands-on has proven that Social Services etc. are in need of a sport that anyone can enter despite disability.

Disability Rights Commission

The Disability Rights Commission have approached BDAA for their information regarding angling, and now use this in order to offer help to others who may need information on the 2004 disability rights act.

It can be seen that the BDAA has become recognised as the first point of call for all things related to disability angling, and so well have the public and angling communities welcomed their work that the gelling of all the types of fishing be it sea, coarse, or game has seen a unity without struggle and central point of information.

Neglected areas are finally being addressed and that disability is at the forefront of angling. The BDAA have worked and continue to strive for new opportunities for disabled people of all ages, who have, or would like an interest in angling and have it laid out to them in a professional manner.

Contact: BDAA, 9 Yew Tree Road, Delves, Walsall, West Midlands WS5 4NQ. Tel: 01922 860912 Website: www.bdaa.co.uk

Exeter & District A.A. Bailiff Steve Moore

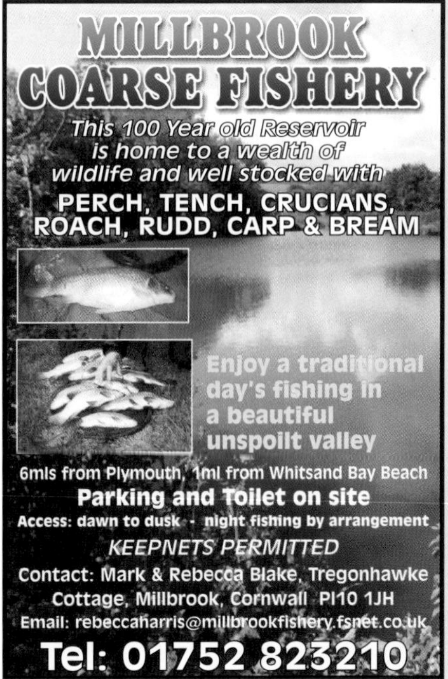

ELMFIELD FARM
COARSE FISHERY

- CANWORTHY WATER, CORNWALL -

1.25 & 2 acre mixed Lakes well stocked with:

Carp to 24lb, Tench 6lb, Bream 6.5lb, Roach 3lb, Rudd 1.5lb, Perch 3.5lb, Orfe 1lb, Chub 3lb

NO CLOSED SEASON

Open Dawn to Dusk - £5 TWO RODS

Children and OAPs £4.00

Hot & Cold Food and Drinks available

Camping/Caravan Site and 6 berth Mobile Home for holiday let

South West Lakes Trust Fisheries

The South West Lakes Trust is an independent charity formed to promote and enhance sustainable recreation, access and nature conservation on and around inland waters in the South West of England for the benefit of the general public. After the setbacks of the previous year, with the Foot and Mouth outbreak , anglers were keen to get back on to the water, and last season proved to be a great success for South West Lakes Trust anglers.

The South West Lakes Angling Association coarse fishing team, captained by Billy Knott, continued last year's success in The Embassy National Championship, and has been promoted to Division 3 for next year. Wimbleball / Kennick anglers Steve Ebdon and Andrew Gooding successfully fished the local and national heats to qualify for the England team for 2003. We plan to build on last year's success, and aim to offer something for all levels of competence (from complete novices through to international match anglers) in both coarse and game disciplines.

The Trust continues with its drive to introduce the sport to all newcomers, from children to pensioners. We intend to follow up on last year's successful introductory and training days in various aspects of coarse angling, (including our specialist pike and carp days), with the help of the E.A., N.F.A. accredited instructors, and local specialists. From this season, Juniors under the age of 12 years will be able to fish for free (providing they are accompanied by an authorised adult angler). Fly fishing tuition and introductory days for both adults and juniors will be available at Wimbleball, Kennick, and sites in Cornwall, all run by qualified professional instructors, throughout the season. All aspects of the sport will be covered, as will the promotion of a responsible and healthy interest in the environment. Juniors again will be encouraged to fish for trout - the parent/child ticket allows the youngster to fish for free and share the parent's bag limit. We will also be building on the success of last year's series of Ladies' Days, starting off at Roadford on 16 March with a pre-season day, run by professional instructors Anne Champion and Sally Pizii. The Trust is keen to encourage club members and other keen anglers to put something back into the sport, and to this end has gained approved centre status to be able to offer the new Joint Angling Governing Bodies recognised coaching qualification scheme to various levels in both coarse and game angling. The first of these are to be offered in early 2003.

The 'Peninsula Classic' bank competition will be held at Kennick on the 18th May, in which there will be a special junior prizes category. The 'Wimbleball 2000' boat competition will be held on 14th September. In addition, there will be a new team event for all clubs based on the Trust's reservoirs - it will be a bank competition held on 20 September, generously supported by Snowbee UK. A number of large carp were transferred from Tottiford to Upper Tamar and Melbury, and Bussow benefited from a number of roach, rudd, and carp from other sites. Fish continue to thrive at Argal - a number of pike and carp in excess of 30lb were landed last season, as well as some excellent bream.

After another successful season of float-tubing at Kennick last year, there is now a committed and growing band of float-tubers in the South West. The Trust will again be organising float tubing days on the first and third Sundays in each month from May onwards. These will be held at Kennick, with local suppliers Snowbee and Orvis helping to promote this aspect of the sport, providing demo equipment on the first Sundays (self-launch only available on the third Sundays from June onwards).

The Trust remains committed to angling and customer care, and welcomes all comments to help us provide what the angler really wants.

For further information, including instruction and competition information, please contact:

Chris Hall, Head of Fisheries on
01837 871565
Or E-mail: chall@swlakestrust.org.uk
Or visit ourwebsite:
www.swlakestrust.org.uk

swlakestrust
www.swlakestrust.org.uk

COARSE FISHING PERMIT AGENTS:

A: The Liscawn Inn, Crafthole, Nr Torpoint, Cornwall PL11 3BD Tel: (01503) 230863
B: Variety Sports, 23 Broad Street, Ilfracombe, Devon. Tel: (01271) 862039
C: Summerlands Tackle, 16-20 Nelson Road, Westward Ho!, Devon, EX39 1LF. Tel: (01237) 471291
D: The Kingfisher, 22 Castle St, Barnstaple, Devon, EX1 1DR. Tel: (01271) 344919
E: Bude Angling Supplies, 6 Queen Street, Bude, Cornwall. Tel: (01288) 353396
F: Bideford Tourist Information Centre, The Quay, Bideford, Devon Tel: (01237) 477676
G: Whiskers Pet Centre, 9 High Street, Torrington, Devon. Tel. (01805) 622859
H: Exeter Angling Centre, Smythen St, Exeter, Devon EX1 1BN Tel: (01392) 436404
I: Exmouth Tackle & Sports, 20 The Strand, Exmouth, Devon EX8 1AF. Tel: (01395) 274918
J: Knowle Post Office, Budleigh Salterton. Tel: (01395) 442303
K: Newtown Angling Centre, Newtown, Germoe, Penzance, Cornwall TR20 9AF. Tel: (01736) 763721
L: Sandy's Tackle, 7 Penryn St., Redruth, Cornwall TR15 2SP. Tel: (01209) 214877
M: Ironmonger Market Place, St Ives, Cornwall. TR26 1RZ. Tel: (01736) 796200
N: Heamoor Post Office, Heamoor, Gulval, Nr Penzance. TR18 3EJ. Tel: (01736) 65265
O: Webby's Tackle, 19 Fore St., Holsworthy, Devon EX22 6EB Tel: (01409) 259300

LOWER SLADE - Ilfracombe, Devon
Stocked with mirror and common carp to 20lb plus bream to 5lb plus, perch to 2.25lb, roach, rudd, gudgeon and pike.
Fishing Times:Open all year, 24 hours per day
Permits: From agents: B,C,D. Tel: (01288) 321262

JENNETTS - Bideford, Devon
Best fish: Common 22lb, Mirror 23lb. Produces quality bags of smaller carp, roach, and tench to float & pole.
Fishing Times: Open all year, 6.30am to 10pm.
Permits: From agents: C,E,F,O. Tel: (01288) 321262

DARRACOTT - Torrington, Devon
Roach up to 1lb. Mixed bags to 20lb plus of roach, rudd, bream, tench, perch to 2.25lb, carp to 15lb.
Fishing Times: Open all year, 24 hours per day.
Permits: From agents: C,D,E,F,G,O.
Tel: (01288) 321262
Seasons Permits - (01837) 871565

MELBURY - Bideford, Devon
Best mirror 27.75lb. Good mixed bags of roach, rudd, bream to pole, float and feeder.
Fishing Times: Open all year. 6.30am - 10pm.
Permits: From agents: C,D,E,F,O.
Limited season permits from our office.
Tel: (01288) 321262

Coarse Fishing

TRENCHFORD - Nr Christow, Devon
Pike weighing up to 30lbs.
Fishing Times: Open all year - 1 hour before sunrise to 1 hour after sunset.
Permits: Self service kiosk at Kennick Reservoir
Tel: (01647) 277587

UPPER TAMAR LAKE - Bude, Cornwall
Carp to 28lbs. 50lb plus bags of bream and 30lb bags of rudd. Regular competitions.
Fishing Times: Open all year, 24 hours a day.
Permits: From agents: C,D,E Tel: (01288) 321262

SQUABMOOR - Exmouth, Devon
Good head of carp to 25lb, roach to 3lb 2oz, Tench.
Fishing Times Open all year, 24 hours a day.
Permits: From agents: H,I,J
Season Permits from our office Tel: (01837) 871565

OLD MILL - Dartmouth, Devon
Carp to over 20lbs, roach to 2lb, tench and bream.
Fishing Times: Open all year, 24 hours a day.
Permits: Season permits from our Office
Tel: (01837) 871565

PORTH - Newquay, Cornwall
Bags of 130lb plus have been caught. Best bream 9lb 2oz, tench 9lb 12oz. rudd to 3lb, roach to 1.25lb plus. Mixed bags of roach, rudd/skimmers to 60lb.
Fishing Times: Open all year, 24 hours a day
Permits: Agent L. Self service at Porth car park.
Season permits from our Office. Great competition water. Tel: (01637) 877959

BOSCATHNOE - Penzance, Cornwall
Common, mirror and crucian carp with fish into the low 20lb range. Roach and bream also stocked.
Fishing Times: Open all year, 1 hour before sunrise to 1 hour after sunset. Season permits from our Office.
Permits: From agents: K,L,M,N. Tel: (01579) 342366

ARGAL - Nr Falmouth, Cornwall
Carp to 20lb plus. Best fish: carp 26lb, bream 8lb 6oz, tench 8lb 8oz and eel 7lb, Pike over 30lb.
Fishing Times: Open all year, 24 hours per day.
Permits: From agents: K,L and self service unit at Argal Reservoir car park. Tel (01579) 342366
Season permits from our Office (01837) 871565.

BUSSOW - St Ives, Cornwall
Rudd to 1.5lb, roach bream and carp.
Fishing Times: Open all year, 24 hours a day.
Permits: From agents: K,L,M. Season permits from our Office. Tel (01579) 342366

CRAFTHOLE - Nr. Torpoint, Devon.
Stocked with carp and tench.
Quality Carp up to 30lb.
Fishing Times: Open all year 1hr before sunrise to 1hr after sunset.
Limited permits from agent A.
Season permits from our office (01837) 871565

Coarse

Coarse

The Get Hooked Top Five Tips

by Des Taylor

I have been catching fish around the country now for over 30 years so hopefully I've picked up a few useful tips along the way! So what I propose today is to give you my top 5 bait tips to catch more and bigger fish.

Follow Des's advice and catch superb fish like this Roach

1) Without doubt my number one tip is to learn how to loose-feed correctly. Too often anglers will have the most expensive rod and reel, the most up to date bait but don't know how to feed a swim. All the great anglers I have fished with like John Wilson, Dave Harrell and Bob Nudd all have the ability to feed the swim correctly. Unfortunately there is no easy way to lean this skill it only comes with experience. The only advice I can give is don't keep doing the same thing if you are not catching fish.

I know that sounds a silly statement but so many unsuccessful anglers keep doing the same thing week in week out and catching nothing. Why not change the amount bait that you are putting in at the start? Change how much bait you use in a session - in fact try a different range of baits.

One thing I do notice when using the likes of maggots and casters, I use twice as much bait as the average angler in summer and as much bait in the winter as most anglers use in the summer! If in doubt put a catapult pouch of bait in every 10 minutes. That way at least out of ten sessions you will over feed the swim twice and ruin the swim, but the other eight sessions you will catch a load!

Don't be conservative with your bait go for it!

2) I know lots of anglers will decry the use of flavours but I rarely use a standard bait nowadays for every bait of mine will have an edge of flavour. My maggots and casters will be flavoured with the likes of Scopex or Strawberry Jam. My luncheon meat will be flavoured with Red Crab or Frankfurter Sausage and baits like boilies will be dipped or soaked in a favourite flavour. I have proved time and time flavouring baits will win hands down over "standard" bait.

3) I use groundbait a lot in my fishing that's on stillwaters and rivers and I rarely use water to mix the ingredients up. I use Corn Steep Liquor Liquid diluted 50/50 with water or throw a handful of Corn Steep Liquor Pellets into a groundbait bowl of water and after 15 minutes they have dissolved I give it a stir with my hands and mix the groundbait up with this solution.

I mentioned early I use groundbait a lot on the river where in a lot of cases the mix needs to be stiffer so it holds together longer. I achieve this by using 20% of crushed hemp and a powdered tare binder available in tackle shops this will set like a rock!

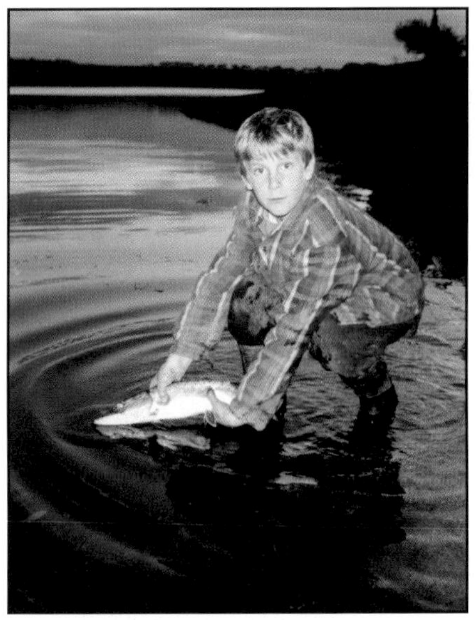

A young angler returns a Pike to do a bit of growing!
South West Lakes Trust

4) I also use a lot of particles like hemp, tares, wheat and maple in my fishing especially when after barbel and carp and for some reason lots of anglers boil their particles before fishing which kills a lot of the vitamins and minerals in the seeds. I think this habit stems from boiling hemp for hook baits, which you have to do to split the seed to get a hook hold. But if you are using particles for baiting up simply soak them in water for 36 hours or even longer so they start to smell a little, fish really like that! Even rock hard maize I only put boiling water on them and leave to soak for 48 hours.

Particles are a very cheap and effective way of keeping fish in your swim but don't ruin them by boiling.

5) But no matter how good your loose feeding is or you have top class baits in your container if you're sitting in the wrong swim with no fish in it you are not going to catch fish! Location is everything and a craft that some anglers never learn.

The criteria of a good swim is not the one nearest to the car or pub. Nor is it the one where your tackle box sits nicely. The criteria of a good swim is one full of fish! My tip here is to stand on the water's edge and ask yourself a few questions:

1) Where would I be if I was a fish today? Try to think like an animal for this one, not a human being.
2) Is the weather going to effect the location today? i.e. which way is the wind blowing, distributing a lot of natural feed at the windward end of the venue or the temperature of the water which will govern if the fish are in deep or shallow water.
3) Where is the safest place for the fish at the venue? i.e. is there a quiet spot on the lake that is difficult to fish or is there an area of weed and snags where the fish feel safe.

All these questions will be easier to answer with experience, sorry that takes time.

But just think for a few minutes scanning over the water before you set up in a swim.

Tight lines.

Fishing is Fun and can be enjoyed by everyone

Rodney Coldron
National Federation of Anglers

MORE than 3.3 million people fish in the UK and that figure easily makes fishing the country's biggest participant sport. But what makes the sport so special for those people who have been hooked on it since being a teenager?

Former Minister for Sport, Tony Banks MP, once told us that we should promote fishing for its 'therapeutic' value. "How can you put a value on a day in the countryside. The opportunity to see a kingfisher working, or a heron waiting patiently for its meal, the rare sight of a grass snake swimming across the river or the real possibility of spotting a fox or even a badger. We are talking about our great countryside and the way angling provides a tremendous back-drop to the countryside which means that the pleasure angler can have a whale of a time without even catching a fish!"

Perhaps we regulars do take our countryside for granted but our passion for the sport means we want to see nature protected. NFA President Ken Ball has often said: "Non anglers can see everything above the water but fish are in a different world because generally speaking the public at large can't see them." But anglers care what goes on beneath the surface and a number of recent pollution cases illustrate the important part we play as conservationists. A deadly pollution wiped out the fish population on a lengthy stretch of the River Smite in Nottinghamshire.

The NFA acted swiftly to ensure the farmer responsible re-stocked the river. The NFA were in action again through its Nemesis scheme when Lincolnshire's Upper Witham was polluted

Jonathan and Thomas Rattenbury, enjoying their fishing.
Spires Lakes

Coarse

through a farm chemical and recently the tiny River Slea in Lincolnshire lost more than 100,000 roach, chub and dace through a spillage of deadly chemical into the high quality river. Anglers have urged the NFA to seek maximum compensation for the loss of fish and amenity.

To anglers a cormorant is an unwelcome sight on the waterside devouring 2.2 lb of fish each day and injuring many more which die as a result of stab wounds. A pair of cormorants can clear all the fish out of a ten-acre lake in little more than a year. This is devastating news to a fishery owner but the law protects this sea-going bird which is increasing in number alarmingly, not just in Britain, but throughout Europe. Of course it may be possible to secure a licence to shoot two of the birds but this would be of little help in the Trent Valley where 100 cormorants can be counted at Cromwell Weir and 50 near Torksey Lock every morning after plundering the Trent's fish stocks. In 1983 there were 100 cormorants in the Trent Valley and now there are more than 15,000 in the UK alone.

The bird lovers want the cormorants left alone but they support the cull of 6,000 ruddy ducks that are mating with the white headed duck (an endangered species) and the result is an emergence of a hybrid species. The slaughter could cost £5 million. The fate of the cormorant is in the hands of Europe where the birds are multiplying at a great pace and destroying habitat. The NFA is a member of the European Alliance and very high on the agenda is the control of cormorant numbers.

The NFA has always argued that fish do not feel pain. A number of studies confirm this and so it was no surprise when American scientist, Professor James Rose declared that fish cannot feel pain. Lets hope that the argument is finally put to rest.

The Minister for Sport, Richard Caborn, MP took a shine to the NFA when he visited the Governing Body recently. He likes the way we are developing schemes to attract youngsters out of the sordid world of crime and drugs and into fishing. The minister was once capable of trotting the Trent with a stick float but nowadays he spends his spare time running marathons.

The NFA's new website is attracting thousands of 'hits' a day and it looks as though at long last we have found a pleasing format. Why not check it out for yourself? www.nfadirect.com

Coaching is now an essential part of angling and the NFA's 125 coaches are working hard to keep up with the classroom, and riverbank lessons. Sport England insist that ALL sports have a recognised coaching structure in place. A copy of our 'Child Protection Policy' was deemed to be so good that a copy was forwarded to every Governing Body organisation.

While the NFA applauds the work of the Environment Agency in cleaning up our rivers we continue to look for ways of introducing some colour to enable us to catch fish in daylight hours. Although the cormorants appreciate clear water anglers want a tinge of colour back and the NFA hopes it has found an expert who can propose how this can be achieved. It would appear that the habitat has been destroyed on some rivers and this has prevented fry survival - we need to ensure the habitat is returned and we have plenty of support from all sorts of groups in this instance.

If you fancy joining our 230,000 members, contact our Membership Services Team:

National Federation of Anglers,
Halliday House, Egginton Junction,
Derbyshire DE65 6GU
Telephone; 01283 734735

or join via our website: www.nfadirect.com

Coarse

Martin King of Plymouth with a 23lb 12oz Pike from an undisclosed westcountry water.
Manadon Angling Supplies

Angling & Conservation.

Developing partnerships to improve habitats

Allan Frake
(Fisheries Recreation & Biodiversity, South Wessex)

The Visitor Centre at Langford Lakes

It is fair to say that over the years Angling and Conservation organisations have not always seen 'eye to eye' or been the best of 'bed-fellows'. Fortunately, things have been changing in recent years and the word 'conflict' is seldom heard echoing up the Avon valley. Both Conservation and Angling interest groups are working extremely hard in the South Wessex Area with a number of exciting initiatives underway and success stories reported.

Opportunities for promoting river management and habitat enhancement to benefit wildlife are achieved by working with those people who make a vital contribution to caring for the river system namely landowners, managers and fishery interests along the river.

On the upper Hampshire /Wiltshire Avon catchment above Salisbury the Wessex Chalk Streams Project Partnership has been running for 3 years focusing on river enhancement and management on the tributaries upstream of Salisbury. The Project is largely funded by Wessex Water with contributions from the Environment Agency, English Nature and Wiltshire Wildlife Trust. The Wiltshire Fishery Association has a significant input and also help to steer the project and ensure that fishing interests are included and well represented.

There is an initial contact point - Jenny Wheeldon who is happy to provide advice on river related management , particularly involving fishing interests and linking up with the plethora of organisations and projects on the catchment. One of Jenny's priority areas of work involves promoting small scale 'opportunistic' river restoration projects which take many different forms, and depending on the level of conservation benefit of the schemes support in the form of grants may be available to assist in the construction and purchase of materials. These have been very well received and successful ranging from projects of just a few metres of river bank and carried out by the owner with a little help from friends, to larger projects of several hundred metres where specialist 'river mending' contractors have to be brought in to effect a sustainable improvement of the habitat. Most of these projects can involve the careful placement of in-river structures to alter the flow characteristics, raising the bed level of the river and creating riffle pool sequences by importing gravel into the channel, or by increasing velocity of specific 'over-widened' channel areas by narrowing using faggots or creating marginal berms. This can dramatically improve the physical diversity of the river which in turn creates and optimises habitat diversity for fish and other species of conservation interest.

The co-operation between the fishing and conservation interests has largely been achieved through excellent liaison and a better understanding of the various issues and potential conflict areas between the groups. The realisation that in general a 'holistic' approach is usually the right one where if the overall riverine habitat is improved then nature is very adept and robust at responding in a positive

A specimen Golden Tench.
West Pitt

- Central Devon location - just half a mile from Crediton
- Two well stocked estate lakes - 4.5 and 1.75 acres
- Day ticket waters
- Predominantly Common Carp (to 31lb)
- Good head of 20 pounders
- Mirror & Koi plus Green and Golden Tench
- On-site parking, level access and toilets

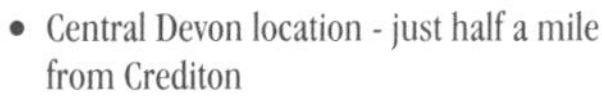

Four Quality Cottage Style Apartments at Manor House opposite the lakes

FREE BROCHURE ON REQUEST

Relax ...

It' Devonshire's Heartland

naturally

Weekly or short stays

Stewart & Sandra Turner

01363 772684

info@creedymanor.com

www.creedymanor.com

way, therefore, if you get the habitat in order then various life stages of fish populations from spawning to fry survival and adult refuge areas will also improve.

Over 30 river habitat enhancent initiatives on this relatively small river-reach scale have been completed on the catchment in the last 5 years. A more ambitious scheme to obtain significant funding from Europe and the Heritage Lottery Fund to carry out extensive habitat enhancements on the River Avon is currently under way with a partnership between English Nature, Environment Agency and Wiltshire Wildlife Trust fronting the initial bid with a view to, if successful, carrying out large scale river restoration projects in the next 3-5 years.

One of the most exciting collaborative partnership projects to promote the integrated relationship between angling and conservation is currently underway at Langford Lakes on the Wylye valley 8 miles west of Salisbury.

Approximately 13 hectares of former gravel pit workings and a half mile of excellent classic chalk stream on the Wylye have been purchased by the Wiltshire Wildlife Trust who have developed a comprehensive partnership with the Salmon & Trout Association, Wild Trout Trust, Wiltshire Fishery Association, with significant financial and practical support from English Nature and the Environment Agency.

The river offers a very interesting fishery predominantly for Trout and Grayling but other good quality coarse fish species are present including dace and perch. A significant amount of habitat enhancement using 'bioengineering' techniques and utilising natural materials including willow and hazel faggots and in-stream current deflectors to increase habitat diversity and holding areas for fish have been installed which will hopefully improve fish populations and will be monitored in subsequent years by a team from the Game Conservancy Trust.

On the still-water side, the Trust has recently purchased an additional lake - the Brockbank Lake where angling will be promoted, swims are to be constructed with facilities for the disabled and tuition particularly for young anglers will be encouraged. The lake is currently being assessed and a fishery management plan developed primarily to improve habitat for coarse fish species to include additional reed beds and submerged vegetation, selective bankside tree clearance to allow more light to improve the quality of aquatic vegetation.

The Langford Lakes project is well on the way to demonstrating 'best-practice' in the management of river and lake habitats accommodating a balance of both angling and conservation interests. As part of this visionary balance a key part is education, and the Langford Centre offer superb potential and facilities for not only angling tuition but environmental education for school parties and courses and seminars for adult audiences as well.

Further details of the Wessex Chalk Stream Project can be obtained from
Jenny Wheeldon, the Project Officer
Tel. 01380 726344 ext 241
jenny.wheeldon@english-nature.org.uk.

Details of fishing opportunities at Langford can be obtained from
Chris Riley at Wiltshire Wildlife Trust
Tel: 01380 725670.
e-mail wwtlangford@btconnect.com.

Habitat improvement at Langford

*Matt from Plymouth with a 17lb 4oz 'Ghostie' known as Patch.
Bake Lakes*

Quality Coarse & Trout Fishing

Six lakes in 32 acres stocked with Carp to over 29lb - plus Tench, Bream, Specimen Roach, Rudd and Perch

PLUS Fly Fishing for Quality Rainbows to 17lb and Browns to 20lb

Open all year - 8am to dusk. FREE Brochure Just 2 miles from Junction 28 on the M5

Email Paul@culmvalley.fsnet.co.uk www.goodifordmillfishery.com

Kentisbeare, Cullompton, Devon. EX15 2AS **Tel: 01884 266233**

Travelling Light

Chris Yates

I was chub fishing the other day, sharing the river with a friend as we went from swim to swim, leapfrogging each other in our search for the fish. With stops for lunch and of course the obligatory photographing of the best looking specimen, we must have taken five hours to fish two miles of river.

We only landed three chub, all over four pounds, but with our surroundings changing every few minutes we'd enjoyed a fascinating day of varied challenges and varied sights and scenes. Yet despite the different demands from all the dozen or so places we fished, we carried all the tackle and bait we needed in our jacket pockets, with just one rod each and a net between us.

At the end of the day we came upon another angler fishing close to a bridge, only 50 yards from where he had parked his car. He was sitting on one of those all purpose seat boxes which, when each drawer is filled with equipment, must weigh a ton - more like a fishing wardrobe than a seat - and he was surrounded by bait buckets, rod rests and several rods. When we asked him how he'd fared he said that the minnows had been driving him mad, though he had managed to justify his keepnet with a small dace. When we told him how far we'd walked for our three fish he blew out his cheeks in astonishment and said he just didn't have the energy for that sort of fishing. Yet it must have taken him more energy just to have heaved his gear the short distance from the bridge, let alone set up all those different rods (and one pole) with different rigs and perfectly lined them up on their adjustable rod rests.

I suppose, especially in fishing, it's 'each to his own' but this amazingly equipped fisherman didn't appear to be very happy in what he was doing. He seemed to think that the quality of his fishing depended on the quantity of tackle he had at his disposal, but he was evidently so tangled up in his multiple rigs and multiple choices that he hardly had a spare moment to simply look at the river. As far as I was concerned he had not only missed the essential delight of

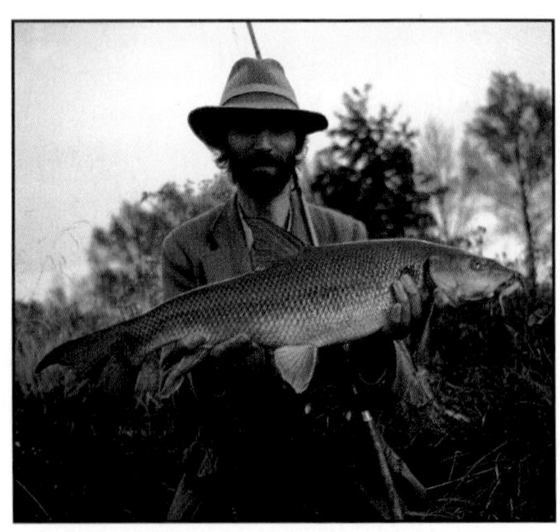

Chris Yates

fishing a lovely water, he'd also made everything appear unbelievably boring. But then some people just love all that technical stuff and even get anxious if they are not in possession of every item of tackle for every eventuality. Personally I call that control freakery and much prefer the idea of improvising with the simplest tackle available. I don't want to have to think through a technical problem, I want to go straight through to the fish, to concentrate on where it might be, how it might be behaving and whether it might be feeding. My belief is that any feeding fish is catchable if you present an acceptable bait to it without arousing it's suspicion.

So all you really need is a hook, a line, a rod, maybe a weight, maybe a float and a simple, preferably natural, bait like a worm. With this minimum of tackle I have caught lots of huge fish - sometimes in quite difficult conditions. The best part of it is that, by always traveling light, on lake or river, I can quietly flit from one feeding area to another and so end up, on average, with many more opportunities for a good fish than the static, sedentary angler. Of course the less quantifiable, but just as important, aspect of lightweight mobility is that you experience far more and ultimately appreciate more. Not just fishing things but the other delights of a natural or semi-natural environment.

After our conversation with the tackle dealers best friend we headed back downstream, walking through an early spring evening that was loud with birdsong and brilliant with the colours of a double sunset - the one in the west and the one in the river.

Newton Abbot Fishing Association

P.O. Box 1, Bovey Tracey, Newton Abbot, Devon TQ13 9ZE

We have more than 18 waters in and around Newton Abbot, the majority of which can be fished on a day ticket.

Rackerhayes Complex, Newton Abbot
6 waters set in 40 acres of countryside less than a mile from the centre of the town. Carp to 36lb, Tench to 11lb 15oz, Bream to over 7lb, Roach, Perch, Pike.

Preston Ponds, Kingsteignton
Peaceful match style waters two miles from Newton Abbot. Carp, Tench, Roach, Perch etc.

Rocombe Complex
Commercial style Carp fisheries with Roach, Tench and Bream. Four ponds on two sites, easily accessible from Torbay. Carp to mid double. Very popular holiday venue.

S.L.A.C. Somerset Levels Association of Clubs
Stretches of rivers and drains throughout the Somerset Levels area.

Details of other waters can be found on our web site or from the tackle shops listed below.

Day Tickets for 2003: £5 Senior. £2 Junior.
1 year Adult Associate licence £43 (fishing for the majority of N.A.F.A. waters).

For advice on how the waters are fishing speak to The Tackle Trader or Abbot Angling or Email: newtonfishing@yahoo.com

Permits from: **Tackle Trader**, Newton Abbot. **Abbot Angling**, Newton Abbot. **Exeter Angling Centre**, Exeter. **Oakford Filling Station**, Kingsteignton (5am-10pm 7 days). **Handy Baits**, Paignton.

www.newtonfishing.com Email: newtonfishing@yahoo.com

Coarse

Help is at Hand for New Anglers

by Dr Bruno Broughton
Technical Director, The Angling Trades Association

Unlike many sports which rely on special skills, like an eye for a ball or a good sense of timing, anybody can fish. Neither is it seasonal - you can fish all the year round. In fact, that is the joy of angling because with each season there are different fish to catch. Carp, tench and bream are usually easier to catch in summer, whereas in the autumn months the fishing for roach and perch may be at its best. Winter is the time for pike and chub, fish you can catch on the move... a good tactic on cold February mornings.

Angling is an ageless pastime. In how many other sports can a child take part on equal terms with his or her grandfather? And it is not limited by number - you can fish alone, with friends or in an organised group. There is fishing to suit everybody's taste and location - casting a fly in spring to a surface feeding trout, stalking a huge carp on a balmy summer evening, or casting beyond the surf when the cod are close to the shore in autumn.

But angling is not only about fish, especially for people living in the inner city. It takes you to the countryside and the magical world of nature. How often do people living in the town see a badger returning home after a night out, spent looking for his dinner, or a stoat taking an early morning stretch? How many people have seen a kingfisher enjoying a hearty breakfast by taking sticklebacks from the top of the water? These are common sights for anglers.

Angling is for all, young and old, male and female, the able and the disabled. Everyone can enjoy this wonderful sport. If you new to angling or thinking about starting - welcome to the world of fish and fishing. It doesn't matter how old you are or where you live because you can be sure that there will be exciting fish to catch somewhere nearby.

You need never be short of further information on angling. Your local tackle shop is a good source of knowledge and tips about local fishing, and most offer a huge range of angling videos for sale or hire, many of them aimed at beginners. You will also be able to obtain free catalogues supplied by the main fishing tackle manufacturers.

A good way of learning more about the sport is by reading. There are about 40 different angling magazines and two weekly newspapers, all sold in tackle shops and/or newsagents. And in large bookshops (and libraries) you will find a wide variety of books on fish and fishing, most of them written by experienced anglers. Schools, youth and angling clubs often organise talks, training sessions and 'fish-ins' for inexperienced anglers. Increasingly, commercial fisheries provide on-the-bank tuition by qualified coaches either for nothing or for a small charge.

Each year there are now several public shows and exhibitions where you can see and handle just about every item of fishing tackle available, listen to angling talks and speak to the experts. Look out for details in the angling press.

Keep warm and safe

It is difficult to enjoy fishing if you are not comfortable, so always wear suitable clothing. In most cases that means a waterproof jacket (with plenty of pockets), stout shoes or rubber boots, and warm undergarments. Several layers of clothes are preferable to one thick one because they can be removed or replaced one or more at a time to keep you at a comfortable temperature.

Hats are also useful - to shade your head and eyes from the summer sun and to keep you warm and dry in cold or wet weather. Unless you are planning only a short trip, remember to take some hot or cold drinks and some food; you won't enjoy yourself if you're cold or hungry! It should be obvious that, potentially, all water is dangerous.

Always remember that when fishing. Look around at the banks or the shoreline where you hope to fish and make sure that it is safe. Never fish underneath or near overhead wires and do

A beautifully conditioned 13lb Common from Pond four.
Upham Farm Ponds

Coarse - Carp
Match - Sea - Game....

- *Top Quality Fresh Coarse & Sea Bait*
- *Match Carp & Sea Specialists*
- *All Local Coarse Licences*
- *Agent for Newton Abbot F.A.*
- *Sole Agents For Lower Teign F.A.*
- *Disabled Access*

Expert Advice Always in stock

FREE PARKING

Tel: 01626 331613

2 Wharf House, Wharf Road, Newton Abbot (behind ATS Tyres)

Town Parks Fishery

Prime Coarse Fishing in the Heart of Devon!

Two Superb Lakes -
Specimen Carp Lake with fish to 35lb
Match Lake with carp to 12lbs, tench, roach, rudd, bream, crucian carp, chub and perch

Open 24hrs, 365 days a year

Easy Parking
Comfortable Swims

Disabled Access
Onsite Shop and Toilets

Tackle Hire
Season Tickets Available

Regular Open Matches
Match Lake available for Club and Corporate Bookings

Friendly, Relaxed Atmosphere
Fantastic Fishing for the Novice or Expert

5 Minutes from Paignton on the A385 Paignton - Totnes Road

CARP LAKE RESTOCKED FOR 2003!

For Bookings and Information contact -
01803 523133 or 07973 433109
or visit us online at www.townparksfishery.co.uk

Town Parks, Totnes Road,
Paignton, Devon. TQ4 7PY.
Telephone: 01803-523133
E-Mail: townparks@btinternet.com

not go out in a boat unless you are wearing a proper life jacket. When you first start fishing - especially if you are young - it is best to go along with a reliable adult.

Starting on a shoestring

As with any sport, you can spend a considerable sum of money on equipment, but this is unnecessary when you begin angling. For somewhere between £30 and £60 you should be able to buy a set of equipment which will enable you to catch most types of fish. The most important features of your tackle are that the rod allows you to cast, the reel works properly, the line doesn't break and the hooks don't bend or snap!

Fishing in the sea is free, whereas in freshwater you need the permission of the fishery owners, which is usually gained by buying a day or season ticket or by joining an angling club. Young anglers and disabled people are usually charged reduced prices. In England and Wales you must also be in possession of a valid rod licence - issued by the Environment Agency - no matter where you fish. They can be bought in post offices and last for one day, eight days, or a year, depending on price. You don't need a rod licence if you are aged 11 or younger, and there are reduced charges for people aged 12-16, for those over 65 years of age and for registered disabled people.

Where and when can I go?

That depends on where you live and what you hope to catch.

Coarse fish - a term for all freshwater fish other than the trout or salmon families - can be caught in rivers and streams, small ponds and large reservoirs, park lakes and canals. A visit to your local fishing tackle shop is the best source of information on good fishing spots nearby, or the directory in this guide of course!

There is a legal close season for coarse fishing between mid-March and mid-June in England and Wales on all freshwater rivers and streams when you are not allowed to go fishing because the fish may be spawning (breeding). On stillwaters - lakes and ponds - the legal close season has been abolished, but some clubs and landowners still operate their own. If details are not on the permit or any notice boards around the fishery, ask at the local tackle shop.

For **sea fish** you can fish at any time. Some species of fish spend all their lives near the shore, by piers, harbours or among the rocks. Others only come near the shore at certain times of year, and some spend all their time in deep waters and can only be caught from a boat. You'll learn the best times for different fish by asking, and watching, other anglers. If you do fish by the sea, take particular care not to get caught by changing tides. Tell someone responsible where you plan to go and, roughly, what time to expect you back.

Game Fish. The close season for salmon varies in different parts of Britain; for brown trout the close season is during the winter, but there is no legal close season for rainbow trout in lakes and ponds because those fish don't normally breed in such waters. Again, if you don't know for sure, ask at the tackle shop.

What are the rules?

Angling is one of the largest sports in the country with millions of people taking part, and one of its appeals is that you can thoroughly enjoy yourself without having to be part of a team or an organised event if that is your wish. It is also one of the most self disciplined, with the majority keeping as a matter of personal pride to the rules and guidelines of various recognised codes of behaviour and practice. They are based on a few sensible principles intended to benefit everybody and everything which uses or lives by, on or in, the water.

The most obvious is not to leave litter, especially nylon line. There is no excuse for not taking it home and disposing of it safely in the dustbin, having first cut it into short sections.

Every effort should be made to safeguard fish welfare. Handle fish gently and return them carefully to the water as soon as possible unless you intend to keep them to eat.

Don't cause a nuisance to other people. Your pleasure shouldn't spoil that of others.

Vic Barnett with a 4lb 2oz specimen Perch.
Little Allers

COOMBE FISHERIES

Two lakes set in a beautiful peaceful valley adjacent to Buckland Abbey

RUDD - ROACH
TENCH - CARP to 28lb - BREAM

Email: schorn@agriplus.net
Miltoncombe, Yelverton, Devon.
Tel: (01822) 616624 or (07899) 958493

Little Allers
COARSE FISHERY

South Brent, Devon

A two acre lake in beautiful surroundings, well stocked with Carp, Bream, Tench & Roach

Day tickets collected at waters edge

Centred in the South Hams we are within easy reach of Plymouth, Torquay and Exeter

Sorry no dogs allowed

For Details phone 01364 72563

East Moore Farm FISHERY

DIPTFORD TOTNES DEVON TQ9 7PE

Two acre Lake well stocked with Carp, Tench, Bream, Roach and Rudd

3 Islands - 51 Pegs

Match Bookings Welcome

Camping & Caravans by prior arrangement

Tel: 01364 73276
www.eastmoorefarm.co.uk

Clubs and fishery owners often have their own local rules which should be printed on the permit. They usually relate to specific methods and baits, or times for angling (such as no night fishing) and should be observed. Again, if you are not sure... ask!

Enjoy yourself but...

Yes, angling does have its rules, but do not let that worry you. Most are simple, sensible measures to try and ensure that everyone can enjoy themselves and keep coming back.

We have already mentioned the need to hold an Environment Agency rod licence if you are to fish in freshwater in England and Wales. Inland, anglers will usually also need a permit from the angling club or landowner controlling the water. Sometimes you can buy a day ticket which allows you to fish for that day only. More frequently you can buy a season permit which lasts for a year between set dates. Make sure you have it (and your rod licence) with you when you go fishing or find out in advance if you can buy one on the bank. In a few places you may be able to fish for free, and some clubs allow young people to fish for free as long as they are with a responsible adult. Ask for details in your local tackle shop.

What about bait?

To catch fish you need some sort of bait to tempt them to 'bite'. For coarse fish that can be bread, cheese, luncheon meat or many of the things you eat yourself. You could also collect worms from your garden, or buy maggots or special 'boilies' from a tackle shop.

Much game fishing involves the use of artificial flies made from silk, fur, feathers or man-made materials tied to a hook in such a way that, when cast onto or into the water, the 'fly' imitates an item of natural food and tricks the fish into taking it.

For sea fish the range of baits can be divided into artificials - metal lures and plastic plugs which imitate fish - and natural baits such as strips of fish, shellfish, rag-worm and lugworm.

In the beginning it is best to try and find what fish you are likely to catch and then use the baits which they prefer. As you become more experienced, you can experiment with different baits and even try your own concoctions.

No Barriers

Angling is one of the most accessible of sports, and it can be enjoyed by people with all forms of physical and mental ability. Indeed, a recent survey has revealed that at least 60,000 disabled people go fishing, and it is among the top five most popular sports for anglers with disabilities.

Increasingly, fisheries are providing safe, comfortable bankside facilities for disabled people, with good access to them, and many trout fisheries are now able to offer fishing afloat on one of the specially constructed 'Wheelyboat' craft. There is still much work to do, but all major angling organisations have pledged their support, and funds, to increasing provision for disabled anglers.

The British Disabled Angling Association (BDAA) exists to help this process and to provide information on angling for people with disabilities. Contact: BDAA, 9 Yew Tree Road, Delves, Walsall, West Midlands WS5 4NQ. Tel: 01922 860912 Website: www.bdaa.co.uk

There's a coach near you!

There are numerous opportunities to learn how to fish from trained, experienced angling coaches, either in one-to-one or group sessions. In addition, every year there are hundreds of local 'try it' events, junior matches and special angling courses throughout the country. Ask your nearby tackle dealer or local angling club for details.

In recent years a large number of experienced anglers have been trained as angling coaches. These qualified people have been taught how to teach others to fish - either individually or in groups - by taking and passing special courses. Every coach has also received first-aid training, is fully insured, has taken courses on child protection and has been cleared by the Criminal Records Bureau. A Government-backed licensing scheme is being extended to angling coaches to verify their qualifications and suitability.

John Scoble with a magnificent 27lb Common.
Stafford Moor (Beatties Lake)

Coarse

Generally, coaches affiliated to angling clubs and associations operate without payment for the benefit of members. Others are linked to specific fisheries or tackle shops and are purely freelance. They usually levy a small fee for their services. Coaching is much more than merely teaching people how to begin angling. Existing anglers can also benefit by using coaches to 'brush up' their skill at a particular style of fishing or to take up a branch of the sport with which they are not familiar. Some coaches also act as angling guides at specific fisheries.

Details of angling coaches can be obtained from the tuition feature in this guide (122-125) or:

Coarse angling

Glyn Williams, National Federation of Anglers, Halliday House, Egginton Junction, Derbys. DE65 6GU. Tel: 012833 734735.

Sea angling

David Rowe, National Federation of Sea Anglers, Hamlyn House, Mardle Way, Buckfastleigh, Devon TQ11 0NS. Tel: 01364 644643.

Game angling

Malcolm Hanson, PO Box 1270, Marlborough,Wilts. SN8 4WD. Tel: 01672 511628.

Professional coaches (all angling styles)

Professional Anglers Association, Trenchard, Lower Bromstead Road, Moreton, Newport, Shropshire TF10 9DQ. Tel: 01952 691515. Website: www.paauk.com

And finally...

To provide new and would-be anglers with more information about the sport, the Angling Trades Association and its partners have prepared special information packs as part of its 'Get Into Angling' campaign. The packs are free and can be obtained from:-

Get Into Angling, Angling Trades Association, Federation House, National Agricultural Centre, Stoneleigh Park, Warks. CV8 2RF. Tel: 02476 414999.

Wherever you fish and whatever you hope to catch, keep safe, respect the environment and - most importantly - enjoy yourself!

Pat Sweeney with an excellent Golden Orfe weighing 3lb 12oz. Spires Lakes

Teaching Good Habits

By Steve Lockett

I have to say at the outset, that I was amazed by the amount of interest. Even given some small degree of apathy amongst the other teaching staff, that resulted in four forms not finding out about this new opportunity, 32 pupils signing up for my fishing tutorials was beyond my expectations.

Brixham is traditionally a hotbed of sea fishing, so when I put a note in the register at the Community College where I work suggesting pupils come to find out about coarse fishing, I wasn't really expecting the response I received. Still, it was very encouraging and dates were set for four groups of eight to attend an evening session in the classroom to look at the basics, followed by two sessions on the bank at local fishery New Barn Farm Angling Centre.

One or two of the pupils had experienced some kind of coarse fishing before, but really, all were raw beginners. First lesson was to be a very simple look at the kinds of venue available for coarse fishing and the kinds of tackle needed to fish effectively. It's amazing sometimes to listen to more experienced anglers trying to pass on tips to youngsters; just imagine for a moment, that you know nothing about fishing whatsoever, I mean - absolutely nothing. Now, if I say "throw a handful of maggots into your swim", that surely does not make any sense at all. So to begin, we have to start to make sense of this incredibly technical sport of ours, explaining that a swim is the area of water immediately in front, or downstream of us. That a hooklength is a thin piece of line with a hook tied to it and is sometimes called a bottom, sometimes called a trace.

First lesson done, now it's time to move on to watercraft. Hands up all those who have a favourite swim they always head for? The first watercraft lesson was on swim selection in the prevailing weather conditions. In the summer, look for the windward bank and floating debris, scum etc. this area is where most of the natural food items will congregate and the fish will follow. Winter time and warmth is the main priority for the fish. This may be in the deepest water, but on sunny days the shallower areas can hold huge shoals where the sun can strike the surface and raise the water temperature by even a fraction of a degree. After all this theory, a bit of light relief was found by learning to tie a few knots, or was it knotting a few ties? Anyway, by now, all the pupils were eager and straining to be let onto a fishery and put all this into practice, the only stipulation from me before they went, was that they buy a disgorger, all the other tackle was provided by myself, a small payment from the Lottery funded New Opportunities Fund and generous discounts at Brixham Bait and Tackle. Off to the bankside we go.

Island Pond at New Barn is a small pond capable of holding maybe eight anglers in comfort with a good stock of roach and perch, the chance of a carp of a couple of pounds and an occasional tench. Maximum depth is around 6 feet and the island is only 7 metres away, making it an ideal venue for a beginner armed with a 4 metre whip. Light floats and ample supplies of maggots bring bites-a-plenty, with 30 or 40 small fish a realistic target in the three hour sessions. The small fish are not particularly tackle shy, so the whip set-up used a 2lb hooklength, enough to stand a chance of subduing the carp should one happen along. At first, I carried a couple of landing nets, strategically placed and netted the fish for the pupils, but soon, most were capable of landing their own fish and getting to grips with using

Tony Savage with a 15lb 12oz Carp.
Bake Lakes (Match Lake)

Coarse

the disgorger, hooking maggots and all the myriad details that experienced anglers take for granted.

The highlights of the entire programme were; Simon Parton taking a small dip! This despite constant warnings, that it is not safe to constantly fidget, stand up, sit down, move his chair and before anyone has a heart attack, there are lifebelts available and, let's face it, he kept still after that. Ricky Gilbey catching a 1lb 4oz roach and his 'Cheshire Cat' grin afterwards. My biggest thrill came from Ross Mogridge, a year 11 pupil who had spent most of his school years in trouble of one sort or another and constantly facing the standard "you'll never make anything of your life" retort. He sat and caught fish after fish and had never believed he could possibly find something so relaxing, enjoyable and that he would actually be good at.

Finally, what more reward could I have than last years pupil's constant hounding and requests for another programme of fishing days.

They are desperate to learn!

The smile says it all - Joe Champness with a typical Roach

Coarse

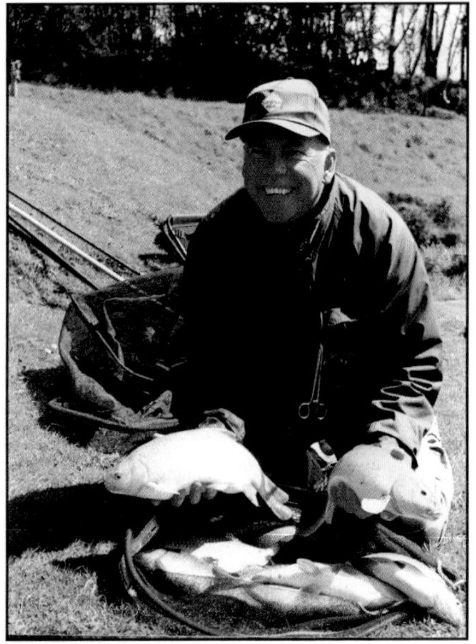

Golden Orfe and Golden Tench in this excellent catch from West Pitt.

South West Lakes Angling Association

Have you joined yet ?

Cost.

For only **£8.00** (£7 junior/OAP) You can become a member of South West Lakes Angling Association

Benefits.

By being a member you will be entitled to a 10% discount on the cost of your season or day ticket to any of the South West Lakes Trust 14 Coarse Fisheries. You will also receive newsletters during the year. You will be entitled to fish in major competitions including the nationals run by the NFA.

Waters include.

Lower Slade - *Ilfracombe*
Jennetts - *Bideford*
Darracott - *Torrington*
Melbury - *Bideford*
Trenchford - *Nr Christow*
Upper Tamar - *Bude*
Lower Tamar - *Bude*
Squabmoor - *Exmouth*
Old Mill - *Dartmouth*
Porth - *Newquay*
Boscathnoe - *Penzance*
Argal - *Nr Falmouth*
Bussow - *St Ives*
Crafthole - *Nr Torpoint*

Application forms from most local tackle shops

or ring South West Lakes Trust on 01837 871565.
Or for more information Contact
Roy Retallick on 01884 256721. Email: r.retallick@btinternet.com

Affiliated to the National Federation of Anglers

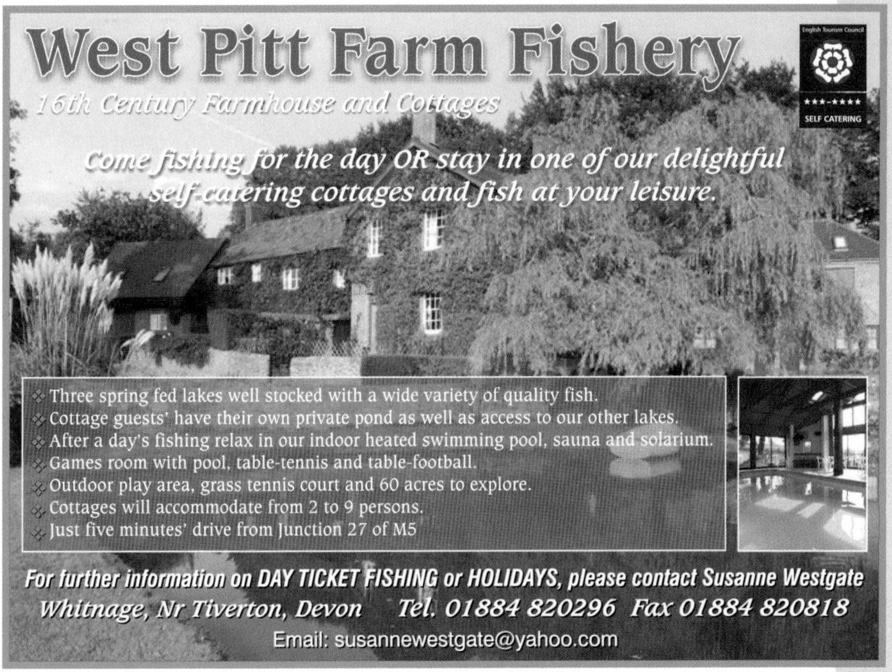

Coarse Fishing in the South Wessex Area

By Steve Carter

The Hampshire Avon

The Hampshire Avon rises in the Vale of Pewsey and with its tributaries the Bourne and Wylye drains the chalk of Salisbury Plain. The River Nadder, which is joined by the Wylye near Salisbury drains part of the South Wiltshire Downs and (more significantly for anglers) the clays of the Wardour Vale. The River Ebble and the Ashford Water enter the Avon downstream of Salisbury and Fordingbridge respectively. Below Fordingbridge a number of New Forest streams enter the Avon. The Avon flows into Christchurch Harbour where it is joined by the River Stour.

The total fall from Pewsey to the sea is 110m, the average gradient downstream of Salisbury is approximately 2m per km. The flow is characterised by a high groundwater component derived from springs rising in the headwaters of the Avon and its major tributaries.

The river and its tributaries are of national and international importance for their wildlife communities. The majority of the river has been designated as a river Site of Special Scientific Interest (SSSI). The river is also a Special Area of Conservation (SAC) under the EU Habitats Directive (Atlantic Salmon are listed as threatened in Annexe II of the EC "Habitats and species" Directive). The catchment is an internationally important area for over wintering waders and wildfowl.

The Hampshire Avon is nationally renowned as one of Britain's premiere coarse fisheries. The name 'Hampshire Avon' distinguishes it from the other seven 'River Avons' found in the UK, while in fact the Hampshire Avon passes through Wiltshire, Hampshire and Dorset.

The Avon is essentially a 'chalk stream'. The chalk aquifer ensures an exceptionally high water quality contributing to the species richness and the abundance of aquatic biota. This has proved a highly advantageous situation for coarse fish populations in the Avon, in terms of growth rates.

The chalk influence of the Avon catchment ensures that the river reacts relatively slowly to rainfall compared to the clay dominated Dorset Stour catchment. However once the chalk aquifer reaches critical saturation level during winter, the springs 'break'. The extra groundwater often maintains a high flow and level through the rest of the winter. Without the influence of floodwater from the Nadder, the Avon would run clear for most of the year.

Species of coarse fish to be found in the Avon include barbel, bream, carp, chub, dace, perch, pike, and roach. All of these species reach

Pete with a nice 3lb 'stripey'. Lands End

Coarse

specimen sizes, in particular barbel, chub, pike and roach. The majority of coarse angling takes place between Salisbury and Christchurch.

The Avon is perhaps best known for its superb roach fishing. Many specimens of 2lb+ are caught every year including several fish over 3lbs. The best roach fishing can be found on the middle and lower reaches of the river. Local roach anglers will often wait until the New Year before targeting specimen roach. By this time the river has flushed out old weed growth and the increased flows will have pushed roach into their winter lies. Roach captures reported in 2002 included many fish between 2lb and 3lb, these fish came from throughout Avon. Exceptional specimens reported in 2002 included fish of 3lb 12oz and 3lb1oz. Notable areas for specimen roach include: Salisbury & DAC and London AA waters around Salisbury; Fordingbridge Rec. (day ticket venue); Christchurch AC stretches (Fordingbridge area and Somerely Estate); Ringwood & DAS (Ibsley and Ringwood area) through to Winkton (day ticket).

Chub fishing has been extremely good over recent years; 2002 was no exception with many fish in the 6lb bracket, several of 7lb+, the largest chub reported included fish of 7lb10oz and 7lb 8oz. Specimen chub are caught throughout the season. Notable areas for chub extend from Salisbury to Hale, but also include the middle to lower reaches: Christchurch AC waters (Somerely Estate, Royalty Fishery); Ringwood & District A.S. (Ibsley and Ringwood area); Lifelands (day ticket).

Barbel captures reported in 2002 included many fish between 10lb+ and 13lb+, most of these fish came from the middle and lower stretches of the Avon. Exceptional specimens reported in 2002 included fish of 14lb 8oz and 14lb 6oz. Barbel are caught throughout the season and are to be found from London AA waters around Salisbury downstream to the Royalty Fishery at Christchurch. Areas of note include: Lifelands, Ringwood, Severalls Fishery, and the Royalty Fishery.

Dace are found throughout the Avon and River Nadder. In 2002 Lifelands and the Severals Fishery, Ringwood produced 30lb nets of dace during the autumn. The Royalty Fishery at Christchurch offers good all round coarse fishing, with barbel 10lb+, carp 20lb+, chub 6lb+, pike 30lb+, nets of dace, and in 2002 a 115lb haul of bream was reported. Interesting captures in 2002 included a 9lb 6oz bass from the Royalty, and an 8lb10oz thick lipped mullet from the Claypool. The Royalty Fishery is now under the control of Christchurch AC, day tickets are available as usual.

Season tickets, guest tickets and day tickets for various club waters can be obtained from local tackle shops. There are also a number of smaller syndicates that offer limited membership and access to estate waters. Day ticket fisheries can be found at Fordingbridge, Ringwood, Bisterne, Winkton and the Royalty at Christchurch.

The Dorset Stour

The Stour rises on the greensand at St Peter's Pump in Stourhead Gardens and flows 96km to the sea at Christchurch: the fall over its entire course is approximately 230m. The catchment lies predominantly within the county of Dorset with smaller areas falling within Somerset and Wiltshire.

From Stourhead, the river flows south to Gillingham where it is joined by the Shreen and Lodden. The Blackmore Vale to the west and

Westcountry Rivers
The Newsletter of The Westcountry Rivers Trust
Summer 2002

Objective One Funding Boost for Cornwall's Rivers!

Coarse

Matt Carter - 22lb 12oz Stour Pike

south is drained by the Stour and a dense network of tributaries. Flowing towards Sturminster Newton, the Stour is joined by several clay influenced tributaries. Fewer tributaries join the Stour as it flows through a narrower valley towards Blandford Forum. Downstream of Blandford the landscape opens up again across pasture and arable fields. Towards the coast, the floodplain widens to form extensive level pastures, marsh and mudflats, meeting the Hampshire Avon at Christchurch Harbour.

The clay influence of the Blackmore Vale ensures that the river reacts more quickly to rainfall compared to groundwater dominated chalk streams in the neighbouring Frome and Avon catchments. Rapidly rising levels and coloured water are regular winter features of this river.

The Dorset Stour has often been perceived as being outshone by its near neighbour the Hampshire Avon. However 'dyed in the wool' Stour anglers have over the years quietly notched up some very impressive specimen coarse fish catches topped by the British record roach of 4lb 3oz from Corfe Mullen in 1990.

Through the summer months the many relatively slow flowing impounded sections on the Stour are highly productive in terms of aquatic plants and invertebrates supporting a wide diversity of coarse fish species with roach being the most abundant. However, the Stour has traditionally been regarded as a winter fishery, fishing well once the weed has blown out, especially after a flood, when the river is fining off but still carrying a little bit of colour.

Species of coarse fish to be found in the Stour include barbel, bleak, bream, carp, chub, dace, perch, pike, roach and tench. Barbel, chub, pike and roach all reach specimen sizes.

Coarse fishing takes place on the Stour from Gillingham to Christchurch Harbour. The upper reaches from Gillingham to Marnhull are noted for throwing up the occasional big roach of 2lb+. Chub, dace, perch and pike are also present. Most of the club water here is controlled by Gillingham & DAA.

At the beginning of 2002 the stretch upstream of Sturminster Newton Mill produced good bags of roach with weights topping 30lb. The waters from Sturminster to Durweston are noted for having produced specimen chub of 6lb+, roach of 3lb+ and pike of 20lb+. Shoals of large bream and the odd large tench are also present. Parts of these stretches are controlled by Sturminster & Hinton AA and Durweston AA; a number of other local clubs also control short sections of fishing within this reach.

The Stour around Blandford has got a good track record for producing roach over 2lb, chub of 5lb+ and pike of 20lb+. Good mixed nets of roach, dace, chub and perch along with bags of large bream are taken in matches. Blandford & DAC control parts of this section, and there is a limited 'free stretch' owned by the council at Blandford (Please note: an Environment Agency rod licence is still required to fish here).

Moving downstream to the Wimborne area, some exceptional specimen chub and barbel have been captured here in recent years including chub of 7lb+ and barbel of 14lb+. The last 7 years have seen an increase in the stocks of perch with 2lb+ specimens appearing regularly; specimens of 3lb+ were captured in 2002. Wimborne & DAC, Christchurch AC and Ringwood & DAS control fishing on various sections around Wimborne.

Longham, Manor Farm, Muscliffe and Throop are well known for the specimen coarse fish produced each season including: 10lb + barbel, 6lb+ chub, 20lb+ pike and 2lb+ roach. At least 13 barbel of 14lb+ were reported from the lower Stour in 2002, with a 15lb 2oz specimen being the largest (inevitably some of these reports may have included recaptured fish). Numerous big chub were reported from

the middle and lower reaches of the Stour in 2002 including 28 over 7lb topped by a massive 8lb8oz specimen that nudged the current British record (again these reports would include fish captured possibly more than once). There is limited 'free fishing' (an Environment Agency rod licence is still required) on the council owned stretches at Longham and Muscliffe. Most of the club controlled waters in this reach come under either Christchurch AC or Ringwood & DAS.

Apart from numerous 6lb+ chub and double figured barbel reported in 2002, Throop is also noted for its bream shoals with a large hauls of bream in 2002.

The tidal Stour includes lower Throop downstream to the Harbour. Here some of the best pleasure and match fishing weights of roach and dace can be made in the area. Throop Fishery is managed by Ringwood & District A.S., whilst the tidal section is largely controlled by Christchurch AC. Both clubs issue day tickets; consult the Directory or contact local tackle shops for more details.

The River Frome

The River Frome rises on the North Dorset Downs near Evershot, and flows down a gradient of 2.2m/km over approximately 60km to the sea at Poole Harbour. The catchment is predominantly rural and lies entirely within the county of Dorset.

From Evershot the Frome flows south to be joined near Cattistock by the Wraxall Brook, and at Maiden Newton by the River Hooke. Two small streams, the Sydling Water and the Cerne, also join the Frome upstream of Dorchester. Below Dorchester, the Win, South Winterbourne and Tadnoll Brook enter from the south, while the Frome itself meanders in an easterly direction to Poole Harbour.

The Frome downstream of Dorchester has been notified as a river Site of Special Scientific Interest (SSSI). This section supports species rich plant communities, rare and scarce aquatic invertebrates and a range of fish species.

The Frome is similar in character to the Hampshire Avon in the fact that both rise from chalk based aquifers. The River Frome is primarily a salmonid fishery controlled by private syndicates and large estates, access to coarse fishing on the River Frome is therefore fairly limited. However the range of coarse fish found in the River Frome is unique in that it represents a more natural assemblage of species. This is because the fishery has been managed almost exclusively for salmon and trout.

Coarse fish species found in the Frome include dace, roach, grayling and pike, these species regularly turn up fish of specimen sized proportions. Of the coarse fish, the Frome is most noted for specimen grayling, regularly producing fish over 2lb, with several fish over 3lb reported each season. Specimen grayling exceeding 4lbs have been recorded in the past.

The fishery at Wareham is owned by the Environment Agency. Coarse fishing in the area around the quay allows good bags of roach and dace to be made from autumn onwards. Several specimen roach of 2lb+ were reported caught in 2002 including fish of 3lb1oz and 2lb10oz along with 'herring sized' dace to 1lb. In early autumn 50lb+ bags of roach and dace were caught.

In 2002 numbers of grayling between 12oz to 2lb and good nets of dace have been caught on various stretches owned by the Wareham & DAS and Dorchester & DAS. Specimen sized grayling are recorded each season at the Pallington Lakes day ticket stretch of the Frome. Christchurch AC lease a stretch of the main river

Matt Carter - 22lb 12oz Avon Pike

Roy Fairchild with an upper double common.
Avalon Fisheries

and carrier at Tincleton, an area which contains specimen sized grayling and dace.

Dorchester FC control stretches of the Frome around Dorchester although this is primarily a premier trout fishery. Some of the most notable specimen grayling have been recorded from the main river and its carriers in this area. Small numbers of 2lb+ roach have also been caught here in recent years.

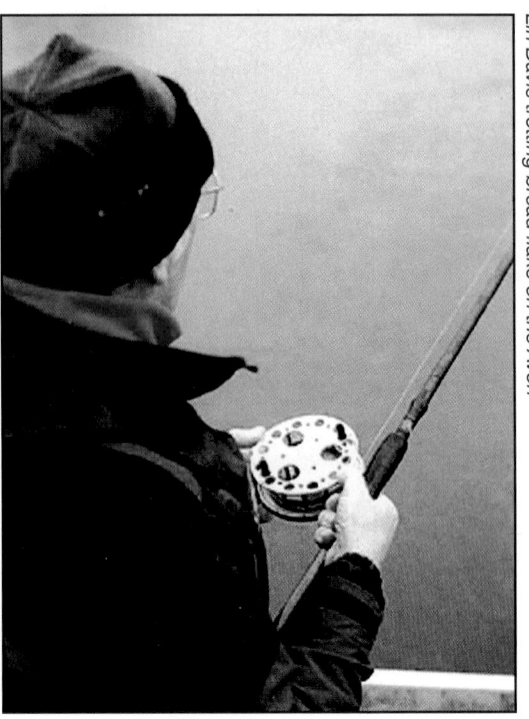

Lin Davis trotting bread flake on the Avon

Stillwaters and Canals

There are many stillwaters offering coarse fishing throughout the South Wessex Area, including ponds, lakes, gravel pits and a short section of the Kennet and Avon Canal near Devizes.

Many gravel pits were dug out in the Ringwood area during the 1950s and 1960s. These are now fully matured coarse fisheries offering anglers the opportunity to catch carp of up to 40lb, tench over 10lb, and large bream and roach. Coarse fish reported from the Ringwood pits in 2002 included: specimen carp (a large number of 20lb fish, several over 30lb and a 38lb specimen); specimen tench (a large number between 6 and 9lb, several 10lb+, with the largest weighing 10lb14oz); crucian over 3lb; pike over 20lb. Christchurch AC and Ringwood & DAS control most of the lakes and pits around Ringwood.

Most of the angling clubs in the South Wessex area have several lakes and ponds under their control, further information can be found in this guide (see fishing directory) or from local tackle shops. Season tickets, guest tickets and day tickets for various club waters can be obtained from local tackle shops. There are also a large number of day ticket fisheries offering a variety of ponds and complexes of lakes, with mixed coarse fish (bream, carp, crucian, perch, pike, roach, and tench).

In the Avon catchment some of the day ticket fisheries include: Hurst Pond, the Longhouse Fishery, New Forest Water Park, Peter's Finger Lake, Walden's Farm, and Witherington Farm. Captures reported in the angling press in 2002 included: Longhouse Fishery (carp bags to 180lb, tench to 6lb12oz, perch 3lb); New Forest Water Park (carp over 30lb, tench of 9lb); Shearwater (bream bags of 50lb+); Witherington Farm (carp bags 100lb+).

Day ticket fisheries in the Stour catchment include Revels Fishery and Todber Manor Fishery. Captures reported in 2002 included: Todber Fisheries (carp bags of 100lb+).

Day ticket fisheries in the Frome catchment include: Luckfield Lake, Pallington Fishery, Radipole Lake, and Warmwell Lakes. Captures reported in 2002 included: Luckfield Lake (carp to 25lb+ with lots of doubles; a massive 8lb8oz eel; roach bags of 20lb with specimens to 3lb; tench to 8lb8oz with excellent bags of tench in the 4 to 6lb bracket); Pallington Lakes (several carp over 20lb, largest 32lb8oz; roach 3lb2oz and tench to 8lb2oz); Warmwell Lakes (carp to 29lb2oz with many 20lb+ fish caught, perch to 3lb14oz; pike to 15lb).

Specimen Chub caught on Christchurch Angling Club waters.

COARSE GAME & CARP SPECIALISTS

Day Tickets - THROOP FISHERIES and LOCAL WATERS

AUTHORISED AGENTS

SHIMANO - DAIWA - FOX - DRENNAN
SOLAR - NASH - ESP - MISTRAL - etc

CENTRE PIN SPECIALISTS

JOIN Ringwood, Christchurch & Wimborne Clubs HERE!

Tel: 01425 475155

www.ringwoodtackle.co.uk

5 The Bridges, West St., Ringwood BH24 1EA

Ringwood & District Anglers Association

www.ringwoodfishing.co.uk

Many miles of excellent fishing on some of the best waters in the South of England on the Hampshire Avon and Dorset Stour including the famous Throop Fishery.

Chub to 8lb, Barbel to 16lb, Bream to 11lb, Carp to 39lb, Tench to 12lb

For more details contact Caroline Groom on 01202 525615
or visit a local Tackle Shop

Day Tickets available for Throop, Severals and our Stillwaters

Coarse

A Taste of Angling in Somerset

By Richard Blackie
Somerset Gazette Columnist

For over 40 years I have fished all over the British Isles, in fact all over the World, as for the first 14 years of my working life I was a sailor. This job took me to every corner of the globe, and I took every opportunity to get ashore and fish.

I have caught tiger fish in the Malayan Jungle, shark off the beaches of Australia, barracuda in Bermuda, fresh water bass in the rivers of the USA. So when I got married and wrapped in my sea going life a decision had to be made as to where to settle down and live. As my wife is a Somerset girl it was decided that Somerset would be the base of our new home. As for fishing it was a decision I have never regretted, as this county is awash with great fishing and places to fish.

When I was on shore leave I stayed with my mother in London and I thought nothing of a two hundred mile round trip drive to fish the Trent or Norfolk Broads. Now I consider a 20 mile drive to be distance fishing!

Over the past 10 years commercial fisheries have come into their own in this County, with year round good fishing for most species (although on some waters carp predominate). As an example how well stocked these fisheries are, some even hold Sturgeon, a fish that twenty years ago was so rare in this country that any caught had to be offered to the Queen(Emerald pool has lots of this species).

Around my home town of Taunton there are four good commercial fisheries that are well worth a visit. The first is Fishponds House which is about mid-way between Taunton and Honiton. The three lakes that are there (only two can be fished) are among this countries' oldest stew ponds. They were originally built by the monks to hold carp for food. Now the monks have gone but a good head of carp remain. Apart from the carp there is a very good head of roach, rudd, bream and tench. The top pool is the biggest, and ranges in depth from five to twelve feet. Best fishing is in summer, although 60 to 70 pound nets are not uncommon in winter. In summer the top lake fishes well in most pegs. In winter, it is best to fish the deeper swims. The smaller pool is very weedy, but tremendous sport can be had with small carp and silver fish. The best swims to fish on this pool are those at the end furthest away from the house. Best baits on both pools are maggots, corn, meat, casters and bread. Fishing one of these baits over a bed of hemp is good for carp. A lot of fun can be had on a warm summers evening with floating crust.

Next we visit Follyfoot Farm which is between Taunton and Bridgwater. This three acre lake is heavily stocked with Koi, common and mirror carp. Although most of these carp are on the smallish side, but there are plenty of double figure fish. Most of the usual baits will catch, although maggots will pull mostly small carp. One day I watched an angler having good sport with carp between 8 and l0lb dog biscuits. Like most commercial fisheries you may only use barbless hooks on this water.

HBS Fisheries, which is also just off the Taunton to Bridgwater road, is another fishery well worth a visit. HBS is made up of two pools, one for specimen fishing and the other which

2lb 9oz Koi caught on caster.
Luccombe

they call the match pool. The specimen pool is stocked with large carp which are caught regularly on various baits, boilies are probably the most successful. Fishing to features or stalking fish are two top methods on this pool. The smaller match pool has carp up to 17lb, although most are in the 8oz to 2lb bracket. There are also some quality roach, tench and the odd surprise fish like the 5.5lb bream my friend caught there last week. For one-a-chuck catch rate maggots are the top bait whereas for the better specimens worm, corn and boilies are tops.

Just the other side of Bridgwater we come to Dunwear lakes where carp and bream feature heavily in this four lake mixed fishery. Apart from the bream and carp there is good all round sport with perch and roach. The north lake, at three and a half acres, holds six known 20lb plus carp, and is heavily stocked with tench. This and the south lake are waters for the specialist carp angler. The south lake, which has produced a 31lb specimen, also has double figure carp which are most frequently taken on boilies. No junior anglers are allowed on the 18 acre seniors lake where swims are cut into the undergrowth. Carp to 30lb are present but rarely caught. Expect mostly commons in the 6 to 9lb range. Roach and rudd show to maggot and caster and bream have provided several 100lb plus bags to feeder with maggot and worm. The two and a half acre railway lake has roach, bream from 4 to 5lb, tench, perch and carp from 8oz to 1lb and has been developed primarily as a beginners water. The corner with the tall reeds is a hotspot and maggots will catch most species Corn tempts bream and perch to 2lb are in all pools. There is disabled access.

Avalon Fisheries, at Westhay, is a 17 acre, two lake complex set among peat workings. Number one lake has 50 pegs and averages eight feet in depth. Number two has 20 pegs, and is of a similar depth. Both pools are well stocked with bream, roach, rudd. tench, perch and carp. Number one has also been stocked with barbel. Both pools have recently been heavily stocked with bream. Be aware that boilies, nuts, bloodworm and joker are banned. Best baits for carp are corn, luncheon meat and bread.

Thorney Lakes, Nr Muchelney Langport, is an established coarse fishery that spans two acres and averages three and a half feet in depth. There is a good head of carp, tench, roach, rudd and bream, which most anglers fish for with pole, using ether corn, meat, maggot or caster. Best pegs are on the island. Shelf life boilies and cereal groundbaits are banned. This is another water where floating crust does well in summer.

We now move across to Wedmore to one of the best kept fisheries I have ever seen. The name of this haven for angling is Lands End Farm Fishery. There are two lakes there; Tadham, which is the specimen lake, and Tealham, the match lake. All the swims on both lakes have rubbish and fag end bins. Tealham lake has a big (and I mean big) platform in every swim and both lakes are heaving with fish. Tadham contains Commons, mirror and ghost carp from 5lb to 22lb, grass carp to 16lb and bream to 8lb. Tealham is stocked with common and mirror carp, tench, golden tench, crucians, ide, roach, rudd, perch, golden orfe, chub, bream and barbel. Best baits are maggot and corn which are best fished on a long pole close to the island or between the pegs close to the bank. This fishery has good paths leading up to the swims (wellies not needed).There is a good car park and toilets and I personally highly recommended this venue.

Fine bag of Bream from Lands End Farm

Immaculate Common Carp.
Upham Farm

The Sedges

Two superb lakes situated just outside Bridgwater on the Somerset levels

Brick Lake - 2 acre general coarse lake stocked with Tench, Roach, Bream, Chub & Carp.
Tile Lake - 3 acres with Carp to 32lb and over 100 doubles!
NEW LAKE with 36 pegs opening in May 2003

Static Caravans 2 mins from the waters edge

Contact Pat & John, The Sedges, River Lane, Dunwear, Bridgwater TA7 0AA. Tel 01278 445221

EDNEY'S FISHERIES

Edney's Farm, Mells, Nr Frome, Somerset.
Tel: 01373 812294. Mobile 07941 280075

Two well stocked lakes, heated by natural springs, in the heart of the Countryside

NEW MATCH & PLEASURE LAKES DUE THIS YEAR

Carp (mirror, common, ghost, linear and leather) **to 30lb.**
Also Tench Roach and Rudd. *100lb BAGS COMMON!*

Match Bookings Taken - Hard Track with Lakeside Parking

CARAVAN & CAMPING ON SITE

Emerald Pool Fishery

1.5 acre Lake stocked with

Carp to 22lb, Sturgeon to 4' long, Tench, Perch, Bream, Golden Orfe, Barbel to 5lb, Roach and Rudd

Excellent Disabled Facilities

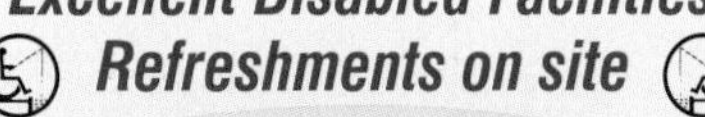

SAPPHIRE POOL

New 20 peg disabled friendly pool for adults and juniors

Self Catering Holiday Cottage beside the lake.

Sleeps four - disabled friendly

For further details contact
Mr Alan Wilkinson, Emerald Pool Fishery,
Puriton Rd, West Huntspill, Highbridge, Somerset.

Tel: 01278 794707 or 01278 685304

THORNEY LAKES

Coarse Fishing
Camping & Caravans

A Beautiful spot to fish, even better to stay in an inspiring landscape in the secret Somerset Levels

FULL FACILITY SITE FOR CAMPING & CARAVANS
MUCHELNEY, LANGPORT, SOMERSET.

Tel: 01458 250811

Email: enquiries@thorneylakes.co.uk www.thorneylakes.co.uk

Lands End Farm Fishery

Heath House, Wedmore, Somerset

Match Lake & Specimen Lake
Open all year - Dawn to Dusk

Stocked with Carp to 23lb, Tench and Bream to 8lb, Grass Carp to 17lb, Roach, Rudd, Golden Rudd, Barbel, Perch, Ide, Chub and Golden Orfe.

Disabled Facilities - Toilets - Refreshments

Please Telephone 07977 545882

At West Huntspill near Highbridge there is a fishery called Emerald Pool. This one and a half acre pool is a family run coarse fishery that boasts big, big catches and a hundred pound net of fish is common. Species include carp up to the mid twenties, bream, perch, roach, golden orfe, rudd, barbel, and sturgeon up to four feet long! Most of the swims have concrete platforms to fish from, the car park is right next to the pool and there is a toilet on site. Most of the usual baits score, although pellets are one of the best. There is disabled friendly holiday accommodation available at this fishery.

Back to Bridgwater now and the Sedges. This fishery was once a brickworks and has two pools, one three and a half acres, the other two and a half acres, with both having an average depth of eight feet. The Tile Pool has carp in the low doubles, and the Brick Pool is stocked with carp to 25lbs and also contains crucians over 2.5lb. Other stock in these ponds includes lots

Carp from The Sedges

of skimmers and bream from 5 to 7lb, tench to 9lb, roach and rudd to llb, big eels and a good head of perch with specimens up to 2lb. Boilies are good for carp throughout the season but in the summer months corn and meat are the tops for this species. Maggots catch lots of small fish and hemp is good for roach. This fishery is disabled friendly, in fact the 45 platforms on these pools will accommodate wheelchairs. Unhooking mats MUST be used.

Staying around Bridgwater we move to Westhay Lake which is between Westhay and Shapwick. This three and a half acre lake was originally dug for peat and its main species is carp (mirrors and commons) which go up to the mid thirties. There are also superb crucians which go up to 3.5lb, tench to 4lb, roach and rudd to 1lb, perch and goldfish. 50 to 60 lb nets are common. For carp. boilies or tiger nuts fished over a bed of hemp works well. Use maggot for smaller fish and pegs 10 and eleven are known hot spots. Carp anglers must have an unhooking mat and no bent or barbed hooks are allowed. There are no pike or bream in this water.

These are just a few of the commercial stillwater fisheries available to anglers. There are plenty more, and this article just gives a taste of the fishing on offer. Browsing the adverts and the directory in the Get Hooked guide will give you information on ALL of them.

Apart from the fisheries above there are a multitude of rivers in this county that offer excellent fishing. The river Tone in Taunton, which has free fishing between the top of French Weir down to the end of the Market car park. The Tone at French Weir, especially above the weir, gives really good sport with a big head of chub, quality roach, bream, grayling and trout. Maggot is a good bait for most of the species although I have caught some thumping big chub on elderberries. The river just below the weir gives a lot of small fish, and this area is popular with youngsters. Between the weir and Priorybridge (the start of the market car park) gives mostly small fish, but be aware there are a number of big carp in this section and the market car park gives some good bream and roach catches. If you accidently catch a grayling or trout (and you will at French Weir) don't put them in your keepnet as you will need a national game licence to do this.

Not far from Taunton, in fact just the other side of Bridgwater, is the river Huntspill. A lot of people call this a drain, but it was originally a river that was widened out to drain water off the

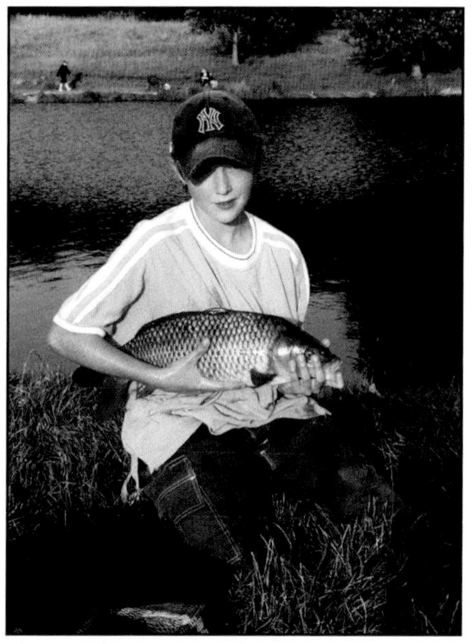

Young angler with a nice Carp.
West Pitt

levels. It runs from the bottom of the south drain to the tidal Parrett. It is famous for its bream fishing, and it is these 'slabs' that most Huntspill anglers are after. A number of 5lb fish are frequently caught but there are some specimens that are a lot bigger. As in all 'drain' bream fishing finding the fish is always the hardest part of catching them. Top method on this water is feeder fishing, with groundbait feeder and worm and caster on the hook. There are also lots of roach and skimmers on this water, and the preferred method is waggler with maggot hookbait. In the winter months bream seem to hold up in the Gold Corner area whearas in the summer the bream spread out all through the river.

Going towards Weston-Super-Mare we come across the river Axe. This delightful little river meanders through the Somerset countryside until it exits into the sea south of Weston. Not always a great favourite with matchmen, as it never seems to produce on the day, but pleasure fish it and you will probably be surprised at the good quality bream and roach you can catch. Another big surprise on this small river is the depth of some of the swims - up to 16 feet! Above Bleadon bridge, between Shiplate and Loxton is usually good, especially on the bends. Below Bleadon bridge is another good spot although it gets very muddy on this section.

Not far from the Axe is Cheddar Reservoir which holds some really big fish. Tench to well over 6lb, 30lb pike, lots of 3lb plus perch and shoals and shoals of quality roach. This water is very clear, so the best way to get among the lumps is long cast straight lead or feeder. Top baits for tench are corn, worm and luncheon meat. For the perch worms and maggots and maggots for the roach. There are brick towers coming out of the water about 50 yards from the bank and these seem to attract the perch, a line cast next to them usually gives good sport with these great fighting fish. I frequently fish successfully to the right of the Yachting Marina.

Back towards Bridgwater we come to one of the best drains in the West Country, the Kings Sedgemoor Drain. This drain has excellent access points at Crandon Bridge, Bawdrip, Parchey, Greylake, and Henley and this water is noted for its good bream, tench and roach fishing. My favourite spot is Greylake Bridge. Upstream from the bridge gives you some big bream and a lot of tench and downstream some very big tench have been caught. If you are feeling lazy fish next to your car in the car park. The last time I fished in the car park I saw a 4lb plus eel caught and a bream just over 6lb. If you feel like a bit of a walk go downstream until you are opposite where the Langacre Drain and the Sowy river enter the main drain as this is a very productive area. Further down stream Parchey is another area where good catches of bream are common. Down stream on the big bend is usually good. Down from Crandon Bridge is a section known as Silver fish. This is another very productive area although it is a bit of walk from the car park.

I have given you only a rough idea of some of the fabulous fishing to be had in Somerset. There is terrific fishing around the Bath area especially on the river Avon. Ilminster has the river Isle running through it (this little river is a chub hotspot). In South Somerset there are the rivers Yeo and Parrett. Try above Yeovilton Weir which is along side the Naval Air Base. Just over the border into Dorset there is Sherborne Castle lake, home to bream the size of dustbin lids. The list goes on......

If you are reading this however you have in your hand the definitive guide to fishing in the south west and with over 800 venues listed in the directory you really are spoilt for choice!

Superb Common - Acorn Carp Fisheries

ALCOVE ANGLING CLUB

Quality Coarse Fishing in the Bristol Area

FOUR COARSE LAKES WITH PARKING

Extensive stocking program
Match & Pleasure angling
Established, friendly club
Open all Year

OPEN MEMBERSHIP - NO WAITING LIST

CONTACT KEN DAVIS on 0117 9025737

Mobile 07941 638680 Email: alcove.a.c.bristol@blueyonder.co.uk

PLANTATIONS

Lakes & Cafe

Carp & Coarse Fishing

NEW CAFE

Opening Summer 2003

Accommodation to follow!

3/4 acre Carp Lake Well stocked with Common, Mirror & Ghost Carp

2.5 acre Coarse Lake Stocked with Tench, Roach, Rudd, Golden Rudd, Bream, Dace, Perch, Chub, Golden Tench, Gudgeon, Crucian Carp, Barbel

Day ticket - Adult £5, Junior/OAP/Disabled £4, Extra Rod £1
Half Days - Adult £4, Junior/OAP/Disabled £2.50

HORSESHOE MATCH LAKE OPEN

Local Country Walks, Camping & Caravan Club Site

For more information Tel: 01934 832325

Middle Lane, Kingston Seymour, Clevedon, North Somerset

Email: watravis@plantations.freeserve.co.uk

Acorn Carp Fishery (S.W.)

Lampley Road, Kingston Seymour, North Somerset (M5 junction 20, B3133 Yatton)

3.5 acres of water stocked with Carp from 10lb to 36lb (mainly upper doubles and twenties)

Day Tickets (12hr) 7am-7pm. Night Fishing, 24hr, 48hr, 72hr and weekly rates available

Facilities include: Hot & Cold Food and Drinks - Tackle and Bait Purchase/Hire - Toilets Car Parking, Hard Standing Paths around entire lake - Sixteen Peg Venue.

Full Disabled Access to EVERY Swim - Professional Tuition

Advanced bookings taken. Call in or call us, Adrian & Bev Bartlett on

01934 833760 or 834050 (lake) 07957 828721

Book Reviews

The Nature of Barbel - Nick Giles
Perca Press. Tel 01202 824245

ISBN 0-9543239-0-4

This is a very comprehensive book dedicated to a species that is becoming an increasingly popular quarry.

It covers pretty well all aspects of Barbel history, location, habitat, behaviour fish management, tackle and fishing methods.

It seems that the Barbel may be becoming the new Carp in so far as a breed of anglers seem to want to pit their wits against the most mysterious and wily of piscatorial opponents. Indeed it was 50 years ago when the famous Dick Walker said 'the barbel is a more mysterious fish than the carp'.

The south west is superb barbel country with the Hampshire Avon, Bristol Avon and Dorset Stour in it's arsenal with fisheries such as The Royalty and Throop synonomous with specimen fish.

The book is interspersed with many a 'fishy tale' and accounts of notable captures which serve to entertain and inform the reader and it features illustrations from Bernard Venables of possibly the greatest angler of all time - Mr Crabtree.

Whether you are a seasoned barbel angler or a beginner there is little doubt this book will increase your knowledge of the species and increase your chances of catching more and better fish.

Fishing's Strangest Days - Tom Quinn
Robson Books, 64 Brewery Road, London N7 9NT

ISBN 1-8610553-5-8

All anglers have experienced strange happenings in pursuit of our sport but this book surely contains the ultimate collection of the most strange!

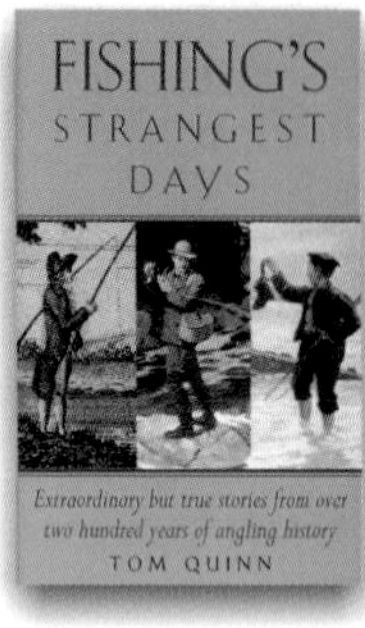

From the Pike that tried to eat a swan and choked to death on it's head to strange baits and strange captures, two hundred years worth of strange but true tales from the world of angling. This one won't improve your skills but it will make you smile!

Waterlog
Tel: 01691 623225.
Web: www.waterlogmagazine.co.uk
Yearly subscription (6 issues) £23.90

Waterlog is a bi-monthly magazine for 'the absolute angler'. Edited by Jon Ward-Allen and Chris Yates and has been going for about 6 years. It's 60 odd A4 pages are full of thoughtful articles covering all branches of the sport. It seems aimed at the more 'traditional' fisherman and many of the advertisements are from traditional tackle makers.

The feel of the Magazine is definitely geared towards the essence of angling and the experiences gained rather than the latest piece of tackle, bite alarms and dozens of pictures of fish being thrust towards the camera to make them appear larger.

There is an underlying humour to the publication and although serious subjects are broached there is much to remind us that we fish because we enjoy it and perhaps we should not take it too seriously - definitely worth a read.

SPECIMEN LAKE

Around 2.5 acres with depths ranging from 2-15ft.
Every swim has underwater features designed and built for big carp.
The stock at the moment is 43 fish between 10-28lbs.

MATCH LAKE

Mature match lake of half an acre with depths to 10ft.
Stocked with roach, rudd, tench,
bream, golden orfe and carp to 15 lbs.

BOTH LAKES AVAILABLE ON DAY AND NIGHT TICKETS.

HBS FISHERIES
ADSBOROUGH
Near Taunton

Car park, toilet and other facilities

Tel: 01823 412389
for further details

Family day out at

LONGLEAT

Warminster, Wiltshire

Set in 500 acres of parkland, 3 lakes containing carp, roach, bream, tench, perch & rudd. Tickets from the bank. Adult £6: Junior/OAP £3.00.

From Warminster take A362 towards Frome, follow signs to Longleat. Further information from the bailiff, Nick Robbins on (01985) 844496

www.longleat.co.uk

Lakes & Fisheries

QUALITY FISHING FOR:
Carp, Bream, Roach,
Tench, Chub and Perch

1 acre and 6 acre lakes
plus canal style sections

BAIT SHOP - CAFE - TOILET FACILITIES

Grittenham, Chippenham, Wiltshire.

Tel: 01666 510368 or 07748 144788

A beautiful seven acre lake well stocked with quality Carp & Tench

Day tickets £5 6am-6pm. OAP's juniors £4

ENQUIRIES WELCOME FOR MATCH BOOKINGS

Home Farm, Rood Ashton, Trowbridge, Wiltshire. ***Tel: 01380 870272***

Barn Moor & Selwood Lakes 1 & 2

2.5 acres. Both stocked with Tench, Bream, Chub, Roach, Golden Rudd, Perch, Common & Mirror Carp - CARP to 27lb in Lake 1

Cottage Lake 3

Bream to 7lb, Roach to 2.5lb, Tench to 3lb Carp to 16lb, small Crucians, Rudd & Dace - IDEAL FOR POLE & WAGGLER

MATCH LAKE

93 pegs designed for matchmen. 13 metres from bank to bank
Available for day ticket use

SITE FACILITIES INCLUDE: flush toilet, hot & cold snacks, drinks, bait and our NEW on-site Tackle Shop

Tackle Shop - TEL: 01722 710088

Toilet facilities for the disabled.
All swims accessible to wheelchairs

COMFORTABLE FARMHOUSE BED & BREAKFAST

FREE FISHING FOR RESIDENTS

CARAVANS WELCOME

Please phone for more details

New Cottage, Witherington Farm, Downton, Salisbury SP5 3QX. TEL: 01722 710021

WALDENS FARM FISHERY
Five lakes offering a variety of quality Coarse Fishing.
Stocked with Pike, Perch, Golden Rudd, Carp, Roach, Barbel, Bream, Orfe, Crucians, Tench & Golden Tench
Plus purpose built Match Lake for Private and Club Hire
Contact: David & Jackie Wateridge
Telephone: 01722 710480
Mobile: 07766 451173
THE nff Walden GROUP
Walden Estate,
West Grimstead,
Salisbury,
Wiltshire SP5 3RJ

Off the Westcountry Coast

- getting started in sea fishing

by Henry Gilbey

Wrasse - plentiful and hard fighters

I suppose the most attractive thing about starting sea fishing is that large parts of our stunning coastline are hugely accessible and of course free to dangle a line from. At certain times of the year we have large numbers of fish that are (fairly) easy to catch, coming as they do right in to the shoreline, and for those starting out, just how important is it to see a few fish? I bet all of us remember that first fish we ever caught.

If you want to get started in sea fishing or want to take a beginner with you, then it seems sensible to take early summer as a good starting time. As you gain experience then you may want to fish all year round for some great fish, but the warmer and calmer months are the time for those first steps, and happily this season coincides with quality fishing.

The humble but plentiful mackerel is a great fish to start off with, for they can be easy to catch, they often shoal around easily accessible places, and one does not need to spend lots of money on a bit of tackle and bait. I am not one who favours hurling out strings of feathers to catch masses of these fish, as to me it seems desperately unsubtle, wasteful and unsporting. Massive a mackerel may not be, but on balanced floatfishing or spinning gear they put up spectacular fights and look impossibly beautiful when fresh out of the sea. Just take a few to eat or to keep for bait and thus avoid removing piles of unwanted fish from the sea.

A simple carp, spinning or pier-type rod and fixed spool reel will the do the job perfectly, teemed up with a big sea float, ball-lead and 1/0 hook. The mackerel is not a fussy feeder and will feed on strips of sandeel, garfish, mackerel (yes!), squid and so on. The same tackle can be used to cast out 2-4oz spinners as well, and often you will pick up the bigger fish at greater depth.

Mackerel - a great starting point

The tail-walking garfish can also be caught using floatfishing methods, but for these weird looking fish, set the hook to lie no deeper than 10' below the surface. Try a little deeper for mackerel, although they can be anywhere. Just look around in the summer at your local piers, headlands and breakwaters and no doubt you will see plenty of people fishing, but of course do not go too

Ian Lewis with a Small Eyed Ray from a Somerset beach.
Combe Martin Sea Angling Club

close to the water. The major holiday resorts all seem to have places for easy summer fishing, so simply get down there and join the throng. First and last light though are often the best times.

Moving on from mackerel and garfish, I reckon the next step up is to start fishing for the bottom dwelling ballan wrasse that are usually fairly plentiful around much of our coastline. Again these fish can often be caught from the above kind of places, but bear in mind that the wrasse is a bottom feeder and tends to live where there are rocks and broken ground. Happily lots of headlands, piers and breakwaters are still worth fishing from, although the biggest wrasse tend to be caught from more out of the way places.....that though is for another time.

The same kind of tackle can be used for wrasse fishing, although a slightly more powerful rod and reel is helpful for the bigger ones. If you use a mainline of about 20lb breaking strain you should be fine, together with a hook of about 2/0 or 3/0. Wrasse are not that fussy and will accept both the lugworm and ragworm that are readily available from so many fishing tackle shops. Thread one of these on the hook and use a lead weight of perhaps 3-5oz to get your offering hard on the sea bed. Bites can often be very savage, and fight these fish hard to get them away from their rocky sanctuary. Deep-set floats also work in some places and it can be a great way of fishing for them; indeed, who doesn't like watching a bite on a float?

If you hook a wrasse of over 3lbs, you will be totally amazed at how a comparatively modest sized fish can fight so hard! Lay your hands on some peeler crab for bait and you are on the road to some great fishing, although at times this bait can be hard to come by; worms tend to sort out plenty of fish, and you never quite know just what you will catch. Please do handle all wrasse very gently and remove the hook as quickly as possible; they make terrible eating and thus every wrasse should be returned to the water to fight another day. Take a quick picture and admire this very pretty fish, but I implore you to put them back alive.

Henry Gilbey : www.henry-gilbey.co.uk

Tackle Test

Harris Lure-Pro 10' Baitcaster - (£70)

This can be considered a multi-purpose lure rod in so far as it will handle Pike, Salmon and Sea fish, such as Bass, with ease.

It's an ideal weapon for the South West coastline, casting 14-56g and an excellent stiffish action which is very advantageous when fishing lures as it gives you better contact and the ability to impart more action to your bait. Being able to add that extra bit of 'life' to your lure could well be what triggers the predatory instinct in your quarry.

As a baitcaster it's designed to be used with a multiplier and has a trigger grip which helps casting and overall rod control. The reel seat is wind down which means your hand is always on the cork and not the thread, much more comfortable especially when you are casting for hour after hour!

The rod is also available in a spinning version for use with a fixed spool and in other lengths from 5'6" to 9'.

Finish is excellent; a top quality carbon blank in matt sage green with green/gold whipping and lined rings throughout to optimise casting ability.

The Harris Lure Pro 10ft Baitcaster is available for £70 post free from

Harris Angling, Whimpwell Green,
Lower Hapisburgh, Norfolk NR12 0AJ,
or from all good tackle shops.
View the full range of Harris tackle at:
www.harrisangling.co.uk

Mr Busniewicz with Bass to over 8lb caught on fly from Lyme Regis under the guidance of Darren Herbert

West is Best

by Jim O'Donnel. Owner/ skipper of Plymouth charter boat "The Tiburon"

Sea Fishing around Devon and Cornwall - the so-called foot of Great Britain.

Using this term makes us sound distant from the rest of the UK. Well I suppose we are distant from the hustle and bustle of real city life. But to be distant from something always means you're closer to something else! The south coasts of Devon and Cornwall face out into the clear, fish rich waters of the western English Channel, placing us closer to arguably the best boat fishing in the country.

Far from the fast life but as close to the dream as you will ever get. This is where the action happens!!

From the busy ports of Plymouth, Brixham, and Falmouth to the small quaint Harbours of Looe, Mevagissy and Salcombe you will find small but enthusiastic teams of expert charter skippers with fast, safe and reliable boats, only too keen give you a superb days sport. This on a good day can be beyond your wildest dreams!! All the skippers that work from the coasts of these two counties are truly passionate about what they do, are anglers themselves and have their own unique stories to tell.

A typical summers day fishing.

It's 6.30am. You've had hardly any sleep because of your imminent fishing trip! The excitement started yesterday evening as you prepared your tackle and packed lunch, ready for an early and well prepared start.

You arrive at you chosen port for the day. All is silent until the sound of an empty fish box hitting a concrete floor at the local fish market breaks the spell and the sound echoes around the old concrete walls of a historic harbour. This is a fisherman's time of day!! Commercial and pleasure fisherman are among the privileged few who know the beauty of this time, sharing in an excitement unknown to those who have never fished. The feeling of nerves and expectation over what catch this day will bring!

You walk down the wooden slipway, across the wooden pontoon to your chosen boat for the day. Others have already arrived, some experienced, some novice but all with one thing in common, they are here to fish and share the same excitement. The boat deck is quiet but there is a tension in the air that feels like everyone's excitement is about to explode!! The skipper emerges from the wheelhouse door with a tray of piping hot tea and coffee. "Morning lads" - his words break the silence and chat breaks out among the expectant crew. Safety instructions and a quick brief on the fishing are given before he turns the key and the boats turbo engine roars into life!!

Fifteen minutes later you are leaving the coastline behind you, to be engulfed by the horizon. Everybody's excitement has now turned to a race to see who will have his or her tackle ready first. The boat slows down as the skipper reaches his chosen destination and you line the sides of the boat ready for the command to drop your tackle to the seabed.

The skipper turns on his electronic fish finder and a huge mark appears on the screen indicating the fish that are beneath the boat. The boat is carefully positioned and a command is

Just perfect!
Brean Sands at Warren Farm Holiday Park

yelled from the wheelhouse "down you go boys". This is it!! Whilst concentrating on your own tackle you can't help but notice somebody to the rear of the boat is shouting. His rod slams over, contorted by a hard fighting fish!! Then another anglers rod bends over, and another, and another until finally it's your turn. Your rod is almost wrenched from your grip and bends as if about to break!! You play the fish savouring the fight all the way to the surface. The skipper nets your catch and places it carefully down so as not to damage it. You triumphantly hold your capture and have your picture taken - a moment saved forever.

There are fish being caught everywhere, many are returned whilst others will be taken home to be cooked and enjoyed by the whole family at the table. The action continues all day until the sun becomes low in the sky and the boat heads back towards land. All aboard have had a superb days sport. Your memories of this day will last forever drawing you back to the western English Channel to chase the dream once more!!

Species that can be sought

Many species inhabit the waters that surround Devon and Cornwall, including specimen pollack, cod, bass, huge conger eels, many flatfish, ray, big blue sharks more. Each port and skipper will have their own speciality. All skippers will provide tackle, copious amounts of tea and coffee and be only to pleased to help, advise, teach, and see the smile on your face when you visit the most productive fishing grounds in the UK and are rewarded with some truly tremendous fishing. Tight lines!!

www.plymouthcharters.co.uk
Email: jim@plymouthcharters.co.uk

Superb Bass - West is definitely best!

Tackle Test

Magellan SporTrak Pro - Handheld GPS - (around £279)

Global positioning devices have been around for a long time now and are the perfect device for marking a favourite location and being able to find it again - optimally down to within just three metres!

All boat anglers will be familiar with GPS systems mounted in the cabin but a handheld device just makes it so convenient. Out on your mates boat and find a real hot spot? Just save it into the unit as a waypoint and it's there forever. Regardless of whose boat you are on you can find that exact spot easily. The unit is waterproof and floats, both very useful attributes.

The SporTrak Pro has several useful optional displays including: map screen, compass screen, position screen and road screen. The last option can be used to navigate on land and shows a graphical display of a road that will indicate when to turn.

The 'Pro' includes a 9mb european mapping database and 23mb of free memory for adding street level maps and, of course, it will all interface with your PC or Laptop. The only limitation really is that the unit really must have an unobstructed view of the sky to get the most satellite 'fixes' possible to work at its' best.

If we all had one of these we could swap info on hotspots, on the sea or on rivers and lakes, or email the co-ordinates of the swim where you caught that 11lb Barbel to your friends, lots of possibilities!

Magellan units are widely available. Major West Country stockist is Mark Dowland Marine, Leanne Business Centre, Sandford Lane, Wareham, Dorset BH20 4DY

Full info on all Magellan products on the web at www.magellangps.com.

Sea Charters & Clubs

Westcountry

National Federation of Sea Anglers
Contact: Head Office, Level 5, Hamlyn House, Mardle Way, Buckfastleigh, TQ11 0NS, 01364 644643, ho@nfsa.org.uk *Water:* Sea Angling, *Species:* All sea fish, *Permits:* None apply, *Charges:* Individual membership £10 per year. Personal membership £15 per year, *Season:* None applicable.

South West Federation of Sea Anglers
Contact: Andy Alcock, 21 Marsh Road, Weymouth, DT4 8JD, 01305 772318, gillian-alcock@btopenworld.com *Water:* South West coastal waters. The Federation is on www.fishingworld.co.uk

Cornwall

Cornish Federation of Sea Anglers
Contact: Mr Ralph Elcox (Hon Sec), 44 Town Farm, Falmouth Road, Redruth, TR15 2XG, 01209 314389, 07876 518777, *Water:* Sea Fishing. Shore and boat. Tidal fishing in estuaries, excluding Bass, *Species:* All sea fish apart from protected species. Minimum weight for all species, *Permits:* None required, other than possible harbour charges, *Charges:* C.F.S.A. affiliation £34 per annum per club. Personal members £7.50. Family membership (i.e. husband, wife and children under 16) £10. *Methods:* Two rods three hooks maximum. No netting.

BOSCASTLE

Boscastle Peganina
Contact: Ken Cave, 01288 353565.

CAMBORNE

Camborne Angling Association
Contact: Mr Ralph Elcox (Hon Sec), 44 Town Farm, Falmouth Road, Redruth, TR15 2XG, 01209 314389, 07876 518777, *Water:* Sea Fishing Association. Shore and boat, *Species:* All sea fish apart from protected species. Minimum weight for all species, *Permits:* None required, other than possible harbour/pier charges, *Charges:* Family membership £10, Couple £8, Senior £7 and £2 Junior. *Methods:* Two rods, three hooks maximum, no netting.

FALMOUTH

Blue Minstrel
Contact: Lance Peters, 01326 250352, 07831 490225, lance.peters@btinternet.com

Leo 1
Contact: Ken Dodgson, 01326 312409/315849, 07779 376641.

Mawnan Angling Club
Contact: Tim Varney, 07766 537221, *Water:* Sea fishing club with boat and shore sections, *Species:* Sea fish, *Charges:* £8 senior, £3 junior. Club meet on 1st Monday of month at Cross Keys, Penryn. New members welcome. Enquiries to Tackle Box, Falmouth or Telephone Tim on number above.

Patrice II
Contact: Michael Tuffery, 01326 313265, 07979 335181.

Segue
Contact: Rob Searle, 01326 312116, 07774 226046, rob@seguecharters.co.uk

HAYLE

San Pablo III
Contact: Dougie Wright, 01209 716970, 07974 409567, divewright@btinternet.com Alternative mobile - 07714 514808.

HELSTON

Helston & District Sea Angling Club
Contact: For further information contact NFSA Head Office: 01364 644643.

LISKEARD

Liskeard & District Sea Angling Club
Contact: For further information contact NFSA Head Office: 01364 644643.

LOOE

Looe Angling Club
Contact: Billy Martin, Quay Street, East Looe, 01506 263337. Clubhouse with club prices on all drinks. Open all day everyday. Membership full, but holiday membership available. Please contact clubhouse.

Mystique
Contact: David Bond, 01503 264530, 07812030008, mystiquebond@aol.com

Shark Angling Club of Great Britain
Contact: The Quay, East Looe, PL13 1DX, 01503 262642, sacgb@bigfoot.com *Water:* Established 50 years. Boat booking agent for 8 boats in Looe for Shark, Reef fishing and Mackerel trips. Club open to new members - required to catch a qualifying length shark prior to joining. For more details please contact above.

MEVAGISSEY

Aquila
Contact: Martin Carrington, 01726 842222.

Venus
Contact: Mevagissey Shark & Angling Centre, Mevagissey, 01726 843430.

Fishing Videos

Henry Gilbey

(Fishing with Henry/Fishing on the Edge)
PMA Video Productions

Many you may have seen these programmes on Sky Discovery Home and Leisure. The videos all feature Plymouth based angler Henry Gilbey who is a fanatical sea fisherman.

There are 6 videos available, two from the original 'Fishing with Henry' series and four from 'Fishing on the Edge', all are about 70 minutes long and each features 3 episodes from the series. The filming is of a very high quality throughout although the background music seems to feature that same guitarist that has accompanied many other T.V. anglers!

There is something for everyone here from basic tackle and wrasse off the rocks (see Henry's article in the guide) to the rather more exotic and extreme 'Skeleton Coast Sharks'. The latter being the only video devoted to one type of fishing features bronze whaler sharks up to 250lb caught off the beach in Namibia!

Although these videos take us to North Africa and Ireland they are very westcountry based, with boat fishing out of Plymouth, Cod on the river Severn, North Cornish Wrasse, Blue Sharks, Wreck Fishing, Jersey Bass and Cornish Rays among the titles.

There is also a great programme on fly fishing for Pike featuring Henry and Nick Hart having a succesful day on Chew.

Videos are available direct from PMA Productions at a price of £12.99 each plus £1 p&p (buy 3 post free).

More details from PMA Productions, 7, Beech Way, Twickenham, Middlesex TW2 5JS
Tel: 020 8898 6395
www.pmavideo.co.uk

Trigger Happy Fishing

Ed Schliffke
Rockhopper Productions

Another very Westcountry video from Cornish fishing personality and guide Ed 'the rockhopper' Schliffke.

A wide variety of techniques and species are covered from both boat and shore at day and night.

Pirking for cod in the English channel produces some great specimens and in true 'predictable' fishing style a session targeting small eyed ray from a North Cornwall beach produces some specimen Smooth Hounds - but no rays. Also there is a surprise species from the Devon coast!

Production quality is not quite up to the PMA offerings but the content is certainly there.

A little more detail on rigs and tackle would have been helpful but at the end of the day it is an entertaining video. Next best thing to fishing!

Ed has five other videos available, all Westcountry based, priced from £15.95. Available from Padstow Angling Centre Tel: 01841 532762

Zoe Jones - learning from Ed Schliffke

All the videos viewed here have one thing in common. The anglers have a true passion for their sport and a huge respect for the fish they catch. Regardless of size or species every fish landed is a 'beauty' and, having outwitted the quarry and enjoyed the fight, as Henry states on many occasions 'the best bit is putting them back'.

Sea Charters & Clubs

NEWQUAY

Treninnick Tavern Angling Club
Contact: For further information contact NFSA Head Office: 01364 644643.

PADSTOW

Blue Fox
Contact: Phil Britts, Padstow, 01841 533293.
Emma Kate
Contact: John Wicks, 01841 533319.
Padstow Angling Centre
Contact: ***Ed Schliffke, 01841 532762,*** **Water:** ***Shore fishing trips.***

PENZANCE

Goldsithney S.A.C.
Contact: For further information contact NFSA Head Office: 01364 644643.
Mounts Bay Angling Society
Contact: David Cains, Shangri-La, 99 Arundel Park, Connor Downs, Hayle, TR27 5EL, 01736 752037, 07919 253065, david-cains@d-cains.freeserve.co.uk *Water:* Regular monthly meetings open to all in area, regular matches fishing on Cornish waters, *Charges:* Seniors £8 per year, Juniors £4 per year, Family membership £13 (2 adults & 2 children).
St Ives S.A.C.
Contact: For further information contact NFSA Head Office: 01364 644643.
The Starfish & The Danda
Contact: Porthlevan Angling Centre, 01326 561885.
Westward Casting Association
Contact: For further information contact NFSA Head Office: 01364 644643.

REDRUTH

Redruth Sea Angling Association
Contact: Treve Opie (Hon Sec), 3 Colborne Avenue, Illogan, Redruth, TR16 4EB, 01209 842622, treve.opie@cornwall.ac.uk *Water:* Founded in 1962 by a group of anglers who regularly fished Porthowan beach which is not far from Redruth. HQ is the Redruth Albany Rugby Football Club at the bottom of Station Hill, Redruth. Meetings are held at 8pm on the first Monday of each month or the first Monday following a Bank Holiday. The club runs it's own competitions, social events, and takes part in team inter club competition, *Charges:* Subscriptions £7 for Seniors over 16 years and £2 for under 16 years.

ST AUSTELL

E.C.C. Ports S.A.C.
Contact: For further information contact NFSA Head Office: 01364 644643.
Mevagissey S.A.C.
Contact: For further information contact NFSA Head Office: 01364 644643.
Roche Angling Club
Contact: For further information contact NFSA Head Office: 01364 644643.

ST IVES

Dolly Pentreath & The James Stevens (No.10)
Contact: Mike Laity, 01736 797269, 07712 386162, mplaity@mlaity.freeserve.co.uk

TORPOINT

Pot Black Sea Angling Club
Contact: For further information contact NFSA Head Office: 01364 644643.
Raleigh Sea Angling Club
Contact: For further information contact NFSA Head Office: 01364 644643.

TRURO

Threemilestone Angling Club
Contact: For further information contact NFSA Head Office: 01364 644643.

WADEBRIDGE

Fulmar
Contact: Chris Ogborne, Kernow Game Fishing, Flora Court, Wadebridge, PL27 6DE, 01208 816266, 07855 038203, *Water:* Boat charter and surf flyfishing around Cornish coast, *Season:* April to October.

Isles of Scilly

Falcon Faldork & Firethorn
Contact: David Stedeford, 01720 422866.

Devon

BARNSTAPLE

Combe Martin Sea Angling Club
Contact: Wayne Thomas, The Shippen, Loxhore Cott, Nr Barnstaple, EX31 4ST, 01271 850586, waesox@shippen99.freeserve.co.uk *Charges:* Family £10, Senior £6, Junior £1.
Triple Hook Club
Contact: Dennis Toleman, 32 Pilton Lawn, Barnstaple, EX31 4AA, 01271 378593, 07815 009260, *Water:* Shore fishing, 8 boat trips, regular fly fishing & coarse fishing matches plus training sessions & tuition, *Permits:* Monthly meeting at Barnstaple & District Social Club (Ex R.B.L.) St Georges Road, Barnstaple, 1st Tuesday in month. New members welcome. Family orientated club, please contact Dennis on number above or come to our meetings, *Charges:* £5 membership, matches £4.

Sea Charters & Clubs

BIDEFORD

Appledore Shipbuilders Angling Club
Contact: M Horrel, 52 Devonshire Park, Bideford, 01237 474614, *Water:* Shore and Boat fishing. Roving monthly competitions. Annual festive competitions. Founded in 1971, 50 plus members. South West Federation member. New members welcome, *Charges:* £4 Adult. £2 Juniors.

Bideford & District Angling Club
Contact: Mr B. Ackland, Honestone Street, Bideford, 01237 478846, *Water:* Bideford based club with coarse, game, boat & sea sections; fishing throughout South West. Competition Friday 23rd May - Monday 26th. Please phone for further details, *Permits:* Membership form from club, open 7pm-11pm, *Charges:* £5 per annum, concessions for juniors/OAPs.

Sanderling
Contact: Randall, Appledore, 01237 479585, 07779 443472, *Water:* Estuary fishing. 2 hour trips in 'Sanderling, fully licenced and insured for 12 anglers. £8 per person. Rod and bait supplied if required, *Species:* Bass, Plaice etc.

Torridge Angling Club
Contact: A.J. Kelly (secretary), 4 Ridgeway Drive, Westward Ho!, 01237 476665, 07779 193085, *Water:* Coarse match fishing at local waters. Boat section. Quarterly meetings. New members welcome. Please contact the secretary, *Charges:* £5 per year. Concessions for juniors.

BRIXHAM

Seaspray III & Bonnie Boys (Mackerel Fishing)
Contact: Chris Willicott, 01803 851328.

CLOVELLY

Jessica Hettie
Contact: Clive Pearson, 01237 431405 (eve), 07774 190359, *Water:* Sea Angling trips around Clovelly and Lundy, *Species:* Shark, Pollack, Mackeral, Bass, *Season:* April to September.

Ralph Atkinson Angling Charters
Contact: Ralph, Isis, Irsha Court, Irsha Street, Appledore, EX39 1RN, 01237 475535, 07774 164086, *Water:* Inshore and offshore reefs, wrecks and banks and deep sea in the Bristol Channel onboard 'Hooker', *Species:* Tope, Shark, Bass, Pollack, Rays, Congers, Huss, *Permits:* 20 mile day or night licence for up to 8 people. Fully equipped with all safety gear and tackle, *Charges:* Individuals £26. To book boat £160, *Season:* Operating all year. Boat leaves Clovelly 9am each day and returns at 5pm.

CREDITON

Crediton Inn Angling Club
Contact: For further information contact NFSA Head Office: 01364 644643.

DART

African Queen
Contact: Alan Hemsley, 07885 246061, alan.hemsley@virgin.net

DARTMOUTH

Dartmouth Angling & Boating Association
Contact: Mervyn G Yalland (Chairman), 5 Oxford Street, Dartmouth, 01548 856254, 07977 843754, *Water:* Predominantly sea fishing, some coarse fishing, *Charges:* Membership £6 individual, £11 couple, £3 Junior.

Gemini III
Contact: Dave Harrison, 01803 851766, 07968 599245, gemini3@domino1.freeserve.co.uk

Saltwind of Dart
Contact: Lloyd Saunders, 01803 883003, 07831 315477.

Samuel Irvin
Contact: Ian Noble, 01803 834598, 07780 970803, samuelirvin@tesco.net

Two Rivers
Contact: Steve Parker, 01803 329414, 07866 806585.

EXETER

Axminster Sea Angling Club
Contact: For further information contact NFSA Head Office: 01364 644643.

Starcross Fishing Cruising Club
Contact: For further information contact NFSA Head Office: 01364 644643.

EXMOUTH

Blue Thunder
Contact: Mike Deem, 01626 891181, mike@bluethundercharters.com *Water:* Operating from Exmouth, Devon using a 420hp 33ft Lochin angling boat, *Species:* Wreck fishing for Bass, Cod and Pollack.

Exmouth Sea Angling Association
Contact: For further information contact NFSA Head Office: 01364 644643.

Restorick III
Contact: Colin Pike, 01363 775316.

Smuggler III
Contact: Colin Dukes, 01626 890852, 07974 437740.

Stuart Line Fishing
Contact: 5 Camperdown Terrace, Exmouth, EX8 1EJ, 01395 275882, 07977 203099, info@stuartlinecruises.co.uk *Water:* Lyme Bay, *Species:* Mackeral, Ling, Pollack, Whiting, Conger Eel, *Permits:* Please phone, *Charges:* Mackeral £5. Deep Sea £10, *Season:* Easter to end of October.

Tamesis
Contact: Nigel Dyke, 01769 580376, 07968 182975.

Sea Charters & Clubs

HONITON

Honiton Sea Angling Club
Contact: Mike Spiller, 6 Charles Road, Honiton, EX14 1QG, 01404 43397, *Water:* A club for family membership. Regular competitions, junior matches, boat & casting competitions held. Casting tuition member of England team, *Charges:* Senior £5, OAP £3, Junior £2. Competitions are free.

ILFRACOMBE

Ilfracombe & District Anglers Association (Sea)
Contact: David Shorney, Victoria Cottage, 8B St Brannocks Road, Ilfracombe, EX34 8EG, 01271 865874, bullfinch@amserve.net *Water:* Beaches and rock marks. Founded in October 1929, the oldest club in North Devon, *Species:* Bass, Pollock, Conger, Mullet, Ray, Coalfish, Cod and various other species, *Permits:* From Variety Sports, Broad Street, Ilfracombe, *Charges:* Fees per year: Family £10, Adult £8, OAP £4, Junior £2. 17 competitions per year and an annual fishing festival in July/August, *Season:* January to January.

Kerry Kim
Contact: Eddie Bennellick, 01271 864143.

Osprey
Contact: Paul Barbeary, Ilfracombe, 01271 864625, 07970 101407.

Silver Fox
Contact: Dave Clemence, Ilfracombe, 01271 863460.

INSTOW

Betty Louise
Contact: Royston, 01271 860889, 07966 428189, *Water:* Licensed for 12, Shark and Tope fishing. All day and 1/2 day trips by arrangement.

Estrella-Domar
Contact: M. Lock, 01271 323270, 07977 538465.

IVYBRIDGE

Bridge Sea Angling Club
Contact: For further information contact NFSA Head Office: 01364 644643.

Plymouth City Engineers Sea Angling Club
Contact: For further information contact NFSA Head Office: 01364 644643.

KINGSBRIDGE

Kingsbridge & District Sea Anglers
Contact: Ray Carr, 17 Barnfield Walk, Kingsbridge, TQ7 1QS, 01548 853331, elaine@barnfield24.fsnet.co.uk *Water:* Regular monthly boat and shore matches, strong junior section, matches with other clubs in region. New members welcome, contact Ray at number above, *Charges:* Seniors £10, juniors £5 (under 16), family £15 (2 adults, 2 children). Child protection policy in force.

PAIGNTON

Charlotte Lousie
Contact: Ashley Lane, 07767 622727, ashley@boyrichard.co.uk

Our Joe-l
Contact: Simon Pedley, 01803 551504, *simon@ourjoe-l.co.uk.*

Paignton Sea Angling Association
Contact: For further information contact NFSA Head Office: 01364 644643.

Seafield Sea Angling Club
Contact: For further information contact NFSA Head Office: 01364 644643.

Tuonela
Contact: Peter Bingle, 01803 666350, 07715 735842.

PLYMOUTH

British Conger Club
Contact: For further information contact NFSA Head Office: 01364 644643.

D.O.E Sea Angling Club
Contact: For further information contact NFSA Head Office: 01364 644643.

Dartmoor Pirates S.A.C.
Contact: For further information contact NFSA Head Office: 01364 644643.

Devonport Sea Angling Club - 'The Peelers'
Contact: For further information contact NFSA Head Office: 01364 644643.

Ford Hotel S.A.C. (Plymouth)
Contact: For further information contact NFSA Head Office: 01364 644643.

Gypsy Mariners Angling Club
Contact: For further information contact NFSA Head Office: 01364 644643.

Naval Stores Sea Angling Club
Contact: For further information contact NFSA Head Office: 01364 644643.

Plymouth Command Angling Association (Sea)
Contact: Mr Vic Barnett Hon.Sec, 5 Weir Close, Mainstone, Plymouth, PL6 8SD, 01752 708206, victor.barnett@talk21.com *Water:* Boat & shore fishing, *Species:* All sea fish, *Permits:* Membership is open to all serving members of HM Forces. Associate membership is also open to ex-serving members of HM Forces, no matter when the time was served, *Charges:* Costs for full membership or associate membership are available on application or enquiry at the above contact.

Plymouth Federation S.A.C.
Contact: For further information contact NFSA Head Office: 01364 644643.

Plymouth Inter Boat A.F.
Contact: For further information contact NFSA Head Office: 01364 644643.

Plymouth S.A.C.
Contact: For further information contact NFSA Head Office: 01364 644643.

The National Federation of Sea Anglers is the National Governing Body of the sport for England and as such is recognised by HM Government and Sport England who grant aid agreed development projects and part fund the National Teams through an International Programme. It represents over Thirty Thousand Sea Anglers through our affiliated clubs, and individual and personal members.

We work alongside our 'sister organisations', the other Governing Bodies for freshwater the National Federation of Anglers and the Salmon & Trout Association for Gamefish on many projects including a Coach Licensing Scheme and with the Environment Agency on major incentives on social inclusion projects to attract people from all backgrounds, into the sport.

Sea angling is a well-established recreational sporting activity, for which the single most important ingredient is that of fish and the UK and the South West in particular should be well placed to provide this as it is surrounded by an extensive continental shelf with potentially rich fish resources.

A fishing rod has been described as being "a fool at one end and a hook at the other", I guess because the idea of an angler outwitting a fish is difficult to comprehend for those who do not understand that angling is about so much more. It is about being in great outdoors, sometimes braving the elements, observing nature and indeed using this knowledge to advantage to catch fish. Therefore we are unhappy about this description, for anglers are proud and passionate about what they do preferring to describe angling as being truly an occupation and sport for all and a measure of the passion is that there have been more books written about angling than most other sports.

There has been some discussion as to whether angling is a recreation or a sport but we believe there is no discussion, it is both, it can be as relaxed as you like or as intense as one wants to make it and UK sea anglers are very successful and have achieved much on the world competition stage.

Sea angling is practised by young and old and, although mainly a male dominated sport, is seeing increasing numbers of female participants. It is carried out by individuals, small groups and, in the case of competitive angling, by organised events where in many cases hundreds of participants fish over a number of days. It is a fact that leisure time and the amount of expendable income continue to increase and the way in which the population spend their time and money is now regarded as significant to a nations overall health. Angling is an ideal outdoor leisure activity contributing to both the physical and mental well-being of society with immense development potential.

It is the one of the largest if not the largest participation sport and it is interesting to note that a recent survey by the English Disabled Federation of Sport showed that Angling was the second most popular sport that disabled persons had tried and the second most popular sport that they wanted to take up. We are informed by the latest reports that there are 1.1 million of us in England and Wales and our economic spend is considerable. The latest study by Nautilus Consultants has quoted angling to be worth £28m in Wales alone, and it is reasonable to submit that considerably more money is spent on angling and its support services in England and in particular in the South West which has many hundreds of miles of coastline and provides a wide variety of venues of interest to anglers.

Therefore the economic impact of sea angling is both immense and diverse. The expenditure on a wide range of specialist fishing tackle, (and many keen sea anglers own tackle valued at thousands of pounds), as well as bait, clothing, footwear, etc., is only the beginning. Many fish from boat, therefore they purchase small boats and engines, also chandlery, trailers to carry the boat on, and vehicles to tow the boat, or alternatively they pay marina fees, thus creating employment. In addition, there are many specialist charter boats who cater for the deep sea angler. The Westcountry was once the

Sea Charters & Clubs

Rodbenders S.A.C.
Contact: For further information contact NFSA Head Office: 01364 644643.
Roving Rods Sea Angling Club
Contact: For further information contact NFSA Head Office: 01364 644643.
Royal Naval & Royal Marines A.A.
Contact: For further information contact NFSA Head Office: 01364 644643.
Scorpion
Contact: Dave Brett, Plymouth, 01752 261261, 07941 261475.
Sea Angler
Contact: Malcolm Jones, Plymouth, 01752 316289, 07977 097690.
Silver Crest
Contact: Silverline Cruises, Derek Smith, 01752 226243.
Size Matters
Contact: Graham Hannaford, Plymouth, 01752 261261, 07941 261475.
Specimen Angling Group of Plymouth
Contact: For further information contact NFSA Head Office: 01364 644643.
Stonehouse Creek Sea Angling Club
Contact: For further information contact NFSA Head Office: 01364 644643.
Storm
Contact: Rod Davies, 01752 492232.
Tiburon
Contact: Jim O'Donnel, 01752 518811, 07855 040015, jim@plymouthcharters.co.uk *Water:* Wreck, reef, bank and Shark fishing, *Season:* Full day, half day and evening trips.
Venture
Contact: Peter Fergus, 01752 709070, 07778 494274, pjfergus@venturecharters.fslife.co.uk

SALCOMBE

Anglo Dawn 11
Contact: Ted Cooke, 01548 531702.
Calypso
Contact: Kevin Oakman, 01548 843784, 07970 651569.
Phoenix
Contact: Mick Allen, 01548 853987.
Salcombe & District Sea Angling Association
Contact: C J Bradford, 5 Portlemore Close, Malborough, TQ7 3SX, 01548 560901, cjbradford@bushinternet.com *Water:* Boat fishing club welcomes new adult members. Please contact above.
Tight Lines
Contact: Kevin Rowe, 01548 843818, 07980 344604.
Tuckers Boat Hire
Contact: Chris Puncher, 01548 842840, info@tuckersboathire.com
Whitestrand Boat Hire
Contact: Debbie or Kevin, 01548 843818, debbie@whitestrand.fsnet.co.uk *Water:* 32 boats.

SEATON

Beer & District Sea Angling Association
Contact: For further information contact NFSA Head Office: 01364 644643.
BJ
Contact: Brian Sanderson, 01297 24774, *Water:* Sailing from Beer in Lyme Bay area, *Permits:* Bookings via Seaton Chandlery.
Cygnet
Contact: Paul Godfrey, 01297 24774, *Water:* Sailing from Beer in Lyme Bay area, *Permits:* Bookings via Seaton Chandlery.

STARCROSS

Torbay & Babbacombe Association of Sea Anglers
Contact: For further information contact NFSA Head Office: 01364 644643.

TEIGNMOUTH

Teignmouth Sea Angling Society
Contact: For further information contact NFSA Head Office: 01364 644643.

TORQUAY

Dalora II
Contact: Kevin Tate, Torquay, 01626 776606, 07989 527180, dalora@deepsea.co.uk
Jubrae
Contact: Geoff and Fred, 01803 213866, 07860 200247, geoff@torbaycharters.co.uk
Torbay S.A.F.A
Contact: For further information contact NFSA Head Office: 01364 644643.

TOTNES

Baywater Anglers
Contact: For further information contact NFSA Head Office: 01364 644643.

Dorset

BOURNEMOUTH

Bay Angling Society
Contact: For further information contact NFSA Head Office: 01364 644643.
Boscombe & Southbourne S.F.C.
Contact: For further information contact NFSA Head Office: 01364 644643.
Bournemouth & District S.A.A.
Contact: For further information contact NFSA Head Office: 01364 644643.
Dorset Police Sea Angling Club
Contact: For further information contact NFSA Head Office: 01364 644643.

Mecca for such angling trips and still today many charter boats operate from ports along the coast, and those who travel from outside the area many as far away as the South East, Birmingham and Liverpool, require accommodation, food and drink to sustain them. Finally anglers like to read about the current sea angling issues and catches and as a result they support a healthy selection of weekly and monthly angling publications

Each Year there are several week long events held in the South West, The YYS Boat and Shore Festival, at Weymouth, the Torbay Festival and here in Plymouth the Plymouth Festival are all major events that attract people and business to the area. The Wyvern National Small Boat Festival at Salcombe has for 24 years attracted 130 anglers in up to 60 boats for a two day event each September, also the National Flounder Festival at Teignmouth now in its sixth year attracts 500 plus anglers, 250 of them in 80 boats many of whom are trailed into the South West from such far away places as Kent, Essex, East Anglia, Midlands and Wales. This collectively makes sea angling an important industry and indeed increasing vehicle ownership has resulted in a significant number of visits to the coast from the inland population. Coastal tourism is undoubtedly a major beneficiary; but this section of the tourism industry is under-recognised and therefore underdeveloped.

In order to address this the NFSA (Wyvern Division) and Bass Anglers Sportfishing Society in conjunction with the Government Office South West, made a presentation at the National Marine Aquarium, Plymouth, in January of this year to make the case for the promotion and development of sea angling in the region.

The aim was to promote the best use of sea fish stocks for sustainable economic value to the South West. Recent studies confirm: the economic impacts from recreational angling exceed that of commercial fishing and much of its associated expenditure contributes significantly to tourism. Examples of successful sport fishing development were highlighted from around the globe and included examples from as close as Ireland and as far away as the Turks & Caicos islands. Two consultants specialising in fisheries management and economics, were flown in from the USA to relate the American experience with particular reference to the restoration of striped bass and the multi billion dollar recreational fishing industry now supported by innovative fisheries policies.

The USA presenters Andy Loftus and Gil Radonski gave a thought provoking and detailed account of how fisheries policy was a much more public affair in the US, providing full participation from the recreational sector. They stressed the key to success was sound fisheries management and demonstrated how sea angling participation levels and the consequential economic impacts, were directly related to fish stock abundance. This was reinforced by Andrew Syvret, a fisheries consultant based in Jersey, Channel Islands, who described other global examples where the potential for developing the sea angling product had been recognised and specific policies to realise the benefits had been implemented. Russell Weston of Snowbee, a fishing tackle company based in Plymouth and just one of thousands of stakeholder businesses who have in the past been overlooked by the fisheries management regime but whose very existence is dependent on fish stocks, confirmed the need for high quality fisheries management to restore those species of direct interest to angling. The final presentation focussed on "What can be done" to enable the South West to capitalise on its multi species fish stock resources, many of particular interest to sea anglers.

The workshop was a big success and the consensus view was that dialogue between the angling sector and the policy makers should be maintained and concluded that improved recognition of the economic impact from the angling sector together with restoration of those fish stocks that are of direct interest to sea angling are essential if the potential is to be realised.

David Rowe

To join the NFSA and help us with our work please contact:
NFSA Head Office, Level 5 Hamlyn House, Mardle Way, Buckfastleigh, Devon, TQ11 0NS.
Tel 01363 644643, Fax 01364 644486
email: ho@nfsa.org.uk,
or visit our comprehensive web site on www.nfsa.org.uk and join on line.

Sea Charters & Clubs

Pokesdown & Southbourne Ex SMC
Contact: For further information contact NFSA Head Office: 01364 644643.
Poole Dolphins Sea Angling Club
Contact: For further information contact NFSA Head Office: 01364 644643.
Post Office Angling Group (Bournemouth)
Contact: For further information contact NFSA Head Office: 01364 644643.
Primo S.C
Contact: Advanced Angling, 499 Christchurch Road, Boscombe, Bournemouth, 01202 303402, advancedangling@hellraiser100.freeserve.co.uk *Water:* Sea match fishing around the Dorset coast, *Charges:* £10 per year including N.F.S.A. membership.
Winton Workmens A.C
Contact: For further information contact NFSA Head Office: 01364 644643.

BRIDPORT

Channel Warrior
Contact: Chris Reeks, 01460 242678, 07785730504.
West Bay Sea Angling Club
Contact: For further information contact NFSA Head Office: 01364 644643.

CHRISTCHURCH

Christchurch & District Fishing Club
Contact: For further information contact NFSA Head Office: 01364 644643.
Christchurch Royal British Legion
Contact: For further information contact NFSA Head Office: 01364 644643.
Christchurch Shore Fishing Club
Contact: For further information contact NFSA Head Office: 01364 644643.
Mudeford Mens Club S.A.A.
Contact: For further information contact NFSA Head Office: 01364 644643.
Poole Charter Skippers Association
Contact: For further information contact NFSA Head Office: 01364 644643.

DORCHESTER

Blandford Sea Angling Club
Contact: For further information contact NFSA Head Office: 01364 644643.

LYME REGIS

Amaretto 11
Contact: Steven Sweet, 01297 445949, 07836 591084, amarettofsh@aol.com
Blue Turtle
Contact: Douglas Lanfear, 01297 34892, 07970 856822, doug@blueturtle.uk.com
Joint Venture
Contact: Paul Blinman, 07720 900235.
Lyme Regis Sea Angling Club
Contact: Ron Bailey, 6/26 Broad Street, Lyme Regis, 01297 443674, 07850 180331, ron@lymeregis.com *Water:* Club restarted in 2002, new members welcome. Boat & shore fishing. Regular monthly matches. Tuition available. Contact Ron at number above, *Charges:* Membership £10, Juniors £5.
Marie F
Contact: Harry May, 01297 442397, 07974 753287.
Neptune
Contact: Peter Ward, 01297 443606, 07768 570437.
Shemara
Contact: Ron Bailey, 01297 443674, 07850 180331, ron@lymeregis.com

POOLE

Albion Sea Angling Club
Contact: For further information contact NFSA Head Office: 01364 644643.
Aries 11
Contact: Duncan Purchase, 01425 278357, 07759 736360, duncan@aries2.freeserve.co.uk
Dawn Louise
Contact: Gary Snook, 07976 252248, dawnlouise@poole1992.fsnet.co.uk
Hamworthy Royal British Legion Sea Angling Club
Contact: For further information contact NFSA Head Office: 01364 644643.
Lychett Bay Angling Club
Contact: For further information contact NFSA Head Office: 01364 644643.
Mistress Linda
Contact: Phil Higgins, 01202 741684, 07860 794183, philip-lindahiggins@mlcpoole.fsnet.co.uk
North Haven Yacht Club (Fishing)
Contact: For further information contact NFSA Head Office: 01364 644643.
Ooker
Contact: Pat Manley, 01202 672849, 07860 320818.
Our Gemma
Contact: Mervyn Minns, 01425 274636, ourgemma.mervyn@virgin.net
Poole & District Sea Angling Association
Contact: For further information contact NFSA Head Office: 01364 644643.
Poole Bay Small Boat Angling Club
Contact: For further information contact NFSA Head Office: 01364 644643.
True Blue
Contact: Steve Porter, 01202 665482, 07967 598669, stevetrueblue33@aol.com

Sea Charters & Clubs

SWANAGE

San Gina Charter Boat
Contact: Swannage Angling Centre, 6 High Street, Swanage, BH19 2NT, 01929 424989, swanageangling@brewer8779.freeserve.co.uk *Water:* Deep sea fishing trips. Fully licenced for 10 anglers. Experienced Skipper.

Swanage and District Angling Club
Contact: Swanage Angling Centre, 01929 424989, swanageangling@brewer8779.freeserve.co.uk *Water:* Fishing around Swanage and Purbeck coast with good fishing on Swanage pier. Open 24 hours a day, *Species:* Bass, Pollack, Rays, Dogfish, Pouting, Mackerel, Plaice, Turbot, Congers, Bream, Flounder.

WEYMOUTH

Atlanta
Contact: Dave Pitman, 01305 781644, 07721 320352.

Autumn Dream
Contact: Len Hurdiss, 01305 786723, 07966 361961.

Bonwey
Contact: Ken Leicester, 01305 821040, 07831 506285, bonwey@aol.com

Channel Chieftain III & IV
Contact: Pat Carling, 01305 787155, 07976 741821, ppcarlin@aol.com

Flamer
Contact: Colin Penny, 01305 766961, 07968 972736, colinpennyfu2@aol.com

Ladygo-Diver
Contact: David Gibson, 01305 750823.

MV Freedom
Contact: Peter, 07976 528054, peterfreecat@aol.com *Water:* Disabled Angling. Totally wheel chair accessible.

Offshore Rebel
Contact: Paul Whittall, 01305 783739, 07860 571615, pwhittal@aol.com

Out-Rage
Contact: Rod Thompson, 01305 822803, 07970 437646, rodfish105@aol.com

Peace & Pleanty
Contact: Chris Tett, 01305 775775, 07885 780019.

Top Cat
Contact: Mr Wellington, 01305 823443, 07966 133979.

Valerie Ann
Contact: Ron Brown, 01305 779217, 07976520607, ronbrown@valerieann.fsnet.co.uk

Weymouth Angling Society
Contact: Mr D Pay, Commercial Road, Weymouth, DT4 8NF, 01305 785032, *Water:* All shore line from Lyme Regis to Christchurch harbour, *Species:* Bass, Pollack, Plaice, Flounder, Cod, Sharks, Ray & Wrasse, *Permits:* N/A, *Charges:* N/A, *Season:* Open, *Methods:* Restrictions in competitions only.

WIMBORNE

Marden - Edwards Sea Angling Association
Contact: For further information contact NFSA Head Office: 01364 644643.

Gloucs

CHELTENHAM

Bass Anglers Sportfishing Society
Contact: For further information contact NFSA Head Office: 01364 644643.

STROUD

South & South West S.A.
Contact: For further information contact NFSA Head Office: 01364 644643.

WITHINGTON

Royal Air Force Sea Angling Association
Contact: For further information contact NFSA Head Office: 01364 644643.

Hampshire

LYMINGTON

Challenger II
Contact: Mike Cottingham, 01425 619358, 07884 394379.

Sundance
Contact: Roger Bayzand, 01590 674652, roger@rogerbayzand.com

The Lymington & District Sea Fishing Club
Contact: Fishing Club HQ, Bath Road, Lymington, SO41 9SE, 01590 674962, *Water:* Boat and shore fishing, with strong Junior section. Fishing for trophies throughout the year. New members welcome, *Charges:* Adults - £6.50 joining fee, plus £13 p/a subs. Juniors - £2 joining fee, plus £4 p/a subs.

Somerset

BATH

Gannet Sea Angling Club
Contact: For further information contact NFSA Head Office: 01364 644643.

Sea Charters & Clubs

BRIDGWATER

Bridgwater Sea Angling Club
Contact: For further information contact NFSA Head Office: 01364 644643.

BRISTOL

Bristol Channel Federation of Sea Anglers
Contact: Keith Reed, 27 St Michaels Avenue, Clevedon, BS21 6LL, 01275 872101, bcfsa@hotmail.com *Water:* Bristol Channel, Hartland Point. North Devon to St Davids Head, Dyfed (all tidal waters eastwards), *Species:* All sea fish, both boat and shore records, yearly update. 53 different species recorded in major (over 1lb) rec.list, 15 different species in minor (under 1lb) rec.list, *Charges:* £40 per CLUB per year inclusive of shore activities insurance, *Season:* All year round activities, shore and boat contests, small boat section with inter-club activities, *Methods:* Fishing to specimen sizes, all specimen fish awarded certificate, best of specie annually, plus fish of the month. Team & Individual annual awards. New for 2003 - Charter Boat contests only. Touch Trace rules. All fish returned alive.

Clevedon Breakaways Sea Angling Club
Contact: J. Aspinall, 6 Lydford Walk, Bedminster, Bristol, BS3 5LJ, 0117 9669869, 07977 393367, *Water:* Boat, Shore and Competitions in the Bristol Channel and South West. Affiliated to B.C.F.S.A. and N.F.S.A, *Species:* All species, *Charges:* Adult £20 plus £2 joining fee. Juniors £6. OAP £6 per year.

BURNHAM-ON-SEA

Burnham Boat Owners Sea Angling Association
Contact: For further information contact NFSA Head Office: 01364 644643.

Kelly's Hero
Contact: Dave Saunders, 01278 785000, 07970 642354, kellyshero@btinternet.com

Three B's Sea Angling Society
Contact: For further information contact NFSA Head Office: 01364 644643.

CHEDDAR

Weston Outcasts S.A.C.
Contact: For further information contact NFSA Head Office: 01364 644643.

HANHAM

Bath & Bristol Civil Service Sea Angling Club
Contact: For further information contact NFSA Head Office: 01364 644643.

STREET

Tor Sea Angling Club
Contact: For further information contact NFSA Head Office: 01364 644643.

WATCHET

Scooby Doo Too
Contact: Stephen Yeandle, 01984 361310/634540, *Water:* 07778 750939 (boat)

WELLINGTON

Blackdown Sea Angling Club
Contact: For further information contact NFSA Head Office: 01364 644643.

WELLS

Wells & District Sea Angling Club
Contact: For further information contact NFSA Head Office: 01364 644643.

WESTON-SUPER-MARE

Weston-Super-Mare Sea Angling Association
Contact: For further information contact NFSA Head Office: 01364 644643.

YEOVIL

Royal British Legion (Yeovil) Sea Angling Club
Contact: For further information contact NFSA Head Office: 01364 644643.

Three Counties Sea Angling Association
Contact: For further information contact NFSA Head Office: 01364 644643.

Yeovil & District Sea Angling Club
Contact: For further information contact NFSA Head Office: 01364 644643.

Alf - well pleased with his first Dogfish

Tuition

Gary & Annie Champion

1 Higher Terrace, Ponsanooth, Truro TR3 7EW
Tel 01872 863551. Mobile 07976 805910
APGAI/STANIC
Devon & Cornwall
Rods Reels Flys etc.

Spey casting. Double haul casting. Fly dressing. For beginners, children and adults. Also advanced angling: Snake roll and Swedish underhand cast. Member of team Loop.

Middle Boswin Lakes

Jonno Johnson, Middle Boswin Farm, Porkellis, Helston TR13 0HR
Tel 01209 860420
Email: jonno@mbos1.fsnet.co.uk
www.middleboswin.co.uk
P.A.A. Coarse
West Cornwall
Tackle and baits.

Beginners a speciality. Please call before arriving at the lake

Bob Tetley Angling

45 Molesworth Terrace, Millbrook, Torpoint Cornwall PL10 1DH
Tel 01752 822954. Mobile 0781 889 8140
Email: bobtetley@aol.com
J.A.G.B. Level 2 licenced coach/instructor in game and coarse angling.
Cornwall and Devon
Tackle available (and bait at Bake Lakes).

Stillwater and river Trout.
Traditional coarse angling methods.

Roger Cannock

Newquay, Cornwall
Tel 01637 879330. Mobile 07979 873279
Email: rogercan2001@yahoo.co.uk
Professional Anglers Ass. coach since 2000
Available across the West Country.
All equipment available. Seat boxes, poles, beachcasters and fly rods. Tackle hire available. Rod Licences.

Coarse fishing techniques specialist.
Match angling techniques.
Guiding and tuition on the Counties festival venues.

How do I become an Angling Instructor?

Malcolm Hanson (Angling Development Officer, Salmon and Trout Association)

Last year I wrote with cautious enthusiasm about the Joint Angling Governing Bodies (JAGB) new Coaching Development Scheme and the introduction of a Coach Licensing Scheme, which would offer a quality assured standard for the coaching of angling in the UK. During the past twelve months the JAGB have worked together with the two professional bodies, the Professional Anglers Association (the PAA) and the Game Angling Instructors' Association (GAIA) to consolidate this vision and to deliver the goods.

In partnership with the Environment Agency, the JAGB will be supporting EA and other initiatives to introduce many thousands of would be anglers into the sport. Young and old, able bodied and disabled, those seeking a new leisure activity and those looking to their halcyon days in retirement, the Angling Participation Plan will be aiming to provide high quality instruction to many people across the three disciplines of angling. To achieve this vision more coaches will be required during the coming year.

One of the most frequently asked questions directed to me is "How do I become a Coach?" The process is straightforward, however, the first thing the 'would-be' coach needs to ask him/herself, is have they got an aptitude to teach. The JAGB Coaching Development Programme believes that we all have a teaching ability… it just needs developing. The JAGB programme focuses on the development of teaching skills and the recognition of learning styles. It is intended to provide the new instructor with the skill and the confidence to work with groups of beginners and individual clients.

The technical ability of the potential coach is also important. After all, she/he will need to be able to demonstrate skills in front of the client, as well as be able to analyse a client's own faults and help correct these. So how technical does a potential coach have to be? To help the 'would-be' coach, explanatory notes are circulated with the application pack, which explain what standard you should have achieved before you attend a course. If the candidate remains uncertain about his/her ability, there is a list of coaches provided whom s/he can visit to have their technical ability assessed. Very often a few minor gaps in the ability level can be put right very quickly.

Once on the course, the coach in training will complete modules and attend workshops. These modules will help to develop best practice through risk assessment, understanding child protection issues and being prepared to deal with the unexpected. Through a specialised training agent, the JAGB now has an angling specific First Aid workshop. Throughout the programme the candidate is prepared for Coach Licensing, which will be the kite mark of their ability to coach.

Unfortunately, many of the people who ask about becoming a coach, have the fond notion that by gaining a qualification they will be able to beat a path to the bosses door, hand in their notice and walk off into the shimmering sunset beyond the water's edge to make their fortune teaching and guiding their beloved sport. Regrettably, very few people are able to make a full time living from coaching. In some areas of the sport, the culture of paying to learn does not exist. It is true that coaches can earn money, but I would encourage anyone considering a qualification not to do so with the intention of making it a primary source of income.

Still interested in becoming a coach? What next? An Application Pack with full details can be obtained from each of the governing bodies for the sport.

For information about Licensed Coaches:

The National Federation of Anglers
(Coarse Fishing) 01283 734735

The National Federation of Sea Anglers
(Sea Fishing) 01364 644643

The Salmon and Trout Association
(Game Anglers) 01672 511628

Or write to me, Malcolm Hanson at either: PO Box 270, Marlborough, Wiltshire, SN8 4WD or email mjhanson@fishcoach.org

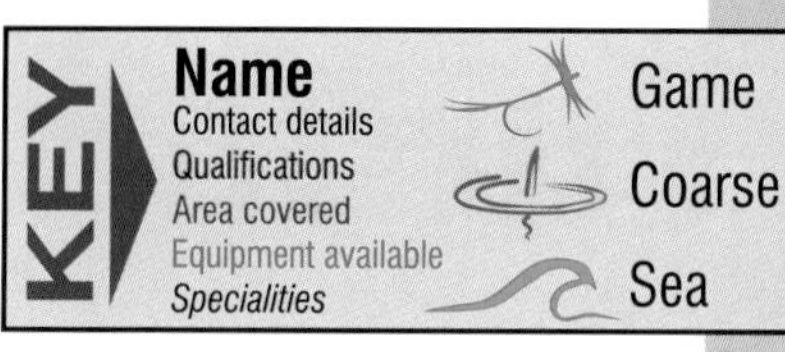

Roy Buckingham

Arundell Arms, Lifton, Devon PL16 0AA
Tel 01566 784666
Fax 01566 784494
Email: reservations@arundellarms.com
www.arundellarms.com
Full member APGAI. STANIC qualified instructor.
Lifton area of Devon. Based at The Arundell Arms Hotel.
Rods, Reels Flies etc.
Spey casting. Individual tuition and courses. Beginners and refresher courses, including Spey casting.

Alex Henderson

Husk Hill, Frithelstock Stone, Torrington EX38 8JR
Tel 01805 624076
Mobile 07791 350156 / 079711 00557
Email: aneilhenderson@hotmail.com
NAC/STANIC Trout & Salmon. Basic and advanced
North Devon
Tackle and Flies.
Fly casting. Spey casting. Double haul. Fly dressing. Children over 12 years only.

Devon & UK Fly Fishing School

Roddy Rae, 6 Hescane Park, Cheriton Bishop EX6 6SP.
Tel 01647 24643. Mobile 077868 34575
Email: roddyrae@btopenworld.com
www.flyfishing-uk.co.uk
STANIC / REFFIS
UK and Worldwide inc. Australia and New Zealand
All tackle available
Single and double Spey casting. Double haul and snake roll casting. Wild Brown Trout, Salmon and Sea Trout. Please Note: Children to be accompanied by an adult.

David Pilkington

Arundell Arms, Lifton, Devon PL16 0AA
Tel 01566 784666
Fax 01566 784494
Email: reservations@arundellarms.com
www.arundellarms.com
Full member APGAI. STANIC qualified instructor.
Lifton area of Devon. Based at The Arundell Arms Hotel.
Rods, Reels Flies etc.
All aspects of fly fishing.

Tuition

Peter Keen

12 The Challices, Eggesford, Devon EX18 7QX
Tel 01769 581127 (home). Mobile 07790 914066
Email: pkeenfisher@postmaster.co.uk

Rivers in Devon - Taw, Mole, Exe and Torridge
Rods, reels, waders, nets for hire or sale.
Local flies supplied.

Individual or group instruction. Fly fishing courses. Casting clinics. Night Sea Trout courses. Ghillie service for the 2003 season. For age 10 and over.

Nick Hart

Exford View, 1 Chapel St, Exford TA24 7PY
Tel 01643 831101. Mobile 079711 98559
Email: nick@hartflyfishing.demon.co.uk
www.hartflyfishing.demon.co.uk
APGAI, STANIC
Somerset and North Devon.
Tackle, waders, course notes and video imaging.

Relaxed, informal, modern fly fishing tuition. Novice to advanced. Overhead, double haul, presentation casts. Guided Trout, Salmon, Sea Trout, Bass, Pollack, Mackerel.

Steve Lockett

The Old Bakehouse, 20 Higher Street, Brixham, Devon TQ5 8HW
Tel 01803 851101. Mobile 07967 043616
Email: steve@coarsefish-torbay.co.uk
www.coarsefish-torbay.co.uk
N.F.A. Regional Coach
Devon, Cornwall, Dorset, Somerset.
General coarse rods & reels, 4m whips. Bait available

Pole and float fishing.
Match style Carping.

Robert Jones

South Lodge, Courtlands, Exmouth EX8 3NZ
Tel 07020 902090 Mobile 0797 0797 770
Email: robertjones@eclipse.co.uk
FRICS. EA Beginners Licence Agent.
The West Country centred on East Devon and rivers Otter, Axe, Teign, Exe, Avon and Camel.
All equipment including EA Licence.

Rivers. Sea Trout by fly at night. Guiding.
For age 10 and over.

R.E.F.F.I.S

The Register of Experienced Fly Fishing Instructors, Schools and Guides (REFFIS) exists to assure the public of the highest standards. All our members are thoroughly vetted before being accepted onto the Register; teaching and guiding skills are rigorously examined to ensure they match the exacting standards set by REFFIS.

We have members well spread across the UK and Eire and even a few overseas. They offer a superb range of locations: small stillwaters, large reservoirs, lush chalk-streams, mighty Scottish and Irish rivers, wild spate rivers and the lovely lochs of Scotland and Ireland - join up with the friendly network of REFFIS members and sample the lot!

REFFIS members introduce many hundreds of people to the delights of game fishing every season. New recruits, young and old, are essential if the aquatic environment is to be safeguarded for future generations. REFFIS takes this responsibility very seriously and we wholeheartedly support the efforts of organisations such as The Salmon and Trout Association, The Game Conservancy, The Atlantic Salmon Trust and The Wild Trout Trust, all of whom work tirelessly for the benefit of game fish and the healthy environment that is so vital for them and indeed for us. We urge you to go game fishing and to choose an experienced mentor from within the ranks of REFFIS.

Bob Wellard

13 Lutyens Fold, Milton Abbot, Tavistock PL19 0NR
Tel/Fax 01822 870277
Email: flyfish@globalnet.co.uk
APGAI. Salmon, Trout and Fly Dressing.
The whole of the West Country.
Tackle and Clothing.

Spey casting. Double Haul. Beginners to advanced catered for.

Kernow Game Fishing

Chris Ogborne, Flora Court, Wadebridge, Cornwall PL27 6DE
Tel 07885 038203

Fully qualified former National fly fishing champion.
National but centered on Devon and Cornwall
Everything needed can be provided

Surf fly fishing for Bass. 'Wild' fly fishing packages. Residential courses/packages.

Tuition

Tuition and Guiding with the REFFIS network in the Westcountry

Simon Cooper	02073 598818
Mike Gleave	01275 472403
Tom Hill	01626 866532
Sally Pizii	01823 480710
Roddy Rae	01647 24643
Richard Slocock	01305 848460

www.reffis.co.uk

Bryan Martin

South Molton, Devon.
Tel: 01769 581463 Mobile 07759 352194
Email: bryan@devonflyfishing.co.uk
www.devonflyfishing.co.uk
STANIC Salmon, Trout and Fly Dressing.
North Devon and West Somerset.
All tackle.

Salmon, Sea Trout and Trout fishing on rivers and stillwaters. Beginners and experienced. Saltwater fly fishing

Colin Nice

17 Lawn Vista, Sidmouth, Devon EX10 9BY.
Tel 01395 577517 Mobile 07989 402650
Email: colin.nicey@virgin.net
Over 40 years experience in game fishing in the West Country, fly tying, sea fishing in East Devon
Throughout the West Country. Based East Devon.
All tackle for fly fishing and sea fishing (bait/lure/fly). Plus all equipment for fly tying.

Tying Brown & Sea Trout flies for rivers Axe, Otter, Exe and Sid. Saltwater fly fishing for Bass. Plugging.

Test Valley School of Fly Fishing

Jerry Wakeford, 44 Butlers Close, Romsey, Hampshire SO51 0LY. Tel 01794 341 990
Email: enquiries@learnflyfishing.co.uk
www.learnflyfishing.co.uk
STANIC Trout. G.A.I.A. (1999), N.CCK, WK (1996)
Hants, Wilts, Oxon, Dorset
Tackle available (up to 10 sets)

The Test Valley School of Flyfishing taught 140 clients in 2002. Ambidextrous casting is a great teaching asset!

Roy Buckland

8 Millington Drive, Trowbridge BA14 9EU
Tel 01225 760465. Mobile 07967 558772
Email: roy@buckland-1.freeserve.co.uk
STANIC Trout.
West Wiltshire and the Chew Valley
Rods, reels, lines etc.

Beginners. Roll casting. Double hauling

Mike Gleave

Dresden, 7 Dundry Lane, Dundry, N, Somerset BS40 8JH
Tel 01275 332339 / 01275 472403
www.bristolwater.co.uk
STANIC & REFFIS
Bristol & the South West, Bristol Water Fisheries.
All Tackle, not clothing.

Stillwater techniques. Fly Tying. Guiding from boat and bank at Blagdon and Chew.

David Griffiths

Tel 01747 871695
Email: d.griffiths@freenet.co.uk
www.flyfishing-tuition.co.uk
APGAI/STANIC Trout, Salmon, Sea Trout.
Exclusive private lake in Wiltshire. Chalk Streams.
Tackle provided by negotiation

Novices and experienced. Hourly and daily rates. All game fishing casting techniques taught. Specialist in Spey casting techniques.

KEY

Name
Contact details
Qualifications
Area covered
Equipment available
Specialities

Game
Coarse
Sea

Tackle Test

Accessories

Snowbee

XS Fishing Bag - (£65)

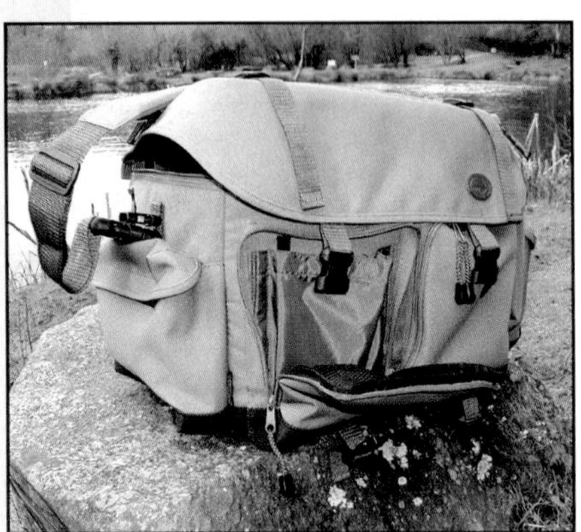

Coarse, Game or Sea fishermen, we all need a fishing bag and although this, being from the Snowbee stable, is aimed primarily at the game angler it will suit all aspects of the sport.

It's a superbly made bag. The polyester outer material is treated with a waterproof and stain resistant coating and the bottom of the bag has an additional layer of PVC to ensure the contents stay 100% dry, very important when it's sitting in the bottom of a boat or on a rain soaked bank. Pockets everywhere, sides, front inside the lid, a priest pocket, rod tube straps, full length zippered rear pocket, 12 permutations for adjusting the internal velcro dividers, a carrying handle and removable shoulder strap, phew! The sides and base are stiffened so it retains it's shape regardless of how much you've got in it, a very good idea. The model shown is the medium size (21"x12"x12") and it is available in large and small as well. £65 makes this a very good value for money and extremely versatile product. For the full range of Snowbee gear view their website or drop in at:

Snowbee UK, Drakes Court, Langage Business Park, Plymouth PL7 5JY.

Tel: 01752 334933

Email: flyfish@snowbee.co.uk

Website: www.snowbee.co.uk

Tilley Clothing

The Tilley range of Travel and Adventure clothing is not designed specifically for anglers but many of their products are very suitable and they are perhaps more stylish than a lot of gear on offer. Tilley are a Canadian family company, (all their products are hand made in Canada) and the U.K. operation is in Helston. We were given a hat, cap and vest to appraise.

Tilley LT5 Hat - (£47)

Guaranteed for life not to wear out, rain resistant, ties on, floats, weighs just 3oz, machine washable, well ventilated and a good size sloping brim make it a perfect fishing hat. Available in several styles and colours this is the LT5 in olive. Only hat I've seen that comes with an owner's manual!

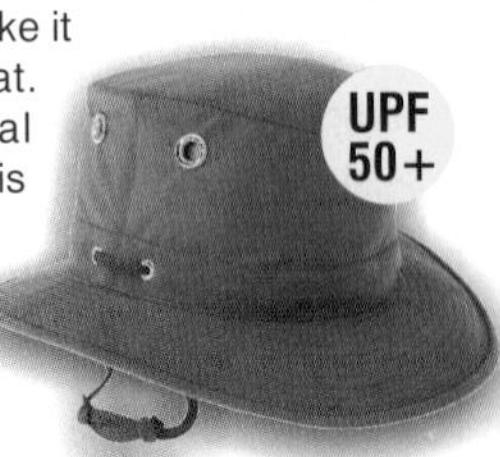

Tilley Tuckaway Cap - (£42)

UPF 50+

Excellent wide brim and a neck cape offering 3 different levels of protection from sun, wind or rain makes this a pretty versatile piece of headgear. Adjustable so two sizes fit all.

Tilley Lightweight Vest - (£115)

Very lighweight with eleven secure pockets with velcro or zippered closure. Two good sized pockets inside the vest and a 'mobile phone' pocket. Made from a polycotton poplin in stone or sagebrush colours it will hang dry overnight. Not as good for the job as a dedicated fishing vest perhaps but a very comfortable and more versatile garment.

More info from Tilley Endurables, Helston Ltd on 01326 574402 or on the web at www.tilley.com.

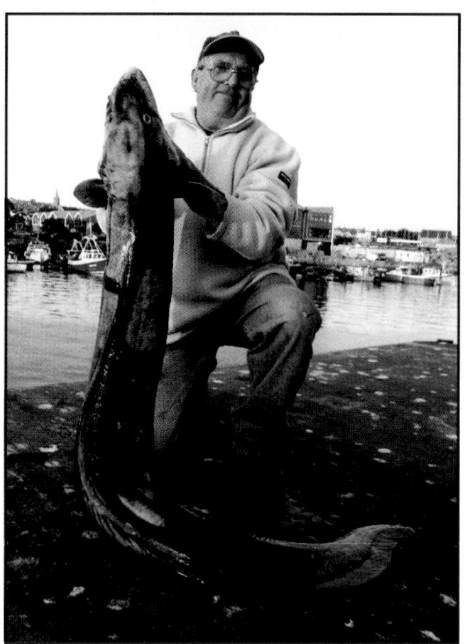

John Murray from Sefton S.A.C. with a 64lb Conger out of Plymouth.
Tiburon

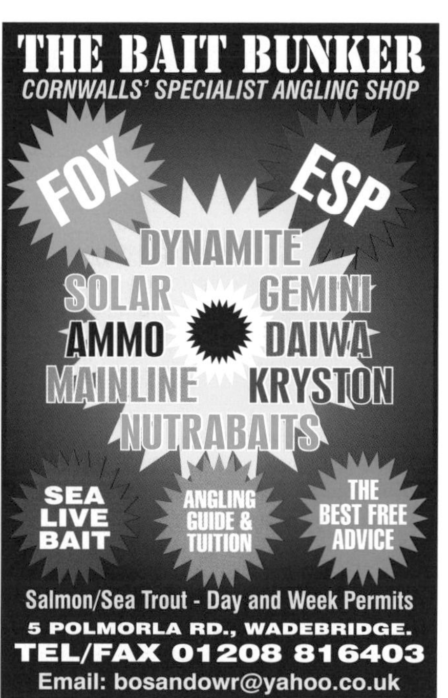

Tackle Test

Fly Tackle

Reviewed this year on a 'changeable' February afternoon at Tavistock Trout Fishery.

First up are a couple of 'matched' outfits from Orvis. If you are buying a whole setup, be it your first or upgrading, this is probably the best way to do it.

Orvis Trident TLS 906 MF rod (£239) with Battenkill LA (£150) and Wonderline Advantage WF floating line (£48.50).

This is a real top of the range set up and certainly feels like it. The two piece rod has a very precise action and, although very light, has a lot of power and made very short work of the 2.5 pound rainbow it deceived. Finish is immaculate with a gold anodised and maple burr reel seat, high grade cork handle and a superb cordura fabric covered rod tube. The Battenkill Large Arbor has been around since 2001, comes with a quality case and, building on the original reels reputation, is one of the best reels you can buy. The line, although brand new and just off the reel, was superbly supple and shot beautifully, a pleasure to use. Lines vary immensely in price but a really good line will make a lot of difference. Profile also is important and weight forward seems to be becoming the favourite over double taper. I always used to buy double taper as a lad because you could turn the line around and double its life but once you have the belly of a weight forward in the air the distance casting advantages are quite considerable.Orvis rods are covered by an unconditional 25 year guarantee so this really could be the only outfit you will ever need. And if you buy the TL5 with the Battenkill LA the Wonderline comes free!

L to R: Sharpes and Battenkill Barstock, Clearwater outfit, Trident and Battenkill LA

Orvis Clearwater Classic 864 MF rod (£120) with Clearwater Classic II Reel (£21) and Clearwater WF Line (£25) or as a kit for £155

The difference in price between the Clearwater and Trident is reflected in the quality, the reel is basic but does the job and, even at this price, still has an adjustable drag, The fittings on the rod are understandably not of the same quality as on the Trident but this is still very usable equipment and would make an excellent small to medium river outfit or moderate stillwater. The rod comes in a plastic tube and there is no reel case but accessories, though desirable, won't help you catch more fish! Outfits are available in weights from 3 to 9. An excellent beginners choice from a quality name.

Orvis Battenkill Bar Stock Reel (£95)

This is the newest version of a very famous reel. The difference being it is machined (in Cornwall!) instead of cast which allows for much finer manufacturing tolerances. This translates to a watch like precision in its use. It's anodised to be totally corrosion proof, and, at the price, would be very hard to better.

Sharpes of Aberdeen AQUAREX 9' 6 piece Travel Rod #8 (£360)

This is a fabulous rod from a very famous maker. State of the art materials and superb building skills have made multi section rods such as this very usable weapons and when collapsed it's only 20" long! Fittings are all of the very highest quality making it suitable for

Chris Cormack, from the crew of Chicago, playing at The Princess Theatre Torquay, on his first deep sea fishing trip in September 2002 caught this 101lb 8oz conger on board Jubrae

saltwater use as well as traditional freshwater, in fact at Sharpes it is often referred to as the bonefish rod. Supplied in a bag and very sturdy tube the rod is finished in a dark green with burgundy windings and an optional butt section (previous page picture) is included. It has a traditional feel and a really sweet tip and middle action that loaded smoothly and handled any length of line with ease. Being an 8 weight rated rod it also shoots very impressively. It still amazes me how carbon fibre has revolutionised the rod buiders art and can provide such a stunning power to weight ratio.

I found it a very 'easy' to use rod, not requiring the precision of technique that some modern rods do, letting you concentrate on fishing rather than casting.A rare attribute in any rod, a real joy to use and an excellent all rounder.

Contacts:

Orvis All Shops and Dealer Outlets, please call 01264-349500 for an Orvis Shop near you
www.orvis.co.uk

Sharpes of Aberdeen:
Tel: 01466 700257
www.sharpes.net

As always I suggest you try before you buy unless you are confident you are getting exactly what you want.

Tackle Test

Coarse Tackle

Harrison Advanced Rods 11' Avon 4 piece - (£135)

This I really like. If there is a multi pupose coarse rod this must be it. You can trot with it, ledger or float fish. Use it at distance or under the bank and I'd happily crust for carp with it.

It will handle very large fish if required and wont knock the stuffing out of the smaller stuff. It's my favourite finish of matt black with black whippings, lined rings throughout and a Fuji DPS reel seat situated at the front of a good length cork handle.

It has a lovely gentle, progressive action behind the 1.6lb test curve that never seems to run out of steam. Being four piece the sections are only some 32" long which makes it very portable. I find two piece rods of 11' and over a real pain to transport and if it makes no difference to the action and usability of the rod I can only see advantages in having a four piece.

This rod has proved very popular as a two piece and this version is sure to be equally popular and at £135 it's very competitively priced.

Ask at your local tackle shop or contact Harrison on 0151 7095981 for a list of dealers
Email: rods@rapid.co.uk
www.harrisonrods.co.uk

A nice Mirror from the Carp Lake. Milemead

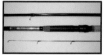

TackleReview

Barbour Clothing

Barbour make one of those rare products where a brand name has become the generally used term for a product. The product is of course the waxed jacket, although their range of products now extends far beyond that.

Duracotton Dryfly Jacket - around £189

This garment has the dark green appearance and 'waxy' feel of a traditional Barbour but the hugely beneficial modifications that it is breathable and washable! Putting your old barbour in the washing machine was the kiss of death and several years accumulation of fish debris and other dubious decaying organic substances did not tend to make your favourite garment 'socially acceptable'. Now all that fish slime can be removed easily and you'll be able to wear your pride and joy down the supermarket as well!

There are five large pockets on the outside of the jacket which are all securely 'poppered' or zipped and another zippered pocket inside plus three external D rings for attaching other equipment and a removable 'sheepskin' patch and reel pocket.

It's really filthy outside today but chuck this on, slip your hands through the warm elasticated cuffs, pull up the lined collar, tighten the draw strings and you know you will stay dry and warm and you're going to look good as well.

Dryfly Endurance Jacket - around £199

This is more specifically a fishing garment although it can certainly be worn anywhere. Barbour Endurance is made from a Cordura® based fabric which is very durable, easy to care for and highly breathable. Although the size is identical to the Duracotton this jacket is somewhat lighter and it's light olive green colour gives it a more 'summery' feel.

The pocket arrangement is the same as the Duracotton apart from the welcome addition of a truly huge 'poachers pocket' which can be unfastened to fold down and make a 'seat' or a lower hem. A removable hood is also included. This garment is completely machine washable at 30 degrees C. The attention to detail is really impressive in all these products. Every fastening, all the zips, every seam, the toggles on the drawstrings - it's all beautifully made right down to the embroidered Barbour logo.

Endurance Chest Waders - £200

Endurance Cordura is also used to manufacture Barbours' new waders. They are available in a stocking foot or as a boot foot with felt soles which are tungsten studded giving the most versatile option for optimum grip. Again these are superbly made and very comfortable with stretch panels giving excellent freedom of movement and foam padding on the knees enhances durability and water proofing. Fully adjustable webbing shoulder and waist straps allow for a very accurate fit. There really is very little comparison between these and 'economy' waders. They are very easy to wear and, being breathable, don't cause excessive sweating which can be very unpleasant on a hot summer day.

Barbour products are not cheap to buy but they are cheap to own. These products are designed and manufactured to last a lifetime.

www.barbour.com
Tel: 0191 454 2944

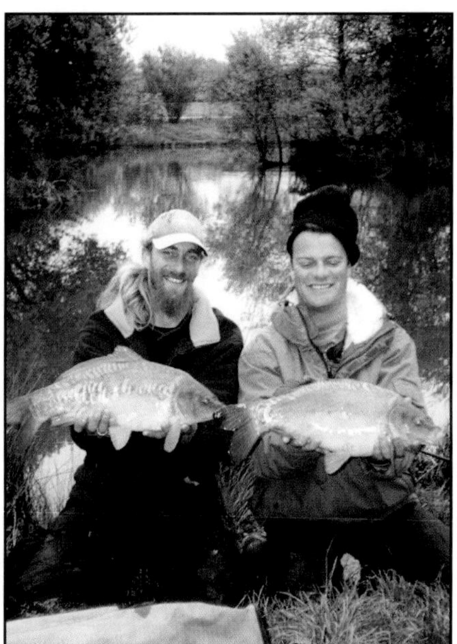

Roger Cannock and Dean Winter with two fine Carp from the Specimen Pool at Gwinear.

Angling at Cadbury GARDEN & LEISURE

Britain's largest covered Garden Centre

OPEN 7 DAYS A WEEK

For a wide range of high quality and value for money tackle and bait for the coarse, game and sea fisherman visit Cadbury's Angling Department.

LIVE BAIT

Many Products at Mail Order Prices

An excellent selection of quality fresh and frozen bait available All year round

STOCKISTS of: Daiwa, Shakespeare, Petzl, Steadfast, Drennan, Mustad, Breakaway, Shimano, Century, Gemini, Coleman, Solar, Kryston, ESP and many more

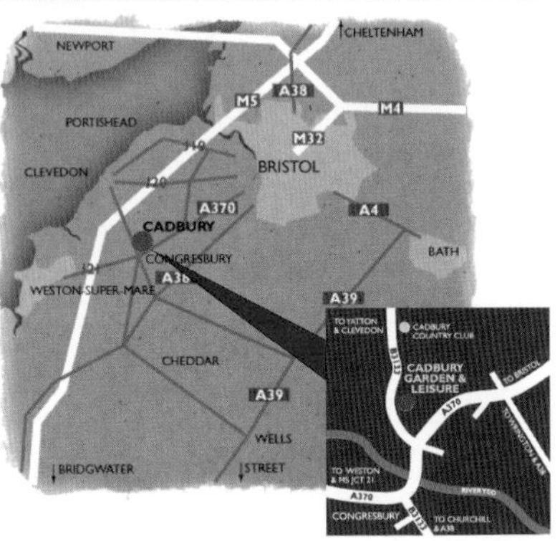

OPENING TIMES

MON	9.00am to 6.00pm
TUE	9.00am to 6.00pm
WED	9.00am to 8.00pm
THU	9.00am to 6.00pm
FRI	9.00am to 6.00pm
SAT	9.00am to 6.00pm
SUN	10.00am to 4.30pm

Late Night Shopping Wednesday Open until 8pm

FRIENDLY, PROFESSIONAL ADVICE FREELY GIVEN

Cadbury Garden & Leisure, Smallway, Congresbury, Bristol BS49 5AA

Tel: 01934 875700 E-mail:info@cadbury.g-l.co.uk

www.cadbury.g-l.co.uk

A superb bag for this partnership.
Innis

Tackle Test - Accessories

Richworth 1st Contact

Richworth is pretty much a household name when it comes to bait, in particular boilies and additives. It seems logical then that they should extend their range into items of tackle. 1st contact is a comprehensive range of rigs and components designed exclusively for the company. Included in the range are: swivels, snap clips, 'Impaler' hooks, cork plugs and balls (pop ups and floaters), beads, PVA products, hair rigs, stops, shrink tubing and 'sorcerer' braid.

Pretty comprehensive then! There is a mind boggling amount of tackle out there for the Carp angler but buying from a company with such a pedigree in this particular branch of the sport means you are getting tackle developed from years of experience in bait manufacture and, of course, presentation.

From all good tackle shops. More information on their web site at www.richworth.com

Owner Hooks

Owner hooks are manufactured and developed in Japan and distributed in the UK by Harrison Advanced Angling.

Supplied were a range of freshwater hooks from size 7 spade end to size 2 eyed carp hooks and trebles. All are superbly finished and very sharp. There is a huge range available for game, coarse and sea and Owner also make lures. One of their innovations are 'cutting point' hooks with a triple-edged cutting blade led by a needle-sharp point that never needs sharpening. They also produce 'circle hooks which look as though they wouldn't work but are proving very popular with catch and release as the fish is almost always hooked in the jaw or scissors. Excellent products well worth trying.

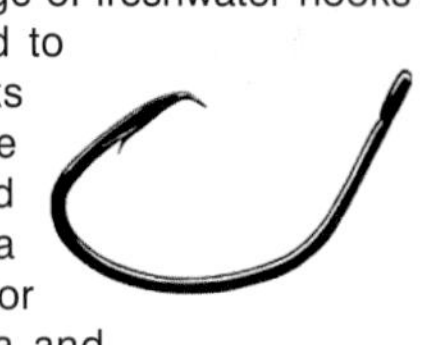

Get them from your local tackle shop or for further information contact Harrison Advanced Angling direct on: 0151 709 5981 or via the web at www.harrisonrods.co.uk

Trev Tomlins TT-PULTS

- (from £5.99)

How many coarse fishermen use a catapult? I didn't for years but now I wouldn't be without one. You may think you can accurately throw in handfulls of hemp or maggots but once you have used a catapult you will realise you can't!

You get much less spread and, of course, much more distance. These models from Trev Tomlin give you an extra advantage in the accuracy department with the unique 'teat pouch' design.

This enables you to plant small amounts of feed exactly where you want it and over a very small area. Available in two sizes with the teat pouch and two with traditional 'aircone' pouches they are very comfortable to use with excellent grip and the non twist latex coming out of the top of the forks means you can use it either way round.

From your local tackle shop or direct from Hopkins & Holloway on: 01527 853822 or at www.hopkinsholloway.co.uk

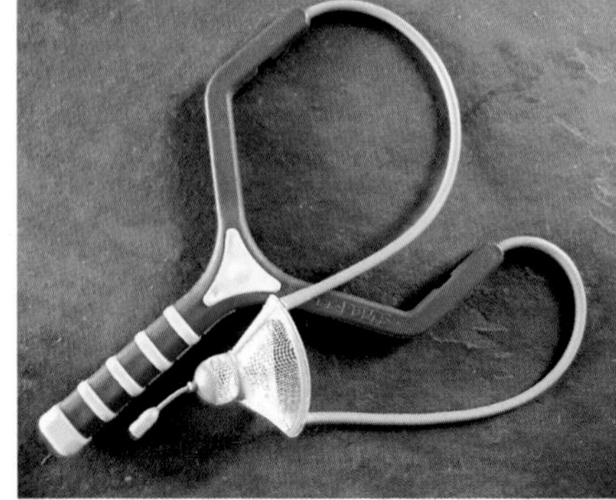

Where to Stay

The following section details some of the increasing number of locations throughout the westcountry offering holidays with a fishing theme. Most have their own lakes, many with residents only fishing.
Advertisers in other sections of the guide mat also offer accommodation. For a complete listing please use the index Don't forget to mention us when you phone them!

Cartwheel Holidays introduce perfect fishing retreats

Head over heels™ with South West farms

Cartwheel farm and country holidays are pleased to present an extensive range of farms and properties with fishing on site, much of which is free to the guest or visitor. Coarse fishing, sea fishing and private river fishing are available on many Bed & Breakfast, Self Catering and Camping & Caravanning Cartwheel properties, throughout Cornwall, Devon and Somerset.

Cartwheel Holidays offer activities for visitors with special interests; one of the most popular being fishing. There is a wide variety of quality inspected accommodation for you to choose from throughout the Westcountry.

Whilst you are here, discover the beauty of the countryside by bicycle. Many farms have paths and lanes to cycle on away from the crowds, and provide secure cycle storage. You could jump into a hot tub, sauna or swimming pool afterwards to relax.

Why not explore on foot and get even closer to the wildlife? Farm trails and walks give the visitor a pleasant, unhurried way to discover nature at its best. Hold your breath and watch a barn owl feed her young. Pick mushrooms, blackberries, and wild strawberries - or enjoy a picnic. You may be able to take your dog along for company.

Cartwheel holidays are the best places to sample the range of delicious, locally produced food the Westcountry has to offer. It is no secret that farmers wives are truly superb cooks and will take great effort and time to source local produce for your meals! Cartwheel proudly presents some of the finest farm shops and restaurants throughout the Westcountry. Imagine the taste of fresh crabs from the quay at Newlyn, apple juice from the orchards in Devon, Cornish Yarg cheese from Liskeard & Penryn, thick clotted cream from Devon and Cornwall, Cornish new potatoes, Somerset cider and tender beef and lamb from our farms to your plate.

Horse and pony rides, for absolute beginners and the very experienced are also featured. Try the new cross-country course in Cornwall - two and a half miles of cliff top riding with stunning views. Some farms even accommodate horses, so you can treat them to a holiday, too!

Alternatively, enjoy a wildlife safari tour, try your hand at woodturning or brush up on your creative skills with an art break. There really is something for everyone, so no need to seek out foreign shores for that something different this year - a Cartwheel holiday is right on your doorstep.

Cartwheel holidays cater for all age groups, offering plenty of opportunity for contact with animals, exploring the countryside, or simply relaxing amongst peaceful surroundings. This makes them an excellent choice for a short break at any time of the year. Cartwheel also promote the top farm and rural attractions that the region has to offer.

For a FREE Cartwheel brochure please call 0870 241 1098, or visit www.cartwheelholidays.co.uk

A nice Pollock for Richard Fishbourne off Boscastle, Cornwall. Combe Martin Sea Angling Club

Nanteague Farm Cottages

Marazanvose, Zelah, Near Truro, Cornwall

1.5 acre Lake stocked with Carp to 22lb plus quality Roach, Rudd, Bream and Perch

LIMITED SEASON TICKETS AVAILABLE

01872 540 351

We have 2 superb self catering cottages surrounded by 130 acres of beautiful open countryside

Contact Classic Cottages on 01326 555 555

Mike Harman with a 3lb 14oz Tench from the Match Lake at Milemead Fisheries.

"Trencreek Farm"

HEWASWATER, St AUSTELL, CORNWALL

Caravans, Bungalows and Camping

4 Small Coarse Fishing Lakes

Carp, Tench,
Roach & Bream

One of Cornwall's Favourite Family Holiday Parks

BROCHURE 01726 882540

www.trencreek.co.uk

Lakeside

Perranporth - Cornwall

Spacious Country House overlooking our well stocked Coarse Fishing Lake.

Carp to 16lb plus Rudd, Roach, Tench and Perch to 3lb

Just two miles from the Beautiful beaches of the north Cornwall coast

Sleeps up to 9 people plus junior bed and cot bed.

For further details phone Mrs S Arthur

01872 572612

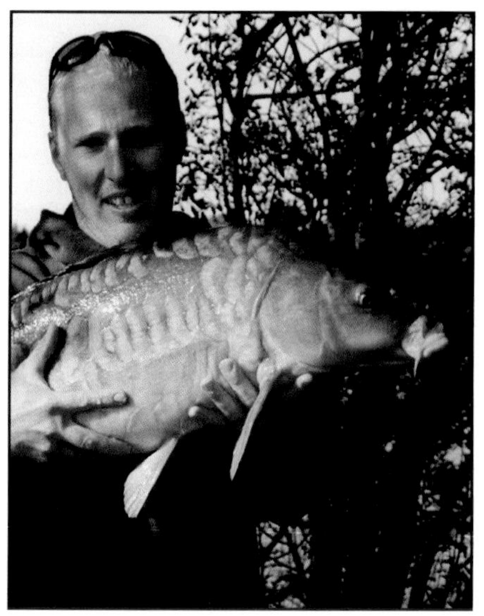

The fisherman's name is 'stupid boy' Pike and the Carp weighed over 20lb.
New Forest Water Park

Caravanning

Perfect for the Angler

The Caravan Club spends millions of pounds each year adding to and improving its sites network. It aims to provide its members with a choice of the top locations with quality facilities. Having more sites across the UK than any other club it can offer its members an unrivalled choice of location. The West Country is no exception, and the Club boasts thirty-seven sites with quality facilities at value-for-money prices in a friendly holiday atmosphere.

Within the extensive borders of the West Country lies a huge variety of scenery and attractions in one of England's most popular holiday destinations. The Club has a site to match every mood and lifestyle, striving to keep sites in tune with the local environment, by making the most of the attractive surroundings and ensuring a better quality of site for everyone, now and for generations to come. By visiting some of the many sites located in the West Country, it gives the traveller/angler the opportunity to visit and stay at many varied locations rather than being tied to one spot. Having the freedom to go where and when one pleases, using Club Sites gives the angler chances to see areas of the countryside, rivers and lakes off the main tourist tracks.

Club sites will come as a pleasant surprise to anyone new to caravanning, old hands already know the quality and advantages they offer. 90% of Club Sites have toilet blocks of the highest standards, but for those who really want to 'get away from it all'; there are simpler with fewer facilities. Exclusively for members of the Caravan Club, there are Certificated Locations which are limited to five vans and are privately owned, possibly in an orchard, next to a public house, or holiday hideaway in a farmer's field. Find the Site that suits you most at: www.caravanclub.co.uk

Many Club Sites attract keen anglers, Lakeside Club Site in Dulverton is a prime example. Lakeside is a spacious site set on the Somerset and Devon border. Not only does the site provide exceptional views towards Exmoor, but also this peaceful retreat has a fishing lake adjacent to the site, attracting many a keen angler, and the river Exe within a short walk. Many anglers staying at this site also visit Oaktree Carp Farm and Fishery, which is close by. Start Bay Club Site in Kingsbridge, is famous for its sea fishing from the beach, so many members take their tackle along with them. However the site is also a paradise for walkers and bird lovers, so remember to bring the binoculars as well.

For those travelling down to Cornwall, thinking of welcoming teas with clotted cream, fresh fish or meat washed down with locally brewed cider, and tasty Cornish pasties. If that alone does not tempt the traveller, the dramatic views of the sea and cliffs and beautiful sandy beaches, which spread along the south coast of Cornwall will draw and captivate. Picturesque locations await, one such that is not to be missed is St Michael's Mount. The Club Site a couple of miles from Marazion, which overlooks St Mounts Bay is Threeways. The site, with a parkland fee,l is an excellent base for walkers and visitors with dogs. From here you are ideally located to visit the many unspoilt coves of West Cornwall and the Lizard Peninsula. Mousehole's busy fishing harbour is a must along with Porthcurno, home of the famous outdoor Minack Theatre.

Many Caravan Club members are avid anglers and tell us of places they like and enjoy, one of these is Hunters Moon Club Site, at Wareham. The site is on the edge of Wareham forest, and it's possible on occasion to catch a glimpse of a Sika Deer, which have given their name to the local nature trail. Close by are the Ringwood Pits, offering some excellent coarse fishing and anglers can expect to catch carp of up to 40lb and tench over 10lb.

So if you are new to caravanning or a frequent tourer, why not consider planning a fishing route around the West Country, test your skills around your choice of lakes, rivers and pits whilst taking in the beauty and wonders the Cornish and West Country can offer.

For more information visit our web site: www.caravanclub.co.uk or call our help line on 01342 318813 quoting GH-SW03.

Perch caught on fly.
Nick Hart Fly Fishing

Wooda Lakes
Holiday Lodges

Secluded accommodation set in 22 acres of glorious, tranquil Devon countryside teeming with wildlife, flora and fauna.

Two well managed lakes,
one mixed and one Carp only.

DAY TICKETS AVAILABLE ON SITE

Just 15 minutes from safe, sandy beaches

For more information and a brochure
Wooda Lakes, Pancrasweek, Holsworthy Devon EX22 7JN

Telephone 01409 241 934

DARTMOOR
LANGSTONE MANOR HOLIDAY PARK

Set in the beautiful & peaceful grounds of a Manor House in a quiet valley, just outside Tavistock, in the National Park

Camping Pitches, Holiday Caravans, Flats and Cottages, Lounge Bar, Evening Meals

Close to Tavistock Trout Fishery plus River & Lake Fishing

Phone/Fax for Brochure 01822-613371

jane@langstone-manor.co.uk www.langstone-manor.co.uk

South Hill

A spacious and comfortable 16th century cottage, sleeping 7 people in centrally heated comfort. Perfect for a peaceful rural holiday or short break. Late availability discounts.

Attractive stretch of fishing on the river Torridge 600 yards from the door.

For further details Contact Gill and Richard Trace
Gortleigh Farm, Sheepwash, Beaworthy, Devon EX21 5HU

Telephone: 01409 231291

email: trace.gortleigh@btclick.com

Kingslake

Fishing Holidays, Devon

Kingslake is a 22 acre estate with Four Coarse lakes.

Lovely cottages and lakeside lodges in an idyllic setting.

Gardens, patios and barbecues. FAMILIES WELCOME
(sorry - no pets)

"A little bit of heaven on earth"
"A fisherman's paradise"
AND MUCH, MUCH MORE!

CARAVANS & CAMPING WELCOME

For Brochure call 01409 231401

or Email: vlangdown@talk21.com
Website: www.kingslakes.co.uk

Garry with a huge Grass Carp from Lands End

'Blue' Trout from Milemead

That's one very happy angler!
Little Comfort

Andy and Debbie Seery invite you to experience the unique atmosphere of Stafford Moor, a gorgeous 67 acre estate hides 30 acres of stunning lakes and luxurious Canadian lodges.

FREE FISHING FOR ALL LODGE RESIDENTS

Stafford Moor Fishery, Toad Hall,
Dolton, Devon EX19 8PP

Please call for our new brochure (01805) 804360
www.staffordmoor.co.uk

Rising Sun Inn

UMBERLEIGH, North Devon (A377/B3227) ☎ 01769 560447

Email: therisingsuninn@btinternet.com Website: www.risingsuninn.com

Fly for it!... Sea Trout Salmon, Brownies - this is <u>**the**</u> place!... eat well too at North Devon's **1999 'Food Pub of the Year'**

The famous "Rising Sun Waters"
Malcolm and Andrew Hogg welcome you to their nine (ensuite) bedroom 13th Century Inn.

Come and fish, then relax in the beautiful Taw valley

Westcountry Salmon Fishing.
Coombe Mill

Modern Toilet & Shower Block
*Disabled Facilities * Hard Standings*
Electric Hook-ups

Write or phone for a brochure

Minnows Caravan Park
Sampford Peverell
Tiverton
Devon EX16 7EN
01884 821770

AA THE CARAVAN CLUB RAC

A rare sight - the editor actually fishing!

HIGHWAY FARM

West Road, Bridport, Dorset

Wonderful views & wildlife

2 COARSE FISHING LAKES

Bed & Breakfast – Ganders S/C Cottage

Short breaks available. All rooms ensuite.

For colour brochure or more info ring 01308 424321

Email: bale@highwayfarm.co.uk www.highwayfarm.co.uk

Warren Park

Farm Holidays

Timber Lodges in secluded position overlooking lake offering excellent fishing.

Centrally situated for Bournemouth, The New Forest & Poole. The Lodges are cosy and warm, ideal for winter and summer holidays. Prices from £140 per week.

For details contact Mrs Huzzey

Tel: 01425 653340 Fax: 01425 650643

SET IN RURAL WEST DORSET & ONLY 3/4 MILE FROM THE SEA

A FAMILY-RUN PARK WITH EXCEPTIONAL FACILITIES

Coarse Fishing Ponds Rod Licences sold Excellent local Sea Fishing
Super Indoor Heated Swimming Pool Tennis Court Children's Playpark
Shop Laundry Spotless Toilet and Shower Blocks Well-kept Grounds
Touring and Tent Pitches Holiday Caravans for Hire and Sale
Self Catering Flat designed for disabled users.

And so much more to do for all the family that you'll want to come back year after year -

Write or phone for a brochure to:

Wood Farm Caravan Park, Axminster Road, CHARMOUTH, Dorset. DT6 6BT

TEL: (01297) 560697 **www.woodfarm.co.uk**

The West Country has Everything!

South West Tourism

The west country is one of the most popular areas in Britain for taking a short break or long. From superb lakes and idyllic rivers to fast waters and slow meandering streams, estuaries, coves, inlets and the open sea, the west country has everything for all the family.

The region starts at the river Thames, beginning as a small trickle at Thameshead in Gloucestershire and extends to the peaceful Isles of Scilly, emerald islands in turquoise seas. Unique views from Lands End can be seen at the most westerly point of England where from the dramatic cliffs different seabirds show off their aeronautical displays. In the north of the region, sand-stoned Cotswold villages provide a wonderful holiday destination whatever the season while the Royal Forest of Dean, the first designated National Forest Park in England offers hours of uninterrupted walking over miles of nature trails. The West Country region also extends to the south coast of Dorset where Regency towns such as Lyme Regis and Sidmouth sit in grandeur, overlooking sandy and shingle beaches with many coastal paths to wander.

Contrasts

This fantastic region of contrasts includes Wiltshire, land of the chalk white horse, magical stone circles and open landscapes less than an hour from London; Rolling sub tropical Dorset, bordered by the sea and almost wholly an Area of Outstanding Natural Beauty filled with wonderful views; Bristol and Bath, individual, exciting and vibrant cities with centuries of culture, stimulating nightlife and excellent shopping; Somerset, a mix of heather covered Exmoor, the level plains of Sedgemoor and wonderful family coastal resorts, brimming with beautiful landscapes and renowned for cider and superb cheeses; Devon with it's fine countryside and two coastlines, The south coast, warm and relaxing ideal for families, and the north coast with views across to the Island of Lundy marine reserve. Further along the more Victorian atmosphere of Lynton and Lymouth present a different age of holiday taking; And the wide open spaces of Dartmoor and Bodmin, each one revealed with its own ever changing characteristics through famous authors such as Jane Austen and Sir Arthur Conan Doyle; Rugged Cornwall, Atlantic facing, wind swept and bounded by the sea, is home also to the awe inspiring and award winning Eden Project which will make any journey to the end of England worthwhile. And don't miss a visit to the fantastic fish markets at Brixham and Looe or Rick Stein's Seafood Restaurant in Padstow.

The West Country cities are some of the most beautiful to be found anywhere and cathedrals spires grace attractive cities like Salisbury, Truro, Exeter or Wells the smallest city in England, while the 2000 year old city of Bath, designated as a World Heritage Site boasts the famous Roman Spa and the sweeping splendour of the Georgian Crescent.

Maritime history features particularly strongly in the West Country and Plymouth, home to the National Marine Aquarium, is where the Pilgrim Fathers, Charles Darwin and Captain Scott of the Antarctic all sailed from.

Gloucester is home to Gloucester Docks, a museum of waterway life on the canals and rivers of the region and in Bristol, the largest city in the West Country, you will find the ss.Great Britain and the award winning science centre, @ Bristol, a fascinating attraction for adults and children.

Spectacular

Wherever you go in the West Country you will see some of the most wonderful scenery and spectacular coastline that England has to offer. Try walking part of the 982 kilometre South West Coast Path from where the sea is never far away. The path is one of many in the west country that allow visitors to experience sandy beaches, dramatic cliffs, secluded coves and estuaries, or picturesque fishing villages and some of the larger and more livelier resorts, each with plenty to do.

Inland, meander through picture postcard villages with thatched cottages and village

Fern, youngest Sleeman, gets in on the act. Avallon Lodges

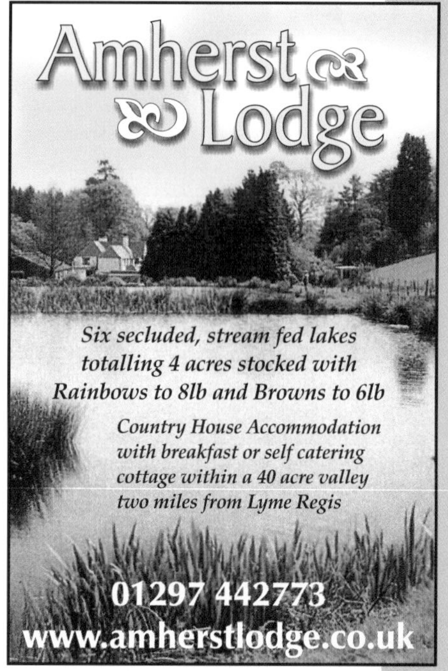

greens, or call in on stately homes with their landscaped gardens - colourful whatever the season, friendly pubs in riverside settings, prehistoric heritage sites, intriguing caves, historic monuments, and of course the wide open spaces of the National Parks, Exmoor and Dartmoor.

If that doesn't give you a taste for more, try the local food and drink - ciders, real ales, gin from Plymouth and locally produced wines, the best of beef, lamb and fish, clotted cream for that delicious cream tea, Cornish pasties, Star Gazey pie, the Bath bun, the Dorset knob. All this plus excellent accommodation, the perfect answer to a perfect holiday.

For more information on west country accommodation, be it in a farm or cottage, historic house, seaside apartments or holiday flats, bed and breakfast or self catering, visit www.westcountrynow.com which also has information on events, attractions and destinations in the region or, for more information on water events and water activities in the region visit www.sw-watersports.com

FISHING

Excellent Chalk Stream Fishing

We also offer accommodation to suit your needs

This ranges from Bed and Breakfast at our 16th century farmhouse to fully self contained premises in a recently converted 18th century barn.

www.chalkstream.co.uk

ALEX and ROZ WALKER, Sutton Veny Fishing, Eastleigh Farm, Bishopstrow, Warminster, Wiltshire BA12 7BE

email: enquiries@chalkstream.co.uk

Tel: 01985 212325 Mobile: 07836 294633

WARREN FARM

Holiday Park

For your touring holiday in Somerset

Our Fishing Lakes are well stocked with a variety of coarse fish - 3 acre main lake!

Fishing to competition level across the moors
Sea Fishing opposite the park

Please phone for a brochure

01278 751227 www.warren-farm.co.uk

Warren Farm Holiday Park, Brean Sands, Somerset TA8 2RP

Wick Farm, Lacock, Nr Chippenham, Wilts

- OPEN ALL YEAR -

DISCOUNTS for anglers staying in our two self-catering Cottages

Small Caravan site at Farm

Stocked with Carp to 26lb, Tench & Bream to 8lb and Pike

DAY or NIGHT TICKETS £5 - *to be purchased at farmhouse*

Tel: 01249 730244 www.cheeseandcyderhouses.co.uk

Lakeside Rendezvous

A 6.5 acre site set In the heart of Wiltshire with our own spring fed offering Carp to 30lb along with Bream, Tench, Roach and Perch

Superb and exclusive lakeside lodge, fully equipped and offering total privacy for your holiday or short break with many attractions just a short distance away.

Rowde, Nr. Devizes, Wiltshire

Tel: 01380 725447 www.lakesiderendezvous.co.uk

FREE FISHING! ***when you stay in our converted barn holiday accommodation - just 50 yds from the lakeside in a picturesque village***

Just 4.5 miles from J20 off the M5 - 4.75 acres of lakes including a Specimen Carp Lake (mirrors to 26lb) plus three mixed coarse lakes. Regularly featured in Anglers Mail, Angling Times, Improve your Coarse Fishing - ***COME AND SEE WHY!***

Open Dawn to Dusk all year - Toilet Facilities - Refreshments available at weekends

Back Lane, Kingston Seymour, N. Somerset BS21 6XA **Tel: 01934 835020**

Email: BullockFarm@kingstonseymour1.freeserve.co.uk Web Site: www.bullockfarm.co.uk

Fresh run 4lb Sea Trout caught 10 miles from the sea on the River Teign.
Robert Jones Fly Fishing

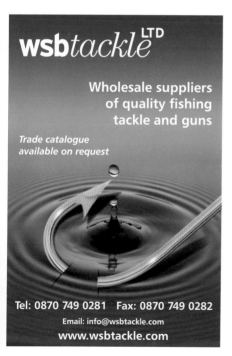

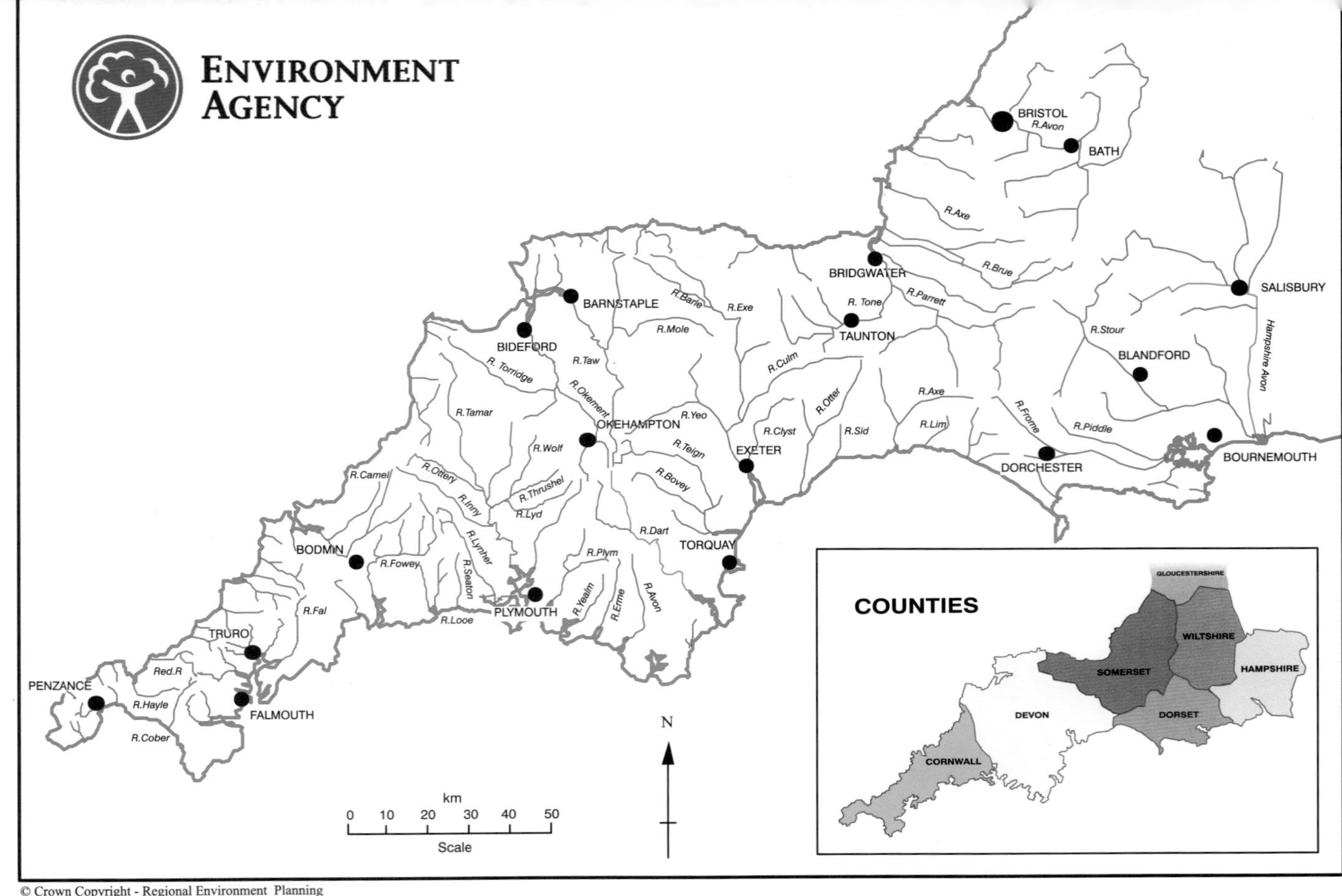
ENVIRONMENT AGENCY
BRISTOL
R.Avon
BATH
R.Axe
R.Brue
BRIDGWATER
SALISBURY
BARNSTAPLE
R.Barle
R.Exe
R. Tone
R.Parrett
BIDEFORD
R.Mole
TAUNTON
R.Stour
R.Taw
R.Culm
BLANDFORD
Hampshire Avon
R. Torridge
R.Okement
R.Otter
R.Axe
R.Tamar
R.Yeo
R.Frome
OKEHAMPTON
R.Clyst
R.Sid
R.Lim
R.Piddle
R.Wolf
R.Teign
EXETER
DORCHESTER
BOURNEMOUTH
R.Camel
R.Ottery
R.Thrushel
R.Bovey
R.Inny
R.Lyd
R.Dart
R.Lynher
TORQUAY
BODMIN
R.Plym
R.Fowey
R.Seaton
PLYMOUTH
R.Yealm
R.Erme
R.Avon
R.Fal
R.Looe
TRURO
Red.R
PENZANCE
R.Hayle
FALMOUTH
R.Cober
N
km
0 10 20 30 40 50
Scale
COUNTIES
GLOUCESTERSHIRE
WILTSHIRE
SOMERSET
HAMPSHIRE
DEVON
DORSET
CORNWALL

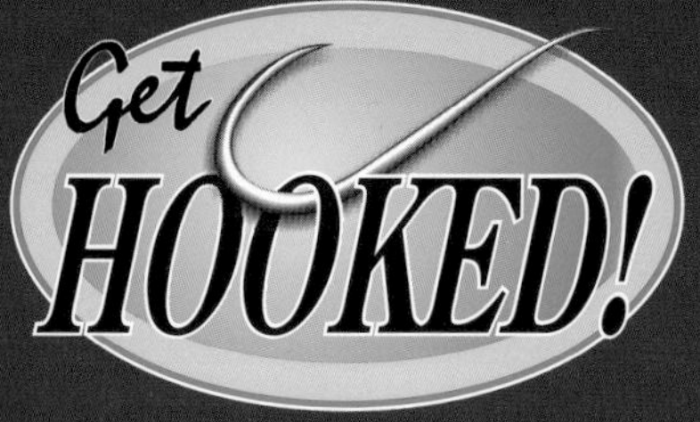

The Directory

**The Directory is divided into counties.
Each county is sub divided and colour coded:**

River Fishing	Stillwater Coarse	Stillwater Trout

Many associations offer both game and coarse fishing on many different rivers and stillwaters.

Each county section starts with river fishing and includes a short description of the river and tributaries followed by entries offering fishing on that river. This section is sorted under river name (see map opposite).

The Stillwater Coarse and Stillwater Trout sections are sorted under the nearest town.

Entries in the Directory highlighted in blue are advertisers and more information will be available elsewhere in the guide via the advertisers index. These entries will also have a map location on the inside back cover.

www.gethooked.co.uk

Every entry in this Directory and the sea fishing Directory also appears on our web site **www.gethooked.co.uk** (unless we have been requested not to do so by the owner)

The 'Fish Finder' on the web site enables you to easily search all of the entries plus a database of Westcountry tackle shops.

ADD YOUR FISHERY!
If you wish to add your fishery or club to the Directory you can use the form on the web site or Email info@gethooked.co.uk, fax to 01271 860064 or post to Diamond Publications Ltd, PO Box 59, Bideford, Devon EX39 4YN.
THERE IS NO CHARGE FOR INCLUSION IN THIS DIRECTORY OR THE WEB SITE DIRECTORY.

CORNWALL River Fishing

CAMEL

The Camel rises on the north west edge of Bodmin Moor and flows past Camelford to its estuary at Wadebridge. The run of Salmon tends to be late with some of the best fishing in November and December. Sea Trout in summer. Brown Trout in upper reaches and tributaries.

Angling 2000 (Camel)
Contact: Simon Evans, Westcountry Rivers Trust, Fore Street, Lifton, PL16 0AA, 01566 784488, simon@wrt.org.uk, *Water:* Beat on the De Lank. Flexible permits fishing for Trout, *Species:* Trout, *Permits:* From the above, *Charges:* £5 per day, *Season:* 1 April to 30 September, *Methods:* Fly only.

Bodmin Anglers Association (Camel)
Contact: Mr Burrows, 26 Meadow Place, Bodmin, 01208 75513, ivanl@breathe.com, *Water:* 11.5 Miles on River Camel, 0.25 miles on River Fowey, *Species:* Salmon, Sea Trout, *Permits:* Roger Lashbrook at Stan Mays Store, Bodmin. D.Odgers, Gwendreath, Dunmere, Bodmin, *Charges:* 1st May - end November £15 per day or £40 per week. Juniors half price. Membership details from Secretary, *Methods:* Fly, Worm, Spinner.

Butterwell
Contact: Tyson & Janet Jackson, Butterwell, Nr Nanstallon, Bodmin, PL30 5LQ, 01208 831515, tyson@butterwell.u-net.com, *Water:* 1.5 miles River Camel, *Species:* Sea Trout (to 10lb 2oz) & Salmon (to 18lb). 5 year average 50 Salmon and 200 Sea Trout, *Permits:* On site, *Charges:* £20/day, maximum 5 rods/day. Priority given to residents, *Season:* 1st May - 30th August, night fly fishing only for Sea trout. 1st September - 15th December for Salmon, *Methods:* Any method for Salmon after 1st September.

Fenwick Trout Fishery (River Camel)
Contact: David & Shirley Thomas, Old Coach Road, Dunmere, Bodmin, PL31 2RD, 01208 78296, *Water:* 570 yards on the river Camel. See also entry under Stillwater Trout, *Species:* Sea Trout and Salmon, *Permits:* On site. EA licence required, *Charges:* Please phone for details, *Season:* As current EA Byelaws, *Methods:* Fly fishing from bank only.

River Camel Fisheries Association
Contact: E.D.T. Jackson, Butterwell, Nr Nanstallon, Bodmin, PL30 5LQ, 01208 831515, *Water:* The association represents all major riparian owners and fishing clubs on the river Camel and agrees fish limits, conservation policy and enhancement projects in co-operation with the Environment Agency.

Wadebridge & Dist. Angling Association
Contact: Jon Evans, Polgeel, Polbrook, Washaway, PL30 3AN, 01208 812447, 07732 921015, jonrevans@aol.com, *Water:* 10 miles River Camel, 1 mile River Allen, *Species:* Salmon to 27lb, Sea Trout to 7lb, *Permits:* Day / Week permits, Bait Bunker, Polmorla Road, Wadebridge: 01208 816403. Padstow Angling Centre, The Drang, Padstow: 01841 532762. Rogers Tackle Shop, Stan Mays Store, Bodmin: 01208 78006, *Charges:* Day £25, Week £100, *Season:* Visitor permits end 31st September, although 4 tickets per week (no day tickets) are available until the end of November - must be pre-booked, *Methods:* No maggots permitted. Fly and spinning, natural baits on some beats.

FAL

Angling 2000 (Fal & Tresillian)
Contact: Simon Evans, Westcountry Rivers Trust, Fore Street, Lifton, PL16 0AA, 01566 784488, simon@wrt.org.uk, *Water:* 2 New beats for 2003 on Tresillian tributary of Fal. Flexible day permits for Trout, Sea Trout and occasional Salmon. *Species:* Sea Trout, Trout and occasional Salmon, *Permits:* From the above, *Charges:* £5 - £10 p/day, *Season:* 1st April - 30th September, *Methods:* Any method.

Fal River Association
Contact: Mr. Tom Mutton, 01872 273858, *Water:* Association protecting the interests of the River Fal.

FOWEY

Rises near the highest point of Bodmin Moor from which it flows south, then turns to the west, and finally south again through Lostwithiel to its long estuary. A late Salmon river. Also good Sea Trout fishing and some Trout fishing.

Bodmin Anglers Association (Fowey)
Contact: Mr Burrows, 26 Meadow Place, Bodmin, 01208 75513, ivanl@breathe.com, *Water:* See entry under Camel. 0.25 miles River Fowey.

Fowey River Association
Contact: Chris Marwood (sec), Withy Cottage, Huish Champflower, Taunton, TA4 2EN, 01398 371384, *Water:* An association of representatives of angling clubs and riparian owners on the Fowey whose aim is to secure and maintain the well being of the river and its ecology. It exists largely as a pressure group and negotiating body on behalf of its members, *Permits:* No permits sold through the Association. For membership details please contact the secretary at the above address, *Methods:* E.A. Byelaws apply. Catch restrictions: Salmon 1/day, 2/week, 5/season; Sea Trout 4/day, all Sea Trout to be returned in Sept.

Lanhydrock Angling Association
Contact: Brian Muelaner, The National Trust, Regional Office, Lanhydrock, Bodmin, PL30 4DE, 01208 265211, cscbdm@smtp.ntrust.org.uk, *Water:* 2 miles on River Fowey, *Species:* Sea trout, Salmon, *Permits:* Available from the above telephone number, *Charges:* £15 Daily, £30 Weekly (maximum 6 tickets daily), *Season:* 1st April - 30th Sept, Sea Trout 31st Aug, *Methods:* Artificial bait only.

Liskeard & District Angling Club (Fowey)
Contact: Bill Eliot (Hon Sec), 64 Portbyhan Road, West Looe, PL13 2QN, 01503 264173, *Water:* 23 Miles of Rivers Fowey, Lynher, Inny, Seaton River, West Looe River; Map of waters with day/week tickets, *Species:* Salmon to 20lb (typically 7-12.5lb) & Sea Trout to 10lb (typically 2.5-4lb), *Permits:* Visitor tickets available until 30 November for winter Salmon. Tremar Tropicals Shop, Liskeard. Lashbrooks Tackle Shop, Bodmin. East Looe Chandlers, The Quay, East Looe. Shillamill lakes, Lanreath. *Charges:* Adult: £15/day, £50/week, Membership £55. Joining fee £10. Membership limited to 250 adults, *Season:* River Fowey 1st April - 15th December; Sea Trout season closes end September, *Methods:* Spinning, fly fishing or bait. Artificials only on some beats. No groundbait, no maggots.

Lostwithiel Fishing Association
Contact: Roger Lashbrook, Rogers Tackle Shop, 1st Floor, Stan Mays Store, Higher Bore Street, Bodmin, PL31 1JZ, 01208 78006, *Water:* 3 miles water, both banks, River Fowey, *Species:* Salmon, Sea Trout, Brown Trout, *Permits:* Rogers Tackle Shop, Bodmin, *Charges:* Season tickets only: £55, *Season:* 1st April - 15th December, *Methods:* All baits.

Newbridge Angling Association
Contact: Mr R Tetley, Trebyan Forge, Lanhydrock, Bodmin, PL30 5AE, 01208 75244, rob.tetley@lanhydrock.com, *Water:* 1.5 miles single bank on River Fowey, *Species:* Trout, Sea Trout & Salmon, *Permits:* Members only - no day tickets. For membership details please contact Mr. Tetley.

Wainsford Fishery (Fowey)
Contact: Paul Elliot, Wainsford Fishery, Twowatersfoot, Liskeard, PL14 6HT, 01208 821432, *Water:* Two miles on the Fowey. See also entry under Stillwater Trout, Liskeard, *Species:* Salmon to 16lb, Sea Trout to 10lb, *Permits:* On site, *Charges:* £15 per day, *Season:* Salmon: 1st April to 15th December. Trout: 1st April to 30th September, *Methods:* Fowey River Association limits apply.

LOOE

The twin rivers, East and West Looe, have their sources near Liskeard and join shortly before reaching the sea at Looe. Although small, there is a run of Sea Trout, and Brown Trout throughout.

LYNHER

Rises on Bodmin Moor and joins the Tamar estuary opposite Plymouth. Brown Trout and runs of Salmon and Sea Trout.

Liskeard & District Angling Club (Lynher)
Contact: Bill Eliot, 64 Portbyhan Rd, West Looe, PL13 2QN, 01503 264173, *Water:* 23 miles of Rivers Fowey, Lynher, Inny, Seaton, West Looe; Map of waters with day/week tickets, *Species:* Salmon to 16lb & Sea Trout to 6lb (some very big ones April/May), *Permits:* Tremar Tropicals Shop, Liskeard. Lashbrooks Tackle Shop, Bodmin. East Looe Chandlers, The Quay, East Looe. Shillamill lakes, Lanreath, *Charges:* Adult: £15/day, £50/week, Membership £55. Joining fee £10. Membership limited to 250 adults, *Season:* River Lynher & Inny; 1st March - 14th October; Sea Trout season closes end September, *Methods:* Spinning, fly fishing or bait. No groundbait, no maggots.

River Lynher Fisheries Association
Contact: Arthur White (hon.secretary), River Lynher Fisheries Association, 14 Wadham Road, Liskeard, PL14 3BD, 01579 345428, efsa@btinternet.com, *Water:* Consultative body for the river Lynher. Membership comprises riparian owners, angling clubs, lessees of fishing rights, individual anglers and others interested in Lynher valley environment, *Species:* Salmon, Sea Trout, Trout, *Permits:* N/A, *Charges:* £5 annual.

Woodcocks Club
Contact: Michael Charleston, The Gift House, Buckland Monachorum, Yelverton, PL20 7NA, 01822 853293, mwcharl@aol.com, *Water:* Two miles of the lower and middle Lynher, *Species:* Salmon, Sea Trout and Brown Trout, *Permits:* Waiting list for very limited number of annual permits. No short term permits, *Season:* Mar 1st to Oct 14th, *Methods:* Fly only for Sea Trout and Brown Trout except in spates. Return of Salmon (catch & release) is encouraged.

MENALHYL

Small stream starting near St. Columb Major and entering the sea north of Newquay. Brown Trout fishing.

St. Mawgan Angling Association
Contact: Mr. T. Trevenna, Lanvean House, St. Mawgan, Newquay, TR8 4EY, 01637 860316, *Water:* Stretch around Mawgan Porth, *Species:* Trout, Brown Trout, *Charges:* Limited day tickets from The Merrymoor, Mawgan Porth. Club membership restricted to those in parish of St. Mawgan, *Season:* Apr 1st - end Sept, *Methods:* See details on site.

SEATON

Small river to the east of Looe with good Sea Trout but very few Brown Trout.

Liskeard & District Angling Club (Seaton & West Looe)
Contact: Bill Eliot (Hon Sec), 64 Portbyhan Road, West Looe, PL13 2QN, 01503 264173, *Water:* Seaton and West Looe Rivers; Map of waters with day/week tickets, *Species:* Good small water Sea Trout, *Permits:* Visitor tickets from: Tremar Tropicals, Liskeard. Lashbrooks Tackle, Bodmin. East Looe Chandlers, The Quay, East Looe. Shillamill Lakes, Lanreath, *Charges:* Adult: £15/day, £50/week, Membership (limited to 250 adults) £55. Joining fee £10. *Season:* River Fowey 1st Apr - 15th Dec; Sea Trout season closes end Sept, *Methods:* Spinning, fly fishing or bait. No groundbait/maggots.

TAMAR

The Tamar rises near the north coast, and for most of its course forms the boundary between Devon and Cornwall. It is always a lowland stream flowing through farmland and this fact is reflected in the size of its Trout which have a larger average size than the acid moorland streams. Around Launceston, the Tamar is joined by five tributaries - Ottery, Carey, Wolf, Thrushel and Lyd - which offer good Trout fishing, as does the Inny which enters a few miles downstream. There is a good run of Salmon and Sea Trout, the latter being particularly numerous on the Lyd. There are also Grayling in places.

Angling 2000 (Tamar)
Contact: Simon Evans, Westcountry Rivers Trust, Fore Street, Lifton, PL16 0AA, 01566 784488, simon@wrt.org.uk, *Water:* 7 beats on the Tamar, Inny, Lyd and Kensey. Flexible permits fishing for Trout, Salmon, Sea Trout and Grayling. New beats for 2003, *Species:* Salmon, Sea Trout, Trout and Grayling, *Permits:* From the above, *Charges:* £5 to £10 per day depending on beat, *Season:* 15 March to 14 October. Grayling fishing to 30 November on selected beats, *Methods:* Fly, spin, (natural baits between 16th June and 31st August only).

Bude Angling Association
Contact: Mr L. Bannister, 2 Creathorn Road, Bude, EX23 8NT, 01288 353986, *Water:* 3 miles on the upper reaches of the River Tamar, *Species:* Brown Trout (Wild), *Permits:* Bude Angling Supplies, Queen Street, Bude. Webby's Tackle, 19 Fore Street, Holsworthy Devon, *Charges:* £3 day, week tickets available £15, *Season:* March 15th - Sept 30th, *Methods:* Fly only.

Dutson Tamar Fishery
Contact: Mr Broad, Lower Dutson Farm, Launceston, PL15 9SP, 01566 773147, 01566 776456, francis.broad@btclick.com, *Water:* Half a mile on the river Tamar at Launceston, *Species:* Brown Trout, Salmon and occasional Sea Trout, Grayling, *Permits:* Homeleigh Angling and Garden Centre, Dutson, Launceston. Tel: 01566 773147, *Charges:* £5 per day, *Season:* 1st March - 14th October, Salmon as current EA Byelaws, *Methods:* See current EA Byelaws.

Launceston Anglers Association
Contact: Colin Hookway, 7 Grenville Park, Yelverton, PL20 6DQ, 01822 855053, *Water:* 6 miles on River Tamar and Carey, 7 miles River Inny, *Species:* Brown Trout, Sea Trout, Salmon, Grayling, *Permits:* The Fishmonger, 16 Southgate Place, Launceston, *Charges:* Salmon & Sea Trout; Day £15, Week £40. Brown Trout: Day £7.50, Week £25, Juniors £2 a day. Day tickets valid for 24 hours from time of purchase. Annual membership from £55, *Season:* From 1st March to 14th October. Grayling all year round on some beats, *Methods:* Brown Trout - fly only, Salmon & Sea Trout - any method subject to byelaws. Grayling - fly only.

CORNWALL Stillwater Coarse

BODMIN

East Rose Farm
Contact: Veronica Stansfield, East Rose Farm, St. Breward, Bodmin Moor, PL30 4NL, 01208 850674, eastrose@globalnet.co.uk, *Water:* Complex of four lakes with 22 permanent pegs (two specially for disabled). 3 acres of water, *Species:* Mixed fishing in two largest lakes: Tench / Roach / Rudd and Crucian. Lower lake has Carp to 8lb. Deep Pool - Carp to 22lb & Tench to 4lb, *Permits:* Day tickets available from Farmhouse at East Rose, *Charges:* Day tickets: £4 adults, £2.75 OAP's, Disabled & U16's. Reduced rate evening tickets, *Season:* No closed season, no night fishing, *Methods:* No keepnets unless by prior arrangement. Barbless hooks only.

Lakeview Coarse Fishery
Contact: Don, Old Coach Road, Lanivet, Bodmin, PL30 5JJ, 01726 810814, 07733 345456, admin@lakeview-country-club.co.uk, *Water:* 3 lakes, 4 acres in total, *Species:* 13 in total inc. Carp to 20lb, Tench to 6lb, Bream to 5lb, Roach to 5lb 3oz & Perch 4lb 9oz, *Permits:* On site Tackle Shop & Main Reception, *Charges:* £5/day/Adult, £3 Junior - O.A.P. - Disabled. Season ticket available, *Season:* Open all year 9am - 5pm. Closed Xmas Day, *Methods:* No boilies or night fishing.

Prince Park Lake
Contact: Prince Park Farm, St Wenn, Nr Bodmin, PL30 5SP, 01726 890095, *Water:* 1/2 acre pond, *Species:* Crucian Carp to 3lb, Common to 9lb, Tench, Roach, Bream to 4lb and Golden Rudd, *Permits:* Please telephone before travelling, *Charges:* £4 Adults, £3 Juniors/ OAP, *Season:* Open all year, dawn to dusk, *Methods:* Nets must be dipped, barbless hooks only, no boilies.

BUDE

Bude Canal Angling Association
Contact: Mr Dick Turner, 2 Pathfields, Bude, EX23 8DW, 01288 353162, *Water:* Bude Canal (1.25 miles), *Species:* Mirror, Common, Crucian Carp, Bream, Tench, Roach, Rudd, Perch, Eels, Gudgeon, Dace, *Permits:* On the bank, *Charges:* Seniors day £4, Seniors week £18, Juniors & O.A.Ps day £2, Juniors & O.A.Ps week £10, *Season:* Closed season April 1st - May 31st inc, *Methods:* Micro barb or barbless hooks only, Strictly one rod only, No camping or any equipment deemed to be associated with camping.

Houndapitt Farm
Contact: Mr Heard, Houndapitt Farm, Sandymouth, Bude, EX23 9HW, 01288 355455, 07968 171255, tony@houndapitt.co.uk, *Water:* Small lake, *Species:* Golden Tench, Rudd, various Carp, *Permits:* From Sandymouth Bay Holiday Park, *Charges:* £2.50 per day, *Methods:* Barbless hooks.

South West Lakes Angling Association
Contact: Roy Retallick, 21 Alstone Road, Tiverton, EX16 4LH, 01884 256721, r.retallick@btinternet.com, *Water:* All 14 South West Lakes Trust fisheries plus 1 exclusive member only water at Lower Tamar, *Species:* All coarse fish - Carp 35lb, Pike 20lb plus, Bream 8lb plus, Tench 7lb plus, Roach 2lb, Perch 3lb 7oz, Eel 4lb, *Permits:* Please contact Roy Retallick, *Charges:* £8 per year membership, £7 junior, OAP and disabled. Entitles 10% discount on day and season tickets to fish any South West Lakes Trust coarse waters, *Season:* Open all year, *Methods:* As South West Lakes Trust rules displayed on site.

Upper Tamar Lake
Contact: South West Lakes Trust, 01837 871565, info@swlakestrust.org.uk, *Water:* Ranger Tel: 01288 321262, *Species:* Carp to 28lb. 50lb plus bags of Bream and 30lb plus bags of Rudd. Regular competitions, *Permits:* See South West Lakes Trust coarse advert. Self service permit hut on site, *Charges:* Full day £4.75, Concession £3.75, 24 Hour £8.75, Season Day £80, Season Concession £60, Season Child (under 16) £35, Season Day & Night £120, Additional Fisheries £20 each. This venue can be booked for competitions, *Season:* Open all year 24 hours a day, *Methods:* No child under 14 years may fish unless accompanied by an adult over 18 years. No child under 16 may fish overnight unless accompanied by an adult over 18 years, and then only with permission of parent or legal guardian (letter to this effect must be produced).

CALLINGTON

Angling 2000 (Penpoll Lake)
Contact: Simon Evans, Westcountry Rivers Trust, Fore Street, Lifton, PL16 0AA, 01566 784488, simon@wrt.org.uk, *Water:* 3.5 acre lake, *Species:* Unfished to date. Carp to 20lb. Rest unknown, *Charges:* £7.50 p/day, *Season:* All season, *Methods:* No Carp in keepnets, no boilies, no particles (previously unfished).

DELABOLE

Ferndale
Contact: Steve Davey, Rockhead, Delabole, PL33 9BU, 01840 212091, 07817 520417, ferndale@agriplus.net, *Water:* Three half acre lakes set in a sheltered valley 3 miles off the North Cornwall coast, *Species:* Roach to 1.5lb, Rudd to 1.5lb, Bream to 4.5lb and Carp to 14lb, Tench to 2lb & Crucian Carp, *Charges:* Adults £4 per day. OAP's and juniors £3 per day. After 5pm £3. Extra rod £1 per day, *Season:* Open all year from dawn to dusk.

FALMOUTH

Argal

Contact: South West Lakes Trust, 01837 871565, info@swlakestrust.org.uk, *Water:* Ranger Tel: 01579 342366, *Species:* Carp to 30lb plus, Bream, Tench, Pike to over 30lb, and Eels, *Permits:* Self service unit at Argal Car Park. See South West Lakes Trust coarse advert, *Charges:* Full day £4.75, Concession £3.75, 24 Hour £8.75, Season Day £80, Season Concession £60, Season Child (under 16) £35, Season Day & Night £120, Additional Fisheries £20 each, *Season:* Open all year 24 hours a day, *Methods:* No child under 14 years may fish unless accompanied by an adult over 18 years. No child under 16 may fish overnight unless accompanied by an adult over 18 years, and then only with permission of parent or legal guardian (letter to this effect must be produced).

HAYLE

Marazion Angling Club

Contact: 7 Chy Kensa Close, Hayle, 01736 365638 or 01736 756767, *Water:* St. Erth Fishery (3 acres), Bills Pool (2.5 acres), Wheal Grey (4 acres), River Hayle (600yd upstream from St. Erth Church), *Species:* Carp, Bream, Tench, Roach, Rudd, Perch, Golden Orfe, Golden Rudd, Gudgeon, Trout, Flounders & Eels; Wheal Grey reputed to hold Cornwall's biggest Carp (30lb plus), *Permits:* Available in local shops: Newtown Angling Centre, Praa Sands. West Cornwall Angling, Penzance. County Angler, Camborne. Post Office, St. Erth plus many more outlets (Please phone for more details) - Permits MUST be obtained prior to fishing, *Charges:* Full Senior £50, Ladies £35, Juniors (up to 16) £17.50, OAP & Disabled £35, Out of county £35. Family membership (2 adults & 2 children) £80. Day £5 - Ladies, Seniors, OAP, Disabled, Juniors £3. Night permit £75. *Season:* Open all year dawn till dusk, night fishing by appointment only, matches held regularly throughout the year, *Methods:* Barbless hooks, full rules & byelaws displayed at lake side (best baits: maggot, worm, pellet, sweetcorn, meat, boilies, nuts).

HELSTON

Middle Boswin Farm

Contact: Jonno, Middle Boswin Farm, Porkellis, Helston, TR13 0HR, 01209 860420, jonno@mbos1.fsnet.co.uk, *Water:* 1 x Pleasure lake, 1 x Beginnners lake, 1 x Match lake (40 pegs), 1 x Carp lake, *Species:* Roach 2lb, Rudd 1.5lb, Bream 4lb, Tench 3lb, Perch 2lb, Hybrid (Roach/Bream) 2.5lb plus single figure Mirror and Common Carp. Carp lake - Carp to 26lb, *Permits:* Day tickets available at farm, *Charges:* Adult £5, concessions/junior £4, Carp lake £6, *Season:* Winter; Dawn to Dusk, Summer 7am - 9 pm. (Night fishing only if pre-booked), *Methods:* Barbless hooks only, no fixed legers, no cereal groundbait, hemp or nuts, no trout pellets. No keepnets (except Matches) or Carp sacks.

LAUNCESTON

Dutson Water

Contact: Mr Broad, Lower Dutson Farm, Launceston, PL15 9SP, 01566 773147, 01566 776456, francis.broad@btclick.com, *Water:* 0.75 acre lake, *Species:* Carp, Tench to 6lb 2oz, Bream to 5lb 2oz, Rudd, Perch to 3lb 4oz etc, *Permits:* Available at farm and Homeleigh Garden and Angling Centre, Dutson. Tel: 01566 773147, *Charges:* Day ticket £5. *Season:* Open all year, *Methods:* No Groundbait, Barbless hooks only.

Elmfield Farm Coarse Fishery

Contact: Mr J Elmer, Elmfield Farm, Canworthy Water, Launceston, PL15 8UD, 01566 781243, *Water:* 2 acre & 1.25 acre lake, *Species:* Carp to 24lb, Tench to 6lb, Roach to 3lb, Perch to 3.5lb, Bream, Orfe to 1lb, Chub to 3lb & Koi, also Barbel, *Charges:* £5 - 2 Rods, £4 Children/OAP's, *Season:* Open all year, *Methods:* No keepnets, ground bait in feeders only, barbless hooks, no boilies.

Hidden Valley Coarse Fishing Lakes

Contact: Mr. P. Jones, Tredidon, Nr Kennards House, Launceston, PL15 8SJ, 01566 86463, hiddenvalley@tredidon.freeserve.co.uk, *Water:* 2 acre & 0.75 acre lake, *Species:* Common, Mirror, Crucian & Ghost Carp to 23lb, Tench to 6lb, Roach, Bream & Rudd, *Permits:* Day tickets from Hidden Valley reception, *Charges:* Adults £5 for 2 rods, Child/OAP £4 for 2 rods, *Season:* Open all year, 6am to dusk, *Methods:* Barbless hooks only. No groundbait.

St. Leonards Coarse Fishing Lake

Contact: Andy Reeve, St. Leonards Equitation Centre, Polson, Launceston, PL15 9QR, 01566 775543, 07860 431225, paintballpolson@totaleyes.co.uk, *Water:* 0.75 acre lake, *Species:* Tench, Crucian, Leather, Mirror and Common Carp, *Permits:* From house, *Charges:* £4 per rod per day, *Season:* Open all year, *Methods:* Barbless hooks only.

LISKEARD

Badham Farm

Contact: Joyce and Robert Brown, St Keyne, Liskeard, PL14 4RW, 01579 343572, *Water:* 0.75 acre lake, *Species:* Carp 15lb, Roach 2.5lb, Tench 3lb and Rudd 2lb, *Permits:* On site, *Charges:* £4/rod/day, *Season:* Open all year dawn to dusk, *Methods:* Barbless hooks only; No boilies; No keepnets; Landing nets to be used at all times; No groundbait.

LOOE

Shillamill Lakes & Lodges

Contact: Shillamill Lakes, Lanreath, Looe, PL13 2PE, 01503 220886, *Water:* 3 Lakes totalling approx 5 acres, *Species:* Main specimen lake: Common, Mirror and Leather Carp. Second lake: Common, Mirror and Ghost, Roach, Perch. Third: Common and Mirror, Golden Rudd, Golden Orfe, Perch, Tench, Roach & Crucian, *Charges:* Private fishing for residents and season ticket holders only, *Methods:* Fishery requirements on application.

NEWQUAY

Goonhavern Fishery

Contact: S. Arthur, Oak Ridge Farm, Bodmin Road, Goonhavern, TR4 9QG, 01872 575052, *Water:* 2 acres, *Species:* Carp, Tench, Rudd, Roach, Perch, *Permits:* On the bank, *Charges:* £4 Adults. £3 children, OAP's, *Season:* Open all year, *Methods:* Barbless hooks, no Carp keepnets.

Gwinear Pools

Contact: Simon & Jo Waterhouse, Gwinear Farm, Cubert, Newquay, TR8 5JX, 01637 830165, *Water:* 3 acre mixed lake, 60 peg match lake. 5 hour match record 294lbs, *Species:* Carp, Roach, Bream, Perch, Rudd, *Charges:* Day tickets from farm and self service kiosk: £5 adult. £3 OAP's & Juniors. Evening £3 & £2, *Season:* No close season, *Methods:* Barbless hooks, no keepnets.

Legonna Farm Fishery
Contact: Mr Trebilcock, Legonna Farm, Lane, Newquay, TR8 4NJ, 01637 872272, *Water:* 1 acre lake, *Species:* Tench, Roach, Rudd, Perch, Carp to 16lbs, *Permits:* Permits/Day tickets available from Farmhouse, *Charges:* Adult £4 (2 rods), Junior/OAPs (2 rods) £3, *Season:* No close season, *Methods:* Barbless hooks, no nuts of any type, no litter, no large fish in keepnets.

Oakside Fishery & Fish Farm
Contact: Brian & Sandra Hiscock, 89 Pydar Close, Newquay, TR7 3BT, 01637 871275, oakside.fishery@btopenworld.com, *Water:* 3 acre lake, *Species:* Carp to 24lb, Tench 6lb, Rudd, Bream 8lb, Perch, Roach 2lb, Crucians 2lb, *Permits:* Pay kiosk, checked by bailiff, *Charges:* Adult £4 (Two rods), Junior, O.A.P's, Disabled £3 (Two Rods), *Season:* All year round, *Methods:* Barbless hooks, no tiger nuts or peanuts and no Carp in keepnets.

Penvose Farm Holidays
Contact: Jonathan Bennett, St. Mawgan, Nr. Newquay, TR8 4AE, 01637 860277 or 860432, enquiries@penvose-farm.fsbusiness.co.uk, *Water:* 3.5 acres of water set in a beautiful valley, *Species:* Carp (Common 15 - 16lb, Mirror 16-17lb, Ghost 19.5 - 20lb), Tench (Green 3 - 4lb, Golden 1/2lb) Bream 4 - 5lb, Crucians 1.5lb, Rudd 1.5lb, Roach 1lb, *Charges:* Adults £5. under 14 £4, *Season:* No closed season, fishing dawn till dusk, *Methods:* Anglers must hold a valid licence. All nets to be dipped in solution tanks, no keepnets except for matches, landing nets must be used. Ground bait up to 2kg maximum. Barbless hooks only.

Porth
Contact: South West Lakes Trust, 01837 871565, info@swlakestrust.org.uk, Ranger Tel: 01637 877959, *Species:* Bags of 130lb plus have been caught. Best Bream 9lb 2oz, Tench 9lb 12oz. Rudd to 3lb. Roach to 1lb 4oz plus. Mixed bags of Roach, Rudd, Skimmers to 60lb. Regular competitions, *Permits:* Self service at Porth car park. See SW Lakes Trust coarse advert, *Charges:* Full day £4.75, Conc. £3.75, 24 Hr £8.75, Season Day £80, Season Conc. £60, Season Child (U.16) £35, Season Day & Night £120, Additional Fisheries £20 ea. Porth can be booked for competitions, *Season:* Open all year 24 hrs, *Methods:* No child U.14 years may fish unless accompanied by an adult over 18. No child U.16 may fish overnight unless accompanied by an adult over 18, and then only with permission of parent or legal guardian (letter to this effect must be produced).

Trebellan Park & Fisheries
Contact: Mr Eastlake, Cubert, Nr. Newquay, TR8 5PY, 01637 830522, treagofarm@aol.com, *Water:* 3 lakes ranging from 1 - 2.5 acres, *Species:* Carp - 20lbs, Roach 3 - 4lbs, Rudd 3 - 4lbs, Tench 3 - 4lbs, *Charges:* Day tickets - £3.50 for 1 rod, £5 for 2 rods. Season ticket (12 months) £60, *Season:* Lakes open all year. No night fishing, *Methods:* No keepnets, barbless hooks only, no ground baiting, no high protein baits, no night fishing.

White Acres Country Park
Contact: Tackle Shop, Newquay, TR8 4LW, 01726 862113, clint@whiteacres.co.uk, *Water:* 14 lakes totalling approx 36 acres, *Species:* Wide range of almost all species (no Pike or Zander), *Permits:* Available from Fishing Lodge, *Charges:* Please call for info, *Season:* Fishery open all year round, *Methods:* 'The Method' is banned, barbless hooks only, some keepnet restrictions, no peas, nuts, or beans.

PADSTOW

Borlasevath
Contact: Robert Hurford, Borlasevath Manor Farm, St. Wenn, Bodmin, PL30 5PW, 01637 880826, 07973 767147, robert.hurford@btclick.com, *Water:* 10 acres of water (5 lakes), *Species:* Carp, Bream, Tench, Rudd, *Methods:* Barbless hooks. All children under 14 years to be accompanied by an adult.

PENZANCE

Boscathnoe
Contact: South West Lakes Trust, 01837 871565, info@swlakestrust.org.uk, *Water:* Ranger Tel: 01579 342366, *Species:* Common Mirror and Crucian carp with fish into the 20lb range. Roach, Tench, Rudd and Bream also stocked, *Permits:* See South West Lakes Trust coarse advert, *Charges:* Full day £4.75, Concession £3.75, 24 Hour £8.75, Season Day £80, Season Concession £60, Season Child (under 16) £35, Season Day & Night £120, Additional Fisheries £20 each, *Season:* Open all year 24 hours a day, *Methods:* No child under 14 years may fish unless accompanied by an adult over 18 years. No child under 16 may fish overnight unless accompanied by an adult over 18 years, and then only with permission of parent or legal guardian (letter to this effect must be produced).

Choone Farm Fishery
Contact: Mr V.B. Care, Choone Farm, St. Buryan, Penzance, 01736 810220, *Water:* 2 lakes, *Species:* Carp, Tench, Perch, Rudd, *Charges:* 1 rod - £4/person, 2 rods - £5.50, *Season:* Please telephone before travelling, *Methods:* Barbless hooks only, no carp in keepnets.

Tindeen Fishery
Contact: J. Laity, Bostrase, Millpool, Goldsithney, Penzance, TR20 9JG, 01736 763486, *Water:* 3 lakes approx 1 acre each, *Species:* Carp, Roach, Rudd, Gudgeon, Perch, Tench, Trout, *Charges:* Adults £3, Juniors under 14 £2, Extra rod £1 each, *Season:* All year, night fishing by arrangement, *Methods:* Barbless hooks to be used.

SALTASH

Bake Fishing Lakes (Coarse)
Contact: Tony Lister, Bake, Trerule Foot, Saltash, 01752 849027, 07798 585836, tony.lister@bakelakes.co.uk, *Water:* 7 lakes adding up to over 15 acres, Coarse and Trout, *Species:* Mirror 28lb, Common 24lb 9oz, Ghost 24lb, Crucian Carp, Tench 6lb, Bream 8lb 4oz, Roach, Rudd, *Permits:* At Bake Lakes, *Charges:* £6.50 per day Specimen Lake, £5 per day Small fish lakes. 2 rods per person, reduced rates for pensioners and juniors subject to change, *Season:* 8am - Dusk. Earlier by appointment, open all year, *Methods:* Barbless hooks, No nuts. No keepnets specimen fish. Landing mats. All nets to be dipped before fishing.

Bush Lakes
Contact: J Renfree, Bush Farm, Saltash, PL12 6QY, 01752 842148, *Water:* 3 Lakes from half to 1 acre, *Species:* Carp to 30lb plus, Tench to 3.5lb, Rudd to 1.5lb, Roach to 1.5lb, Bream, Perch to 4.5lb, *Charges:* £5.50 per person, two rods max, *Season:* Open all year, *Methods:* Barbless hooks, landing mat, no nets for big carp.

ST AUSTELL

Glenleigh Farm Fishery

Contact: Mr & Mrs A Tregunna, Glenleigh Farm, Sticker, St Austell, PL26 7JB, 01726 73154, 07816 953362, fishglenleigh@btinternet.com, *Water:* One acre lake. New access to enable parking adjacent to lake, allowing easy access for disabled persons and new fully disabled friendly fishing platforms, *Species:* Carp (Common, Ghost, Mirror, Leather), Tench, Rudd, Roach, Eels, Gudgeon, Perch, *Permits:* Tickets from lakeside, permits from Sticker post office, *Charges:* £4.50 day, £3.50 child /OAP. £2.50 evening, £1.50 child /OAP. 12 month membership available, *Season:* Open all year dawn to dusk, *Methods:* Barbless hooks. No nuts, peas or beans. Max 2 rods per person. Mats to be used. No groundbait.

Roche (St Austell) Angling Club

Contact: Mr Ian Holland (Membership Secretary), Elmfield House, Trekenning, Newquay, TR8 4JD, 01637 880948, kelvinpyke@aol.com, *Water:* 6 fresh water lakes in St Austell area, *Species:* Roach, Perch, Rudd, Tench, Eels, Carp, Pike & Bream, *Permits:* Fishing restricted to Members and their guests only. Membership applications available from membership secretary direct, *Charges:* Full Annual membership £35, concessionary £15 plus initial joining fee. Membership to Game and Sea sections only at reduced rates, *Season:* Open all year, *Methods:* As specified in club byelaws.

Sunnyview Lake

Contact: Philip Gale, 01726 890715, *Water:* Half acre lake, *Species:* Roach, Rudd, Tench, Perch & Carp, *Permits:* Limited day tickets available by prior booking only - please phone number above, *Charges:* £4 /day /person (maximum 4) Sole hire £16 per day, *Season:* All year, dawn to dusk.

ST COLUMB MAJOR

Meadowside Fishery

Contact: M Early, Meadowside Farm, Winnards Perch, St. Columb, TR9 6DH, 01637 880544, info@meadowsidefisheries.co.uk, *Water:* 2 lakes. one mixed coarse fishery, one carp lake, *Species:* Carp 15lb, Roach 2lb, Perch 3lb, Rudd 1lb, Tench 5lb, Bream 6lb, *Permits:* Block permit on site from E.A. *Charges:* £3.50/1rod, concessions & juniors £2.50/1 rod, £1/extra rod, max. 2 rods, *Season:* No close season, 7.30am to dusk daily all year round, *Methods:* Barbless hooks, no keepnets, unhooking mats.

Retallack Waters

Contact: Retallack Waters, Winnards Perch, Nr St Columb Major, 01637 881160, 01637 880057, fishing@retallackwaters.co.uk, *Water:* 6.5 acre main lake, separate match canal, *Species:* Common, Mirror and Ghost Carp, Pike, Bream, Tench, Roach and Rudd, *Permits:* Night fishing only available to season ticket holders. Please enquire for details, *Charges:* Canal: £5 adults, £4 children/OAPs. Main specimen lake: £6 adult, £5 children/OAP's, *Season:* Open all year, *Methods:* Barbless hooks only. Unhooking mats and specimen landing net required on specimen lake. Dogs allowed by prior arrangement, please phone first.

ST IVES

Bussow

Contact: South West Lakes Trust, 01837 871565, info@swlakestrust.org.uk, *Water:* Ranger: 01579 342366, *Species:* Rudd to 1.5lb. Roach, Bream and Carp, *Permits:* See South West Lakes Trust coarse advert, *Charges:* Full day £4.75, Concession £3.75, 24 Hour £8.75, Season Day £80, Season Concession £60, Season Child (under 16) £35, Season Day & Night £120, Additional Fisheries £20 each, *Season:* Open all year 24 hours a day, *Methods:* No child under 14 years may fish unless accompanied by an adult over 18 years. No child under 16 may fish overnight unless accompanied by an adult over 18 years, and then only with permission of parent or legal guardian (letter to this effect must be produced).

Nance Lakes

Contact: Mr or Mrs Ellis, Nance Lakes, Trevarrack, Lelant, St Ives, TR26 3EZ, 01736 740348, *Water:* Three lakes, various sizes, *Species:* Carp, Roach, Bream and Tench, *Permits:* No E.A. Licence required. Permits at site, *Charges:* £5 per day. Evening tickets - £3 after 5pm, *Season:* Open all year 8am to 5pm, *Methods:* Barbless hooks, no keepnets unless competition.

St. Ives Freshwater Angling Society

Contact: Dr. Charles Franklin, Chy-An-Meor, Westward Road, St. Ives, TR26 1JX, 01736 798251, *Water:* 1.5 acre spring-fed lake with depths from 6 to 24 feet, situated in farmland, 5 miles from St.Ives, *Species:* Bream, Carp, Tench, Roach, Rudd, Perch, Gudgeon, and Eels, *Permits:* 1) Symons Fishing Tackle, Market Place, St Ives. 2) Mr. K. Roberts, Woonsmith Farm, Nancledra, Nr. Penzance. 3) Newtown Angling Centre, Newtown, Germoe, Penzance. Location maps available with permits, *Charges:* Adults: Day £5, Weekly £15. Juniors (under 16): Day £3, Weekly £9, *Season:* Open all year. No night Fishing, *Methods:* Barbless hooks only. No fish over 3 lb to be retained in a keepnet. All nets to be dipped in disinfectant tank before use. Good baits are maggots, casters, sweetcorn and trout pellets.

TORPOINT

Crafthole

Contact: South West Lakes Trust, 01837 871565, info@swlakestrust.org.uk, *Species:* Carp and Tench. Quality Carp up to 30lb, *Permits:* See South West Lakes Trust coarse advert, *Charges:* Full day £5 (limited availability from agent), Season Day £150, Concession £135.Family £250 (Husband, wife and up to 2 children under 16). Additional Fisheries £20 each, *Season:* Open all year 1hr before sunrise to 1hr after sunset, *Methods:* No child under 14 years may fish unless accompanied by an adult over 18 years. No child under 16 may fish overnight unless accompanied by an adult over 18 years, and then only with permission of parent or legal guardian (letter to this effect must be produced).

Millbrook

Contact: Mark or Rebecca Blake, Tregonhawke Cottage, Millbrook, PL10 1JH, 01752 823210, *Water:* 1 Acre water in sheltered, wooded valley. 150 year old reservoir, *Species:* Perch, Tench, Ghost Carp, Crucians, Common Carp, Mirror Carp, Roach, Rudd, Bream. *Permits:* Not applicable, *Charges:* £5 per day, £3 evening after 5 p.m.-. £10 night fishing ticket. Annual permits £120, *Season:* Dawn until dusk, no closed season, *Methods:* No barbless hooks. Keepnets permitted, landing nets and disgorgers to be used.

TRURO

Mellonwatts Mill Coarse Fishery
Contact: Pensagillas Farm, Grampound, Truro, 01872 530808, pensagillas@farming.co.uk, *Water:* 2 acre lake, *Species:* Carp to 25lb, Common & Mirror, Roach, Tench, Golden Rudd, *Charges:* Day ticket £5, Evening £3, *Season:* Open all year. Night fishing by arrangement only.

Nanteague Farm Fishing
Contact: Maraznvose, Zelah, Truro, TR4 9DH, 01872 540351, nanteague@aol.com, *Water:* 1.5 acre lake, *Species:* Carp to 22lb, Roach, Rudd, Bream and Perch, *Permits:* Limited season tickets by prior arrangement. Please telephone/e-mail. No day tickets.

Rosewater Lakes
Contact: Mike Waters, Hendravossan Farm, Rose, Truro, TR4 9PL, 01872 573040, 07977 666025, *Water:* Lake closed.

Threemilestone Angling Club
Contact: Mrs T. Bailey, 9 Sampson Way, Threemilestone, Truro, TR3 6DR, 01872 272578, tbbailey@aol.com, *Water:* Langarth Pools (2 Pools), *Species:* Carp, Tench, Roach, Rudd, Bream, Perch, Goldfish, *Permits:* At lakeside, *Charges:* Seniors £4, Juniors £3, *Season:* All season, no night fishing, *Methods:* Barbless hooks only, no Peanuts etc.

Tory Farm Angling
Contact: Andy Ayres, Tory Farm, Ponsanooth, Truro, TR3 7HN, 01209 861272, *Water:* 2.5 acre lake, *Species:* Mirror, Common, Wild and Ghost Carp to 28lb. Crucian to 1.5lb. Tench to 5lb. Rudd to 2lb, *Charges:* £6 per day, daylight hours only. Club membership available £50 per season (or part of). Ticket commences 1st June, *Season:* Open all year, *Methods:* Barbless hooks only, no keepnets, unhooking mats to be used.

CORNWALL Stillwater Trout

BODMIN

Colliford Lake
Contact: South West Lakes Trust, 01837 871565, info@swlakestrust.org.uk, *Water:* Ranger Tel: 01579 342366, *Species:* Brown Trout, *Permits:* Colliford Tavern, *Charges:* Full day £9.50, Season £125, Reduced day £7.25, Season £95, Child/Wheelchair £2, Season £30, *Season:* Opens 15th March - 12th October, *Methods:* Catch & Release operates. Barbless hooks only.

Fenwick Trout Fishery
Contact: David & Shirley Thomas, Old Coach Road, Dunmere, Bodmin, PL31 2RD, 01208 78296, *Water:* 2 acre lake plus river fishing. See also entry under Camel, *Species:* Rainbow 1.5lb - 12lb, Browns to 10lb plus, *Charges:* £20/Full day (4 fish, 8hrs), £13/Half day (2 fish, 4hrs), *Season:* All year, *Methods:* Fly fishing only.

Temple Trout Fishery
Contact: Mr Julian Jones, Temple Trout Fishery, Temple Road, Temple, Bodmin, PL30 4HW, 01208 821730, 07787 704966, jj@templetroutfishery.freeserve.co.uk, *Water:* 2.7 acre lake. Plus 4.5 acre 'any method' lake, *Species:* Rainbows (16lb 4oz) & Brown trout (16lb 6oz), *Permits:* Available at fishery Tel: 01208 821730, *Charges:* Club membership £7 (2002 price) entitles members to 10% discount on tickets, to fish club events and to purchase a season ticket at £118.20 for 25 Trout - full day £22.50, 5 fish - 3/4 day £20, 4 fish - 1/2 day £15.75, 3 fish - evening £11.50, 2 fish - child under 16 & disabled £11.50, 2 fish all day, extra fish £6. Single fish on any method lake £6, *Season:* Open all year round from 9 a.m to dusk, in winter open 4 days a week Wednesday, Thursday, Saturday and Sundays or by appointment, *Methods:* Fly fishing on 2.7 acre lake. Any legal method on one bank of 4.5 acre lake and a sporting ticket available on 4.5 acre lake.

BOSCASTLE

Venn Down Lakes
Contact: Ted & Sue Bowen, Trebowen, Trevalga, Boscastle, 01840 250018, *Water:* 2 pools, 3 acres, *Species:* Rainbow Trout, *Charges:* Ticket to fish £5, plus fish at £1.85/lb. Junior ticket £3 - 1 fish, *Season:* Open all year except Christmas Day, *Methods:* Max hook size 10, single fly only.

CAMELFORD

Crowdy
Contact: South West Lakes Trust, 01837 871565, info@swlakestrust.org.uk, *Species:* Brown Trout, *Charges:* Free to holders of a valid Environment Agency Licence, *Season:* 15th March - 12th October, *Methods:* Angling by spinning, fly or bait.

HAYLE

Tree Meadow Trout Fishery
Contact: John Hodge, Tree Meadow, Deveral Road, Fraddam, Hayle, TR27 5EP, 01736 850899, 07971 107156, enquiries@treemeadow.co.uk, *Water:* Two lakes. 4 acres in total. Sedge lake to 14lb, Willow lake to 20lb plus, *Species:* Rainbow and Brown Trout & Blues, *Permits:* At Lodge Shop, *Charges:* Contact for details, *Season:* Open all year 9am to 1 hour after dusk, *Methods:* Catch and release after fish limit. Max hook size 10.

LAUNCESTON

Rose Park Fishery
Contact: Rose Park Fishery, Trezibbett, Altarnun, Nr Launceston, PL15 7RF, 01566 86278, roseparkfishery@bushinternet.com, *Water:* Two lakes, *Species:* Rainbow 13lb Wild Browns 2.5lb. Stocked Brown Trout 9lb 5oz, *Permits:* From the fishery, *Charges:* No catch, no charge. Rainbows £1.70 per lb, Browns £2.25 per lb. Fishin charge £2.50 on 1st & 2nd fish only, *Season:* Open all year from 8am till Dusk *Methods:* Fly fishing. No catch and release.

LISKEARD

Siblyback

Contact: South West Lakes Trust, 01837 871565, info@swlakestrust.org.uk, *Water:* Ranger Tel: 01579 342366, *Species:* Premier Rainbow Fishery - Boat & Bank (boats may be booked in advance: 01579 342366). Rod average 2002: 3 fish per rod day, *Permits:* Self Service Kiosk at Watersports Centre, *Charges:* Full day £16.75, Season £390. Concession day £13.50, Season £290, Child/Wheelchair £3, Season £90. Evening Monday - Friday £13.50. Season Permits can be used on any Premier Fishery only. Boats £10 per day inc. 2 fish extra to bag limits, *Season:* Opens 22nd March 2003 - 31st October, *Methods:* Fly fishing only. No child under 14 years may fish unless accompanied by an adult over 18 years.

Wainsford Fishery (Trout Lake)

Contact: Paul Elliot, Wainsford Fishery, Twowatersfoot, Liskeard, PL14 6HT, 01208 821432, *Water:* Three Trout lakes. See also entry under River fishing - Fowey, *Species:* Brown Trout to 5.5lb. Rainbows to 12.5lb, *Permits:* On site, *Charges:* £15 per day, *Season:* Open all year.

PENZANCE

Drift Reservoir

Contact: Estate Office, Penzance, 01736 363021, mail@bolithoestates.co.uk, *Water:* 65 acre reservoir, *Species:* Stock Rainbows (3 per day, 9 weekly) Wild Browns. Browns (3 per day, 9 weekly), *Permits:* Enquiries to Estate Office: 01736 363021 re. tickets and permits, *Charges:* Permit Charge - Rainbow/Brown. Season £120 - 9 Rainbows per week, 3 Brownies per day. Week £30 - 9 Rainbows per week, 3 Brownies per day. Day £10 - 3 Rainbows per day, 3 Brownies per day. Evening £7 - 2 Rainbows per evening, 2 Brownies per evening (after 4pm) (Sept-Oct after 2pm), *Season:* 1st April - 12th October Brown trout, 1st April - 31st October Rainbows, *Methods:* No static with boobies, any other traditional fly or lures.

REDRUTH

Stithians

Contact: South West Lakes Trust, 01837 871565, info@swlakestrust.org.uk, *Water:* Ranger Tel: 01579 342366, *Species:* Intermediate Rainbow & Brown Trout Fishery. Trout to 6lb. 2002 rod average 2.6 fish per rod day, *Permits:* Stithians Watersports Centre (01209 860301), Sandy's Tackle, Redruth (01209 214877), *Charges:* Full day £9.50, Season £195, Concession day £10.50, Season £175, Child/Wheelchair £2, Season £40. Boats £10/day, *Season:* Opens 15 March - 31st October, *Methods:* Fly fishing only. Catch and release - barbless hooks.

SALTASH

Bake Fishing Lakes (Trout)

Contact: Tony Lister, Bake, Trerule Foot, Saltash, PL12 5BU, 01752 849027, 07798 585836, tony.lister@bakelakes.co.uk, *Water:* 7 Lakes adding up to 14 plus acres, Coarse and Trout. Troutmaster Water, *Species:* Rainbow 16lb 7oz, Brown Trout 10lb, *Permits:* At Bake lakes, *Charges:* Sporting ticket £11 per day. Catch only £6.50 plus £5 - 1 fish, £14 - 2 fish, £18.50 - 3 fish, £23 - 4 fish, £26 - 5 fish, specimen to 15lb. £12 - 2 fish to £20 - 5 fish, Dunes, *Season:* 8am - Dusk, earlier by appointment, *Methods:* Catch and release on 1 lake. Barbless or debarbed hooks when releasing.

ST AUSTELL

Innis Fly Fishery

Contact: Mrs Pam Winch, Innis Fly Fishery & Innis Inn, Innis Moor, Penwithick, St. Austell, PL26 8YH, 01726 851162, innis@tiscali.co.uk, *Water:* 15 acres (3 lakes), stream fed enclosed water, *Species:* Rainbow Trout, *Permits:* As above, *Charges:* Full day £20 (5 Fish), half day £10.50 (2 Fish), Catch and release £12, *Season:* All year, 8.00 a.m. to dusk, *Methods:* Barbless hooks when catch & release, no static fishing.

TRURO

Gwarnick Mill Fishery

Contact: Sue Dawkins, Gwarnick Mill, St. Allen, Truro, TR4 9QU, 01872 540487, *Water:* 1.5 Acre spring and river fed lake, *Species:* Rainbow Trout to 10lb, *Charges:* 4 Fish £18, 3 Fish £15, 2 Fish £11. *Season:* Open all year, *Methods:* Barbless hooks preferred.

Ventontrissick Trout Farm

Contact: Gerald Wright, St. Allen, Truro, TR4 9DG, 01872 540497, 07762 781200, *Water:* Half acre, *Species:* Rainbow Trout 1.25lb - 10lb, *Charges:* £5.50 per day rod ticket, £1.60 per lb fish killed, first two fish to be killed, thereafter release optional. £10 sporting ticket, *Season:* 8.00am till 1hr after sunset 10 p.m, *Methods:* Fly only, barbless if releasing.

DEVON River Fishing

AVON

South Devon stream not to be confused with Hampshire Avon or Bristol Avon. Rises on Dartmoor and enters sea at Bigbury. Brown Trout, Sea Trout and Salmon.

Avon Fishing Association

Contact: Dr Paul Kenyon, 16 Kimberley Villas, Western Road, Ivybridge, PL21 9AS, 01752 893382, *Water:* 14.5 miles on the river Avon, *Species:* Salmon, Sea Trout and Brown Trout, *Permits:* From the above. No day tickets, *Charges:* £45 weekly, £65 fortnightly, £70 monthly. Plus a £2 donation to the N.A.S.T, *Season:* 15th March to 30th September. 30th November for Salmon only, *Methods:* Fly only except spinning below Silveridge Weir 1st October - 30th November.

Newhouse Fishery (River Avon)
Contact: Newhouse Farm, Moreleigh, Totnes, 01548 821426, kirsty.cook@btinternet.com, *Water:* 0.25 mile on the river Avon (also see entry under Stillwater Trout, Totnes, Devon), *Species:* Brown Trout, Sea Trout and Salmon, *Permits:* On site, *Charges:* £10 Brown Trout, £25 Salmon. Various tickets available, *Season:* As current E.A. Byelaws, *Methods:* As current E.A. Byelaws.

South West Rivers Association
Contact: Michael Charleston (secretary), The Gift House, Buckland Monachorum, Yelverton, PL20 7NA, 01822 853293, mwcharl@aol.com, *Water:* South West Rivers Association is the regional organisation of the river associations of Devon and Cornwall and is a consultative and campaigning body for the protection and improvement of south west rivers, their fish stocks and ecology.

AXE & TRIBUTARIES

This quiet meandering stream rises in the hills of west Dorset, runs along the boundary with Somerset before flowing past Axminster to the sea at Seaton. The Axe is a fertile river with good Trout fishing and a run of Salmon and Sea Trout. The two main tributaries, the Coly and Yarty, are also Trout streams and the Yarty has a good run of Sea Trout.

Axmouth Fishing
Contact: Seaton Chandlery, The Harbour, Axmouth, 01297 24774, tombuoys@aol.com, *Water:* Axmouth from lower end Pool below Coly-Axe confluence to Axmouth Bridge, *Species:* Mullet, Bass, Sea Trout, *Permits:* Seaton Chandlery, *Charges:* £5 Day Adult, £2.50 Child. £25 week Adult, £12.50 Child, *Methods:* Fishing from East Bank of Estuary Only.

Stillwaters (Axe)
Contact: Michael Ford, Lower Moorhayne Farm, Yarcombe, Nr Honiton, EX14 9BE, 01404 861284, info@land-own.demon.co.uk, *Water:* One Sea Trout rod on River Axe also 1 acre lake see entry under Stillwater Trout Honiton.

Taunton Fly Fishing Club
Contact: Mr G. Woollen, Graylings, Frog Lane, Combe St. Nicholas, Chard, TA20 3NX, 01460 65977, *Water:* Large sections Rivers Tone and Axe plus Otterhead Lakes, *Species:* Sea Trout, Brown Trout, *Permits:* No permits available, *Charges:* Prices on application, *Season:* 1st April - 15th October, *Methods:* Fly only.

BRAY

Nick Hart Fly Fishing (Bray)
Contact: Nick Hart, Exford View, 1 Chapel Street, Exford, Minehead, TA24 7PY, 01643 831101, 0797 1198559, nick@hartflyfishing.demon.co.uk, *Water:* 1 1/3 miles on river Bray. Many new bankside improvements creating new pools. (see also entries under Devon River Fishing - Torridge and Exe), *Species:* Brown Trout to 1lb, Sea Trout to 5lb, *Permits:* From Nick Hart Fly Fishing, *Charges:* £12 per day Brown Trout and Sea Trout (night fishing allowed), *Season:* 15 March - 30 September, *Methods:* Fly only. Catch & release of Wild Brown Trout compulsory. E.A. byelaws apply.

CLAW

Tetcott Angling Club (Claw)
Contact: Mr & Mrs J Miller, The Old Coach House, Tetcott, Holsworthy, EX22 6QZ, 01409 271300, *Water:* Approx half a mile of the river Claw, *Species:* Brown Trout, *Permits:* No day tickets - private club, *Season:* 16th March to 30th September. Daylight hours only, *Methods:* Artificial lures, fly, spinning, worm.

COLY

Higher Cownhayne Farm
Contact: Mrs Pady, Higher Cownhayne Farm, Cownhayne Lane, Colyton, EX24 6HD, 01297 552267, *Water:* Fishing on River Coly, *Species:* Brown & Sea Trout, *Charges:* On application, *Methods:* Fly fishing, no netting.

DART & TRIBUTARIES

Deep in the heart of lonely Dartmoor rise the East and West Dart. Between their separate sources and Dartmeet, where they join, these two streams and their tributaries are mainly owned by the Duchy of Cornwall and provide many miles of Salmon, Sea Trout and Trout fishing for visitors. The scenery is on the grand scale and the sense of freedom enjoyed when you know that you can fish away over miles and miles of river is seldom realised on this crowded island. This is a moorland fishery - swift flowing, boulder strewn, usually crystal clear. Below Dartmeet the river rushes through a spectacular wooded valley before breaking out of the moor near Buckfastleigh and flowing on to its estuary at Totnes. Although there are Brown Trout throughout the river, these middle and lower reaches are primarily Salmon and Sea Trout waters.

Buckfastleigh
Contact: South West Lakes Trust, Higher Coombepark, Lewdown, Okehampton, EX20 4QT, 01837 871565, info@swlakestrust.org.uk, *Water:* 1/4 mile on River Dart. Austins Bridge to Nursery Pool, *Species:* Salmon & Sea Trout, *Permits:* From South West Lakes Trust at above address, *Charges:* Season - £80. Limit of 16 rods, *Season:* 1st February - 30th September.

Dart Angling Association
Contact: D.H. Pakes - Hon. Secretary, Holly How, Plymouth Road, South Brent, TQ10 9HU, 01364 73640, *Water:* 9 miles on river Dart. (3.9 miles of main river open to visitors plus the tidal Totnes weir pool), *Species:* Salmon, Sea Trout, Brown Trout, *Permits:* All permits - Sea Trout Inn, Staverton Tel: 01803 762274, *Charges:* Membership details from secretary. Totnes weir pool £20 per day (only 1 day Salmon, 1 night Sea Trout ticket available). Buckfast (Austin's Bridge) - Littlehempston (left bank) only 2 per day (unless resident at the Sea Trout Inn), *Season:* Salmon 1st February - 30th September. Sea/Brown Trout 15th March - 30th September, *Methods:* Fly (some stretches fly only), spinning, prawn (below Staverton) see club regulations i.e. conservation measures in force.

Duchy Of Cornwall
Contact: Duchy Of Cornwall Office, Duchy Hotel, Princetown, Yelverton, PL20 6QF, 01822 890205, cgregory@duchyofcornwall.gov.uk, *Water:* East & West Dart Rivers and its tributaries down to Dartmeet, *Species:* Salmon and Trout, *Permits:* Charles Bingham Fishing Ltd, West Down, Warrens Cross, Whitchurch, Tavistock. The Old Post Office, Poundsgate, Newton Abbot. Two Bridges Hotel, Two Bridges, Princetown, Yelverton. The Post Office, Postbridge, Yelverton. Princetown Post Office, Princetown, Yelverton. Prince Hall Hotel, Two Bridges, Princetown, Yelverton. The Arundell Arms, Lifton. James Bowden & Sons, The Square, Chagford. Badger's Holt Ltd, Dartmeet, Princetown. Exeter Angling Centre, Smythen Street, Exeter. The Forest Inn Hexworthy, Poundsgate, Yelverton. Peter Collings, Huccaby's News, 33 Fore St, Buckfastleigh, *Charges:* Salmon Season: £125, Week £70, Day £20. Trout Season: £55, Week £15, Day £4, *Season:* Salmon: 1st February to 30th September. Trout: 15th March to 30th September, *Methods:* Fly only. Additional information on permit.

Hatchlands Trout Farm
Contact: Malcolm Davies, Greyshoot Lane, Rattery, South Brent, TQ10 9LL, 01364 73500, madavies@onetel.net.uk, *Water:* 600 yards, both banks of the river Harbourne (tributary of the Dart), *Species:* Brown Trout, *Charges:* On application, *Season:* See current E.A. Byelaws, *Methods:* Barbless hooks only.

Nurston Farm Fishery (River)
Contact: Mabin Family, Nurston Farm, Dean Prior, Buckfastleigh, TQ11 0NA, 01364 642285, *Water:* 3 miles River Dart (see entry under Stillwater Coarse, Buckfastleigh, Devon), *Charges:* On application.

Prince Hall Hotel
Contact: Mr Adam Southwell, Nr. Two Bridges, Dartmoor, PL20 6SA, 01822 890403, gamefish@princehall.co.uk, *Water:* Access to all Duchy water, *Species:* Wild Brown Trout 1.5lb, Sea Trout 6lb, Salmon 11lb, *Permits:* Duchy. EA Licences on sale 7 days a week at the hotel, *Charges:* Trout £5 per day. Salmon £22. Trout week £16. Salmon week £75, *Season:* March - September, *Methods:* Fly only.

Two Bridges Hotel
Contact: Two Bridges Hotel, Two Bridges, Dartmoor, PL20 6SW, 01822 890581, twobridges@warm-welcome-hotels.co.uk, *Water:* Stretch of 600yds double bank fishing, *Species:* Trout & Salmon, *Permits:* At hotel reception, *Charges:* See Duchy permit, *Season:* E.A. Byelaws apply.

DEER

Tetcott Angling Club (Deer)
Contact: Mr & Mrs J Miller, The Old Coach House, Tetcott, Holsworthy, EX22 6QZ, 01409 271300, *Water:* Approx one mile of the river Deer, *Species:* Brown Trout, *Permits:* No day tickets - private club, *Season:* 16th March to 30th September. Daylight hours only, *Methods:* Artificial lures, fly, spinning, worm.

ERME

A small Devon stream rising on Dartmoor and flowing south through Ivybridge to the sea. The Erme is probably best known for its Sea Trout, but there is also a run of Salmon and Brown Trout are present throughout its length.

EXE & TRIBUTARIES

The Exe rises high on Exmoor and flows through open moorland until it plunges into a steep wooded valley near Winsford. By the time Tiverton is reached the valley has widened and from here to the sea the Exe meanders through a broad pastoral vale until it flows into the estuary near Exeter and finally into the sea between Exmouth and Dawlish Warren. It is the longest river in the south west.

Throughout most of its length the Exe is a good Trout stream, the fast flowing, rocky upper reaches abounding in fish of modest average size, which increases as the river becomes larger and slower in its middle and lower reaches, where fish approaching a pound feature regularly in the daily catch. The Exe has a good run of Salmon and can produce big catches when the grilse arrive in summer. In the deep slow waters around Exeter there is a variety of coarse fish, as there is in the Exeter Ship Canal which parallels the river from Exeter to the estuary at Topsham.

The Exe only has a small run of Sea Trout, but Grayling are plentiful in the middle and lower reaches. The two main tributaries - the Barle and the Culm - could not be more different in character.

The Barle is a swift upland stream which rises high on Exmoor not far from the source of the Exe, and runs a parallel course, first through open moor and then through a picturesque wooded valley, before joining the parent river near Dulverton. It has good Trout fishing throughout and Salmon fishing on the lower reaches.

The Culm issues from the Blackdown Hills and in its upper reaches is a typical dry fly Trout stream, with good hatches of fly and free-rising fish. From Cullompton until it joins the Exe, the Culm becomes a coarse fishery, with the Dace in particular of good average size.

Bridge House Hotel
Contact: Brian Smith, Bridge House Hotel, Bampton, EX16 9NF, 01398 331298, *Water:* 1 Mile on River Exe, *Species:* Salmon, Trout and Grayling; (2000 Season: 12lb Salmon, 3lb Brown Trout), *Permits:* As above, *Charges:* Salmon £25 per day, Trout £15 per day, *Season:* March 15th - Sept 30th, *Methods:* Fly, occasional spinner.

Devon & UK Fly Fishing School (Exe)
Contact: Mr Roddy Rae, 6 Hescane Park, Cheriton Bishop, EX6 6SP, 01647 24643, 07786 834575, roddy.rae@btopenworld.com, *Water:* 3.5 miles of prime fishing on the river Exe divided into 3 beats, 4 rods per beat per day. Also 1 mile of river Taw and access to rivers Yeo, Creedy, Mole and Torridge, *Species:* Salmon, Brown Trout & Grayling on the Exe, *Permits:* Daily weekly and occasional season lets, *Charges:* Exe - £35 day, *Season:* Exe: 14th February - 30th September for Salmon. Brown Trout 15th March - 30th September, *Methods:* Fly & Spinner on Exe. All other waters fly only.

Exe Duck's Marsh (River Exe)
Contact: Exeter City Council, River & Canal Manager, Civic Centre, Exeter, EX1 1RP, 01392 274306, river.canal@exeter.gov.uk, *Water:* River Exe, left bank 1 mile downstream Salmonpool weir, *Species:* Salmon (Trout), *Permits:* River & Canal Office, Canal Basin, Haven Rd, Exeter, EX2 8DU. Angling Centre, Smythen Street, Exeter, *Charges:* Day tickets only: £6.00, *Season:* 14th February - 30th September; no night fishing, *Methods:* Permit restrictions & E.A. byelaw controls; only artificial fly & lures and all fish returned before June 16th.

Exe Valley Fishery (River Exe)
Contact: Andrew Maund, Exebridge, Dulverton, TA22 9AY, 01398 323328, info@exevalleyfishery.co.uk, *Water:* Half a mile of single bank, *Species:* Salmon Trout and Grayling, *Permits:* Day Tickets from Exe Valley Fishery, *Charges:* Contact for details, *Season:* EA Byelaws apply, *Methods:* Trout and Grayling fly only. Salmon fly or spinner.

Exeter & District Angling Association (River Creedy)
Contact: Terry Reed (Hon. Sec.), PO Box 194, Exeter, EX2 7WG, 07970 483913, exeteranglingassociation@yahoo.co.uk, *Water:* Cowley Bridge; just a short walk from the Exe, *Species:* Roach, Dace, Gudgeon, *Permits:* Exeter Angling Centre, Smythen Street (Off Market Street Exeter). Bridge Cafe, Bridge Road, Exeter. Exmouth Tackle & Sport, The Strand, Exmouth. Tackle Trader, Wharf Road, Newton Abbot. Exe Valley Angling, West Exe South, Tiverton, *Charges:* £27 Adults, £2 for Juniors (annual). Day and week tickets depending on water, ask at agent, *Season:* Different on each water. Details in association handbook or from agents, *Methods:* Different restrictions on each water. Details in association handbook.

Exeter & District Angling Association (River Culm)
Contact: Terry Reed (Hon. Sec.), PO Box 194, Exeter, EX2 7WG, 07970 483913, exeteranglingassociation@yahoo.co.uk, *Water:* Stoke Canon, Paddleford Pool, Killerton and Beare Gate; Smaller faster flowing river, *Species:* Superb catches of Chub, Roach and Dace possible throughout. An excellent, yet relatively easy Pike water, *Permits:* Exeter Angling Centre, Smythen Street (Off Market Street Exeter). Bridge Cafe, Bridge Road, Exeter. Exmouth Tackle & Sport, The Strand, Exmouth. Tackle Trader, Wharf Road, Newton Abbot. Exe Valley Angling, West Exe South, Tiverton, *Charges:* £27 Adults, £2 for Juniors (annual). Day and week tickets depending on water, ask at agent, *Season:* Different on each water. Details in association handbook or from agents, *Methods:* Different restrictions on each water. Details in association handbook.

Exeter & District Angling Association (River Exe)
Contact: Terry Reed (Hon. Sec.), PO Box 194, Exeter, EX2 7WG, 07970 483913, exeteranglingassociation@yahoo.co.uk, *Water:* Tidal stretch of Exe at Countess Wear; big catches of Mullet, Dace and Bream. Non tidal stretch at Weirfield; big bags of Bream and Carp from 15 to 20lb. Shillhay runs nearly through the City centre; can produce big bags of Bream and Roach. Exwick is a faster flowing section adjacent to St David's railway section; good nets of quality Roach and Dace, fishes well in the autumn. Cowley Bridge is a relatively under fished stretch; good nets of Roach and Dace along the whole length. Oakhay Barton; fewer fish but good size and high quality fish, *Species:* Roach, Dace, Bream, Chub, Perch, Carp, Mullet, *Permits:* Exeter Angling Centre, Smythen Street (Off Market Street Exeter). Bridge Cafe, Bridge Road, Exeter. Exmouth Tackle & Sport, The Strand, Exmouth. Tackle Trader, Wharf Road, Newton Abbot. Exe Valley Angling, West Exe South, Tiverton, *Charges:* £27 Adults, £2 for Juniors (annual). Day and week tickets depending on water, ask at agent, *Season:* Different on each water. Details in association handbook or from agents, *Methods:* Different restrictions on each water. Details in association handbook.

River Exe & Tributaries Association
Contact: Ian Cook, 01392 254573, *Water:* Association to protect and enhance the natural Trout & Salmon fisheries of the River Exe, *Permits:* No day tickets to fish available.

River Exe (Exeter)
Contact: Exeter City Council, River & Canal Manager, Civic Centre, Exeter, EX1 1RP, 01392 274306, river.canal@exeter.gov.uk, *Water:* River Exe, 10 beats between Head Weir & Countess Wear, *Species:* Salmon (Trout), *Permits:* Annual, available by post with payment and photograph to Exeter City Council, Community & Enviromental Directorate, Civic Centre, Exeter. EX1 1RQ, *Charges:* £57.50, limited permits, *Season:* 14th Feb - 30th Sept, *Methods:* Permit restrictions and E.A. Byelaws apply. Only artificial fly & lures. All fish returned before Jun 16th.

Robert Jones Fly Fishing (Exe)
Contact: The Estate Office, Courtlands, Exmouth, EX8 3NZ, 07020 902090, 07970 797770, robertjones@eclipse.co.uk, *Water:* River Exe. Private and Hotel water, *Species:* Brown Trout, Sea Trout and Salmon, *Permits:* Day permits. E.A. Beginners Licence agent, *Charges:* From £25 per day, *Season:* 15th Mar - 30th Sept, *Methods:* Fly and spinner.

Tiverton & District Angling Club (River Culm)
Contact: Exe Valley Angling, 19 Westexe South, Tiverton, EX16 5DQ, 01884 242275, *Water:* 0.75 miles river Culm at Stoke Cannon. Various stretches on several rivers in Somerset. See also entry under stillwater coarse, Tiverton, *Species:* Roach, Dace, Chub, Perch, Pike and Eels. Salmon and Trout in season, *Permits:* Please ring Exe Valley for details. Also available from: Exeter Angling Centre, Enterprise Angling Taunton, Topp Tackle Taunton & Minnows Caravan Park - beside Grand Western Canal, *Charges:* Senior: Day £4, Annual £20. Conc: Junior & OAP Day £2.50, Annual £8, *Season:* Coarse: closed 15th Mar to 16th Jun. Trout: open from 15th Mar to 30th Sept. Salmon: open 14th Feb to 30th Sept, *Methods:* Canal Methods: Any. Restrictions: Fish from permanent pegs, no night fishing, no cars on bank, no digging of banks or excessive clearance of vegatation. Lakeside Methods: Any. Restrictions: No night fishing, boilies, Trout pellets or nuts, one rod only, fishing from permanent pegs, no dogs, nets to be dipped. Ring Exe Valley Angling for full details.

Tiverton Fly Fishing Association
Contact: Exe Valley Angling, 19 Westexe South, Tiverton, EX16 5DQ, 01884 242275, *Water:* 3.5 Miles on River Exe, *Species:* Trout & Grayling, *Permits:* Exe Valley Angling: 01884 242275, *Charges:* Senior £15, Conc. £4, Guests £5, *Season:* 15th Mar - 30th Sept, *Methods:* Fly only.

LYN

Chalk Water, Weir Water, Oare Water, Badgeworthy Water - these are the streams that tumble down from the romantic Doone Country of Exmoor and join to form the East Lyn, which cascades through the spectacular wooded ravine of the National Trust's Watersmeet Estate. The main river has good runs of Salmon and Sea Trout, and wild Brown Trout teem on the Lyn and the tributary streams.

Cloud Farm Fishing
Contact: Cloud Farm, Oare, Lynton, 01598 741278, holiday@doonevalley.co.uk, *Water:* Badgeworthy Water, tributary of the Lyn - 0.75 miles single bank fishing, *Species:* Salmon and Brown Trout, *Charges:* From £5 per day.

Environment Agency - Watersmeet and Glenthorne
Contact: 01392 444000, *Water:* The fishery is in two parts: The Watersmeet Fishery, leased by the Agency from the National Trust - Tors Road, Lynmouth to Woodside Bridge, right bank only; Woodside Bridge to Watersmeet both banks; upstream of Watersmeet right bank only to Rockford. The Glenhorne Fishery - right bank only upstream of Rockford to 300 yards downstream of Brendon Road Bridge. Half a mile of Trout fishing is available on the Hoaroak Water between Hillsford Bridge and Watersmeet; this is specifically for children, who only require a Trout rod licence when fishing this particular stretch if they are aged 12 years or over. WARNING: Anglers are advised that parts of the river are exceptionally steep and rocky and can be dangerous. River Lyn information line - 01398 371119.
The Glenthorne Fishery - right bank only upstream of Rockford to 300 yards downstream of Brendon Road Bridge. Half a mile of Trout fishing is available on the Hoaroak Water between Hillsford Bridge and Watersmeet; this is specifically for children, who only require a Trout rod licence when fishing this particular stretch if they are aged 12 years or over. WARNING: Anglers are advised that parts of the river are exceptionally steep and

rocky and can be dangerous. River Lyn information line - 01398 371119, *Permits:* Mr & Mrs Rigby, Brendon House Hotel, Brendon. Tourist Information Centre, Town Hall, Lynton; Mrs J. Fennell, Variety Sports, 23 Broad Street, Ilfracombe; Mrs Topp, Topp Tackle, 63 Station Road, Taunton. Porlock Visitor Centre, West End, High Street, Porlock. Rockford Inn, Brendon, Lynton, N.Devon, *Charges*: Salmon & Sea Trout, season withdrawn for conservation reasons, week £35, day £13.50, evening (8 pm to 2 am) £4; Brown Trout, season £27.50, week £10, day £3. Bag Limits: 2 Salmon, 4 Sea Trout, 8 Brown Trout per day. 2 Salmon week, 6 Salmon per season, *Season*: Salmon 1st March - 30th September; Sea Trout & Trout 15th March - 30th September. Fishing permitted 8 am to sunset, except from 1st June - 30th September when fishing by traditional fly fishing methods is permitted until 2 am between Tors Road & Rockford, *Methods:* Brown Trout, fly only. Salmon, no shrimp or prawn. Artificial fly or lure only before 16th June. Catch and release of all salmon prior to 16th June. No weight may be used whilst fly fishing. The weight used for worm fishing and spinning must be lead free and not weigh more than 0.5 ounce and must be attached at least 18 inches from the hook.

Southernwood Farm
Contact: John Ralph, Southernwood Farm, Brendon, EX35 6NU, 01598 741174, southernwoodfarm@totalise.co.uk, *Water:* 900 metres on the East Lyn river, 6 named pools for a maximum of 3 anglers, *Species:* Salmon, Sea Trout and Brown Trout, *Permits:* Day and Weekly, *Charges:* Day tickets at £12 per day for Salmon and Sea Trout. £5 per day for Brown Trout. Weekly tickets at £35 and £18, *Season:* June 16th to October 31st (catch and return pre - June 16th), *Methods:* Any within Environment Agency restrictions.

OTTER

The Otter springs to life in the Blackdown Hills and flows through a broad fertile valley to join the sea near the little resort of Budleigh Salterton. This is primarily a Brown Trout stream noted for its dry fly fishing for Trout of good average weight. There is also an improving run of Sea Trout.

River Otter Association
Contact: Alan Knights (Secretary), Cottarson Farm, Awliscombe, Honiton, EX14 3NR, 01404 42318, *Water:* Comprises riparian owners, anglers and conservationists concerned with the preservation of the total ecology of the river Otter, *Species:* Brown Trout, Sea Trout.

Clinton Devon Estates
Contact: Water: 3.4 mile single bank fishing on the River Otter from Clamour Bridge (footpath below Otterton) to White Bridge near Budleigh Salterton, *Species:* Brown Trout, *Charges:* Free to EA rod licence holders, *Season:* 1st April to 30th September.

Deer Park Hotel
Contact: Reception, Deer Park Hotel, Weston, Nr Honiton, EX14 3PG, 01404 41266, admin@deerparkcountryhotel.com, *Water:* 6 miles on River Otter, *Species:* Brown Trout, *Permits:* From reception desk at hotel, *Charges:* £30 per day. Season permits available. Prices on application, *Season:* 15th March - 30th September, *Methods:* Dry Fly only.

Otter Falls (River)
Contact: John or Carol, New Road, Upottery, Nr Honiton, EX14 9QB, 01404 861634, hols@otterfalls.fsnet.co.uk, *Water:* 400 metre section of River Otter (see entry Stillwater Trout, Honiton), *Species:* Brown Trout, *Charges:* £10 per session, *Season:* Booking only, 8am to 1 hour after sunset, *Methods:* On application.

Robert Jones Fly Fishing (Otter)
Contact: The Estate Office, Courtlands, Exmouth, EX8 3NZ, 07020 902090, 07970 797770, robertjones@eclipse.co.uk, *Water:* River Otter. Private and Hotel water, *Species:* Brown Trout and Sea Trout, *Permits:* Day permits. E.A. Beginners Licence agent, *Charges:* £25 per day, *Season:* 15th March - 30th September, *Methods:* Fly only.

PLYM

A short stream rising on Dartmoor and running into Plymouth Sound. Trout fishing on the Plym and its tributary the Meavy, with some Sea Trout on the lower reaches and a late run of Salmon.

Plymouth & Dist Freshwater Angling Assoc. (Plym)
Contact: Mr D.L.Owen, 39 Burnett Road, Crownhill, Plymouth, PL6 5BH, 01752 705033, douglas@burnettrd.freeserve.co.uk, *Water:* 1 mile on River Plym, 1.5 miles on River Tavy, *Species:* Salmon, Sea Trout, Brown Trout, *Permits:* Snowbee, Drakes Court, Langage Business Park, Plymouth. D.K.Sports/Osborne and Cragg, 37 Bretonside, Plymouth, *Charges:* £10 a day Mon to Fri up to 30th Sept incl.; £15 a day Mon to Fri from 1st Oct to 30th Nov. To join the association, contact secretary. Annual subscription is about £105, *Season:* Plym: Apr - 15th Dec; Tavy: Mar - 14th Oct, *Methods:* Artificial baits only.

Plymouth Command Angling Association (River)
Contact: Mr Vic Barnett Hon.Sec, 5 Weir Close, Mainstone, Plymouth, PL6 8SD, 01752 708206, victor.barnett@talk21.com, *Water:* Fishing rights on the Plym, Tavy and Walkham plus a small private pond near Ivybridge. Access to rivers for serving members only, *Species:* Salmon, Sea Trout and Trout, *Permits:* Membership is open to all serving members of HM Forces. Associate membership is also open to ex-serving members of HM Forces, no matter when the time was served, *Charges:* Costs for full membership or associate membership are available on application or enquiry at the above contact, *Season:* Plym, Tavy and Walkham as per Environment Agency Byelaws.

Tavy,Walkham & Plym Fishing Club (Plym)
Contact: John Soul, Trevenevow, Crapstone Road, Yelverton, PL20 6BT, 01822 854923, johnsoul@globalnet.co.uk, *Water:* See entry under Tavy, *Species:* Salmon, Sea Trout and Brown Trout, *Permits:* From: DK Sports, Barbican, Plymouth. Moorland Garage, Yelverton. Tavistock Trout Fishery, Mount Tavy, Tavistock, *Charges:* Season Tickets: Salmon £110. Sea Trout £110. Brown Trout £45. Day Tickets available, *Season:* As E.A. byelaws. No day tickets after 30 September, *Methods:* No worm, prawn or shrimp fishing. Complete rules are issued with permit. Full returns must be made to the club secretary as a condition of purchase.

TAMAR

The Tamar rises near the north coast, and for most of its course forms the boundary between Devon and Cornwall. It is always a lowland stream flowing through farmland and this fact is reflected in the size of its Trout which have a larger average size than the acid moorland streams. Around Launceston, the Tamar is joined by five tributaries - Ottery, Carey, Wolf, Thrushel and Lyd - which offer good Trout fishing, as does the Inny which enters a few miles downstream. There is a good run of Salmon and Sea Trout, the latter being particularly numerous on the Lyd. There are also Grayling in places.

Arundell Arms
Contact: Mrs Anne Voss-Bark, Lifton, PL16 0AA, 01566 784666, reservations@arundellarms.com, *Water:* 20 miles of private fishing on Rivers Tamar, Lyd, Carey, Thrushel, Wolf and Ottery. Also 3 acre private lake stocked with Rainbow and Brown Trout, *Species:* Rivers: Salmon, Sea Trout and Brown Trout. Lake: Rainbow & Brown Trout, *Permits:* Arundell Arms, *Charges:* Trout £20. Salmon & Sea Trout £20 to £25. Lake £24, *Season:* Salmon March 1st to October 14th. Trout and Sea Trout March 15th to September 30th. Lake open all year, *Methods:* Fly and spinner for Salmon (1 fish limit per day after June 16 then catch and release). Fly only for Trout and Sea Trout.

Endsleigh Fishing Club
Contact: M.D.S. Healy, Endsleigh House Hotel, Milton Abbot, Tavistock, PL19 0PQ, 0207 6101982, mdsh@ukonline.co.uk, *Water:* 12 miles double bank River Tamar, *Species:* Salmon maximum 23lb & Sea Trout maximum 9lb, *Permits:* EA licences sold at the hotel, *Charges:* Per rod per full day all species, £20 March - April; £25 May to June 15th inclusive; £34 June16th to August 31st; £54 1st September - October. £12 5pm - midnight April - August inclusive Sea Trout only, *Season:* March 27th - October 8th 2003 incl, *Methods:* Fly. Spinning only under certain conditions.

TAVY

A Salmon and Sea Trout river which rises high on Dartmoor and flows through Tavistock to its junction with the Tamar estuary north of Plymouth. There is moorland Brown Trout on the upper reaches and on the Walkham, its main tributary.

Plymouth & Dist Freshwater Angling Assoc (Tavy)
Contact: Mr D.L. Owen, 39 Burnett Road, Crownhill, Plymouth, PL6 5BH, 01752 705033, douglas@burnettrd.freeserve.co.uk, *Water:* River Tavy above Tavistock, *Species:* Salmon, Sea Trout and Brown Trout, *Charges:* Tavy fishing is available to members of the association. Contact the secretary for membership details. See entry under River Plym, *Season:* 1st March to 14th October, *Methods:* Artificial baits only.

Tavy,Walkham & Plym Fishing Club (Tavy)
Contact: John Soul, Trevenevow, Crapstone Road, Yelverton, PL20 6BT, 01822 854923, johnsoul@globalnet.co.uk, *Water:* Rivers Tavy, Walkham, Plym, Meavy, *Species:* Brown Trout, Salmon, Sea Trout, *Permits:* Only through D.K.Sports, Barbican, Plymouth. Moorland Garage, Yelverton. Tavistock Trout Fishery, Tavistock, *Charges:* Season Trout £45, Season Salmon / Sea trout £110, plus other permits. Please phone for details, *Season:* See Environment Agency season dates. Please note, no day tickets after 30th September, *Methods:* No worm, prawn, shrimp on club permit waters. Please note club rules on back of permit including the dates by which accurate returns must be made as a condition of taking a permit.

TAW

The Taw is a noted Salmon and Sea Trout river that rises high on Dartmoor and then flows through the rolling farmland of North Devon to its estuary at Barnstaple. Its main tributary, the Mole, also has good Salmon and Sea Trout fishing, and the Moles own tributary, the Bray, is a good little Trout stream.

Angling 2000 (Taw)
Contact: Simon Evans, Westcountry Rivers Trust, Fore Street, Lifton, PL16 0AA, 01566 784488, simon@wrt.org.uk, *Water:* Beats on the Little Dart. Flexible permits fishing for Trout, *Species:* Trout, Sea Trout and occasional Salmon, *Permits:* From the above, *Charges:* £5 to £10 per day, *Season:* 1 March to 30 September, *Methods:* Fly only.

Barnstaple & District Angling Association (River)
Contact: S.R. Tomms (Secretary), Barnstaple & District Angling Association, Upcott Farm, Brayford, EX32 7QA, 01598 710857, *Water:* Approx 3 miles on the river Taw plus a stretch on the river Yeo. See also under Stillwater coarse, Barnstaple, *Species:* Salmon, Sea Trout, Brown Trout, Rainbows, *Permits:* No day tickets. Fishing by membership only. Details from the Secretary above or Kingfisher Tackle Shop, Barnstaple Tel. 01271 344919, *Charges:* Membership £30, Juniors £10, *Season & Methods:* Current EA byelaws apply.

Crediton Fly Fishing Club (Taw)
Contact: info@fly-fishing-club.co.uk, *Water:* See entry under Yeo. 1.5 miles River Taw, *Charges:* £11 surcharge. Membership £67. Joining fee £20.

Devon & UK Fly Fishing School (Taw)
Contact: Mr Roddy Rae, 6 Hescane Park, Cheriton Bishop, EX6 6SP, 01647 24643, 07786 834575, roddy.rae@btopenworld.com, *Water:* 1 mile of river Taw also 3.5 miles of prime fishing on the river Exe divided into 3 beats, 4 rods per beat per day and access to rivers Yeo, Creedy, Mole and Torridge, *Species:* Salmon, Sea Trout & Brown Trout on River Taw, *Permits:* Daily weekly and occasional season lets, *Charges:* Taw - £30 per day, *Season:* Exe: 14th Feb - 30th Sept for Salmon. Brown Trout 15th Mar - 30th Sept, *Methods:* Fly & Spinner on Exe. All other waters fly only.

Eggesford Country Hotel
Contact: Eggesford, Chulmleigh, EX18 7JZ, 01769 580345, relax@eggesfordhotel.co.uk, *Water:* Fishing on Rivers Taw & Little Dart, *Species:* Prime Salmon, Sea Trout & Brown Trout, *Charges:* Prime Salmon & Sea Trout £30/day (24 hrs), Brown Trout £20/day. Salmon, Trout and Sea Trout full week permit (7 days) £100, *Season:* 1st Mar - 30th Sept, *Methods:* Spinning March only. Rest of season fly only.

Highbullen Hotel
Contact: Chris Taylor, Chittlehamholt, Umberleigh, EX37 9HD, 01769 540561, info@highbullen.co.uk, *Water:* 3 miles River Mole & over 2 miles River Taw, *Species:* Salmon 24.5lb (2000), Sea Trout 12lb (1998) & Brown Trout 2lb (2002), *Permits:* From Highbullen Hotel, *Charges:* Brown Trout £15 per rod day. Salmon and Sea Trout from £25 per rod to £40 per day, *Season:* Salmon 1st March - 30th Sept, Brown and Sea Trout 15th Mar - 30th Sept, *Methods:* Spinner Mar. Fly Mar - Sept. Local byelaw, Aug and Sept all Salmon over 70cm have to be returned.

Nick Hart Fly Fishing (Taw)
Contact: Nick Hart, Exford View, 1 Chapel Street, Exford, Minehead, TA24 7PY, 01643 831101, 0797 1198559, nick@hartflyfishing.demon.co.uk, *Water:* 1 mile on Taw available Fridays for 2 rods (see also entries under Torridge, Bray and Exe), *Species:* Salmon (to double figures), Sea Trout (excellent numbers), *Permits:* From Nick Hart Fly Fishing, *Charges:* £25 per day, 2 rods available, *Season:* 1st March - 30th September, *Methods:* Fly only. E.A. byelaws apply.

Rising Sun Inn
Contact: Malcolm & Andrew Hogg, Rising Sun Inn, Umberleigh, Nr Barnstaple, EX37 9DU, 01769 560447, risingsuninn@btinternet.com, *Water:* Access arranged (for residents only) to approx 6 miles of Taw fishing, *Species:* Sea Trout 11.5lb, Brown Trout, Salmon 23lb. A reasonable 2002 but 2003 shows a lot of promise!, *Permits:* Post Office, Umberleigh for licence, *Charges:* £35 to £45, *Season:* Salmon 1st March - 30th Sept, Sea/Brown Trout 15th March - 30th Sept, *Methods:* As per E.A. rules.

Taw Fishing Club
Contact: Mr J.D.V. Michie, Hillside Farm, Bratton Clovelly, Okehampton, EX20 4JD, 01837 871156, *Water:* 3.25 miles on River Taw between Brushford and Hawkridge bridges, *Species:* Brown Trout, Sea Trout and Salmon, *Permits:* Fishing by membership of club only, *Charges:* £60 season, *Season:* 15th March to 30th September, *Methods:* Fly only, barbless encouraged.

The Rising Sun Water
Contact: David Judge, No. 1 Telegraph Street, London, EC2R 7AR, 0207 2569013, 07736 628971, hayrish@easynet.co.uk, *Water:* 2 1/4 miles (4 beats) on River Taw. Fishing from the favoured left bank. Please call for brochure, *Species:* Salmon, Brown Trout & Sea Trout, *Permits:* Umberleigh Post Office, *Charges:* £40 (24 hrs) per beat - ex vat. £625 for season rod (1 beat per week) - ex vat, *Season:* Salmon - 1st March to 30th September. Sea & Brown Trout - 15th March to 30th September, *Methods:* Spinning March only. Rest of season, fly only.

Tremayne Water
Contact: J.G. Smith, 0208 9958109, gilbert.smith@virgin.net, *Water:* 1.5 miles single & double bank fishing on the upper Taw and Little Dart, *Species:* Salmon, Sea Trout, *Charges:* Limited season rods only, *Season:* E.A. Byelaws apply, *Methods:* E.A. Byelaws apply.

TEIGN

The Teign has two sources high up on Dartmoor which form the North and South Teign but the two branches of the Teign quickly leave the moor to join west of Chagford while still very small streams. Between Chagford and Steps Bridge the river runs through a dramatic wooded gorge which is at its most spectacular at Fingle Bridge, a popular beauty spot. All along the Teign the Spring fisherman is greeted by myriads of daffodils, which are at their most numerous around Clifford Bridge. The upper Teign offers good fishing for wild Trout and Sea Trout, with Salmon fishing in suitable conditions from April to the end of the season. Much of the upper river is controlled by the Upper Teign Fishing Association. From just south of the Moretonhampstead - Exeter road to the estuary at Newton Abbot. the Teign is mostly controlled by the Lower Teign Fishing Association. This water has plenty of Brown Trout but is essentially a Sea Trout and Salmon fishery.

Lower Teign Fishing Association
Contact: Mr R Waters (Secretary), 121 Topsham Road, Exeter, EX20 4RE, 01392 251928, *Water:* 14 miles River Teign, *Species:* Salmon, Sea Trout, *Permits:* 3 Beats with 3 tickets on each (beat 3 only available between 1st May and 31st August). One junior ticket per beat per day available, *Charges:* £20 per day (24 hour period - night-time Sea Trout fishing). Beat 3 - September £25 per day. Available from Tackle Trader, Newton Abbot. 01626 331613, *Season:* 1st Febuary - 30th September, *Methods:* Spinning, fly (fly only at night), no worming or maggots.

Mill End Hotel
Contact: Sandy Park, Chagford, TQ13 8JN, 01647433106, millendhotel@talk21.com, *Water:* 3 miles plus access to a further 8 miles, *Species:* Brown Trout, Salmon and Sea Trout, *Permits:* At Hotel, *Charges:* £5 per day.

River Teign Riparian Owners Association
Contact: Mr Clive Tonkins, WBB Minerals, Lovering Lodge, East Gold Works, Kingsteignton Rd, Newton Abbot, TQ12 2PA, 01626 322331, *Water:* Riparian Owners Association representing interest of owners of fishing waters on River Teign, *Permits:* No day tickets available through the association.

Robert Jones Fly Fishing (Teign)
Contact: The Estate Office, Courtlands, Exmouth, EX8 3NZ, 07020 902090, 07970 797770, robertjones@eclipse.co.uk, *Water:* River Teign. Private and Hotel water, *Species:* Brown Trout, Sea Trout and Salmon, *Permits:* Day permits. E.A. Beginners Licence agent, *Charges:* From £25 per day, *Season:* 15th March - 30th September, *Methods:* Fly and spinner.

Upper Teign Fishing Association
Contact: Roddy Rae, 6 Hescane Park, Cheriton Bishop, EX6 6SP, 01647 24643, enquiries@upper-teign-fishing.org.uk, *Water:* Approx 8 miles on upper Teign, *Species:* Brown Trout to 1lb 4oz, Sea Trout to 8lb & Salmon to 18lb, *Permits:* From: Fingle Bridge Inn, Drewsteignton (01647 281287). Drewsteignton Post Office. Bowdens, Chagford. Abbott Angling, Newton Abbot (01626 200198). Mill End Hotel, Sandy Park, Chagford (01647 432282). Clifford Bridge Caravan Park (01647 24226). Exeter Angling Centre (01392 436404). Orvis, Exeter (01392 272599) Post Office & General Stores, Cheriton Bishop. All anglers must be in possession of a current Environment Agency licence. *Charges:* Ordinary Member - Annual Subscription £153. Full season for Salmon, Sea Trout & Brown Trout. Trout Member - Annual subscription £56. Full season for Brown Trout. Temporary Members' Tickets - Salmon & Sea Trout £15 per day (6 ticket limit per day from Anglers Rest plus 4 ticket limit - Salmon and Sea Trout from Drewsteignton Post Office). Sea Trout £7 per day (4 ticket limit per day from Bowdens, Chagford). Membership Enquiries to Secretary. Brown Trout Adult season £40, Juvenile (under 16) £15. Week £17.50. Juvenile £7. Day £5. Juvenile £2.50, *Season:* Brown Trout: March 15th - September 30th. Sea Trout: March 15th - September 30th. Salmon: February 1st - September 30th.

TORRIDGE

Throughout its length the Torridge flows through the rolling farmland of North Devon. It rises close to the coast near the Cornish border and swings in a great arc before flowing into the estuary that it shares with the Taw. The middle and lower reaches are best known for their Salmon and Sea Trout, but can offer surprisingly good Trout fishing.
The upper reaches and its tributaries, the Waldon and Lew, offer plenty of opportunities for Brown Trout fishing.

Angling 2000 (Torridge)
Contact: Simon Evans, Westcountry Rivers Trust, Fore Street, Lifton, PL16 0AA, 01566 784488, simon@wrt.org.uk, *Water:* Beats on the Walden, Lew, Okement & Torridge. Flexible day permits. New beats for 2003, *Species:* Trout, Salmon and Sea Trout, *Permits:* From the above, *Charges:* £5 to £12.50 per day, *Season:* 1 March to 30 September, *Methods:* Fly only after 31st March.

Clinton Arms
Contact: Wendy, Clinton Arms, Frithelstock, Torrington, EX38 8JH, 01805 623279, wendy@clintonarms.com, *Water:* Approx 1.5 mile of double bank on River Torridge (left hand bank only last 200yds), *Species:* Brown Trout, Sea Trout, Salmon, *Permits:* The Clinton Arms on 01805 623279, *Charges:* £20/day/rod, *Season:* March to September.

Gortleigh Fishing
Contact: Gortleigh Farm, Sheepwash, Beaworthy, EX21 5HU, 01409 231291, trace.gortleigh@btclick.com, *Water:* 1.5 miles double bank fishing, *Species:* Brown Trout, Sea Trout and occasional Salmon, *Charges:* From Farmhouse by prior arrangement. Please phone first, *Season:* E.A. Byelaws apply, *Methods:* No dogs.

Half Moon Inn
Contact: Half Moon Inn, Sheepwash, Beaworthy, EX21 5NE, (01409) 231376, lee@halfmoon.demon.co.uk, *Water:* 12 miles river Torridge, 3 x 2 acre lakes, *Species:* River: Sea, Brown & Wild Brown Trout, Salmon; Lakes: Rainbow Trout 2-3lb, *Permits:* Day tickets for residents & non-residents, *Charges:* Sea Trout & Salmon: £17.50, Brown Trout: 3 - fish £10, Lakes: 2 - fish £10, 4 - fish £15, *Season:* Mid March - 30th September, *Methods:* Dry & Wet Fly only, Spinning in March.

Little Warham Fishery
Contact: Group Captain P. Norton-Smith, Little Warham House, Beaford, Winkleigh, EX19 8AB, 01805 603317, fishyns@aol.com, *Water:* 2 miles of River Torridge, *Species:* Salmon, Sea Trout, Brown Trout, *Permits:* As above, *Charges:* £20/day/rod, all species, *Season:* March 1st - September 30th, *Methods:* Fly only.

Mill Leat (River Fishing)
Contact: Mr Birkett, Thornbury, Holsworthy, EX22 7AY, 01409 261426, cottages@mill-leat.fsnet.co.uk, *Water:* Half mile of single bank on the Waldon (tributary of the Torridge), *Species:* Brown Trout & Coarse fish, *Charges:* £5 to fish the river, *Season:* E.A. Byelaws apply, *Methods:* E.A. Byelaws apply.

Nick Hart Fly Fishing (Torridge)
Contact: Nick Hart, Exford View, 1 Chapel Street, Exford, Minehead, TA24 7PY, 01643 831101, 07971 198559, nick@hartflyfishing.demon.co.uk, *Water:* Approx 0.5 mile single bank, superb tidal stretch of Sea Trout fishing, *Species:* Sea Trout & occasional Salmon, *Charges:* £20 per day. Night fishing by arrangement, *Season:* 15th March - 30th September, *Methods:* Fly only, E.A. byelaws apply.

South Hay Fishery (Torridge)
Contact: Gill and Reg Stone, South Barn Farm, South Hay, Shebbear, Beaworthy, 01409 281857, *Water:* See entry under Stillwater Trout, Beaworthy. 2 miles on Torridge.

Torridge Fishery Association
Contact: Charles Inniss, Beeches, East Street, Sheepwash, Beaworthy, EX21 5NL, 01409 231237, charles.inniss@btopenworld.com, *Water:* An association of riparian owners and Torridge fishermen, whose aim is to secure and maintain the well being of the river and its ecology. Several day permits available, please phone for details, *Species:* Salmon to 15lb. Sea Trout to 8lb. Brown Trout to 1lb, *Permits:* Half Moon Inn, Sheepwash, Beaworthy, Devon 01409 231376. Group P. Norton-Smith, Little Warham, Beaford, Winkleigh, Devon 01805 603317, *Charges:* Salmon and Sea Trout from £15 to £20 daily. Brown Trout from £5 to £10 daily, *Season:* March 1st to September 30th, *Methods:* Fly Only.

YEALM

Upper Yealm Fishery
Contact: Snowbee U.K. Ltd, Drakes Court, Langage Business Park, Plymouth, PL7 5JY, 01752 334933, flyfish@snowbee.co.uk, *Water:* 1 mile both banks River Yealm, *Species:* Sea Trout, Brown Trout (Stocked), Salmon, *Permits:* Snowbee U.K. Ltd, *Charges:* Full membership £100, Half rod £50, day ticket (All species) £10, *Season:* Brown Trout & Sea Trout 15th March - 30th Sept, Salmon 1st April - 15th December, *Methods:* Fly fishing & spinning.

YEO

Crediton Fly Fishing Club (Yeo)
Contact: David Pope, 21 Creedy Road, Crediton, EX17 1EW, 01363 773557, info@fly-fishing-club.co.uk, *Water:* 5 miles Rivers Yeo & Creedy, 1.5 miles River Taw, *Species:* Brown Trout, Sea Trout & Salmon, *Permits:* 01363-773557, *Charges:* Weekly (5 days) £20, Season £67, Juniors £10. Two day weekend (Sat-Sun) £20. Joining fee £20, *Season:* Environment Agency Season, *Methods:* Fly only.

DEVON Stillwater Coarse

AXMINSTER

Summerleaze Pond
Contact: Summerleaze Farm, Kilmington, Axminster, EX13 7RA, 01297 32390, *Water:* 1 coarse fishing lake, *Species:* Carp, Roach, Perch. Best Carp 20lbs, *Charges:* On site, £3 adults, £1.50 children under 16, *Season:* Open all year, dawn to dusk, *Methods:* Please ask at fishery.

BAMPTON

Four Ponds
Contact: Mr Valentine, Bowdens Lane, Shillingford, Bampton, EX16 9BU, 01398 331169, fredvalentine@yahoo.co.uk, *Water:* 2 ponds totalling approx 1.5 acres, *Species:* Carp to 20lb, Roach, Rudd, Tench to 5lb, Perch to 4lb, *Permits:* At pond, *Charges:* £4/day, *Season:* Open all year, 6am to dusk, *Methods:* Barbless hooks only, all children under 12 must be accompanied by an adult, no keepnets.

BARNSTAPLE

Barnstaple & District A. A. (Coarse Ponds)

Contact: S.R. Tomms (Secretary), Barnstaple & District Angling Association, Upcott Farm, Brayford, EX32 7QA, 01598 710857, *Water:* 4 mixed coarse fishing ponds in the Barnstaple area ranging from 0.5 acres to 2 acres, *Species:* Roach, Rudd, Carp, Perch, Bream, Tench and Eels, *Permits:* Members only. Details from the secretary or Kingfisher Tackle Shop, Barnstaple Tel. 01271 344919, *Charges:* £30 per year adult. Children (18 and under) £10 per year, *Season:* All year, dawn to dusk, *Methods:* Full rules in the membership book. Barbless hooks only.

Little Comfort Farm

Contact: Little Comfort Farm, Braunton, EX33 2NJ, 01271 812414, jackie.milsom@btclick.com, *Water:* 1.5 acre lake approx, *Species:* Carp - 15lbs, Rudd, Roach, Bream. *Permits:* Lakeside, *Charges:* £6 all day, £5 half day, £3 evening. Concessions £1 off all prices for OAPs and under 14. 2 rods each angler, *Season:* Open all year dawn to dusk, *Methods:* Barbless hooks, no keepnets.

Riverton House & Lakes

Contact: Dave Shepherd or Sue Bryant, Riverton House & Lakes, Swimbridge, Barnstaple, EX32 0QX, 01271 830009, fishing@riverton.fsnet.co.uk, *Water:* Two 2 acre lakes, *Species:* Carp to 25lb, Bream, Tench, Roach, Perch, Chub, Rudd & Eels, *Permits:* Agent for Environment Agency rod licences, *Charges:* Adult day £5, Junior £3, Match bookings £4 (min 10 pegs). Specials: 'Dads and Lads' (one adult & one junior) £7. Family ticket (2 adults and 2 juniors) £12. Half day ticket available. Night fishing by appointment, *Season:* Open all year, *Methods:* Barbless hooks, care and consideration.

BEAWORTHY

Anglers Eldorado

Contact: Zyg, The Gables, Winsford, Halwill,, Beaworthy, EX21 5XT, 01409 221559, info@anglers-paradise.co.uk, *Water:* Four lakes from 1 acre to 4 acres, *Species:* Carp to 25lb, Grass Carp to 18lb, Wels Catfish to 20lb, Golden Tench to 5lb, Golden Orfe to 6lb, Blue orfe to 2lb, Golden Rudd to 2lb, Koi to 10lb, *Permits:* Also from Halwill Newsagents, *Charges:* £4 per day per rod, £3 Juniors & O.A.Ps. £2 excess if fishing without permit, *Season:* All year, 8am-9pm or dusk (Which ever is earlier), *Methods:* Barbless hooks, No keepnets or sacks.

Anglers Shangrila

Contact: Mr Zyg Gregorek, The Gables, Winsford, Halwill, Beaworthy, EX21 5XT, 01409 221559, info@anglers-paradise.co.uk, *Water:* Three match only lakes, 240 pegs, *Species:* Carp, Golden Tench, Golden Orfe. Top weights of 100lbs possible, *Permits:* From Zyg only, *Charges:* You can book the whole lake, charges depending on how many people, *Methods:* Barbless hooks.

Braddon lake

Contact: G. E. Ridge, Braddon Cottages, Ashwater, Beaworthy, EX21 5EP, 01409 211695, holidays@braddoncottages.co.uk, *Water:* 2.5 acre lake, *Species:* Mirror Carp to 30lbs, Bream 3lbs, Roach 1lb, Common Carp to 10lbs, Rudd 1lb, *Permits:* Limited day ticket available by prior booking only, *Season:* All year, *Methods:* Barbless hooks only.

BIDEFORD

Bideford & District Angling Club

Contact: Mr B. Ackland, Honestone Street, Bideford, 01237 478846, *Water:* Bideford based club with coarse, game, boat & sea sections; fishing throughout South West. Competition Friday 23rd May - Monday 26th. Please phone for further details, *Permits:* Membership form from club, open 7pm-11pm, *Charges:* £5 per annum, concessions for juniors/OAPs.

Fosfelle Country House Hotel (Coarse)

Contact: Hartland, Bideford, 01237 441273, *Water:* Approx half acre pond, *Species:* Carp, Tench, Roach, Rudd, *Charges:* £5 per day, *Season:* Open all year, *Methods:* Displayed on site.

Jennetts

Contact: South West Lakes Trust, 01837 871565, info@swlakestrust.org.uk, *Water:* Ranger Tel: 01288 321262, *Species:* Commons to 22lb, Mirrors to 23lb. Quality bags of smaller Carp, Roach and Tench to pole and float, *Permits:* See South West Lakes Trust coarse advert, *Charges:* Full day £4.75, Concession £3.75, 24 Hour £8.75, Season Day £80, Season Concession £60, Season Child (under 16) £35, Season Day & Night £120, Additional Fisheries £20 each, *Season:* Open all year 6.30am to 10pm. Please note that there is no access to the car park outside these times, *Methods:* No child under 14 years may fish unless accompanied by an adult over 18 years. No child under 16 may fish overnight unless accompanied by an adult over 18 years, and then only with permission of parent or legal guardian (letter to this effect must be produced).

Little Weach Fishery

Contact: 1 Weach Cottage, Westleigh, Bideford, EX39 4NG, 01237 479303, *Water:* 2 lakes totalling approx 1 acre, *Species:* Crucian, Common, Mirror and Koi Carp to 16lb, Tench 7lb, Roach 1.5lb, Rudd, Bream, Goldfish 1lb, *Charges:* £4 per day, £2 Children. Under 12's must be accompanied by an adult, *Season:* Open all year dawn to dusk, *Methods:* No keepnets or boilies.

Melbury

Contact: South West Lakes Trust, 01837 871565, info@swlakestrust.org.uk, *Water:* Ranger Tel: 01288 321262, *Species:* Best Mirror 27.5lb. Good mixed bags of Roach, Rudd and Bream to pole, float and feeder, *Permits:* See SW Lakes Trust coarse advert. Limited season permits from South West Lakes Trust, *Charges:* Full day £4.75, Conc. £3.75, Season Child (u.16) £35, Season Day £80, Conc. Season £60, Additional Fisheries £20 each, *Season:* Open all year from 6.30am to 10pm, *Methods:* No child U.14 years may fish unless accompanied by an adult over 18. No child U.16 may fish overnight unless accompanied by an adult over 18, and then only with permission of parent or legal guardian (letter to this effect must be produced).

Torridge Angling Club

Contact: A.J. Kelly (secretary), 4 Ridgeway Drive, Westward Ho!, 01237 476665, 07779 193085, *Water:* Coarse match fishing at local waters.Boat Section. Quarterly meetings. New members welcome. Please contact the secretary, *Charges:* £5 per year. Concessions for juniors.

BOVEY TRACEY

Bradley Pond

Contact: Newton Abbot Fishing Association, Clive Smith (membership secretary), PO Box 1, Bovey Tracey, Newton Abbot, TQ13 9ZE, 01626 836661, newtonfishing@yahoo.com, *Water:* See entry under Newton Abbot Fishing Association. Full members only. 4 acre former clay pit, *Species:* Popular match and Carp venue with Roach to 2lb, Perch to 3lb 9oz, Tench, Skimmers, Carp to 28lb and large Trout.

BUCKFASTLEIGH

Castoffs Angling Club

Contact: Mr Pete Burgess, 01803 856990, *Water:* 3 acre 'Nurston Lake' near Buckfastleigh, *Species:* Roach, Rudd, Perch, Tench and Carp, *Permits:* Club open to membership from Brixham residents, *Charges:* £10 annual membership. No charge for children under 13 when accompanied by an adult, *Season:* Open all year, *Methods:* Barbless hooks only. No keepnets.

Nurston Farm Fishery (Coarse)

Contact: Mabin Family, Nurston Farm, Dean Prior, Buckfastleigh, TQ11 0NA, 01364 642285, *Water:* 2.5 acre lake (also see entry under River Fishing, Dart, Devon), *Species:* Roach to 2.5lb, Tench to 5lb, Rudd to 1lb, Bream to 4lb, Carp (different species) to 15lb, *Charges:* Dawn till dusk £5 / u14s £3 / 4pm till dusk £3, *Methods:* Barbless hooks, no keepnets, no boilies / match bookings.

CHUDLEIGH

Trenchford

Contact: South West Lakes Trust, 01837 871565, info@swlakestrust.org.uk, *Water:* Ranger Tel: 01647 277587, *Species:* Pike up to 30lb, *Permits:* Self service kiosk at Kennick Reservoir, *Charges:* Full day £4.75, Concession £3.75, 24 Hour £8.75, Season Day £80, Season Concession £60, Season Child (under 16) £35, Season Day & Night £120, Additional Fisheries £20 each. Full day boat + fishing £8.50 (boats must be booked 48 hrs in advance), *Season:* Open all year 24 hrs/day, *Methods:* No child under 14 years may fish unless accompanied by an adult over 18 years. No child under 16 may fish overnight unless accompanied by an adult over 18 years, and then only with permission of parent or legal guardian (letter to this effect must be produced).

COMBE MARTIN

Newberry Farm Coarse Fishing

Contact: Mr. & Mrs. Greenaway, Newberry Farm, Woodlands, Combe Martin, EX34 0AT, 01271 882334, enq@newberrycampsite.co.uk, *Water:* 2 acre lake, *Species:* Carp to 17lb & Green Tench to 4kg (8lb), Roach, Rudd & Perch, *Permits:* From above address. Environment Agency rod licence required. Available from local Post Office or by 'Telesales' service on 0870 1662662, *Charges:* £5/day, max 2 rods; evening or half day tickets also available, *Season:* Open Easter till end October 8am - 8pm (please book in advance to fish Nov - March), *Methods:* Barbless hooks only, No ground bait or keepnets. Children under 16 must be accompanied by an adult over 18 years. No dogs.

CREDITON

Creedy Lakes

Contact: Sandra Turner, Longbarn, Crediton, EX17 4AB, 01363 772684, info@creedylakes.com, *Water:* 4.5 acre & 1.75 acre spring fed lakes, *Species:* Common to 31lb 3oz, Mirror to 25lb 6oz. Koi Carp plus Tench, *Charges:* Day ticket £6 (up to 2 rods). £8 (3 rods), Evening ticket £3 (up to 2 rods). £4 (3 rods), *Season:* March through to end December, *Methods:* Barbless Hooks, minimum line 8lbs, no keepnets or nut baits. No poles or beachcasters. Unhooking mats and 'Klinik' antiseptic compulsory. No night fishing.

Lower Hollacombe Fishery

Contact: Mr. C. Guppy, Lower Hollacombe, Crediton, EX17 5BW, 01363 84331, *Water:* Approximately 1 acre, *Species:* Common Carp, Koi Carp, Rudd, Tench, Mirror Carp, Crucian Carp, Roach, Perch, *Permits:* At bank side, *Charges:* £5 per day. £3 per day under 14. £2.50 evenings. under 16 must be accompanied by adult, *Season:* All year round, *Methods:* Barbless hooks, no boilies or nut baits.

Oldborough Fishing Retreat

Contact: Wendy Wilshaw, Oldborough Fishing Retreat, Morchard Bishop, Crediton, EX17 6SQ, 01363 877437, wendywilshaw@eclipse.co.uk, *Water:* 2 acres of lakes, *Species:* Mirror, Leather and Common Carp, Tench, Roach, Rudd, Perch and Eels, *Permits:* By prior arrangement, *Charges:* £5 per person per day, *Season:* Open all year, *Methods:* Barbless hooks only. No keepnets. No Boilies. No night fishing.

Salmonhutch Coarse Fishery

Contact: Mr Mortimer, Uton, Crediton, EX17 3QL, 01363 772749, *Water:* Three 1 acre spring fed lakes, *Species:* Mirror to 26lb 1oz and Common Carp to 20lb 12oz, Tench to 5lb, Rudd, *Permits:* On Site, *Charges:* Day fishing 7am to 10pm, from £4 for Adults. Night fishing 9pm to 7am, from £4 (prior booking required) Evening fishing from £2.50, *Season:* All Year, *Methods:* Barbless hooks, no long shank bent hooks, no permanently fixed lead rigs. Minimum 8lb line for carp, 4lb for general fishing. No carp in keepnets. Full rules from the fishery.

Shobrooke Lake

Contact: Clare Shelley, Shobrooke Park, Crediton, EX17 1DG, Tel: 01363 775153, fish@shobrookepark.com, *Water:* 9 acre lake in superb parkland setting, *Species:* Tench, Carp, Mirror, Rudd, Perch, Roach, *Permits:* Not from above address - Ladd's Sport Shop, Exeter Rd, Crediton 01363 772666 or Crediton Tourist Information Centre, Town hall, High Street, Crediton 01363 772006, *Charges:* Adult: £6/day, £12/week, £80/year; Under 16/Student & Pensioner: £3/day, £6/week, £40/year, *Methods:* Fishing by rod or line from bank only, no night fishing, no keepnets.

CULLOMPTON

Coombelands Coarse Fishery

Contact: Mr & Mrs Berry, Higher Coombelands, Bunneford Cross, Knowle, Cullompton, EX15 1PT, 01884 32320, rosemary@billingsmoor.fsnet.co.uk, *Water:* 4 lakes totalling approx 3 acres & 3 lakes in 1 acre, *Species:* 1 Carp lake, mixed coarse fishing ponds, *Permits:* Higher Coombelands, *Charges:* From £3.50 - £5.50 /day, evening and season tickets available, *Season:* Open all year, *Methods:* Barbless hooks only, no keep nets, no boilies, night fishing with prior permission only, no dogs.

Exeter & District A.A. (Kia Ora)
Contact: Terry Reed (Hon. Sec.), PO Box 194, Exeter, EX2 7WG, 07970 483913, exeteranglingassociation@yahoo.co.uk, *Water:* A recently built Association water, *Species:* Heavily stocked with mixed species coarse fish, *Permits:* Exeter Angling Centre, Smythen Street (Off Market Street Exeter). Bridge Cafe, Bridge Road, Exeter. Exmouth Tackle & Sport, The Strand, Exmouth. Tackle Trader, Wharf Road, Newton Abbot. Exe Valley Angling, West Exe South, Tiverton, *Charges:* £27 Adults, £2 for Juniors (annual). Day and week tickets depending on water, ask at agent, *Season:* Different on each water. Details in association handbook or from agents, *Methods:* Different restrictions on each water. Details in association handbook.

Goodiford Mill Fishery (Coarse Lakes)
Contact: David Wheeler, Goodiford Mill, Kentisbeare, Cullompton, EX15 2AS, 01884 266233, paul@culmvalley.fsnet.co.uk, *Water:* 7 acre Coarse lake with over 100 doubles & 20lbs to 29lbs, *Species:* Carp: Common, Mirror, Crucian, Leather and Ghost. Tench: Roach and Bream, *Permits:* At Lodge, *Charges:* £6 day ticket (1 rod). £5 concession/Children under 14 must be accompanied by an adult (1 rod). Extra rod £1 each, *Season:* All year, *Methods:* Full rules on application, no keepnets, barbless hooks, nets must be dipped.

Millhayes Fishery
Contact: Mr Tony Howe, Millhayes, Kentisbeare, Cullompton, EX15 2AF, 01884 266412, tonyhowe@mill-hayes.fsnet.co.uk, *Water:* 2 acre spring fed lake, 0.5 acre Tench lake, *Species:* Carp 20lb, Tench, Roach, Rudd, *Charges:* £5 Adults, £3 Under 16, £3 Evenings, *Season:* 1st March - 31st December, *Methods:* Barbless hooks only, no boilies, no night fishing, no carp over 1lb in nets, nets to be dipped, no dogs.

Newcourt Ponds
Contact: Andy Hitt, Newcourt Barton, Langford, Cullompton, EX15 1SE, 01884 277326, *Water:* Four lakes totalling 1.5 acres, *Species:* Carp, Tench, Bream, Golden Orfe, Rudd, Golden Tench, *Permits:* Collected on bank, *Charges:* Adults £3 two rods. under 16 £2 one rod. Extra rods £1, *Season:* Open all year dawn to dusk. No night fishing, *Methods:* No Boilies. Barbless Hooks. No Carp over 2lb in nets.

Padbrook Park
Contact: Richard Chard, Padbrook Park, Cullompton, EX15 1RU, 01884 38286, padbrookpark@fsmail.net, *Water:* 3 acre lake, *Species:* Many Carp up to 20lb, *Charges:* £5 Day. £2.50 half day, *Methods:* No keepnets.

Pound Farm
Contact: Mrs A.M.Davey, Butterleigh, Cullompton, EX15 1PH, 01884 855208, *Water:* Small spring fed pond, *Species:* Mirror, Common Carp, Roach, Tench, Perch, Rudd, *Charges:* £3 per rod per day, £1.50 children, *Season:* All year, *Methods:* Barbless hooks only. No Boilies.

South Farm Holiday Cottages & Fishery
Contact: Mrs. Susan Chapman, Blackborough, Blackdown Hills, Cullompton, EX15 2JE, (01823)681078, chapmans@southfarm.co.uk, *Water:* 4 lakes (1/3-2/3 acre each), *Species:* Carp, Roach, Chub, *Permits:* N/A, *Charges:* £5/day, *Season:* All year, *Methods:* Barbless hooks, no keepnets, no boilies, net dip.

Upton Lakes
Contact: Richard Down, Upton Farm, Cullompton, EX15 1RA, 07968 029022, richdown11@hotmail.com, *Water:* 1.5 acre and 1.25 acre match lake (day tickets available), *Species:* Carp 26lb 4oz, Bream 9lb 12oz, Tench 6lb, Perch 3lb, Crucian Carp, Roach & Rudd to 1lb plus, *Charges:* From April 2002 - £4 adults, £3 juniors, up to 3 rods; season tickets £70 adults, £40 juniors. Season tickets run on a 364 day basis. Pay as you arrive system, in place April 2003. Correct money therefore necessary, *Season:* Dawn until dusk, night fishing by prior arrangement only, *Methods:* Barbless hooks, no boilies, no peanuts.

DARTMOUTH

Old Mill
Contact: South West Lakes Trust, 01837 871565, info@swlakestrust.org.uk, *Species:* Carp to over 20lb, Roach to 2lb. Tench and Bream, *Permits:* See South West Lakes Trust coarse advert, *Charges:* Season Child (u.16) £35, Season Day & Night £150, Concession £135. Family (husband, wife & up to 2 children u.16) £250. Additional Fisheries £20 each, *Season:* Open all year 24 hours a day, *Methods:* No child under 14 years may fish unless accompanied by an adult over 18 years. No child under 16 may fish overnight unless accompanied by an adult over 18 years, and then only with permission of parent or legal guardian (letter to this effect must be produced).

DAWLISH

Ashcombe Fishery
Contact: Ashcombe Adventure Centre Ltd, Ashcombe, Near Dawlish, EX7 0QD, 01626 866766, info@ashcombeadventure.co.uk, *Water:* 3 Lakes approx 3 acres, *Species:* Carp 18lb, Tench 4lb, Roach 2lb, *Permits:* Day tickets/permits available from lakes (fishing inspector), *Charges:* Adults £4.50, Juniors / OAP's £3.50, *Season:* Open all Year, *Methods:* Barbless Hooks, No large Carp to be kept in keepnets, No boilies.

Hazelwood Park
Contact: Reception, Warren Road, Dawlish Warren, EX7 0PF, 01626 862955, info@hazelwood.co.uk, *Water:* Lake within Holiday Park, *Species:* Carp, Roach, Tench, *Charges:* £2.50 day, £10 week Adults, *Methods:* Barbless hooks.

EXETER

Broadclyst Pond
Contact: Jarvis Hayes, Broadclyst, Exeter, EX5 3AD, 01392 461268, jarvishayes@btopenworld.com, *Water:* One half acre lake, *Species:* Carp to 20lb plus.Tench 3.5lb, Perch 1.5lb, Rudd 12oz, *Permits:* On site - contact for details, *Charges:* £4 per day, *Season:* Open all year, *Methods:* No keepnets, barbless hooks only.

Bussells Farm
Contact: Lucy or Andy Hines, Bussells Farm, Huxham, Exeter, EX5 4EN, 01392 841238, 07802 435934, hinesandrew@netscape.net, *Water:* Three lakes covering 2.5 acres, *Species:* Carp to 20lb, Bream to 7lb, Tench to 7lb. Roach, *Charges:* £5 per day, £3 after 2pm, *Season:* Open all year, *Methods:* Barbless hooks only. No night fishing. No boilies.

Darts Farm Fishing Lakes
Contact: Darts Farm, Clyst St George, Topsham, Nr Exeter, EX3 0QH, 01392 878200, julie@dartsfarm.co.uk, *Water:* 3 acres lakes, *Species:* Carp max 27lb, Bream max 8-10lb, Roach, *Permits:* Available from Darts farm shop. E.A. licence required, *Charges:* Adult: 1 rod - £3.50, 2 or more rods £4.50. O.A.P/Child (under 16): 1 rod - £2.50, 2 or more rods £3.50 (2002 prices), *Season:* All year round; Night Fishing by arrangement, *Methods:* Barbless hooks, do not encourage keep nets, disinfectant tanks for dipping tackle.

Exeter & District A.A. (Fennick Ponds)
Contact: Terry Reed (Hon. Sec.), PO Box 194, Exeter, EX2 7WG, 07970 483913, exeteranglingassociation@yahoo.co.uk, *Water:* Two very prolific ponds, *Species:* Tench, Carp, Crucians, Roach and Rudd, *Permits:* Exeter Angling Centre, Smythen Street (Off Market Street Exeter). Bridge Cafe, Bridge Road, Exeter. Exmouth Tackle & Sport, The Strand, Exmouth. Tackle Trader, Wharf Road, Newton Abbot. Exe Valley Angling, West Exe South, Tiverton, *Charges:* £27 Adults, £2 for Juniors (annual). Day and week tickets depending on water, ask at agent, *Season:* Different on each water. Details in association handbook or from agents, *Methods:* Different restrictions on each water. Details in association handbook.

Exeter & District A.A. (Sampford Peverall Ponds)
Contact: Terry Reed (Hon. Sec.), PO Box 194, Exeter, EX2 7WG, 07970 483913, exeteranglingassociation@yahoo.co.uk, *Water:* Two ponds, *Species:* All coarse fish present with Carp to 20lb, *Permits:* Exeter Angling Centre, Smythen Street (Off Market Street Exeter). Bridge Cafe, Bridge Road, Exeter. Exmouth Tackle & Sport, The Strand, Exmouth. Tackle Trader, Wharf Road, Newton Abbot. Exe Valley Angling, West Exe South, Tiverton, *Charges:* £27 Adults, £2 for Juniors (annual). Day and week tickets depending on water, ask at agent, *Season:* Different on each water. Details in association handbook or from agents, *Methods:* Different restrictions on each water. Details in association handbook.

Exeter & District Angling Association (Exeter Canal)
Contact: Terry Reed (Hon. Sec.), PO Box 194, Exeter, EX2 7WG, 07970 483913, exeteranglingassociation@yahoo.co.uk, *Water:* This very old waterway is approximately 12ft deep, throughout its six mile length, *Species:* Carp to 40lb, Tench, Chub, Roach and specimen Pike to 30lb, *Permits:* Exeter Angling Centre, Smythen Street (Off Market Street Exeter). Bridge Cafe, Bridge Road, Exeter. Exmouth Tackle & Sport, The Strand, Exmouth. Tackle Trader, Wharf Road, Newton Abbot. Exe Valley Angling, West Exe South, Tiverton, *Charges:* £27 Adults, £2 for Juniors (annual). Day and week tickets depending on water, ask at agent, *Season:* Different on each water. Details in association handbook or from agents, *Methods:* Different restrictions on each water. Details in association handbook.

Exeter Ship Canal
Contact: Exeter City Council, River & Canal Manager, Civic Centre, Exeter, EX1 1RP, 01392 274306, river.canal@exeter.gov.uk, *Water:* 5.25 miles of canal, both banks; upper 2 miles free permits, *Species:* Roach, Bream, Tench, Carp, Pike & Eels, *Permits:* Free permits from: River & Canal Office, Canal Basin, Haven Rd, Exeter, EX2 8DU and Exeter City Canal, Civic Centre, Phase II Reception, Paris Street. Angling Association permit from tackle shops, *Charges:* Free permits with proof of identity or E.A. licence. Lower level 3.25 miles on Exeter & District A.A. permit, *Season:* Open all year, *Methods:* No live or dead bait coarse fish.

Hogsbrook Lakes
Contact: Desmond & Maureen Pearson, Russett Cottage, Greendale Barton, Woodbury Salterton, Exeter, EX5 1EW, 01395 233340, *Water:* One 1.5 acre and one 2 acre lake, *Species:* Bream, Tench, Roach, Rudd, Golden Rudd, Carp, *Permits:* At lakeside from bailiff, Night fishing by prior arrangement, *Charges:* Day ticket £4 per day (One Rod) £1 extra per rod, Junior £2. Night £6 (One Rod) £1 extra per rod, *Season:* Open all year, *Methods:* Barbless hooks, keepnets by arrangement, no Carp in nets or sacks, all Carp anglers must have unhooking mats.

Home Farm Fishery
Contact: Mr F Williams, Home Farm, Mamhead, Kenton, Exeter, EX6 8HP, 01626 866259, *Water:* 1 lake approx one acre, *Species:* Carp 20lb plus, Roach to 2lb, Tench to 4lb, Rudd to 12oz, *Permits:* From the cabin by the lake, *Charges:* 1 rod - £5, 2 rods - £5.50, weekly ticket £25 max two rods, concessions for children. Night fishing by arrangement, *Season:* Open all year, *Methods:* No groundbaiting with boilies, no tiger nuts.

Luccombes Coarse Fishery
Contact: Julian Harrod, Towsington Lane, Exminster, EX6 8AY, 01392 832858, 07748 568316, jenga22@hotmail.com, *Water:* Five medium sized ponds set in 9 acres. New Tench and Bream pond open. Bream to 5lbs, Tench to 7lbs, *Species:* Carp to 21lb. Tench to 6.5lb, Bream, Rudd, Koi and Roach, *Permits:* Season tickets available from the above, *Charges:* £5 day tickets on the bank. £3.50 after 4.30pm. £3.50 junior (under 16 accompanied). £100 season ticket (12 months), *Season:* Open all year from 6am to half hour before dark, *Methods:* No keepnets (except in matches) Barbless hooks ONLY, no nuts or seeds with the exception of hemp and sweetcorn.

Pengellies Carp Ponds
Contact: Mr Carr, Shillingsford Abbot, Exeter, EX2 9QH, 01392 832286, *Water:* Two small ponds totalling 1/4 acre, *Species:* Carp to 15lb, Roach, *Charges:* Tickets from office, £10 per day up to 3 rods; lake can be prebooked for exclusive fishing, *Season:* Open all year dawn to dusk, night fishing by arrangement only, *Methods:* Barbless hooks only, no boilies.

South View Farm
Contact: Mr R.K.Gorton, South View Farm, Shillingford Saint George, Exeter, EX2 9UP, 01392 832278, 07799 198498, keithgorton@btinternet.com, *Water:* 3 lakes totalling 3 acres, *Species:* Mirror, Common up to 28lb & Ghost Carp 15lb, Roach 2.5lb, Rudd 2.5lb, Perch 4lb, Bream, Green & Gold Tench to 3.5lb, *Permits:* Tickets on the bank, *Charges:* £5 for two rods, Juniors (under 16, must be accompanied) £4. Evening ticket after 5pm £3 adult, £2 junior, *Season:* Open all year round, *Methods:* Barbless hooks, no boilies, no keepnets.

Upham Farm Ponds
Contact: S.J.Willcocks, Upham Farm, Farringdon, Exeter, EX5 2HZ, 01395 232247, 07971 827552, mail@uphamfarm.com, *Water:* 6 well stocked ponds, *Species:* Carp 27lb 1oz, Tench 8lb 8oz and Bream, *Permits:* Day tickets on bank, *Charges:* £5/day (concessions for O.A.P's, Junior), *Methods:* Barbless hooks, no keepnets, no groundbait.

EXMOUTH

Squabmoor
Contact: South West Lakes Trust, 01837 871565, info@swlakestrust.org.uk, *Water:* Ranger Tel: 01647 277587, *Species:* Good head of Carp to 25lb. Roach to 3lb 2oz, Tench, *Permits:* See South West Lakes Trust coarse advert, *Charges:* Full day £4.75, Concession £3.75, 24 Hour £8.75, Season Day £80, Season Concession £60, Season Child (under 16) £35, Season Day & Night £120, Additional Fisheries £20 each, *Season:* Open all year 24 hours a day, *Methods:* No child under 14 years may fish unless accompanied by an adult over 18 years. No child under 16 may fish overnight unless accompanied by an adult over 18 years, and then only with permission of parent or legal guardian (letter to this effect must be produced).

HATHERLEIGH

Legge Farm Coarse Fishery

Contact: Graham Hall, Church Road, Highampton, Beaworthy, EX21 5LF, 01409 231464, legge_farm@yahoo.com, *Water:* 1.25 acre lake & two other ponds, *Species:* Carp (common to 20lb plus), Tench, Perch to 4.3lb, Roach, Rudd, Crucians, Grass Carp, Bream, *Permits:* E.A. licences sold on site, *Charges:* Adults £5, O.A.Ps & evenings after 4pm £3.50, juniors £3, *Season:* All year 7am - Dusk, *Methods:* Barbless hooks, landing nets, no radios or keepnets.

HOLSWORTHY

Clawford Vineyard

Contact: Clawton, EX22 6PN, 01409 254177, 07786 332332, john.ray@clawford.co.uk, *Water:* 10 lakes totalling over 30 acres of water, *Species:* Common, Mirror, Crucian, Ghost & Grass Carp, Tench, Roach, Rudd, Orfe, Barbel, Golden Tench, Blue Tench, Golden/Pink Orfe, Green Rudd, Gold Carp, Goldfish, Catfish, Ide, Chub, *Charges:* On application, *Season:* Open all year, *Methods:* No live or deadbait. No particles or nuts except hemp or sweetcorn. Barbless hooks only. No carp whatsoever in keepnets. Full rules at the fishery.

Eastcott Farm & Lodges

Contact: Mrs C. Whitmill, Eastcott Farm, North Tamerton, Nr Holsworthy, EX22 6SB, 01409 271172, eastcott@fsmail.net, *Water:* One Lake approx 0.75 acres, *Species:* Carp & Rudd, *Charges:* Day ticket £2.50, Under 16 & OAP £1.50, *Season:* Open all year, *Methods:* Barbless hooks, no keepnets.

Exemoor Farm

Contact: Mr A R Mills, Week St. Mary, Holsworthy, EX22 6UX, 01566 781366, *Water:* Half acre lake, *Species:* Tench 4 - 5lb, Golden Orfe, Rudd, Crucian, Common 13lb & Mirror Carp, *Charges:* £3 per rod per day, cheaper rates after 5pm, *Season:* Open all year, *Methods:* No boilies or hemp.

Simpson Valley Fishery

Contact: Simpson Farm, Holsworthy, EX22 6JW, 01409 253593, simpson@valleyfishery.fsnet.co.uk, *Water:* 7 lakes, including new 2.5 acre specimen lake & syndicate water, please enquire for details, *Species:* Carp to 23lb, Tench 8lb, Roach 2lb, Rudd 1lb, Gudgeon near to British record, Chub 5lb, *Charges:* £5 per day - 2 rods, £3 Juniors and O.A.P's. Limited membership available for syndicate water, *Season:* Open all year dawn to dusk, *Methods:* Barbless hooks only. No Carp in keepnets.

Wooda Fisheries

Contact: C.J. Pickett, Pancrasweek, Holsworthy, EX22 6DJ, 01409 241934, *Water:* 3 lakes - 1 general, 1 intermediate and 1 specimen, *Species:* Carp, Tench, Perch, Bream & Roach, *Permits:* On site, *Charges:* £5 per day, *Season:* All year, *Methods:* Barbless hooks only, no keepnets.

Woodacott Arms

Contact: Len Sanders, Woodacott Cross, Thornbury, Holsworthy, EX22 7BT, 01409 261358/261237, woodacottarms@aol.com, *Water:* 2 lakes, 1.25 acre, 1 acre, *Species:* Carp 23lb, Tench 7lb, Bream 3lb, Rudd 1.5lb, Roach 1.5lb, Perch 4.5lb, *Charges:* Adults: Day Tickets 2 Rods £5, Juniors: 2 Rods £3, *Methods:* Barbless hooks, no keepnets, no boilies or peanuts.

HONITON

Fishponds House

Contact: Fishponds House, Dunkeswell, Honiton, EX14 4SH, 01404 891358, jim@fishpondshotel.com, *Water:* 2 Lakes each over 1 acre, *Species:* Carp to 20lb, Rudd, Roach and Tench, *Charges:* £6.00 per day, Children under 11yrs £3.00 per day, *Season:* Open all year dawn to dusk, *Methods:* Barbless hooks, no boilies, no keepnets.

Hartsmoor Fisheries

Contact: John Griss, Bolham Water, Clayhidon, Cullompton, EX15 3QB, 01823 680460, *Water:* Two day ticket lakes - 2 acres and 1.25 acres, One syndicate lake - 3.5 acres, plus one 5 acre lake being developed, *Species:* Roach and Rudd to 2lb, Tench 6lb, Bream 7lb, Barbel 4.5lb, Perch 3lb, Crucians 3.5lb (not hybrids!), Blue Orfe 2.5lb, Chub 5lb, Carp 26.5lb (syndicate 35lb) Gudgeon 4oz, *Permits:* Day tickets on the bank, Syndicate - get your name on the waiting list, *Charges:* £5 per day. £5 per night by arrangement, *Season:* Day tickets dawn to dusk all year round, *Methods:* Barbless hooks. No nuts of any kind. No Carp over 2lb in keepnets. Loose feed and groundbait is permitted.

Hollies Fishery

Contact: Fiona Downer, Sheldon, Honiton, EX14 4QS, 01404 841428, info@holliestroutfarm.co.uk, *Water:* Spring fed lake, *Species:* Carp and mixed coarse fish, *Charges:* Please enquire at number above.

Milton Farm Ponds

Contact: Milton Farm, Payhembury, Honiton, EX14 0HE, 01404 850236, *Water:* 5 lakes approx 2 acres, *Species:* Carp to 22lb, Tench 7lb, Roach, Bream, *Permits:* Collected on bank, *Charges:* £3.50/person/day - no charge for extra rods, £2.50 children 14 or under, *Season:* Open all year round, *Methods:* No groundbaiting with boilies.

ILFRACOMBE

Ilfracombe & District Anglers Association (Coarse)

Contact: David Shorney, Victoria Cottage, 8B St Brannocks Road, Ilfracombe, EX34 8EG, 01271 865874, bullfinch@amserve.net, *Water:* No Club waters. Use Slade reservoir and Mill Park at Berrynarbor, *Species:* Carp, Bream, Perch, Roach, Rudd, Gudgeon and Pike, *Permits:* From Agents: Variety Sports, 23 Broad street, Ilfracombe and The Post Office, Slade, Ilfracombe, Devon, EX34 8LQ, *Charges:* Annual fee combines Sea & Coarse plus licence and permits, *Season:* January to December. Open charity competition in June, *Methods:* Barbless hooks. No Carp in keepnets.

Lower Slade

Contact: South West Lakes Trust, 01837 871565, info@swlakestrust.org.uk, *Water:* Ranger Tel: 01288 321262, *Species:* Mirror & Common Carp to 20lb plus. Bream to 5lb plus. Perch to 2lb 4oz, Roach, Rudd, Gudgeon and Pike, *Permits:* See South West Lakes Trust coarse advert, *Charges:* Full day £4.75, Concession £3.75, 24 Hour £8.75, Season Day £80, Season Concession £60, Season Child (under 16) £35, Season Day & Night £120, Additional Fisheries £20 each, *Season:* Open all year, 24 hours a day, *Methods:* No child under 14 years may fish unless accompanied by an adult over 18 years. No child under 16 may fish overnight unless accompanied by an adult over 18 years, and then only with permission of parent or legal guardian. (letter to this effect must be produced).

Mill Park Coarse Fishing Lake
Contact: Brian & Mary Malin, Mill Park, Mill Lane, Berrynarbor, Ilfracombe, EX34 9SH, 01271 882647, millpark@globalnet.co.uk, *Water:* 1.5 acre lake between Ilfracombe and Combe Martin, *Species:* Bream, Carp, Perch, Roach, Rudd, Tench, Golden Orfe, Golden Tench, Crucian Carp, *Charges:* Adult £4.50, Junior £2.50, Adult & Junior £6.50. Reduced rates for residents of touring and camping site; All juniors (under 16) must be accompanied by adult, *Season:* Lake open all year; day ticket 8am-9pm or dusk (whichever is earlier), *Methods:* Barbless hooks only, dip all nets, no night fishing.

KINGSBRIDGE

Bickerton Farm Fishery
Contact: Mr Graham Tolchard, Bickerton Farm, Hallsands, Kingsbridge, TQ7 2EU, 01548 511220, *Water:* 1/3 acre & 3/4 acre ponds, *Species:* Carp 15lb, Roach, Rudd, Perch, Tench, Bream, *Charges:* £3 Under 16's, £4 per rod Adults, Two rods £5 & £7, *Methods:* Barbless hooks, No keepnets unless fishing match.

Coombe Water Fisheries
Contact: J.W. Robinson, Coombe Farm, Kingsbridge, TQ7 4AB, 01548 852038, *Water:* 3 Lakes, *Species:* Carp to 25lb, Bream to 4lb, Tench to 3lb, Roach to 2.5lb, *Permits:* No E.A. licence required. Lakes are covered by general E.A. licence, *Charges:* £5 day ticket, £2.50 Under 16. 1/2 day ticket £3, *Season:* All year dawn to dusk. Night fishing by arrangement only, *Methods:* Barbless hooks, no ground bait, no Carp over 1lb in keepnets.

Slapton Ley National Nature Reserve
Contact: Nick Binnie, Slapton Ley Field Centre, Slapton, Kingsbridge, TQ7 2QP, 01548 580685, *Water:* 180 acre freshwater lagoon, *Species:* Pike, Perch, Roach, Rudd, *Permits:* Hired rowing boats only, *Charges:* Dependent on number in boat e.g. £18 for 2 anglers, *Season:* No close season, *Methods:* No bank fishing, barbless hooks, no keepnets. Livebait is not to be used. All fish caught are to be returned.

Valley Springs Coarse and Trout Fishery (Coarse)
Contact: J. Bishop, Sherford, Nr Kingsbridge, TQ7 2BG, 01548 531574, info@valley-springs.com, *Water:* 2 lakes totalling approx 3 acres, Trout & Coarse, *Species:* Coarse Fish - Carp to 32lb, Tench to 4.5lb, Roach/Rudd to 2lb, *Charges:* Seniors £10 per day, Juniors £5 per day including E.A. Rod Licence, *Season:* Fishing by appointment only. Please ring, *Methods:* Barbless hooks.

LAUNCESTON

Angling 2000 (Rexon Cross)
Contact: Simon Evans, Westcountry Rivers Trust, Fore Street, Lifton, PL16 0AA, 01566 784488, simon@wrt.org.uk, *Water:* 1.5 acre lake, *Species:* Carp to 18lb, Tench to 5lb and Crucian to 1lb, *Methods:* No Carp in keep nets, barbless hooks only.

LEWDOWN

Alder Lake
Contact: Mr Bob Westlake, Alder, Lewdown, Okehampton, EX20 4PJ, 01566 783397, bobwestlake@aldersportswear.com, *Water:* 4 acre Lake, *Species:* Perch, Carp to 25lb, Bream to 8.25lb, Specimen Roach and Tench. Plus natural stock of Trout, *Charges:* £5 per rod per day, *Season:* No closed season, *Methods:* No restrictions. Night fishing allowed.

LIFTON

Rexon Cross Farm
Contact: Mrs A. Worden, Broadwoodwidger, Lifton, PL16 0JJ, 01566 784295, john.worden@btclick.com, *Water:* 1.5 acre lake, *Species:* Tench, Bream, Carp up to 18lb, *Charges:* £5 per day (1 rod per person), *Methods:* Barbless hooks, rules displayed at site, one rod per person.

NEWTON ABBOT

Exeter & District A.A. (Abrook Pond)
Contact: Terry Reed (Hon. Sec.), PO Box 194, Exeter, EX2 7WG, 07970 483913, exeteranglingassociation@yahoo.co.uk, *Water:* Good looking pond with rustic bridges and plenty of lily pads, *Species:* Tench, Beam, Roach and Carp to mid twenties, *Permits:* Exeter Angling Centre, Smythen Street (Off Market Street Exeter). Bridge Cafe, Bridge Road, Exeter. Exmouth Tackle & Sport, The Strand, Exmouth. Tackle Trader, Wharf Road, Newton Abbot. Exe Valley Angling, West Exe South, Tiverton, *Charges:* £27 Adults, £2 for Juniors (annual). Day and week tickets depending on water, ask at agent, *Season:* Different on each water. Details in association handbook or from agents, *Methods:* Different restrictions on each water. Details in association handbook.

Finlake Holiday Park
Contact: Tony Irving (Bailiff) Ext 230, Nr Chudleigh, TQ13 0EJ, 01626 853833, *Water:* 1 Acre - 30 Peg, *Species:* Crucians 1-4lb, Bream to 4lb, Tench 2-4lb, Skimmers, Roach to 2.5lb, Golden Orfe 12 inches, Rudd 1.5lb, Golden Rudd 8 inches, No Carp, *Permits:* On entry at security, *Charges:* £4 Adult, £2.50 to 14yrs, *Season:* All year round, Winter opening times: 8.30am - Dusk, Summer opening times: 8.30am - 6pm every day, *Methods:* Barbless hooks, no keep nets, no boilies, nuts, floating baits, pellets or paste. Strictly no ground bait, landing nets essential.

Learn To Fish In Newton Abbot
Contact: Paul Power, Newton Abbot, 01626 205941, paulpower@blueyonder.co.uk, *Water:* Open to all who would like to learn to fish in Newton Abbot area. NFA qualified Coach, all types of angling covered. Tuition free of charge.

Newton Abbot Fishing Association (Coarse Ponds)
Contact: Clive Smith (membership secretary), PO Box 1, Bovey Tracey, Newton Abbot, TQ13 9ZE, 01626 836661, newtonfishing@yahoo.com, *Water:* 17 coarse ponds in the Newton Abbot Area. Also member of S.L.A.C. (Somerset Levels Association of Clubs) with stretches of the Parret, Brue and Isle, *Species:* Carp to 36lb, Tench to12lb, Bream to 8lb, Roach to 2lb, Perch to 3lb 9oz, Rudd to 1.5lb, *Permits:* From Tackle Trader, Newton Abbot. Abbot Angling, Newton Abbot. Oakford Filling Station, Kingsteignton. Sporting Lines, Torquay, Handy Baits, Paignton. Brixham Bait & Tackle, *Charges:* Day Tickets: £5 senior, £2 junior. Associate licence £41 senior (1 year fishing majority of waters). Full member £46 adult. £13 junior, £23 OAP/ conc. (must live within 20 miles of Newton Abbot), *Season:* Ponds and lakes are open 24 hours a day, 365 days a year. Rivers are controlled by the national close season for coarse fish; Rocombe Ponds and Wapperwell Ponds open from dawn to dusk, *Methods:* Barbless or crushed barbs. 2 rods 1st April to 30th September. 3 rods 1st October to 31st March. No lead shot. No nut baits. No fires. No dogs. No keepnets at Rocombe.

Preston Ponds
Contact: Newton Abbot Fishing Association, newtonfishing@yahoo.com, *Water:* See entry under Newton Abbot Fishing Association. 4 ponds at Kingsteignton. Key Transport: Popular match water (full members only). Eddison Pond: small water. Sawmills: about 3 acres coloured by run off from local clay works but don't be put off! New Cross: Extremely deep former clay pit, *Species:* Key Transport: Skimmers, Bream, big Roach, Rudd, Perch, Tench and Crucians to over a pound. Eddison Pond: Most species with Tench, Crucians and mid-double Carp. Sawmills: Skimmers, Bream, Perch, Tench Carp and Roach to over 1lb with odd Perch to 3lb, Carp to 20lb & rumours of one large Catfish! New Cross: Some good Roach, Perch, the odd Tench.

Rackerhayes Complex
Contact: Newton Abbot Fishing Association, newtonfishing@yahoo.com, *Water:* See entry under Newton Abbot Fishing Association. 6 waters just outside Newton Abbot. Island Pond 5 acres (full members only), First Pond 2 acres, Dores Pond 9 acres, Linhay Pond 3 acres, Weedy Pond (just under 1 acre) and Wheel Pond (juniors only). *Species:* Island Pond: most species, numerous Carp over 30lb.Tench over 10lb. Good sized Roach, Rudd, Pike, Bream and Eels. First Pond: Good head of Carp to 28lb, Tench, Roach, Bream etc. and a large number of jack Pike. Wheel Pond: Carp to 14lb, Roach, Rudd, Perch, Golden Orfe, Tench and occasional small Pike. Linhay Pond: Most coarse species with some excellent Bream. Dores Pond: Very large head of Carp to 30lb, superb Tench averaging 6lb and up to 11lb 15oz. Weedy Pond: most coarse fish including good Tench and some large Carp.

Spring Ponds
Contact: Newton Abbot Fishing Association, newtonfishing@yahoo.com, *Water:* See entry under Newton Abbot Fishing Association. Three small farm ponds, *Species:* Middle pond has been heavily re-stocked. Top and bottom ponds well stocked with Carp averaging 2lb. Odd Carp to low double plus Tench, Roach and Bream. Almost guaranteed action.

West Golds
Contact: Newton Abbot Fishing Association, newtonfishing@yahoo.com, *Water:* A tidal water that is incorporated in the local flood defence system. Extreme care should be taken as flash tidal flooding is common, *Species:* Dace, Roach, Skimmers, Mullet and Carp to over 20lb. Stock changes with flow of higher tides.

NORTH TAWTON

North Tawton Angling Specimen Group
Contact: Mr. J.D. Mansfield, 4 Taw Vale Close, North Tawton, EX20 2EH, 01837 880048, 07812 155035, *Water:* Fishing waters in Avon, Somerset, Devon & Cornwall. Lake, River & Sea fishing from shore only, *Species:* Any species listed in the British records, *Charges:* Membership £8/year, *Season:* June 1st - May 31st, *Methods:* Abide by regulations laid out on lake or river that the group are fishing.

Spires Lakes
Contact: Barry Ware, Riverside, Fore Street, North Tawton, EX20 2ED, 01837 82499, *Water:* Two lakes, 30 peg match lake and 2 acre lake, *Species:* Carp 30lb, Tench 5lb, Roach 1lb 8oz, Rudd 1lb, Bream 3.5lb, Perch 1.5lb, Orfe 4lb, Ghost Carp 1lb, *Permits:* On site kiosk, self service, *Charges:* £5.50 Day ticket, £4.00 Evening, £4.00 Juniors & O.A.Ps, *Season:* Dawn to dusk, *Methods:* Barbless hooks, no boilies, no tiger or peanuts.

OKEHAMPTON

Millaton - Wrigley Fishing Syndicate
Contact: Mr Vic Barnett (Syndicate Sec.), 5 Weir Close, Mainstone, Plymouth, PL6 8SD, 01752 708206, victor.barnett@talk21.com, *Water:* 3 small ponds, each cannot be seen from the other. A very private and secluded fishery, *Species:* Carp, Tench, Golden Tench, Bream, Perch, Gudgeon, Roach, Rudd, Large Brown Goldfish (2.5lb), Gold Carp, *Permits:* To join the syndicate, costs in the first year are: £10 joining fee, £50 for year. After the first year cost is £50 p.a. 5 day tickets - price on booking (around £5 per day). More details from the above contact or phone 01837 861100, allowing for a long ring please, *Charges:* As above, *Season:* No close season, *Methods:* Barbless hooks only. No Carp over 2lb to be retained in keepnets. Knotless nets only. No boilies. All spawning fish to be returned to the water immediately after photographing or weighing. Syndicate members may camp overnight and generally come and go as they wish.

Millaton Farm Coarse Fishery
Contact: Gareth or Jessica Charles-Jones, Millaton Farm, Bridestowe, Okehampton, EX20 4QG, 01837 861100, *Water:* 3 large lakes, 2 small (from 0.75 to 2 acres), *Species:* Carp - Koi 9lb, Ghost 10.5lb, Mirror 15lb, Common 14lb, Crucian 2.5lb, Leather. Tench, Bream 4lb, Perch 1lb, Roach, Rudd, American Sun Bass 2oz. *Permits:* Up to 5 day tickets allowed. You MUST RING day before to book space before setting out, *Charges:* £5 per day per rod, *Season:* Dawn to dusk all year round, *Methods:* Barbless hooks only. No boilies, hemp, peanuts. Groundbait in moderation. No keepnets, dogs, radios.

Stowford Grange Farm Fisheries
Contact: H Vigers & Sons, Stowford Grange Farm, Lewdown, Okehampton, EX20 4BZ, 01566 783298, 07771 798363, *Water:* 2.5 acre, 1 acre and 1.25 acre lakes, *Species:* Roach, Rudd, Carp 20lb, Bream 10lb 2oz, Tench 6lb 4oz, Perch 4lb 14oz, Gudgeon, Golden Tench, *Permits:* At the farm, *Charges:* On application at the Farm, *Season:* Open all year, *Methods:* Barbless or whisker barbs, no boilies in bottom lake, no nuts, no large carp in nets.

Week Farm
Contact: John & Grenville Hockridge, Bridestowe, Okehampton, EX20 4HZ, 01837 861221, 07866 854121, accom@weekfarmonline.com, *Water:* 2 x 0.5 acre lakes & 0.25 acre lake, *Species:* Mixed Carp (Common, Mirror, Crucian), Bream in 0.25 acre, Roach, Rudd & Green Tench, *Charges:* £4/day plus £1 extra rod, £2/evening, children & OAP half price, *Methods:* Barbless hooks only, all nets to be dipped, night fishing by arrangement, no dogs.

OTTERY ST MARY

Escot Lake
Contact: Escot Aquaculture, Parklands Farm, Escot, Ottery St. Mary, EX11 1LU, 01404 822188, escot@eclipse.co.uk, *Water:* 1 acre lake, *Species:* Mixed Coarse Fish, Bream, Crucion, Tench, Mirrors and Commons, *Permits:* On site at Aquatic Centre, *Charges:* £5 per day, £10 for 24 hour ticket, *Season:* Open 1st February - 1st October, *Methods:* No restrictions.

PAIGNTON

New Barn Angling Centre

Contact: Andrew & Callie Buchanan, Newbarn Farm, Totnes Road, Paignton, TQ4 7PT, 01803 553602, info@newbarnfarm.com, *Water:* 6 ponds up to 1.25 acre suitable for juniors (parent supervision), beginners, pleasure and specimen anglers, *Species:* Carp to 27lb, Ghost Carp to 17lb, Tench to 6.5lb, Roach to 2lb 12oz, Bream to 5lb, Perch to 4lb, Rudd to 2lb 4oz, Eels (mirror lake only) 7lb 8oz, *Permits:* No EA rod licence required. Purchase day tickets on arrival, *Charges:* £6 for 1 rod, 2nd & 3rd rod £1 each - Junior £3.50. Adults (14+) 3 day ticket £16, 7 day ticket £32 (n.b. days taken anytime over a year), *Season:* Open all year 7am to dusk (6am June to August). Night fishing only available to holiday guests. 9 fishing shelters around main lake, first come first served, *Methods:* Barbless hooks only, no keepnets, no nuts. All baits eff.: maggots, luncheon meat, sweetcorn, boilies, bread & pellets. Sensible ground baiting allowed, float fishing and ledgering (ledger rigs will be checked to ensure safety), summer time good for floating dog biscuits.

Town Parks Coarse Fishing Centre

Contact: Mr Paul Gammin, Town Park Farm, Totnes Road, Paignton, TQ4 7PY, 01803 523133, 07973 433109, townparks@btinternet.com, *Water:* Specimen Carp lake 1.5 acres (max 10 anglers at any one time). Match lake 2 acres (21 pegs) available for club/block bookings, phone for details, *Species:* Carp lake - Mirror and Common Carp to 35lbs. Match lake - Carp 10lbs, Crucian Carp 3lbs, Tench 5lbs, Chub 4lbs, Bream 4lbs, Roach 2lbs, Rudd 1lb, Perch 4lbs, *Permits:* No E.A. Rod licence required, *Charges:* Carp lake - Full day £8, Night (6pm - 9am) £10, Evening (4pm - Dusk) £5, 24 hrs £15. Match lake - Full day £5, Night (6pm - 9am) £7, Evening (4pm - Dusk) £4, 24 hrs £10, *Season:* 24hrs, 365 day a year, but please book night fishing in advance, *Methods:* A full list of rules are posted on site.

PLYMOUTH

Plymouth & District Angling Club

Contact: Mr Brian Morrell, 20 Pinehurst Way, Ivybridge, PL21 9UL, 01752 894199, *Water:* 3 ponds at Cadover Bridge, two at St. Germans and one at Dellamare (pure Tench) - ranging in size from 0.5 to 2 acres, *Species:* Carp to 29lb 8oz, Tench 6lb, Bream 8lb 8oz, Rudd 11lb 6oz Roach 2lb 8oz and Crucians, *Permits:* Clive's Tackle and Bait, 182 Exeter St, Plymouth. Tel: 01752 228940, *Charges:* £30 membership fee (1st Jan - 1st Feb). Other times £40 membership. Seniors £35. Juniors £10. Disabled and OAP's £15, *Season:* Open all year. St Germans and Cadover 24 hrs, *Methods:* Barbless hooks. No Carp in keepnets. Unhooking mats for all Carp.

Plymouth Command Angling Association (Ponds)

Contact: Mr Vic Barnett Hon.Sec, 5 Weir Close, Mainstone, Plymouth, PL6 8SD, 01752 708206, victor.barnett@talk21.com, *Water:* Two lakes of 0.75 and 1.25 of an acre for coarse fishing within ten minutes of Plymouth, plus several other accesses to associated waters in the Southwest open to members, *Species:* Carp, Tench, Bream, Perch, Roach, Rudd, Crucians, Goldfish, Eels, Golden Carp and some Koi, *Permits:* Membership is open to all serving members of HM Forces. Associate membership is also open to ex-serving members of HM Forces, no matter when the time was served. Day tickets available from Manadon Angling Supplies, Plymouth @ £5 per person, up to 5 per day, *Charges:* Costs for full membership or associate membership are available on application or enquiry at the above contact, *Season:* No close season for coarse fish, *Methods:* Barbless hooks only at the coarse fishery. Knotless keepnets to be used as per E.A. guidelines on minimum 3 metres length. No trout pellets in any form allowed. Only Carp friendly and proven pellets are to be used. All spawning fish are to be returned to the water immediately. No Carp over 2lb to be kept in keepnets.

Sunridge Fishery

Contact: RM and M Hammett, Sunridge Nurseries, Worston, Yealmpton, Plymouth, PL8 2LN, 01752 880438, 07734 557212, sunridgenurseriesuk@yahoo.co.uk, *Water:* Approx half acre private lake that can be reserved for exclusive use. Est. 29 years, *Species:* Mirror and Common Carp up to 22lb, *Permits:* From above at the Nurseries, *Charges:* £5 adult day, £3 child/OAP, *Season:* Open all year dawn to dusk, night fishing by arrangement only, *Methods:* Barbless hooks only, no keepnets (except by prior arrangement).

Warleigh Barton Fishery

Contact: Andrew Kent, Tamerton Foliot, Plymouth, PL5 4LG, 01752 771458, 07811 339569, *Water:* 2 acre lake, *Species:* Mirror and Common - Now up to 30lbs, *Charges:* Syndicate £50 to join, £100 per year, *Season:* All year, *Methods:* Barbless hooks, no keep nets.

SEATON

Horriford Fishing

Contact: Mr Pady, Horriford Farm, Colyford, Colyton, EX24 6HW, 01297 552316, horriford@aol.com, *Water:* 2 ponds - 1 with access for disabled, *Species:* Bream (5lb), Roach (1lb), Tench (5lb), Carp (8-10lb), Perch (2lb), Rudd (1.5lb), *Permits:* From farmhouse, *Charges:* Day ticket £4. Half day ticket £2.50, *Season:* Open all year dawn to dusk, *Methods:* Barbless hooks only, no boilies.

Wiscombe Park Fishery

Contact: Mike Raynor, Wiscombe Park Fishery, Colyton, EX24 6JE, 01404 871474, 07860 222342, michael@wiscombe.co.uk, *Water:* Half acre lake & Trout fishing, *Species:* Carp, Tench, Bream, *Permits:* Self-service (No booking), *Charges:* £3.50/day, Reduced rates for O.A.Ps & Children, Children (under 15) free if accompanied by permit holding adult, *Season:* All year, *Methods:* Single rod.

SOUTH BRENT

Hatchlands Coarse Fishery

Contact: Malcolm Davies, Greyshoot Lane, Rattery, South Brent, TQ10 9LL, 01364 73500, madavies@onetel.net.uk, *Water:* Two acre lake, *Species:* Carp, Tench, Roach, Bream, Rudd and Gudgeon, *Permits:* No E.A. licence required. Block EA licence held by fisher *Charges:* £5 per person per day, *Season* Open all year, *Methods:* Barbless hooks only. No large Carp in keepnets.

Little Allers Coarse Fishery
Contact: M & J Wakeham, Little Allers Farm, Avonwick, South Brent, 01364 72563, 07855 427510, *Water:* 2 acre lake, *Species:* Carp, Bream, Tench, Roach, Rudd, *Permits:* On the bank, *Charges:* £5 per day adults, £3 under 16, £2.50 evening ticket after 5pm, *Season:* Open all year dawn to dusk, *Methods:* Barbless hooks only, no carp in keepnets.

SOUTH MOLTON

Dunsley Farm
Contact: Mr and Mrs Robins, Dunsley Farm, West Anstey, South Molton, EX36 3PF, 01398 341246, *Water:* Half acre lake, *Species:* Roach, Rudd, Carp and Tench, *Permits:* At the farmhouse, *Charges:* £3 adults. £1.50 children, *Methods:* Children under 16 must be accompanied by an adult.

Oaktree Fishery
Contact: George Andrews, Bottreaux Mill, West Anstey, South Molton, EX36 3PU, 01398 341568, oaktreefishery@btinternet.com, *Water:* 3 x 2 acre lakes, *Species:* All Carp, Tench, Bream, Roach, Perch, Koi Carp, Catfish, *Permits:* On site only, *Charges:* Day tickets: Adults from £5, Specimen lake £6, Junior/OAP from £4, Specimen lake £5, Eve tickets: Adult £3.50, Specimen lake £5, Junior/OAP £3.50 Specimen lake £4, *Season:* Open all year 24hrs, *Methods:* Barbless hooks only. No nut type baits. See board at fishery.

TAVISTOCK

Milemead Fisheries (Coarse Lakes)
Contact: Mr Harry Dickens, Mill Hill, Tavistock, PL19 8NP, 01822 610888, *Water:* Two Lakes of 2 acres each. Match Lake available for bookings, please phone for details. Regular Sunday open matches and Thursday evening matches in the summer, *Species:* Carp to 15lb, Tench to 4lb, Bream to 4lb, Roach to 2lb, Rudd to 1.5lb, Crucians to 1lb, *Permits:* Available from lakeside tackle and bait shop, *Charges:* Adult £5, Conc. £4, Evening tickets available (2002 prices), *Season:* All year, 7am to Dusk, *Methods:* Barbless hooks, All nets to be dipped prior to fishing, Please read the rule boards.

TIVERTON

Coombe Farm Fishponds
Contact: Mrs Curtis, Coombe Farm, Cadleigh, Tiverton, EX16 8HW, 01884 855337, *Water:* 3 lakes totalling 0.5 acre, *Species:* Carp to 20lb, Roach, Tench to 4lb, Bream to 1.5lb, *Charges:* £3 per day, *Season:* Open all year, *Methods:* No boilies.

Tiverton & District Angling Club
Contact: Exe Valley Angling, 19 Westexe South, Tiverton, EX16 5DQ, 01884 242275, *Water:* 11.5 Miles on Grand Western Canal, 1.25 acre mixed fishery lake at Exebridge. Various stretches on several rivers in Somerset, *Species:* Canal: Carp, Bream, Tench, Roach, Perch, Pike, Eels. Lakeside: Carp, Bream, Roach, Tench, Eels, Crucian Carp, *Permits:* Please ring Exe Valley for details. Also available from: Exeter Angling Centre, Enterprise Angling Taunton, Topp Tackle Taunton & Minnows Caravan Park - beside Grand Western Canal, *Charges:* Senior: Day £4, Annual £20. Conc: Junior & OAP Day £2.50, Annual £8, *Season:* Canal: Closed March 1st - May 31st inc, except 3 mile section (Basin to Halburton - ring for details). Lakeside: Open all year, Weekends full members only, Maximum five day permits per day, *Methods:* Canal Methods: Any. Restrictions: Fish from permanent pegs, no night fishing, no cars on bank, no digging of banks or excessive clearance of vegetation. Lakeside Methods: Any. Restrictions: No night fishing, no boilies, Trout pellets or nuts, one rod only, fishing from permanent pegs, no dogs, nets to be dipped. Ring Exe Valley Angling for full details.

West Pitt Farm Fishery
Contact: Susanne Westgate, Whitnage, Nr. Tiverton, EX16 7DU, 01884 820296, 07855 582374, susannewestgate@yahoo.com, *Water:* 3 lakes up to 1.25 acres, *Species:* Common & Mirror Carp, Bream, Tench, Roach, Rudd, Crucians, Golden Tench, Chub, Golden Orfe, *Permits:* Self service day tickets £4.50 per day (correct money please), *Charges:* £4.50/day,. £3.50 evenings, *Season:* All year, no closed season. Open dawn till dusk, *Methods:* No boilies, barbless hooks, nets to be dipped, groundbait in moderation.

TORRINGTON

Bakers Farm
Contact: Mr & Mrs Ridd, Bakers Farm, Moortown, Torrington, EX38 7ES, 01805 623260, *Water:* 1 acre lake, *Species:* Mirror & Common Carp, Tench, Roach & Rudd, *Charges:* £4/rod/day, *Methods:* Barbless Hooks, No large carp in keepnets.

Darracott
Contact: South West Lakes Trust, 01837 871565, info@swlakestrust.org.uk, *Water:* Ranger Tel: 01288 321262, *Species:* Roach up to 1lb. Mixed bags to 20lb plus of Roach, Rudd, Bream and Tench. Perch to 2.25lb. Carp to 15lb, *Permits:* See South West Lakes Trust coarse advert, *Charges:* Full day £4.75, Concession £3.75, 24 Hour £8.75, Season Day £80, Season Concession £60, Season Child (under 16) £35, Season Day & Night £120, Additional Fisheries £20 each, *Season:* Open all year 24 hours a day, *Methods:* No child under 14 years may fish unless accompanied by an adult over 18 years. No child under 16 may fish overnight unless accompanied by an adult over 18 years, and then only with permission of parent or legal guardian (letter to this effect must be produced).

Great Torrington Anglers Association (Coarse)
Contact: Paul Martin, 67 Calf Street, Torrington, EX38 7BH, 01805 623658, paul@olmargamesdevon.fsbusiness.co.uk, *Water:* Coarse fishing on local reservoirs, open to anglers from Torrington and surrounding areas, *Permits:* No day tickets sold by club, *Charges:* Annual membership Adult £5, Junior £3.

Stevenstone Lakes
Contact: Alan & Rebecca Parnell, Deer Park, Stevenstone, Torrington, EX38 7HY, 01805 622102, parnellaj@yahoo.co.uk, *Water:* Three lakes, total of six acres in a parkland setting, *Species:* Mirror Carp 23lb, Common 13lb, Tench 6lb, Rudd 1lb, Eels 3lb, *Permits:* Only at Deer Park, *Charges:* Day tickets £10 per day per person, *Season:* Open 7am to sunset from 1st April to 30th September, *Methods:* Barbless hooks only, no boilies, no nut type baits, no fish over 2lb in keepnets, no dogs, no litter. Unhooking mats essential.

TOTNES

East Moore Farm Fishery
Contact: John & Kelly Bowden, Diptford, Totnes, TQ9 7PE, 01364 73276, 07976 559090, *Water:* 1 lake totalling 2 acres, *Species:* Carp to 7lb, Rudd, Tench, Bream, Roach, *Charges:* On site, £5 day (2 rods per person). Under 13 half price, but must be accompanied by an adult, *Season:* Dawn to Dusk, open all year, night fishing by prior arrangement, *Methods:* No keepnets, except in matches, landing mats must be used, no boilies, barbless hooks only. Full rules at Fishery.

UMBERLEIGH

Bridleway Cottages
Contact: Fiona Gordon, Golland Farm, Burrington, Umberleigh, EX37 9JP, 01769 520263, golland@btinternet.co.uk, *Water:* 2 half acre lakes, *Species:* Carp, Tench and Roach, *Charges:* Occasional day tickets available, *Season:* Open all year, *Methods:* Barbless hooks only.

WINKLEIGH

Okehampton Coarse Fishing Club
Contact: Mrs Paisey, 68 Moyses Meadow, Okehampton, EX20 1JY, 01837 53746, *Water:* Enclosed still water. Brixton Barton Farm, *Species:* Common Carp to 8lb, Roach, Rudd, *Permits:* Fishing only with a member, *Charges:* £3.50 Guest, £6.50 Adult, £5 Junior, £12.50 Family ticket for full membership, *Season:* 12 months, sunrise to sunset, *Methods:* Barbless hooks. No fish over 2lb in keepnets.

Stafford Moor Fishery
Contact: Andy or Debbie Seery, Dolton, Winkleigh, EX19 8PP, 01805 804360, *Water:* 8 acre specimen lake, 100 pegs match fishery (bookings available); 2 acre pleasure lake. 4 acre Carp bagging water (3lb to 10lb fish). 3 acre lake with Tench, Crucians and Bream, *Species:* Carp 30lb, Tench 5lb, Bream 5lb, Roach 2lb, Rudd 1.5lb, Eels 5lb, *Permits:* At lodge at Stafford Moor. Specimen lake pre-booking only, *Charges:* £5 pleasure/day, £3.50 conc./OAP/Junior; £6 specimen/day £6 night, £4 conc./OAP/Junior. *Season:* All year, *Methods:* The method is banned, max. 6 pints of bait (incl. 2 pints of trout pellets), max. 2 kg groundbait, barbless hooks (max. size 6), night fishing by arrangement.

YELVERTON

Coombe Fisheries
Contact: Mr Stephen Horn, Yelverton, Nr Plymouth, 01822 616624, 07899 958493, schorn@agriplus.net, *Water:* Two 1 acre lakes, *Species:* Coarse fish: Rudd, Roach, Tench, Bream + various Carp (28lb), *Permits:* Local Post Office and also mobile phone 07788 715470, *Charges:* £4/day, £2.50/evening, *Season:* No close season, dawn to dusk, *Methods:* Barbless hooks, no peanuts.

DEVON Stillwater Trout

ASHBURTON

Venford
Contact: South West Lakes Trust, 01837 871565, info@swlakestrust.org.uk, *Species:* Brown Trout, *Charges:* Free to holders of a valid Environment Agency Licence, *Season:* 15th March - 12th October, *Methods:* Angling by spinning, bubble float & bait.

AXMINSTER

Lower Bruckland Fishery
Contact: David Satterley, Lower Bruckland Farm, Musbury, Axminster, EX13 8ST, 01297 552861, 0421 429077, info@fishing4trout.co.uk, *Water:* 2 x 2 acre lakes, *Species:* Tringle Lake: Rainbows to 30lb & Wild Browns, Serpentine Lake: Rainbows, *Permits:* Available at Angler's Hut by car park, *Charges:* Tringle: £16/day, £12/half day, £10/evening - Serpentine: 4 - fish £18, 2 - fish £12.50, *Season:* All year, *Methods:* Tringle: Catch & Release, max hook 10, Barbless - Serpentine: Catch & Keep, any method except Spinners.

BARNSTAPLE

Blakewell Fisheries
Contact: Mr Richard & John Nickell, Blakewell Fisheries, Muddiford, Barnstaple, EX31 4ET, 01271 344533, info@blakewellfisheries.co.uk, *Water:* 5 Acre Lake, *Species:* Rainbow to 22lb 11oz. Brown to 8lb 8oz and Brook Trout to 4lb 12oz, *Permits:* On Site, *Charges:* 5 Fish £22, 4 Fish £20, 3 Fish £18, 2 Fish £16, *Season:* All Year, *Methods:* Fly Only.

Southwood Fishery
Contact: Bratton Flemming, 01271 343608/344919, nigel.early@btopenworld.com, *Water:* 2.5 acre lake, max 10 rods, *Species:* Rainbow to 20lbs plus, *Permits:* Must be obtained in advance. Please phone numbers above or contact Kingfisher Tackle Shop, The Strand, Barnstaple, 01271 344919, *Charges:* £12 for 2 fish, £16 for 3 fish, £20 for 4 fish, *Season:* Tickets to fish for 7am - 12 noon, 12 noon - 5pm, 5pm - Dusk Summertime. Open all year, *Methods:* Tickets must be pre-booked. Fly only, children under 16 must be accompanied by a fishing adult.

BEAWORTHY

South Hay Fishery
Contact: Gill and Reg Stone, South Barn Farm, South Hay, Shebbear, Beaworthy, 01409 281857, r.d.stone@btinternet.com, *Water:* 2 acre Trout lake, 2 miles of River Torridge, *Species:* Rainbow Trout (lake), Brown Trout, Sea Trout, Salmon (river), *Charges:* Lake £5 per day plus £1.50 per lb, River £10 per day, *Season:* Lake - all year, River - Mid March to End September, *Methods:* Fly only.

BIDEFORD

Fosfelle Country House Hotel (Game)
Contact: Hartland, Bideford, 01237 441273, *Water:* Pond approx half acre, *Species:* Rainbow & Golden Trout, *Charges:* £7.50 half day - 2 Trout, *Season:* Open all year, *Methods:* Displayed on site.

Torridge Fly Fishing Club
Contact: Mr W.H. Akister (secretary), "Ebroch", North Down Rd, Bideford, EX39 3LT, 01237 475906, *Water:* 2 x 4 acre reservoirs situated 2 miles east of Bideford, *Species:* Stocked Rainbow Trout from 1.5 to 8lb. Natural Browns to 5lb, *Permits:* 2 day tickets allowed each day, *Charges:* Day tickets: £12.50 per day (3 fish limit) to be obtained at Summerlands Fishing Tackle, Westward Ho!, Tel. 01237 471291; Season tickets: £130 (waiting list: membership limited to 25), *Season:* 14th April - 16th December for Rainbow Trout, 14th April - 30th September for Brown Trout, *Methods:* Floating fly lines only.

CHAGFORD

Fernworthy

Contact: South West Lakes Trust, 01837 871565, info@swlakestrust.org.uk, *Species:* Brown Trout, *Permits:* Self Service Kiosk, *Charges:* Full day £9.50, Season £125, Reduced day £7.50, Season £95, Child/Wheelchair £2, Season £30, *Season:* Opens 1st April 2001 - 12th October, *Methods:* Catch & Release operates. Barbless hooks only.

CHUDLEIGH

Kennick

Contact: South West Lakes Trust, 01837 871565, info@swlakestrust.org.uk, *Water:* Ranger Tel: 01647 277587, *Species:* Premier Rainbow Fishery Bank & Boat. 2002 average 2.8 fish per rod day, *Permits:* Self Service Kiosk - Boats may be booked in advance: 01647 277587, *Charges:* Full day £16.75, Season £390. Concession day £13.50, Concession Season £295, Child/Wheelchair £3, Season £90. Evening Monday - Friday £13.50. Season Permits can be used on any Premier Fishery only. Boats £10 per day inc. 2 fish extra to bag limits. 'Wheelie Boat' available for disabled anglers (must be booked at least 48 hrs in advance), *Season:* Opens 22nd March 2003 - 31st October, *Methods:* No child under 14 years may fish unless accompanied by an adult over 18 years.

Kennick Fly Fishers Association

Contact: Mike Boston, 5 Shirburn Rd, Torquay, TQ1 3JL, 01803 325722, *Water:* 45 acre reservoir, *Species:* Rainbow & wild Brown Trout, *Permits:* Club members able to obtain SWLT discounted tickets, *Charges:* Membership fee for club is £8 annual subscription, *Methods:* I.A.W. SWLT byelaws.

CULLOMPTON

Goodiford Mill Fishery (Trout Lakes)

Contact: David Wheeler, Goodiford Mill, Kentisbeare, Cullompton, EX15 2AS, 01884 266233, paul@culmvalley.fsnet.co.uk, *Water:* 2 lakes set in 20 acres, *Species:* Rainbow - 17lb 5oz, Brown Trout - 20lb 4oz, Tiger, *Permits:* Rod licence required, *Charges:* £24 - 4 fish, £21 - 3 fish, £18 - 2 fish. Children under 14 must be accompanied by an adult, *Season:* All year, *Methods:* Max 10 longshank. Full rules on application.

HATHERLEIGH

Half Moon Fishery (Trout Lake)

Contact: Half Moon Inn, Sheepwash, Beaworthy, EX21 5NE, (01409) 231376, lee@halfmoon.demon.co.uk, *Water:* See also entry under Torridge. 3x 2 acre Trout lakes, *Species:* Rainbow Trout up to 3lb, *Permits:* Day tickets available to residents and non-residents, *Charges:* £10 - 2 fish, £15 - 4 fish.

HOLSWORTHY

Mill Leat Trout Fishery

Contact: Mr Birkett, Thornbury, Holsworthy, EX22 7AY, 01409 261426, cottages@mill-leat.fsnet.co.uk, *Water:* Two lakes totalling 3 acres, *Species:* Rainbow Trout, *Charges:* £5 plus £1.50 per lb. No Limit, *Season:* 1st April - 31st October, *Methods:* Fly only.

HONITON

Hollies Trout Farm

Contact: Fiona Downer, Sheldon, Honiton, EX14 4QS, 01404 841428, info@holliestroutfarm.co.uk, *Water:* Spring fed lake, *Species:* Rainbow & Brown Trout, *Charges:* 2 fish - £15, 3 fish - £20, 4 fish - £25, 5 fish - £30. Concessions for O.A.P. and under 12's, *Season:* Open all year dawn to dusk, *Methods:* Fly only, dry or wet.

Otter Falls (Game)

Contact: John or Carol, New Road, Upottery, Nr Honiton, EX14 9QB, 01404 861634, hols@otterfalls.fsnet.co.uk, *Water:* One Trout lake - circa 2.5 acres (see entry under River Otter, Devon), *Species:* Rainbow Trout to 12lbs, *Charges:* Trout £25 day, £15 half day - 2 fish, *Season:* Booking only, 8am to 1 hour after sunset, *Methods:* Barbless hooks. No keepnets.

Stillwaters

Contact: Michael Ford, Lower Moorhayne Farm, Yarcombe, Nr Honiton, EX14 9BE, 01404 861284, info@land-own.demon.co.uk, *Water:* 1 acre lake. 1 Sea Trout rod on River Axe at the Sea Pool, *Species:* Trout up to 17lb 10oz in lake. Sea Trout of average size in river, *Charges:* From £25 per day for River Axe fishing - 1 rod only. £10 per session on stillwaters lake, *Season:* March 1st - November 1st, *Methods:* Fly only.

IVYBRIDGE

Mill Leat Trout Farm

Contact: Chris Trant, Ermington, Nr Ivybridge, PL21 9NT, 01548 830172, chris@millgallery.com, *Water:* 0.75 acre lake, *Species:* Rainbow Trout average 2 to 4.5lb, *Permits:* E.A. Licence required, *Charges:* 2 fish £10, 4 fish £18, then £1.75/lbs, *Season:* Open all year - booking advisable, *Methods:* No lures.

KINGSBRIDGE

Valley Springs Coarse and Trout Fishery (Trout)

Contact: J. Bishop, Sherford, Nr Kingsbridge, TQ7 2BG, 01548 531574, info@valley-springs.com, *Water:* 2 lakes totalling approx 3 acres, Trout & Coarse, *Species:* Rainbow & Brown Trout, *Charges:* £10/Adult and £5/Child to fish plus fish caught at £2 per lb including E.A. Licence, *Season:* Fishing by appointment only, please telephone, *Methods:* Barbless hooks, traditional fly fishing methods only.

NEWTON ABBOT

Watercress Fishery

Contact: Mr Paul Cook, Kerswell Springs, Chudleigh, Newton Abbot, TQ13 ODW, 01626 852168, kirsty.cook@btinternet.com, *Water:* 3 spring fed lakes totalling approx 5 acres. Alder lake (specimen lake) Tiger, Brown & Rainbow, *Species:* Rainbow, Brown, Tiger Trout, *Permits:* On site. No E.A. rod licence required, *Charges:* Various tickets available. Please enquire. *Season:* Open all year, 8am to 1 hour after sunset, *Methods:* Rules on notice board at fishery.

OKEHAMPTON

Meldon

Contact: South West Lakes Trust, 01837 871565, info@swlakestrust.org.uk, *Species:* Brown Trout, *Charges:* Free to holders of a valid Environment Agency Licence, *Season:* 15th March - 12th October, *Methods:* Angling by spinning, fly or bait.

Roadford
Contact: South West Lakes Trust, 01837 871565, info@swlakestrust.org.uk, *Water:* Ranger Tel: 01409 211514, *Species:* Brown Trout Fishery - Boat & Bank (boats may be booked in advance: 01409 211514). 2002 rod average 2.9, *Permits:* Angling & Watersports Centre at Lower Goodacre, *Charges:* Full day £13.50, Season £290, Reduced day £11.50, Season £230, Child/Wheelchair £3, Season £60, Evening Mon-Fri £11. Boats £10 per day, *Season:* Opens 22 March 2003 - 12th October, *Methods:* Fly fishing only. Catch and release operates - Barbless hooks only. No child under 14 years may fish unless accompanied by an adult over 18 years.

Roadford Fly Fishing Club
Contact: Rod Dibble, 25 Pine View, Gunnislake, PL18 9JF, 01822 834188, rodneydibble@hotmail.com, *Water:* Club fishing at Roadford Lake, *Species:* Brown Trout, *Methods:* Fly only.

PLYMOUTH

Drakelands
Contact: Mr Elford, Higher Drakelands, Hemerdon, Plympton, Plymouth, 01752 344691, *Water:* 1.75 acre lake, *Species:* Brown Trout, Rainbow Trout, *Charges:* Ticket to fish £3 plus fish @ £1.85/lb, 1/2 day ticket £12 - 4 hrs (2 fish), £16 - 6 hrs (3 fish), £20 - 8 hrs (4 fish), £22 - 8 hrs (5 fish). Catch and release £12 day, *Season:* Open all year, Tuesday - Sunday, *Methods:* Barbless hooks only. Catch and release on all Brown Trout.

SEATON

Wiscombe Park Fishery (Trout Lakes)
Contact: Mike Raynor, Wiscombe Park Fishery, Colyton, EX24 6JE, 01404 871474, 07860 222342, michael@wiscombe.co.uk, *Water:* Two half acre lakes plus Coarse fishing, *Species:* Rainbow Trout, Brown Trout, *Permits:* Self-service (No booking), *Charges:* £17/day (8 fish limit), £12/4hrs (3 fish), £8.50/2 hrs (2 fish), Children under 15 free (accompanied by permit holding adult), *Season:* All year, *Methods:* Fly fishing (singles).

SOUTH BRENT

Avon Dam
Contact: South West Lakes Trust, 01837 871565, info@swlakestrust.org.uk, *Species:* Brown Trout, *Charges:* Free to holders of a valid Environment Agency Licence, *Season:* 15 March - 12 October, *Methods:* Angling by spinning, fly or bait.

Hatchlands Trout Lakes
Contact: Malcolm Davies, Greyshoot Lane, Rattery, South Brent, TQ10 9LL, 01364 73500, madavies@onetel.net.uk, *Water:* 6 acres, 2 lakes, *Species:* Rainbow, Brown, Golden, Blue and Brook Trout, *Permits:* No E.A. Permit required, *Charges:* Prices from £10 for 2 fish. Other prices on application. Sporting ticket from £16, Catch and Release £12, *Season:* Open all year, *Methods:* Barbless hooks on catch and release.

Somerswood Lake
Contact: S.A. Goodman, Brent Mill Farm, South Brent, TQ10 9JD, 01364 72154, *Water:* 2 acres in Avon valley, *Species:* Rainbow Trout, *Permits:* At farmhouse, *Charges:* Please enquire, *Season:* Open all year, *Methods:* Fly.

SOUTH MOLTON

Wistlandpound
Contact: South West Lakes Trust, 01837 871565, info@swlakestrust.org.uk, *Water:* Ranger Tel: 01288 321262, *Species:* Intermediate Rainbow Trout Fishery. Trout to 6lb, *Permits:* Post Office in Challacombe: (01598) 763229, The Kingfisher, Barnstaple: (01271) 344919. Lyndale News, Combe Martin: (01271) 883283, Variety Sports, Ilfracombe: (01271) 862039, *Charges:* Full day £11.50, Season £195, Reduced day £10.25, Season £175, Child/Wheelchair £2, Season £40, *Season:* Opens 15th March - 31sth October. *Methods:* Fly fishing only. Catch and release - barbless hooks.

TAVISTOCK

Milemead Fisheries (Trout Lake)
Contact: Mr Harry Dickens, Mill Hill, Tavistock, PL19 8NP, 01822 610888, *Water:* 2 acre spring fed lake, max 10 anglers at any one time, *Species:* Rainbow, Blue and Brown Trout from 1.5lb to 10lb plus, *Permits:* Available from lakeside tackle and bait shop, *Charges:* 2 fish - £12. 3 fish - £16. 4 fish - £19. 5 fish - £22 (2002 Prices), *Season:* Open all year 8.30 am to dusk, *Methods:* Fly fishing only, no catch and release, please read the rule boards.

Tavistock Trout Farm & Fishery
Contact: Abigail Underhill, Parkwood Road, Tavistock, PL19 9JW, 01822 615441, abigail@tavistocktroutfishery.co.uk, *Water:* 5 lakes totalling approx 4 acres, *Species:* Rainbow Trout, Brown Trout, *Charges:* Full day 4 fish permit - Osprey Lake £34, Full day 4 fish Kingfisher and Heron Lakes £16.50, *Season:* Open all year 8am - dusk, *Methods:* Max hook size 10.

TIVERTON

Bellbrook Valley Trout Fishery
Contact: Mr Chris Atwell, Bellbrook Farm, Oakford, Tiverton, EX16 9EX, 01398 351292, chris@bellbrookfishery.com, *Water:* 7 Lakes totalling 6.75 acres, *Species:* Rainbow Trout (25lb 12oz), Exmoor Blue (8lb 6oz) and Wild Brown Trout (7lb 8oz), *Charges:* Evening ticket £10, 3 fish normal £18, 2 fish specimen £22. Range of rover tickets, allowing mix of normal and specimen, start @ £25. Catch and release - £15 ticket, plus 1st fish can be taken, *Season:* Open all year 8.00am / dusk (No later than 9.00pm), *Methods:* Fly only, some catch & release available.

Bickleigh Mill
Contact: Bickleigh Mill, Bickleigh, Nr Tiverton, EX16 8RG, 01884 855419, general@bickleighmill.freeserve.co.uk, *Water:* Bickleigh Mill fishing ponds, *Species:* Rainbow Trout, *Permits:* Only at above, *Charges:* £10 for 3 fish, *Season:* Easter to end of September, *Methods:* Rod supplied.

TORRINGTON

Great Torrington Anglers Association (Trout)
Contact: Paul Martin, 67 Calf Street, Torrington, EX38 7BH, 01805 623658, paul@olmargamesdevon.fsbusiness.co.uk, *Water:* Fly fishing on local reservoirs and canal fishing, *Permits:* No day tickets sold by club, *Charges:* Annual membership Adult £5-00, Junior £3-00.

TOTNES

Newhouse Fishery

Contact: Newhouse Farm, Moreleigh, Totnes, 01548 821426, kirsty.cook@btinternet.com, *Water:* 4 acre lake (also see entry under River Fishing, Avon, Devon), *Species:* Rainbow Trout, Brown Trout, *Permits:* At above. No E.A. rod licence required, *Charges:* Various tickets available, *Season:* Open all year, *Methods:* Fly only, barbed hooks.

YELVERTON

Burrator

Contact: South West Lakes Trust, 01837 871565, info@swlakestrust.org.uk, *Species:* Low Cost Rainbow & Brown Trout, *Permits:* Esso Garage, Yelverton, *Charges:* Full day £9.50, Season £195, Reduced day £10.50, Season £175, Child/Wheelchair £2, Season £30, *Season:* Opens 15 March 2001 - 12th October, *Methods:* Catch & release operates. Barbless hooks only.

Burrator & Siblyback Fly Fishing & Angling Association

Contact: Derek Friend (Hon Sec), 01752 224822, pfleagues@hotmail.com, *Species:* Regular fortnightly competitions fishing South West Lakes Trust waters and sea fly fishing trips, *Permits:* Open to all, *Charges:* Family membership £15, members £10. All Juniors under 18 must be accompanied by an adult, *Season:* Contact Derek at the above number.

Burrator Fly Fishers Association

Contact: Geoff Riley (secretary), 6 Hazel Drive, Elburton, Plymouth, PL9 8PE, 01752 401370, geoff.riley@lineone.net, *Water:* Burrator Reservoir, *Species:* Stocked Rainbow and Brown Trout, *Permits:* From the Esso Garage at Yelverton, *Charges:* £9.25 for full day, *Season:* 15 March to 12 October, *Methods:* Fly with limited spinning. Barbless hooks encouraged.

DORSET River Fishing

THE 'HAMPSHIRE' AVON

For detailed description of the Hampshire Avon and tributaries, see under Hampshire River fishing.

RIVER AVON PEWSEY - CHRISTCHURCH

Fisheries located between Pewsey and Salisbury are predominantly managed for Brown Trout fly fishing. A mixture of Coarse, Salmon and Trout fishing is available on the main river between Salisbury and Christchurch.

Christchurch Angling Club (Game)

Contact: John Cheetham, 19b Willow Way, Christchurch, BH23 1JJ, 01202 490014, 07720 671706, jrcheetham@msn.com, *Water:* Largest club on the river Avon, mainly mid/lower Avon, Burgate - Christchurch, also Fishing on River Stour between Gains Cross and Christchurch. Stillwater Coarse fishing at Whitesheat. Various other stillwaters. Sea Trout at Christchurch Harbour. Please telephone the secretary for full details, *Species:* Salmon, Sea Trout, Rainbow Trout & Brown Trout, *Permits:* Steve Richards (Membership Secretary) Tel: 01202 474648 or Local Tackle shops, *Charges:* Adult £122, Junior £51, OAP/Concession £87. Salmon £222, *Season:* Rainbow Trout all year round. Brown Trout: 1st April to 15th October. Salmon 1st February to 31st August. Sea Trout 1st July - 31st October, *Methods:* See rules for individual waters.

Royalty Fishery

Contact: John Cheetham, 19b Willow Way, Christchurch, BH23 1JJ, 01202 490014, 07720 671706, jrcheetham@msn.com, *Water:* Approx 1 mile of double bank fishing. Lowest beat on the river. Controlled by Christchurch Angling Club, *Species:* Roach 3lb, Chub 8lb, Dace 1lb, Barbel 14lb, Pike 38lb, Bream 11lb, Perch 4lb, Carp 31lb, Tench 7lb, Salmon 40lb, Sea Trout 15lb, *Permits:* Tickets available from Davis Tackle only, *Charges:* Tel: 01202 485169. Free for Christchurch Angling Club members. Day tickets Adults Summer £8/ Winter £6, *Season:* Coarse: 16th June - 14th March. Sea Trout 15th April - 31st October. Salmon 1st February - 31st August, *Methods:* No spinning, no night fishing. No Barbel, Carp or game fish to be kept in keepnets.

Winkton Fishery

Contact: John Cheetham, 01202 490014, 07720 671706, jrcheetham@msn.com, *Water:* Approx 1 mile of fishing. Lower river near Christchurch, *Species:* Roach to 3lb 10oz, Chub to 6lb, Dace to 1lb, Barbel 13lb, Pike to 30lb, Perch to 3lb, *Permits:* Davis Tackle only as above, *Charges:* £8 per day (2 rods per day, coarse only), Block bookings for clubs available. Please call 01202 490014, *Season:* June 16th - March 14th, 7am to 2 hours after sunset, *Methods:* No spinning. Coarse only: No Barbel or game fish to be placed in keepnets.

FROME

The Frome rises through chalk on the North Dorset Downs near Evershot, and flows south east through Dorchester, and finally Wareham, where it confluences with the River Piddle in Poole harbour. The River Frome is well known for its excellent Salmon, Brown Trout and Grayling fishing. There are also good numbers of coarse fish in certain areas; although access is limited sport can be very rewarding. Salmon and Trout fishing is generally controlled by syndicates and local estates.

Dorchester Fishing Club
Contact: Mr J.Grindle (Hon. Sec.), 36 Cowleaze, Martinstown, DT2 9TD, 01305 889682, 07810 555316, john@36cowleaze.freeserve.co.uk, *Water:* Approx 6.5 miles of double bank on the Frome near Dorchester, Brown Trout fly fishing, *Species:* Brown Trout, Grayling, *Permits:* John Aplin, Dorchester (01305) 266500, *Charges:* Day tickets and membership available. Please telephone John Aplin for day tickets and John Grindle for membership details, *Season:* Apr 1st - Oct 14th, *Methods:* Dry fly and Nymph only. Barbless hooks are encouraged.

Frome, Piddle & West Dorset Fishery Association
Contact: R.J. Slocock, 01929 471274, *Water:* An amalgamation of of riparian owners with an interest in the welfare of river fisheries in their locality. Information can be obtained concerning estate waters from the contact above.

River Frome (Town Section)
Contact: Purbeck Angling Centre / Deano, 28 South Street, Wareham, BH20 4LU, 01929 550770, *Water:* 1 mile stretch of River Frome, *Species:* Roach, Dace, Grayling, Eels, Pike, Salmon, Trout, Sea Trout, Mullet, Bass, Flounder, Carp and Perch, *Permits:* Enquiries to Purbeck Angling Centre, *Charges:* Free fishing on public section. Enquiries to Purbeck Angling Centre, *Season:* Normal closed seasons, *Methods:* This stretch is run as a Coarse Fishery only. All Game and Saltwater fish to be returned immediately.

Wessex Chalk Streams Ltd. (Frome)
Contact: Richard & Sally Slocock, Lawrences Farm, Southover, Tolpuddle, Dorchester, DT2 7HF, 01305 848460, sally.slocock@virgin.net, *Water:* 5 Lakes & Pools totalling 4 acres for Rainbow Trout. Plus 16 Beats on Rivers Piddle & Frome for Brown Trout, *Species:* Brown Trout, *Permits:* From the above address, *Charges:* from £19 to £65, *Season:* 1st Apr - 1st Oct, *Methods:* Barbless hooks.

PIDDLE AND WEST DORSET STREAMS

'West Dorset' streams include the River Brit, Asker, Bride and Char. These streams are relatively short, 'steep' water courses supporting populations of mainly Brown Trout and Sea Trout.

The River Piddle rises at four major springs near Alton St. Pancras, initially flowing south before turning east at Puddletown towards Poole Harbour, where it confluences with the River Frome. This small chalk stream offers excellent Brown Trout fishing, with Salmon, Sea Trout and coarse fish in the lower reaches. Other fish species can be found in the River Piddle including, Roach, Dace, Pike and Perch. Much of the fishing is controlled by local syndicates and estate waters; further information about these groups can be obtained from the aforementioned Frome, Piddle and West Dorset Fishery Association.

Environment Agency - Piddle Fishery
Contact: Fisheries Recreation & Biodiversity Officer, Environment Agency, Rivers House, Sunrise Business Pk, Higher Shaftesbury Rd, Blandford, DT11 8ST, 01258 456080, *Water:* 3km of bank fishing on Lower Piddle, *Species:* Salmon & Sea Trout, *Permits:* 14 permits per annum, *Charges:* £199 plus vat (£34.82), subject to annual review.

Manor of Wareham
Contact: Guy Ryder, The Estate Office,, Manor of Wareham, Cow Lane, Wareham, BH20 4RD, 01929 552666, *Water:* Stretch on river Piddle single bank fishing, *Species:* Brown Trout and Sea trout, *Charges:* Season tickets only. Price on application, *Season:* E.A. Byelaws, *Methods:* E.A. Byelaws.

Wessex Chalk Streams Ltd. (Piddle)
Contact: Richard Slocock, Lawrences Farm, Tolpuddle, Dorchester, DT2 7HF, 01305 848460, sally.slocock@virgin.net, *Water:* 5 Lakes & Pools totalling 4 acres for Rainbow Trout. Plus 16 Beats on Rivers Piddle & Frome for Brown Trout, *Species:* Lakes: Rainbow Trout, Rivers: Brown Trout, *Permits:* At above address, *Charges:* Minimum £19 day, Max £65, *Season:* April 1st to October 15th, *Methods:* Fly Fishing only, most river beats are catch & release using barbless hooks.

STOUR

The River Stour in Dorset is well known by anglers across the country for quality of its fishing. Over the years many British record captures have been made here, for example the current Roach record stands at 4lb 3oz, taken from the Stour near Wimborne.

The Stour rises on the Greensand at St. Peters Pump in Stourhead Gardens and flows through Gillingham near by where it is joined by the Shreen Water and the River Lodden. The Stour stretches out for 96 km, passing through the Blackmoor Vale down to the sea at Christchurch; the total fall over this distance is approximately 230m. Other notable tributaries along its length include the River Tarrant confluencing near Spetisbury, the River Allen at Wimborne and the Moors River coming in near Christchurch. The Stour confluences with the River Avon at the 'Clay Pool' in Christchurch, before flowing into the harbour area and ultimately out into the English Channel.

Blandford & District Angling Club
Contact: Peter Brundish, 10 Windmill Road, Blandford Forum, DT11 7HG, 01258 453545, *Water:* 4 mls of Dorset Stour (Crown Meadows and Nutford) and 1 ml river at Bugs Water between Blandford and Charlton Marshell A350, *Species:* Roach to 1.5lb, Bream to 8lb 10oz, Perch to 3lb 2oz, Carp to 17lb, Chub & Pike to 25lb. Common Carp 28lb 12oz (Crown Meadows 2002), *Permits:* Conyers Tackle Shop, Market Place, Blandford Tel 01258 452307. Todber Manor Fishing Tackle Shop, Tel: 01258 820384. Or from the secretary, *Charges:* Senior £27.50, O.A.P. £16.50, Junior £8.50, Day tickets £4. Enquire for family membership, *Season:* Normal coarse season, *Methods:* Boilies in small amounts. Carp over 5lb to be weighed and released, not kept in keepnets.

Dorchester & District Angling Society
Contact: W. Lucy, Secretary, 7 Celtic Crescent, Dorchester, DT1 2QJ, 01305 264873, *Water:* 4 miles on Dorset Stour, 1.5 miles Dorset Frome plus lakes at Kingcombe and West Knighton. R. Brue Somerset plus water sharing agreements and Federation waters on Somerset Levels, *Species:* Roach, Dace, Chub, Pike, Gudgeon, Perch, Eels, Carp, Bream, Grayling, *Permits:* 'Reels & Deals', Weymouth, Aplins Tackle Dorchester, Weymouth Angling Centre, Surplus International, Dorchester, *Charges:* Adult members £40. Reductions for Juniors & Spouses. Members guest tickets, no day tickets, half-year membership from Dec 1st, *Season:* Jun 16th - Mar 14th, Stillwater open all year, *Methods:* Various, specific to particular waters.

Durweston Angling Association
Contact: Mr Vernon Bell (secretary), "Endcote", Durweston, 01258 451317, *Water:* 2 miles River Stour (including Weir & Mill Pool), *Species:* Bream, Roach, Rudd, Gudgeon, Dace, Eels, Chub, Pike, Perch, *Permits:* "The White Horse" Public House, Stour Paine, *Charges:* Day tickets: £3, River permit £30/adult, £5/under 16. *Season:* Close season 14th March - 16th June, *Methods:* Children under 10 years must be accompanied by an adult.

Gillingham & District A A (Stour)
Contact: Simon Hebditch (Hon. Secretary), 30 Meadowcroft, New Road, Gillingham, SP8 4SR, 01747 825931, 07990 690613, ditch@ham5.fsnet.co.uk, *Water:* 7 miles Upper Stour - Gillingham to Marnhull. Also Turners Paddock lake at Stourhead. Mappowder Court 4 lakes at Mappowder, *Species:* Roach 3lb, Chub 4lb 8oz, Barbel 6lb, Pike 21lb, Dace 1lb, Bream 6lb, Gudgeon 3oz, Perch 3lb, Tench 3lb, Carp 10lb, Eels 4lb. Trout, Grayling 2lb 8oz, *Permits:* Mr P Stone (Treasurer) The Timepiece, Newbury, Gillingham, Dorset, SP8 4HZ. Tel: 01747 823339. Mr J Candy, Todber Manor Fisheries Shop, Tel: 01258 820384, *Charges:* £4 day ticket, £23 season ticket. £12 juniors and concessions. (probable charges for 2003), *Season:* June 16th to March 14th, *Methods:* Best stick float with maggot casters and bread. Large lump of bread for Chub.

Muscliffe & Longham
Contact: Ivor Brittain, Bournemouth, 01202 514345, ivorbri@ntlworld.com, *Water:* 1.5 miles river Stour at Muscliffe and quarter mile at Longham, *Species:* Chub, Barbel, Roach, Dace, Pike, Eels, Minnow, Gudgeon and Perch, *Permits:* Free (owned by Bournemouth Council), *Charges:* Free. E.A. licence required, *Season:* 16th June to 14th March, *Methods:* No restrictions.

Ringwood & District A.C. (Stour)
Contact: Mr Steve Martin, 2 Oakmead Road, Creekmoor, Poole, BH17 7XN, 01202 777892, 07812 360278, steve.martin1@ntlworld.com, *Water:* 11 stretches on Stour including total control of Throop fishery and various stretches upstream to Stourpaine, *Species:* Throop - Barbel to 16lb, Chub 7lb. Middle regions good general Roach, Chub, Bream, Pike, Perch, some Trout, Grayling and Carp, *Permits:* Local tackle shop or contact Caroline Groom (Membership Secretary) on: 01202 525615, *Charges:* Adult £100, Junior £40, concessions for OAP's and disabled; Throop day tickets £8.00. Concessions, O.A.P's, Disabled and Juniors available from local tackle dealers, *Season:* As per coarse season, *Methods:* All on reverse of ticket.

Stalbridge Angling Association (Stour)
Contact: 01963 362291, *Water:* 2.5 miles Stour, 3 Lakes (Buckland Newton), *Species:* Bream, Tench, Roach, Dace, Pike, Chub, Carp, Rudd, *Permits:* Stalbridge Angling 01963 362291, *Charges:* Senior Annual £22 no joining fee, Junior (under 17 years) £8 & Concessions (Reg. Disabled & OAPs) £12 no joining fee. Husband and wife ticket £30. Day Tickets £4 senior, £2 junior, *Season:* No closed season on Lakes, *Methods:* No boilies on ponds, no braided lines, no fixed method feeders or fixed leads. Full rules available with permit.

Sturminster & Hinton A.A
Contact: S. Dimmer, 38 Grosvenor Rd, Stalbridge, DT10 2PN, 01258 472788/ 01963 363291, steve@dimmer.freeserve.co.uk, *Water:* 14 miles mid River Stour, 3 small lakes (Stoke Wake Lake & High Bench Lake) members only, *Species:* Roach, Chub, Tench, Bream, Perch, Carp, Pike, *Permits:* Harts Garden Supplies, Kevs Autos or S. Dimmer (Membership Secretary) 01963 363291(evenings), *Charges:* £4/day, £10/ week, Juniors £3/season, Adults £17.50 & £5 joining fee, *Season:* March 14th - June 16th, *Methods:* No dogs, radios, no live baiting, no night fishing, one rod, second rod for Pike only.

Throop Fisheries
Contact: Ringwood & District Angling Club, Mr Steve Martin, 2 Oakmead Road, Creekmore, Poole, 01202 777892, 07812 360278, steve.martin1@ntlworld.com, *Water:* See entry under Coarse Fisheries - Bournemouth. 10 miles on Dorset Stour.

Wareham & District Angling Society
Contact: Mr. Abrams, 114 Portland Rd, Weymouth, 01305 783145, denning_tackle@yahoo.co.uk, *Water:* River waters on North Dorset Stour and the Frome. 3 lakes Wareham area, *Species:* Coarse, *Permits:* Wessex Angling, Poole, Dorset Tel: 01202 668244; Dennings Tackle, Wyke Regis, *Charges:* Senior £35, Ladies / O.A.P's £16, Junior £15. Membership runs Jun 1st to May 31st (2002 prices), *Season:* One lake open during Coarse closed season, *Methods:* Barbless, no litter/cans, variations as per membership book.

Wimborne & District Angling Club (Stour)
Contact: G.E.Pipet (chairman), 12 Seatown Close, Canford Heath, Poole, BH17 8BJ, 01202 382123, *Water:* 10 miles River Stour, 16 lakes, 1 mile River Avon, *Species:* Trout & Coarse Fisheries, *Permits:* Certain waters are available on Guest Tickets £6 from Wessex Angling Centre, 321 Wimborne Rd, Oakdale, Poole, Dorset, *Charges:* £75 plus £8 joining fees, *Methods:* Barbless hooks on Coarse Stillwaters, no floating baits.

Dorset Stillwater Coarse

BEAMINSTER

Higher Kingcombe Coarse Fishing
Contact: Mr Crocker, Higher Kingcombe, Dorchester, DT2 0EH, 01300 321079, kingcombe@eurobell.co.uk, *Water:* 5 lakes - approx 4 acres of water in total, *Species:* Carp (Mirror, Common & Ghost), Perch, Roach, Rudd, Bream, Tench. Specimen lake - Carp to 27lb, *Charges:* Day ticket £5, Evening (after 6pm) £3, Night (10pm - 6am) £4, 24hrs ticket £7.50, Juniors (16 and under) £2.50 per day, *Season:* Open all year, *Methods:* Max 2 rods per person, barbless hooks only, U.14's must be accompanied by an adult.

BLANDFORD

Milton Abbas Lakes
Contact: Wayne Little / Lesley Woodcock, Milton Abbas, Blandford, DT11 0BW, 01258 880919, 07780 966117, *Water:* 8 acre syndicate lake - waiting list - phone for application form. 3 acre day ticket lake (new for 2003). *Species:* Carp 10lbs up to 18lbs, Grass Carp to 16lbs, Tench to 6lbs, Roach to 2lbs, Crucian Carp, Bream, Tench, Perch & Eels, *Permits:* Telephone Bookings only. Maximum of 10 anglers per day. Tickets on the bank, *Charges:* Adult £10.00 per day, £15 - 24 hours. Juniors £5 per day, £10 - 24 hours (Must be under 16 and accompanied by an adult), *Season:* Day ticket lake opening April 2003. No close Season. Fishing times 7am until Sunset. *Methods:* No keep nets or Carp sacks, 2 rods only. No peas, nuts or beans, a suitable landing net and unhooking mat if Carp fishing, no dogs, fires, swimming or bait boats.

BOURNEMOUTH

East Moors Lake

Contact: Mr. Nicolas Hoare, East Moors Farm, East Moors Lane, St. Leonards, Ferndale, Nr Bournemouth, 01202 872302, *Water:* 1.5 acre lake, *Species:* Carp: Common, Mirror, Ghost, Leather, Purple Blushing; Tench, Gold Tench, Roach, Perch, Rudd, Chub & Pike, *Charges:* Members only, Country/Holiday membership available - Please telephone for details, *Methods:* Barbless hooks only, no boilies, no keepnets, no dogs. Children under 14 must be accompanied by adult.

Throop Fisheries (Coarse Lake)

Contact: Ringwood & District Angling Club, Mr Steve Martin, 2 Oakmead Road, Creekmore, Poole, 01202 777892, 07812 360278, steve.martin1@ntlworld.com, *Water:* Northern edge of Bournemouth. 10 Miles of river bank on Dorset Stour & Stillwater Mill Pool. *Species:* Barbel, Chub, Carp, Roach, Tench, Perch, Dace, Pike, *Permits:* Yeovil Angling Centre - Tel. 01935 476777, Ringwood Tackle - Tel. 01425 475155, Bournemouth Fishing Lodge - Tel. 01202 514345, or contact Caroline Groom (Membership Secretary) 01202 525615, *Charges:* Prices on application & list, *Season:* 16th June - 14 March (Open every day between these dates), *Methods:* No night fishing.

BRIDPORT

Highway Farm

Contact: John & Pauline Bale, West Road, Bridport, DT6 6AE, 01308 424321, bale@highwayfarm.co.uk, *Water:* 2 small lakes in quiet, secluded valley, *Species:* Carp, Tench, Roach, Rudd, *Permits:* From the Post Office, *Charges:* £4.50 day / £3 half day, *Season:* Open all year, dawn to dusk. No night fishing, *Methods:* No boilies or keep nets. Barbless hooks only. No dogs.

Mangerton Valley Coarse Fishing Lake

Contact: Clive & Jane Greening, New House Farm, Mangerton Lane, Bradpole, Bridport, DT6 3SF, 01308 458482, jane@mangertonlake.freeserve.co.uk, *Water:* 1.6 acre lake, *Species:* Carp to 26lb (Common and Mirror), Roach, Tench, *Permits:* From Post Office, *Charges:* £5 day, £3 half day, £2 evening, *Season:* Possibly closed March - April - May (please ring first), *Methods:* Barbless hooks. No boilies or beans. No nuts, no dogs. Night fishing by arrangement. All children under 12 to be accompanied by an adult.

Washingpool Farm Fishing

Contact: West Bay Watersports, 10a West Bay, Bridport, DT6 4EZ, 01308 421800, sales@anglingmailorder.com, *Water:* 2 lakes, *Species:* Carp to 10lb, Mirror Common Crucian, Ghost 15lb, Wild Carp, Tench, Roach, Rudd & Bream, *Charges:* Limited Day tickets in advance from West Bay Watersports. £5 per day 2 rods, *Season:* Open all year dawn to dusk, *Methods:* Barbless hooks only, no keepnets.

CHRISTCHURCH

Avon Tyrrell Lakes

Contact: Richard Bonney, Avon Tyrrell House, Bransgore, Christchurch, BH23 8EE, 01425 672347, info@avontyrrell.org.uk, *Water:* Two lakes totalling approx 2.5 acres, *Species:* Carp, Tench, Roach, Bream, Perch and Rudd, *Permits:* On site from reception, *Charges:* £6 Day Tickets Adults. £3 Juniors(Under 16). Season Tickets also available, please note Night Fishing only available on a season ticket, *Season:* Open mid June to Mid March 8am to 8pm, *Methods:* Barbless Hooks, No keepnets, No nut baits. See rules on site.

Christchurch Angling Club (Coarse Ponds)

Contact: John Cheetham, 19b Willow Way, Christchurch, BH23 1JJ, 01202 490014, 07720 671706, jrcheetham@msn.com, *Water:* Various coarse ponds including Blashford, Somerley and Cranebrook lakes. Please telephone the secretary for full details. See entry under Hampshire Avon, *Species:* Carp to 44lbs, Pike to 36lbs, Bream 14lbs, Perch 4lbs, Tench 10lbs, Roach, Rudd, *Permits:* Steve Richards (Membership Secretary) Tel: 01202 474648 or Local Tackle shops, *Charges:* Adult £122, Junior £51, OAP/Concession £87, *Season:* 16th June - 14th March. Night fishing available with prepaid permit, *Methods:* See individual fishery rules.

Hordle Lakes

Contact: M.F. Smith, Hordle Lakes, Golden Hill, Ashley Lane, Hordle, Nr New Milton, 01590 672300, 07778 954799, *Water:* Seven spring fed lakes set in 11 acres, *Species:* Double figure Carp. Tench, Roach, Rudd, Bream and Perch, *Permits:* At the fishery, *Charges:* Adults £7 per day. OAPs £5. Kiddies pool £3, *Season:* Open all year 8am to dusk, *Methods:* All fish returned immediately. No groundbaiting, loose feeding only. Barbless hooks only, no larger than size 6. No boilies, beans, nuts, trout bait or floating crust/biscuit. Full rules at the fishery.

Mudeford Wood Angling Club

Contact: 01202 484518, *Water:* Contact Pro Angling. Half acre lake, *Species:* Carp, Tench, Roach, Rudd, *Permits:* Pro Angling, Barrack Road, Christchurch. Limit of 3 day tickets per day, *Charges:* £5 per rod per day, *Season:* Closed 31st Mar 03 - 1st Jun 03, fishing from 7am till one hour after sunset, *Methods:* Barbless hooks only, no boilies, no keepnets.

Orchard Lakes

Contact: Mr R Southcombe, New Lane, Bashley, New Milton, BH25 5TD, 01425 612404, 07973 963304, *Water:* 3 small lakes, largest 2 acres. New 50 peg match lake opening Summer 2003 (bookings being taken), *Species:* Carp, Tench, Bream, Roach, Rudd, Perch, *Permits:* Day tickets on the bank, *Charges:* From £6/ day main & Tench lake; £5 on Match Pool, *Season:* Open all year 7am to dusk, *Methods:* Barbless hooks only. No keepnets.

Sopley Farm PYO

Contact: Sopley Farm PYO, Sopley, Christchurch, 01425 475155, *Water:* 8 acre lake. 1000 yard perimeter, *Species:* Carp, Bream, Roach, Rudd, *Permits:* At local Tackle shops, *Charges:* £5 Day, £4 OAP, *Season:* All year.

Whirlwind Lake

Contact: Mr & Mrs Pillinger, Whirlwind Rise, Dudmore Lane, Christchurch, BH23 6BQ, 01202 475255, ww@whirlwind86.freeserve.co.uk, *Water:* Secluded lake, *Species:* Common, Crucian and Mirror Carp, Roach, Rudd, Tench, Chub etc, *Permits:* On site and local fishing tackle shops. Davis Tackle, 75 The Bargates, Christchurch: 01202 485169. Pro Tackle, 258 Barrack Road, Christchurch: 01202 484518. Advanced booking advisable, limited number available, *Charges:* Adults £7.50 day ticket. £5 half day (Limited places). Children (must be accompanied) £5 day, *Season:* Open all year, *Methods:* Barbless hooks only, no keepnets, no boilies.

CORFE

Arfleet Mill Lakes

Contact: Mr B Charron, Dairy Cottage, Knitson, Corfe Castle, BH20 5JB, 01929 427421, *Water:* 1 acre spring fed lake, 1 acre deep water lake and a young anglers pool. Situated off the B3351 near Corfe Castle, *Species:* Carp to 29lb 3oz, Roach, Rudd, Tench, Perch and Eel, *Permits:* Local Tackle shops or on Telephone number above, *Charges:* £6.50 day - 2 rods, £3.95 1/2 day and concessions for children under 16, *Season:* Opens March 29th 2003. Night fishing by arrangement only, *Methods:* No Trout pellets, no keepnets, barbless hooks only, no ground bait.

CRANBORNE

Gold Oak Fishery

Contact: Mr J Butler, Gold Oak Farm, Hare Lane, Cranborne, 01725 517275, *Water:* 7 small lakes, *Species:* Carp to 20lb, Green + Golden Tench to 5-6lb, Perch 2.5lb, Roach 2lb, Chub 4lb, Bream 3lb, *Charges:* Summer day - £7 Adult, £5 Junior. 1/2 day - £5 Adult, £3 Junior. Eve - £3 Adult, £1 Junior. Winter day - £5 Adult, £3 Junior. 1/2 day - £3 Adult, £2 junior, *Season:* All year, *Methods:* No large fish in keepnets, barbless hooks, dogs on lead.

Martins Farm Fishery

Contact: Mr Ball, Martins Farm, Woodlands, Nr Verwood, 01202 822335, *Water:* 2.5 acre spring fed lake, *Species:* Carp, Tench, Perch, Roach, Rudd, *Permits:* Tel: 01202 822335, *Charges:* £8 Adult day ticket, £4 Juniors (under 14), *Season:* Closed 16th March - 16th June, *Methods:* No keepnets, barbless hooks, no hemp/boilies.

Wimborne & District Angling Club (Coarse Lakes)

Contact: G.E.Pipet (chairman), 12 Seatown Close, Canford Heath, Poole, BH17 8BJ, 01202 382123, *Water:* 11 coarse lakes, 10 miles river Stour, 1 mile river Avon. 5 Trout lakes. See also entry under Stour, *Species:* Mixed Coarse, *Permits:* Certain waters are available on guest tickets. £6 from Wessex Angling, 321 Wimborne Rd, Oakdale, Poole, *Charges:* £75 plus £8 joining fees, *Methods:* Barbless hooks on Coarse Stillwaters, no floating baits.

DORCHESTER

Dorchester & Dist. Angling Society (Coarse Lake)

Contact: W. Lucy, Secretary, 01305 264873, *Water:* See entry under Stour. Coarse lakes at Kingcombe and West Knighton, *Species:* Carp, Tench, Perch and Roach, *Season:* Lakes open all year, *Methods:* Barbless hooks only. No boilies or bivvies on lakes.

Gillingham & District A.A. (Mappowder Court)

Contact: Simon Hebditch (Hon. Secretary), 30 Meadowcroft, New Road, Gillingham, SP8 4SR, 01747 825931, 07990 690613, ditch@ham5.fsnet.co.uk, *Water:* Mappowder Court Fishing Complex (4 lakes), Mappowder Nr Dorchester. (see also entry under river fishing Stour), *Species:* Crucian/Crucian cross 2lb, Carp 22lb, Tench 4lb, Eels 3lb, Roach 2lb, Rudd 1lb, Gudgeon, Perch 2lb, Bream 3lb, Barbel 1lb, Grass Carp 8lb, *Permits:* Mr P Stone (Treasurer) The Timepiece, Newbury, Gillingham, Dorset, SP8 4HZ. Tel: 01747 823339. Mr J Candy, Todber Manor Fisheries Shop, Tel: 01258 820384. Kings Stag Garage, Kings Stag, Nr Hazelbury Bryan, *Charges:* £4 day ticket, £23 season ticket. £12 juniors and concessions. (probable charges for 2003), *Season:* Open all year, *Methods:* Barbless hooks. Mainly pole fishing.

Hermitage Lakes (Coarse)

Contact: Nigel Richardson, Common Farm, Hermitage, Cerne Abbas, Dorchester, DT2 7BB, 01963 210556, *Water:* Half acre lake, *Species:* Carp, *Charges:* Day ticket £4, *Season:* Closed 14th March - 16th June, *Methods:* Barbless hooks, no keepnets.

Luckfield Lake Fishery

Contact: John Aplin, 1 Athelstan Road, Dorchester, DT1 1NR, 01305 266500, 07889 680464, *Water:* 1.5 acre clay pit in beautiful surroundings, *Species:* Carp to 23lb, Tench to 9lb plus, Roach to 3lb plus, *Permits:* As above, *Charges:* Day £6, Night £10, 1/2 season £40, *Season:* Open all year, *Methods:* No keepnets, barbless hooks.

Lyons Gate Fishing Lakes

Contact: Lyons Gate, Nr Cerne Abbas, Dorchester, DT2 7AZ, 01300 345260, *Water:* Five lakes totalling approximately 3.5 acres, *Species:* Top lake: Carp to approx 20lb, Roach and Rudd. Carp only lake. Bream and Sturgeon lake. Three island lake with Carp, Roach, Rudd and Tench, *Charges:* £4 per day (2 rods), *Season:* Open all year dawn to dusk, *Methods:* No night fishing, barbless hooks only. No groundbaiting - loose feed only. Full details at the fishery.

Pallington Lakes

Contact: Mr Simon or Mrs Tini Pomeroy, Pallington, Dorchester, DT2 8QU, 01305 848141, 07887 840507, pallatrax@aol.com, *Water:* 3 lakes and a stretch of the river Frome, *Species:* Lakes: Carp to 33lb, Tench to 12lb 3oz, Perch to 4lb 13oz, Grayling to 3lb 12oz, Roach 3lb, Bream 10lb, Rudd 3lb, *Permits:* As above, *Charges:* Lakes: Day £8, Evening £4, 24 hours £15. Juniors half price. Extra charge for third rod. River by arrangement, *Season:* All year round. Ticket office open daily 8 to 10am and 4 to 5pm. Otherwise fishing by appointment only, *Methods:* Barbless hooks, No keepnets. No nut baits. All anglers must be in possesion of a fish antiseptic. All Carp anglers must have min. 36" landing net and unhooking mat. Nets to be dipped.

GILLINGHAM

Culvers Farm Fishery

Contact: V.J. Pitman, Culvers Farm, Gillingham, SP8 5DS, 01747 822466, *Water:* One 1.5 acre lake. One 3 acre lake, *Species:* Carp, Bream, Roach and Tench, *Charges:* Day £5. Half Day £3. OAP's and under 16 £3 all day, *Season:* Open all year. No night fishing, *Methods:* Barbless hooks only. No Boilies. No keepnets allowed on Middle Mead. Lower Mead - keepnets permitted.

LYME REGIS

Wood Farm Caravan Park

Contact: Jane Pointing, Axminster Road, Charmouth, DT6 6BT, 01297 560697, holidays@woodfarm.co.uk, *Water:* 2 ponds totalling approx 1 acre, *Species:* Carp, Rudd, Roach, Tench & Perch, *Permits:* Rod licences sold, *Charges:* £3.50 day ticket. £15 week. £35 season, *Season:* All year, *Methods:* No boilies, keepnets. Barbless hooks only.

POOLE

Alder Hills Fishery

Contact: Dave Cates, Sharp Road, Talbot Heath, Poole, 07939 514346, alderhillsfishing@hotmail.com, *Water:* Mature 2.5 acre clay pit situated on the Poole / Bournemouth border, *Species:* Carp (common, Mirror and Koi) to 20lb plus, Tench 6lb plus, Roach 2lb plus, Pike 10lb plus, Perch, Eels and Rudd, *Permits:* Day tickets must be puchased in advance from: Wessex Angling Centre, Castaways Tackle, AC Angling, Bournemouth Fishing Lodge or the Dorset Knob Pub at the end of Sharp Road. All are situated locally. Annual tickets available from Dave Cates on 07939 514346, *Charges:* Adult day ticket (16-64 years) £5. Junior day (under 16-over 64) £2.50. Annual tickets from £15. Please call Dave Cates on 07939 514346, *Season:* Open 16 June to 14 March from 7am to dusk. Night fishing by arrangement only, *Methods:* Barbless hooks only. 2 rods per person maximum. Tickets in advance only. All litter must be taken home.

STALBRIDGE

Stalbridge Angling Association (Coarse Lake)

Contact: 01963 362291, *Water:* See also entry under Stour. Buckland Newton Lakes - 3 lakes.

STURMINSTER NEWTON

Sturminster & Hinton A.A (Coarse Lakes)

Contact: S. Dimmer, 38 Grosvenor Rd, Stalbridge, DT10 2PN, 01258 472788/ 01963 363291, steve@dimmer.freeserve.co.uk, *Water:* 3 small lakes (Stoke Wake Lake & High Bench Lake) members only. Also see entry under Stour.

Todber Manor Fisheries

Contact: John Candy, Manor Farm, Todber, Sturminster Newton, DT10 1JB, 01258 820384, 07974 420813, info@todbermanor.co.uk, *Water:* Two acre canal style lake; one acre Specimen Lake; 2 x 1 acre small Carp lakes & other species i.e. Roach, Tench, Rudd, *Species:* Roach, Skimmers, Tench, Gudgeon, Crucians, Perch and Barbel. Specimen Lake Carp 20lb plus, *Permits:* As above, *Charges:* £5 per day. Specimen Lake £20 for 24 hours, *Season:* Open all year, *Methods:* Barbless hooks only. No keepnets on specimen lake.

WAREHAM

Wareham & District Angling Society (Coarse Lakes)

Contact: Mr. Abrams, 114 Portland Rd, Weymouth, 01305 783145, denning_tackle@yahoo.co.uk, *Water:* See entry under Stour - 3 lakes including Breach Pond, Pitmans Pond & Lily Pond.

WEYMOUTH

Osmington Mills Holidays

Contact: Reception, Osmington Mills, Weymouth, DT3 6HB, 01305 832311, holidays@osmingtonmills.fsnet.co.uk, *Water:* 1 acre lake, *Species:* Carp, Tench, Bream, Roach, *Permits:* Caravan Park reception, on bank, *Charges:* £6 per day Adults, £3 under 16, £3.50 Evening ticket after 5pm, *Season:* May 23rd - March 15th, *Methods:* Barbless hooks, no keepnets, no particle bait.

Radipole Lake

Contact: Mr D.Tattersall, Council Offices, North Quay, Weymouth, DT4 8TA, 01305 206234, 07980 730069, davidtattersall@weymouth.gov.uk, *Water:* 70 acres plus, *Species:* Carp to 20lb, Eels, Roach to 2lb, Dace, Pike, Mullet, *Permits:* Reels and Deals, 61b St. Thomas Street, Weymouth: 01305 787848. Weymouth Angling Centre, 24 Trinity Road, Weymouth: 01305 777771, *Charges:* Day - Junior £2, Adult £4, 60 plus £3; Monthly - Juniors £5, Adult £16, 60 plus £10; Annual - Adult £38, 60 plus £28, Junior £12, *Season:* 16th June - 14th March, *Methods:* 2 rod max, barbless hooks only, no bivvies.

Warmwell Holiday Park

Contact: John Aplin - Fishery Manager, Warmwell, Nr Weymouth, DT2 8JE, 01305 257490, 07889 680464, *Water:* 3 lakes. 2 acre specimen lake - 20 swims pre-booking only. 2 mixed fishing lakes, *Species:* Carp to 30lb, Perch to 4lb, Pike to double figures, Rudd, Crucians, Eels, *Permits:* Day tickets available all year, but must be purchased in advance. Contact fishery manager on number above, *Charges:* Day tickets £7 dawn to dusk on specimen lake. Other lakes £4 per day, *Season:* Open all year, *Methods:* Specimen Lakes: Barbless hooks. No nuts, beans or pulses. 2 rods max. No keepnets. No remote control boats. Unhooking mats must be used. Minimum 10lb line.

WIMBORNE

Crooked Willows Farm

Contact: Mr & Mrs VJ Percy, Mannington, Wimborne, BH21 7LB, 01202 825628, *Water:* 1.5 acres, *Species:* Carp to 20lb, Tench to 6lb, Chub 4lb, Roach, Rudd & Crucians, *Permits:* Available on bank, *Charges:* £5/day, Juniors £3, *Season:* Dawn to Dusk all year round, *Methods:* Barbless hooks only, no groundbait, no keepnets.

Environment Agency - Little Canford Ponds

Contact: Fisheries Recreation & Biodiversity Officer, Environment Agency, Rivers House, Sunrise Business Pk, Higher Shaftesbury Rd, Blandford, DT11 8ST, 01258 456080, *Water:* Approx. 2 acres with facilities for the Disabled including fully accessible fishing platforms, *Species:* Carp, Bream, Roach, Perch Tench, Rudd, Pike, *Charges:* Adult £42, Conc. £21, Junior £21, under 12 years free (subject to annual review).

Riverside Lakes

Contact: Tony Perkins, Riverside Farm, Slough Lane, Horton, BH21 7JL, 01202 821212, tony@riverside-lakes.co.uk, *Water:* 3 lakes over 6 acres, *Species:* Carp, Koi, Rudd, Tench, Perch, Roach, Bream, Orf & Eels, *Permits:* Bailiff collects money & issues tickets on-site, *Charges:* £6.50 Day ticket, £4.50 Senior & under 14, *Season:* All year, *Methods:* No barbs, no night fishing, no keepnets, no improper equipment, no boilies.

Whitemoor Lake

Contact: 400 Colehill Lane, Colehill, Wimborne, BH21 7AW, 01202 884478, *Water:* 2 acre lake and half acre canal, *Species:* Carp 25lb, Tench 7lb, Perch 4 to 9lbs, Roach 2lb, Rudd 1 to 8lbs, *Permits:* Minster Sports (Wimborne), Bournemouth Fishing Lodge (Bournemouth), *Charges:* Adults £6, Juniors £3.50, O.A.P's £4, *Season:* No close season, *Methods:* No barbed hooks, no keepnets.

DORSET Stillwater Trout

BRIDPORT

Mangerton Mill

Contact: Mr Harris, Mangerton Mill, Mangerton, Bridport, DT6 3SG, 01308 485224, *Water:* 1 acre lake, *Species:* Rainbow Trout, *Permits:* Post Office, *Season:* 1st April - 31st December, *Methods:* Max hook size 10.

CRANBORNE

Wimborne & District Angling Club (Trout Lakes)

Contact: Mr J Burden, 35 Hardy Crescent, Wimborne, BH21 2AR, 01202 889324, *Water:* 5 Trout lakes plus Brown Trout on the river Avon. See also entry under Stour, *Charges:* £75 plus £8 joining fees.

DORCHESTER

Flowers Farm Fly Fishers

Contact: Alan.J.Bastone, Flowers Farm, Hilfield, Dorchester, DT2 7BA, 01300 341351, *Water:* 5 lakes total 3.75 acres, *Species:* Rainbow & Brown Trout. Best fish in 2002 - 13lb Rainbow and 5lb 4oz Brown, *Permits:* Some 25 and 50 fish tickets available. Prices on request (Tel/Fax: 01300-341351), *Charges:* £20 per day, £15 half day, £11.50 evening, *Season:* Open all year 5.30am to dusk, *Methods:* Single fly, max size 10, Bank fishing only.

Hermitage Lakes (Trout)

Contact: Nigel Richardson, Common Farm, Hermitage, Cerne Abbas, Dorchester, DT2 7BB, 01963 210556, *Water:* 3 half acre lakes, *Species:* Rainbow & Brown trout, *Charges:* Day (4 fish) £15, Half day (3 fish) £12, Evening (2 fish) £9, *Season:* Open all season, *Methods:* Max size 10 longshank.

Wessex Fly Fish. Trout Lakes & Chalk Streams Ltd

Contact: Richard & Sally Slocock, Lawrences Farm, Southover, Tolpuddle, Dorchester, DT2 7HF, 01305 848460, sally.slocock@virgin.net, *Water:* See entries under Piddle and Frome. 5 clearwater lakes and pools totalling 4 acres, *Species:* Lakes: Rainbow Trout only. Rivers: Brown Trout only, *Permits:* From the above address, *Charges:* Lakes: Day £26, £22/6hrs, £18/4hrs, £15/evening, conc.(OAP) £18 (3 fish - usual £18 ticket only 2 fish) and favourable hours, *Season:* Lakes: March 1st - January 2nd, *Methods:* Fly only. Lakes: Max 10 h/s. Rivers: Barbless or de-barbed.

LYME REGIS

Amherst Lodge

Contact: Darren Herbert or B Stansfield, Amherst Lodge, St Mary's Lane, Uplyme, Lyme Regis, DT7 3XH, 01297 442773, 07765 817206, *Water:* 6 stream fed Trout lakes totalling 4 acres, *Species:* Rainbow to 7lb, Brown Trout to 4lb (catch and release only), Tiger Trout to 1lb and Blue Trout 2lb, *Permits:* Go to rod room on arrival, *Charges:* From £13 for two fish bag. Catch & release £15 day. £11 half day. £8 evening. (2002 Prices), *Season:* Open all year 9am to dusk. Must book if arriving before 9am, *Methods:* Small imitative patterns only. Barbless for catch & release.

WIMBORNE

Whitesheet Trout Lakes

Contact: John Cheetham, 19b Willow Way, Christchurch, BH23 1JJ, 01202 490014, 07720 671706, jrcheetham@msn.com, *Water:* 3 lakes totalling 7 acres. See Christchurch Angling Club main entry under River Avon, Hampshire, *Species:* Rainbow & Brown Trout, *Permits:* On site, *Season:* Open all year dawn to dusk, *Methods:* Fly only.

GLOUCS River Fishing

LITTLE AVON

Berkeley Estate Fishing Syndicate

Contact: T. Staniforth, 68 Firgrove, Chipping Sodbury, BS37 7AE, 01454 881719, *Water:* 6.5 miles of Coarse and Game fishing Little Avon from Berkeley Castle to Damery-Tortworth, *Species:* Chub, Dace, Roach, Brown Trout, Rainbow Trout and Grayling, *Permits:* From above, *Charges:* Annual membership £35. Guests may accompany members @ £5 per day, *Season:* Statutory, *Methods:* Trout season fly only. From June 16 any method. No spinning.

Charfield Angling Association

Contact: Mr Mark Lewis, Langford Mill House, Charfield Road, Kingswood, Wotton-Under-Edge, GL12 8RL, 01453 843130, 07787 573468, mark@hblewis.co.uk, *Water:* Approx. 3 miles of Little Avon and Ozleworth Brook, *Species:* Brown Trout, Rainbow Trout, Roach, Grayling and Chub, *Permits:* As above, *Charges:* £30 per season seniors. £15 OAPs, £7.50 juniors, *Season:* Severn Trent byelaws apply, *Methods:* Severn Trent byelaws apply.

CAM

Gloucestershire Disabled Angling Club

Contact: Wally Dewsnip, 56 Lower Meadow, Quedgeley, Gloucester, GL2 4YY, 01452 724366, j.dewsnip@blueyonder.co.uk, *Water:* G.D.A.C. have 38 members of which 75% are disabled. The club fish waters on the river Cam and share Paulton lakes with the Newent Angling Club. We are taking part in the canal users festival at the Saul Junction on July 4th, 5th, 6th, *Permits:* We are holding an open match on Lemmington lakes, contact the Secretary for more details on 01452 501465. *Charges:* Membership £5 per annum. We run a junior section which is open for membership at present time.

GLOUCS Stillwater Coarse

CIRENCESTER

Swindon Isis Angling Club Lake No1

Contact: Peter Gilbert, 31 Havelock St, Swindon, SN1 1SD, 01793 535396, *Water:* 6 acre mature gravel pit at Cotswold Water Park (Water Park Lake 19), South Cerney, Cirencester, *Species:* Tench 9lb, lake with Carp to 30lb, Rudd to 2lb12oz, odd big Bream, usual Roach, Perch & good Pike, *Permits:* Tackle shops in Swindon, Cirencester, Chippenham and Calne, *Charges:* Club Permits: Senior £34.50. OAP and disabled £12. Juniors £8. The club permit contains two free day tickets and more day tickets can be obtained for £5 each. Year starts 1 April, *Season:* Open all year round. Club cards start 1st April, *Methods:* No bans.

FAIRFORD

Milestone Fisheries (Coarse)

Contact: Sue & Bob Fletcher or Andy King, London Road, Fairford, GL7 4DS, 01285 713908, *Water:* 3.5 acre mixed coarse lake. 56 acre Pike lake, *Species:* Well stocked with Carp 26lb, Tench 9.5lb, Bream 11lb, Roach 3.5lb, Rudd, Perch 4.5lb. Separate 56 acre Pike lake 33lb, *Permits:* Day tickets available from fishery office - above address, *Charges:* £5.00 per day (2 rods) Junior £3.00 per day, £8 day & night. Pike lake - Day ticket £8, Night ticket £8, day & night ticket £13, *Season:* No closed season, open every day except Dec 25th. Night fishing by arrangement. Pike lake Open from 1st October to end of April, *Methods:* No keepnets, no dogs, barbless hooks only. Pike lake - Barbless & semi - barbless hooks, minimum of 12lb b.s. line. Traces min 18lbs, 36" soft mesh landing net, unhooking mat, strong wire cutters.

GLOUCESTER

Huntley Carp Pools

Contact: John Tipper - Frank Morris, 14 Thoresby Ave, Tuffley, Gloucester, GL4 0TE, 01452 505313, *Water:* 2 x 4 acre lakes. 1 with Carp to 30lb. 1 with general fish, Carp, Tench, Perch, Bream, Roach, Rudd, Crucian, *Species:* Carp: to 30lb. Coarse: Carp to 20lb, Bream 4lb, Perch 3lb, Tench 5lb, Roach/Rudd 2.75lb, *Permits:* Only from above, *Charges:* To be advised, *Season:* 16th June - 30th April, *Methods:* No keepnets, barbless hooks.

Lemington Lakes

Contact: Ann, Todenham Road, Moreton-in-Marsh, GL56 9NP, 01608 650872, enquiries@lemingtonlakes.co.uk, *Water:* 1 x 5 acre lake, 1 x 2.5 acre lake, 2 x 1.25 acre lakes. 4 ponds varying sizes all with coarse fish, *Species:* Carp up to 34lbs (ranging from 1lb - upwards), Rudd up to 4 - 5lbs, Roach up to 4 - 5lbs, Tench up to 3/4lbs, Perch up to 3/4lbs, *Permits:* As above, *Charges:* £5 - 1 rod, £6 - 2 rods, £3 - Children up to 14th Birthday & 1 rod only, *Season:* 7am - Dark (all year), match bookings taken, *Methods:* Barbless hooks - maximum size allowed 10, no boilies, tiger nuts, peanuts, bloodworm/ joker. Keep nets allowed. No 'Method' but inline feeders permitted.

WOTTON-UNDER-EDGE

Lower Killcott Farm Fishing

Contact: Lower Kilcott Farm, Nr Hillesley, Wotton-Under-Edge, GL12 7RL, 01454 238276, 07967 280574, *Water:* 1 acre lake, *Species:* Carp to 20lb, Roach, Rudd, *Charges:* £5 day, £3 half day, *Season:* Open all year, *Methods:* Barbless hooks only, no keepnets or boilies.

The Willow Fishery

Contact: Bill Davis, The Mill House, Horlsey Bridge, Nailsworth, GL6 0PL, 01453 832053, 07831 774624, bill@swindonhiggloss.com, *Water:* 1.5 acre spring fed, *Species:* Brown Trout to 12lbs, Rainbow to 9lbs, Carp to 10lbs, *Permits:* As above, *Charges:* All day - £12, evening £6 (catch and release only), *Season:* Open all year dawn to dusk, *Methods:* Fly only, barbless hooks only, wet or dry, max size 10, max people 8.

GLOUCS Stillwater Trout

DURSLEY

Great Burrows Trout Fishery

Contact: Vernon Baxter (Manager), North Nibley, Nr Dursley, 01453 542343, 07754 502134, *Water:* Two acre lake, *Species:* Brown Trout, Rainbow Trout (triploid) stocked from 2lb to 5lb, *Permits:* From V. Baxter on site, *Charges:* Day tickets: 2 fish - £14. 3 fish £16. 4 fish £20. 5 fish £24. 6 fish £30, *Season:* Open all year except Christmas day. Fishing from 8am to one hour after sunset, *Methods:* Fly only. No lures. Barbless hooks only. Max hook size 12 longshank. No static fishing. No catch and release except for Brown Trout. Breeding fish to be returned if caught. No wading, fishing from platforms. Knotless landing nets only. E.A. Licence required.

FAIRFORD

Milestone Fisheries (Trout Lakes)

Contact: Sue or Bob Fletcher or Andy King, Milestone Fisheries, London Road, Fairford, GL7 4DS, 01285 713908, *Water:* 10 acre lake and 2 acre lake, *Species:* 10 acre lake: Brown trout, Rainbow trout 2lb - 20lb. 2 acre lake: Rainbow trout 1lb - 1.25lb (bank fishing only). Also Blue/ Golden Trout and doubles only pool 10lb - 23lb, *Permits:* Day tickets & Season tickets plus a limited number catch and release (take first fish - not available when water temperature is high), *Charges:* 10 acre lake: Day & season tickets. Bank (Boats & Float tube for hire) Day ticket 5 fish £35, 1/2 day 3 fish £25. 2 Acre lake: bank fishing only. Catch and take only £12 for 5 fish (top pool), *Season:* No closed season (Return all browns), *Methods:* Catch & take or catch & release on ten acre lake only (Barbless hooks on catch & release). Fly fishing only.

GLOUCESTER

The Cotswolds Fishery

Contact: Mrs Celia Hicks Beach/Mr J. Hunter, Witcombe farm, Great Witcombe, GL3 4TR, 01242 603594, 07890 657279, 01452 864413. jimstanicwit@aol.com, *Water:* 3 reservoirs - 15 acres, 5 acres and 2 plus acres. *Species:* Rainbow Trout max weight 8lbs, *Permits:* Witcombe Farm Estate, Great Witcombe, Gloucester GL3 4TR, *Charges:* Seasonal permits available, various prices on application. Day visitor tickets - Full day £30 (6 fish), Half day (6 hrs) £20 (3 fish), Evening £12 (2 fish). Boats £10 Full day, £5 Half day, £3 Evening. Novice 6 hrs £15, pay £3.50 per fish taken. *Season:* 6th March - 18th October, from 8am to Dusk, *Methods:* Normal Game fishing for Trout, knotless nets. No catch and release.

LECHLADE

Lechlade & Bushyleaze Trout Fisheries

Contact: Tim Small, Lechlade & Bushyleaze Trout Fisheries, Lechlade, GL7 3QQ, 01367 253266, tim@timtrout.co.uk, *Water:* Lechlade - 8 acres. Bushyleaze - 20 acres, *Species:* Lechlade - Rainbows to 27lb, Browns to 18lb. Bushyleaze - Rainbows to 17lb, Browns to 9lb, *Charges:* Lechlade: £40 full day, 4 fish. £30 half day, 2 fish. £20 evening, 1 fish. Bushyleaze: £30 full day, 6 fish. £25 full day, 4 fish. £20 half day, 3 fish. £15 evening, 2 fish. Season tickets available for both lakes. Discounted day tickets for juniors (2002 Prices), *Season:* Open all year, *Methods:* Fly only. Boat hire and float tube hire.

HAMPSHIRE River Fishing

THE 'HAMPSHIRE' AVON

The River Avon is one of England's most famous rivers, and is revered by all anglers for the quality of fish that live in it. This river creates a certain mystique that captivates the attentions of fishers from all walks of life.

The River Avon rises in the Vale of Pewsey and, with its tributaries the Bourne and Wylye, drains the chalk of Salisbury Plain. The River Nadder, which is joined by the Wylye near Salisbury, drains the escarpment of the South Wiltshire Downs and the Kimmeridge clays of the Wardour Vale. The River Ebble and Ashford Water also drain the South Wiltshire Downs and join the Avon downstream of Salisbury and Fordingbridge respectively.

Below Fordingbridge, a number of streams drain the New Forest area. The Avon finally drains into Christchurch harbour, where it is joined by the Rivers Stour and Mude before discharging into the English Channel.

AVON HAMPSHIRE

Bickton Mill

Contact: Simon Cooper, Fishing Breaks, Walton House, 23 Compton Terrace, N1 2UN, 020 7359 8818, info@fishingbreaks.co.uk, *Water:* Extensive fishing on well stocked carriers south of Fordingbridge, *Species:* Brown and Rainbow Trout, *Permits:* By phone or e-mail from Fishing breaks, *Charges:* £65 per person per day, *Season:* April to October, *Methods:* Dry Fly and Nymph.

Britford (Coarse)

Contact: London Angler's Association, Izaak Walton House, 2A Hervey Park Road, E17 6LJ, 0208 5207477, admin@londonanglers.net, *Water:* Several stretches of the Hampshire Avon, *Species:* Roach 3lb, Barbel 10 lb, Chub 7 lb, plus specimen Dace, Grayling, Perch & Pike, *Permits:* Day membership tickets available from Fishery Keeper on the bank - £5 Seniors per rod, maximum of 2 rods. £2.50 Juniors & OAPs per rod, maximum of 2 rods, *Charges:* Senior: £39 - Junior: £21 - OAP/Reg. Disabled: £22 - Husband & wife: £58 - Club affiliated membership available on request, *Season:* Current EA byelaws apply, *Methods:* See members handbook.

Britford (Game)

Contact: London Angler's Association, Izaak Walton House, 2A Hervey Park Road, E17 6LJ, 0208 5207477, admin@londonanglers.net, *Water:* Several stretches of the Hampshire Avon, *Species:* Trout & Salmon, *Permits:* Salmon & Sea Trout - Day membership permit available from Fishery Keeper on bank - £20 per day. Trout fishing - £10 per day (available from Fishery Keeper on bank), *Season:* Current EA byelaws apply, *Methods:* See members handbook.

Christchurch Angling Club (Coarse River)

Contact: John Cheetham, 19b Willow Way, Christchurch, BH23 1JJ, 01202 490014, 07720 671706, jrcheetham@msn.com, *Water:* Largest club on the river Avon, mainly mid/lower Avon, Burgate - Christchurch, including the Royalty Fishery as of 1.4.01, also Fishing on River Stour between Gains Cross and Christchurch plus various coarse ponds including Blashford, Somerly and Whitesheat lakes. Please telephone the secretary for full details, *Species:* Roach (3lb), Chub (7lb), Dace (1lb), Barbel (14lb), Pike (36lb), Bream (11lb), Perch (4lb), Carp (40lb), Eels (5lb), Crucian Carp (4lb), Grayling (3lb), Tench (9lb), *Permits:* Steve Richards (Membership Secretary) Tel:01202 474648 or for rivers and stillwaters enquire at Local Tackle shops, *Charges:* Adult £122, Junior £51, OAP/Concession £87, *Season:* Coarse: 16th June to 14th March. Salmon: 1st Feb to 31st August. Rainbow Trout all year round. Brown Trout: 1st April to 15th October, *Methods:* See rules for individual waters.

Fordingbridge Park Day Ticket Fishing

Contact: Dave Cates, Fordingbridge Recreation Ground, Fordingbridge, 07939 514346, fordingbridgefishing@hotmail.com, *Water:* 500 yards of excellent fishing on the Hampshire Avon, *Species:* Chub 6lb 2oz, Roach 2lb 10oz, Dace 1lb, Rainbow Trout 6lb, Eels 1lb, Pike 23lb, Perch 1lb, Carp 10lb, *Permits:* Day Tickets must be purchased in advance from one of the following outlets: Fordingbridge Service Station (Q8 Garage, 500 yds from fishery). Ringwood Tackle. Avon Angling Centre (Ringwood). Sandy Balls Holiday Park (Godshill, Nr Fordingbridge). Fordingbridge Tourist Information Centre, *Charges:* £5 Adults per Day age 16-64. £2.50 per day for Juniors (15 and under) and Senior Citizens (65 plus), *Season:* Coarse Fishing June 16th, March 14th 7.30am - Darkness. Trout Fishing April to June by arrangement only - Contact Dave Cates on 07939 514346, *Methods:* Max 2 rods per person. No fishing under power lines or in play area. Tickets must be purchased in advance.

Ringwood & District Angling Club (Hampshire Avon)
Contact: Mr Steve Martin, 2 Oakmead Road, Creekmoor, Poole, BH17 7XN, 01202 777892, 07812 360278, steve.martin1@ntlworld.com, *Water:* Between - Severals fishery at Ringwood upstream to Fordingbridge including Ibsley, *Species:* Barbel to 14lb, Chub to 7lb, Roach 3lb plus, Pike 30lb plus, Bream 10lb plus, Perch, Carp, Dace, Salmon, Sea Trout, Brown Trout, *Permits:* Local tackle shop or contact Caroline Groom (Membership Secretary) on: 01202 525615, *Charges:* Adult £100, Junior £40, Concessions, O.A.P's, Disabled £62 (Joining fee-£15 adult, £5 junior). Severals day tickets £7.50. Concessions for O.A.P's, Disabled, Juniors. Prices subject to seasonal review, *Season:* Slight variations to coarse season due to Salmon fishing, Current E.A. byelaws apply.

DUN

Holbury Lane Lakes (River Dun)
Contact: Tim Weston / Jerry Wakeford, Holbury Lane, Lockerley, Romsey, SO51 0JR, 01794 341619, *Water:* 1000yds of river Dun, a tributary of the river Test, plus four Trout Lakes (see Stillwater Trout, Romsey), *Species:* Brown Trout 1 1/2lb average, *Permits:* 10 or 25 fish tickets, *Methods:* Single fly, max size 10, no catch and release, priest and net must be carried by anglers.

HAMPSHIRE Stillwater Coarse

FORDINGBRIDGE

Cranborne Fruit Farm
Contact: Cranborne Fruit Farm, Alderholt, Fordingbridge, 01425 475155, *Water:* 3 acre lake, *Species:* Carp, Bream, Roach, Rudd, *Permits:* At all local tackle shops, *Charges:* £5 Day. £4 day OAP, *Season:* January to November.

Lake Farm Fishery
Contact: P.S. Birch, Lake Farm, Sandleheath, Fordingbridge, SP6 3EF, 01425 653383, phil@birch50.fsnet.co.uk, *Water:* 3 acre lake, *Species:* Carp to 25lb, *Charges:* Day tickets £6 at lakeside, *Season:* Open all year 8am to sunset, *Methods:* Barbless hooks only, no keepnets.

New Forest Water Park
Contact: Mark Jury, Hucklesbrook Lakes, Ringwood Road, Fordingbridge, SP6 2EY, 01425 656868, 07939 273388, info@newforestwaterpark.co.uk, *Water:* 19 acre lake, 11 acre lake, *Species:* Pike to 35lb plus, Carp to 40lb plus, Roach, Rudd and Perch in 11 acre lake. Carp to 32lb, Tench to 10lb, Roach to 3lb, Rudd to 2lb in 19 acre lake, *Permits:* From Clubhouse (After 10 a.m.) or on bank. No E.A. licence required. Clubhouse facilities Easter to early November, *Charges:* Day ticket: £6 for 2 rods, £9 for 3 rods. 24hrs ticket £15 for 2 rods, £22.50 for 3 rods bookable in advance, *Season:* All year round, *Methods:* Barbless hooks, no nut baits, no keepnets, no live bait.

RINGWOOD

Blashford Lakes
Contact: John Cheetham, 19b Willow Way, Christchurch, BH23 1JJ, 01202 490014, 07720 671706, jrcheetham@msn.com, *Water:* Series of former Gravel Pits. Fishing available to members of Christchurch Angling Club. See entry under Hampshire Avon. Includes Spinnaker lake Rockford lake, Roach pit, *Species:* Carp to 44lb, Pike to 36lb, Bream to 14lb, Perch to 4lb, Roach, Tench & Rudd, *Permits:* Steve Richards (Membership Secretary) Tel: 01202 474648 or local tackle shops, *Charges:* Adults - £122 Junior - £51 OAP/ Concession - £87, *Season:* 16th June - 14th March. Night fishing available with prepaid permit from Tackle shops, *Methods:* See individual fishery rules.

Hurst Pond
Contact: Ringwood Tackle, 01425 475155, *Water:* 1.5 acre pond at Hedlands Business Park, Blashford, Ringwood, Hants, *Species:* Carp 18lb, Tench 6.5lb, Roach 2.5lb, Rudd 2lb, Perch 3lb 12oz, Crucians 2.5lb, Eels 5lb, *Charges:* £5 per day. Limited night fishing, £10 - 24hr ticket, *Season:* Open all year.

Moors Valley Country Park
Contact: Andy Beale, Horton Road, Ashley Heath, Nr Ringwood, BH24 2ET, 01425 470721, mvalley@eastdorset.gov.uk, *Water:* The Moors Lake covers an area of 9 acres. Maximum depth 2 meters. *Species:* Tench to 6lb, Carp to 10lb, Roach to 2lb, Perch to 2lb, Rudd 2lb, Pike to 20lb. Most river species ie Dace/Gudgeon etc, *Permits:* Fishing is from the bays marked by wooden posts on the west bank and has disabled access. Permits from visitor centre, *Charges:* £3.00 Adults (17 - 65yrs), £2.50 65yrs plus, £2.00 Junior (Up to 16yrs). Car park charges vary throughout the year, pay and display, *Season:* Moors lake from 16th June to 14th March, *Methods:* Rod licence for 12yrs plus, one ticket per rod, fishing from 8-30am to dusk, no keepnets, no boilies, barbless hooks, wooden bays only, float/ledger/feeder/dead bait for Pike.

Ringwood & District A.A. (Coarse Lakes)
Contact: Mr Steve Martin, 2 Oakmead Road, Creekmoor, Poole, BH17 7XN, 01202 777892, 07812 360278, steve.martin1@ntlworld.com, *Water:* 4 lakes at Hightown plus Northfield on outskirts of Ringwood, *Species:* Hightown - Mixed fishery with Carp to 38lb 14oz, Tench, Bream, Roach, Rudd, Pike, Eels. Northfield - Big Carp to 30lb, Tench to 12lb, Bream, Roach, Rudd, Pike, *Permits:* Local tackle shop or contact Caroline Groom (Membership Secretary) on: 01202 525615, *Charges:* Adult £100, Junior £40, concessions for OAP's and disabled; day tickets £7.50 plus night options available at Ringwood Tackle, West St, Ringwood, 01425-475155. Prices may change for 2003, please enquire, *Season:* All year fishing available, *Methods:* All on reverse of ticket.

Turf Croft Farm Fishery
Contact: Keith, Stephen, Christine Duell, Forest Road, Burley, Nr Ringwood, BH24 4DF, 01425 403743, 07753 183909, *Water:* 8 acre lake - naturally spring fed, *Species:* Ghost Carp to 18lbs, Mirror Carp to 23lbs, Tench to 5lbs, Bream to 4lbs, Roach & Crucians to 2.5lbs, *Permits:* Day ticket only. No Night fishing, *Charges:* £7 per two rods maximum, *Methods:* No boilies, no nut baits, no hemp, no keepnets, natural bait.

Hampshire Stillwater Trout

FORDINGBRIDGE

Damerham Fisheries

Contact: Mike Davies, The Lake House, Damerham, Fordingbridge, SP6 3HW, 01725 518446, *Water:* 6 lakes. 1.5 mile Allan River, *Species:* Rainbow Trout (Sandy, Lavender, White & Electric Blue Rainbow Trout), *Permits:* Season Rods, *Charges:* Full Rod £1,650 (30 days), 1/2 Rod £900 (15 days), 1/4 Rod £600 (10 days). Guest Rod £60. Please phone to confirm prices. *Season:* March - October, *Methods:* Fly only.

Rockbourne Trout Fishery

Contact: Rockbourne Trout Fishery, Rockbourne Road, Sandleheath, Fordingbridge, SP6 1QG, 01725 518603, 07802 678830, rockbourne@talk21.com, *Water:* 6 Spring fed lakes & 3 chalkstream beats on the Sweatford water, *Species:* Rainbow / Brown Trout, Triploids, *Permits:* From the fishery, *Charges:* 5 fish £45. 4 fish £36. 3 fish £30. 2 fish £20. Junior/novice 1 fish catch and release lake £10, age limit 16yrs, *Season:* All year, *Methods:* Fly only, max hook size 10lb, no droppers, tandem/double/treble hooks, no dogs.

ROMSEY

Holbury Lane Trout Lakes

Contact: Tim Weston / Jerry Wakeford, Holbury Lane, Lockerley, Romsey, SO51 0JR, 01794 341619, *Water:* 4 lakes totalling 7.5 acres plus 1000yds on the river Dun (see River Dun entry), *Species:* Rainbow Trout to 2lb to 5lb, Blue Trout 2lb to 5lb and Brown Trout 3lb plus, *Permits:* 10 or 25 fish ticket, *Charges:* 2 fish 1/2 Day £20. 4 fish full day £35, *Season:* 9am to dusk, *Methods:* Single fly, max size 10, no catch and release, priest and net must be carried by anglers.

STOCKBRIDGE

John O ' Gaunts

Contact: Mrs E Purse, 51 Mead Road, Chandlers Ford, SO53 2FB, 01794 388130, 02380 252268, *Water:* 2 Lakes approx 7 acres in Test Valley, *Species:* Rainbow Trout (various sizes), *Permits:* Available from Fishery Tel: 02380 252268 or 01794 388130, *Charges:* £34/day -4-fish, £18/half day - 2-fish, *Season:* February 1st - November 30th inclusive, Wednesdays & Saturdays throughout December and January, *Methods:* Fly and Nymph only.

WINCHESTER

Dever Springs

Contact: Mr N. Staig and Miss P. Bull, Barton Stacey, Winchester, SO21 3NP, 01264 720592, pippa@deversprings.freeserve.co.uk, *Water:* Two lakes totalling 6 acres plus a half mile stretch of the river Dever, *Species:* Rainbow Trout - British record holder at 36lb 14oz. Brown Trout - British record holder at 28lb 2oz, *Permits:* EA rod licence required, *Charges:* 4 fish £60. 3 fish £48. 2 fish £35, *Season:* Open all year, *Methods:* Fly only. Max hook size 12, single wet or dry fly.

SOMERSET River Fishing

AXE

The River Axe emerges from the Mendip Hills at Wookey Hole and from here to below Wookey the river is Trout water. The river deepens as it crosses low lying land at the foot of the Mendips to the sluices at Bleadon and Brean Cross, the tidal limit. Fish species in the lower reaches include Bream, Roach, Tench, Dace and Pike.

Weston-super-Mare A.A

Contact: Weston Angling Centre, 25a Locking Road, Weston-super-Mare, BS23 3BY, 01934 631140, *Water:* River Axe, River Brue, South Drain, North Drain. Summer Lane Pond, Locking Pond, *Species:* Bream, Tench, Roach, Carp, Gudgeon, Perch, Rudd, Chub & some Dace, *Permits:* Weston Angling Centre, *Charges:* Season £22, Week £10, Day £4, *Season:* Old River Axe, Summer Lane and Locking Ponds - year round, *Methods:* No boilies/nuts.

BARLE

Fly Fishing in Somerset (Barle)

Contact: R.M. Gurden, 3 Edbrooke Cottages, Winsford, Nr Minehead, TA24 7AE, 01643 851504, 07814 243991, complete.angling@virgin.net, *Water:* 2 miles on the Barle, *Species:* Wild Brown Trout, Salmon, *Season:* March 15th to September 30th, *Methods:* All waters fly only.

Paddons

Contact: Mrs M. McMichael or Mr P. Jones, Northmoor Road, Dulverton, TA22 9PW, 01398 323514, marymm@paddons.fsnet.co.uk, *Water:* 400 yards single bank on River Barle, *Species:* Brown Trout & Salmon, *Charges:* Day ticket - Adults £5, Juniors £1, *Season:* March 15th to September 30th, *Methods:* Fly fishing.

BRIDGWATER AND TAUNTON CANAL

Cut in 1827 the canal provided a good commercial waterway between the two towns. The canal has been recently restored for navigation but there is only infrequent boat traffic. The canal offers excellent coarse fishing from the towpath for Roach, Bream, Tench, Rudd, Perch & Pike.

HUNTSPILL RIVER / SOUTH DRAIN / CRIPPS RIVER / NORTH DRAIN

The Huntspill River is a man made drainage channel, excavated in the 1940s and connected to the River Brue and South Drain via the Cripps River. The North Drain was dug c1770 to drain low lying moors to the north of the River Brue. The Huntspill is a notable coarse fishery and is often the venue for national and local match fishing competitions. Catches consist primarily of Bream and Roach. The North and South Drain and Cripps River contain similar species and also offer good sport for the coarse angler.

Bridgwater Angling Association
Contact: Mr M Pople, 14 Edward Street, Bridgwater, TA6 5EU, 01278 422397, *Water:* 6 miles on the Bridgwater & Taunton Canal, Fishing on the rivers Cripps, Brue, North & South Drain, King's Sedgemoor Drain, Langacre Rhine & The Huntspill. Stillwater fishing at Combwich, Walrow, Dunwear & Screech Owl and Bridgwater Docks, *Species:* All types of Coarse Fish, *Permits:* Available from Tackle outlets throughout Somerset area including Somerset Angling, 74 Bath Rd, Bridgwater, Tel: 01278 431777 & Thyers Tackle, 1a Church Street, Highbridge, Tel: 01278 786934. Veals Fishing Tackle, 61 Old Market Street, Bristol 0117 9260790. Topp Tackle, 63 Station Road, Taunton 01823 282518. Further information on Bridgwater A.A. available from Watts News, Edward Street, Bridgwater. Open: Mon-Sat 5am-7pm, Sunday . 5am-4pm. Tel: 01278 422137, *Charges:* Adult season £26, Junior (12-17yrs) £6, Senior Citizens £9, Disabled £9, Junior (7-11yrs) £3.Day tickets £3.50, enquire at outlets. (2002 prices), *Season:* E.A. byelaws apply. Bridgwater and Taunton Canal open all year, *Methods:* Full rules and map with permits.

Taunton Angling Association (Bridgwater & Taunton Canal)
Contact: Mr. J.Helyer, 40 Albemarle Road, Taunton, TA1 1BA, 01823 257559, jonhelyer@btinternet.com, *Water:* 6 miles on Bridgwater & Taunton Canal (also see entries under Stillwater Coarse), *Species:* Roach 2lb, Bream 8lb, Eels 3lb, Rudd 2lb, Perch 2lb, Pike 27lb, Tench 7lb, *Permits:* Topp Tackle, Taunton, (01823) 282518. Enterprise Angling, Taunton (01823) 282623. Somerset Angling, Bridgwater (01278) 431777. Street Angling, Street (01458) 447830. Wellington Country Sports, Wellington (01823) 662120. Thyer's Tackle, Burnham-on-sea (01278) 786934. Yeovil Angling Centre, Yeovil (01935) 476777. Planet Video & Angling, Chard (01460) 64000. Exe Valley Angling, Tiverton (01884) 242275. Exeter Angling Centre, Exeter (01392) 436404. Thatcher's Pet & Tackle, Wells (01749) 673513. Weston Angling Centre, Weston-Super-Mare (01934) 631140, *Charges:* Season £25. Day tickets £5 Senior, £2 Junior, *Season:* Closed 14th March - 16th June, Ponds and canal open all year, *Methods:* Barbless hooks on stillwaters. All fish (including Pike and Eels) to be returned alive.

BRISTOL AVON

The River Avon flows from its sources near Sherston and Tetbury to its confluence with the Severn at Avonmouth some 117 kilometers and is fed by many tributaries on its way. The headwaters of the River Avon, the Tetbury and Sherston branches join at Malmesbury. Both are important Trout streams where fishing is strictly preserved and there is little opportunity for the visiting angler to fish these waters.

Malmesbury to Chippenham
Coarse fisheries predominate in this section, although Trout are stocked by fishing associations in some areas. Arguably one of the best fisheries in the country, this section contains a wide range of specimen fish. Local records include: Roach 3lb 2oz, Perch 3lb 3oz, Tench 8lb 5 1/2oz, Bream 8lb 8oz, Dace 1lb 2oz, Chub 7lb 10oz, Carp 20lb 8 1/4oz and Pike 33lb 3oz. Also many Barbel to 12lb have been reported.

Chippenham to Bath
Upstream from Staverton to Chippenham the Avon continues to be an important coarse fishery, both for the pleasure angler and match fisherman. The river flows through a broad flood plain and provides a pastoral setting. In the faster flowing sections chub, Roach, Dace and Barbel can be caught in good numbers.

Bath to Hanham
Between Hanham and Bath much of this length retains a rural character and is an important coarse fishery used by pleasure and match anglers. The National Angling Championships have been held here. Roach, Bream and Chub are the main catches and, in some favoured swims, Dace. Very good catches of Bream are to be had with specimen fish. 'Free' fishing is available through Bath from the towpath side between Newbridge and Pulteney Weir. Carp of 20lb have been reported caught downstream of Pulteney and Keynsham Weirs.

Hanham to Avonmouth
Between Netham Dam and Hanham Weir the river is affected by spring tides. The water has a very low saline content and this length of river provides reasonable coarse fishing. Below Netham Dam the river contains mostly estuarine species but some sea Trout and Salmon have been seen.

Bathampton Angling Association (Bristol Avon Claverton)
Contact: Dave Crookes, 25 Otago Terrace, Larkhall, Bath, BA1 6SX, 01225 427164, dave@bathampton.org, *Water:* 2.5 miles Bristol Avon up and downstream from Claverton, *Species:* Bream to 6lbs, Chub to 5lbs, Roach to 2.5lbs, Pike to 25lbs, Barbel to 12lbs, *Permits:* Local fishing tackle shops, *Charges:* Adults £22, combined lady and gent £30, juniors £7, O.A.P £7. Registered disabled £7, Under 12's free. To year end 31/12/03. Members only, *Season:* Standard river close season, night fishing on application, *Methods:* Club byelaws apply.

Bathampton Angling Association (Box Brook)
Contact: Dave Crookes, 25 Otago Terrace, Larkhall, Bath, BA1 6SX, 01225 427164, dave@bathampton.org, *Water:* 3 miles of Box brook (tributary of Avon). Split into 2 beats at Middle Hill and Shockerwick, *Species:* Brown Trout (occasional Rainbows) Grayling, *Permits:* Local fishing tackle shops, *Charges:* Adults £22, combined lady and gent £30, juniors £7, O.A.P £7. Registered disabled £7, Under 12's free. To year end 31/12/03. Members only special day permits must be purchased before fishing, *Season:* Fishing from 1st Apr to 15 Oct inclusive, *Methods:* Traditional Fly/Nymph only.

Bathampton Angling Association (Bristol Avon Kelston)
Contact: Dave Crookes, 25 Otago Terrace, Larkhall, Bath, BA1 6SX, 01225 427164, dave@bathampton.org, *Water:* 2 miles of Bristol Avon at Kelston. *Species:* Bream to 8lbs, Roach to 2lbs, Pike to 20lbs, Chub to 3lbs, Barbel to 8lbs. *Permits:* Local fishing tackle shops, *Charges:* Adults £22, combined lady and gent £30, juniors £7, O.A.P £7. Registered disabled £7, Under 12's free. To year end 31/12/03. £3 day tickets available to Non-Members. Tickets must be purchased before fishing. *Season:* Standard river close season, *Methods:* Club byelaws apply.

Bathampton Angling Association (Bristol Avon Newbridge)
Contact: Dave Crookes, 01225 427164, dave@bathampton.org, *Water:* 1.5 miles of Bristol Avon at Newbridge, downstream of Bath, *Species:* Bream to 10lbs, Chub to 4lbs, Roach to 2.5lbs, Pike to 16lbs, *Permits:* Local fishing tackle shops, *Charges:* Adults £22, combined lady/gent £30, juniors £7, O.A.P £7. Registered disabled £7, Under 12's free. To year end 31/12/03. £3 day tickets available to Non-Members. Tickets must be purchased before fishing. *Season:* Standard river season, *Methods:* Club byelaws apply.

Bathampton Angling Association (Bristol Avon Saltford)
Contact: Dave Crookes, 25 Otago Terrace, Larkhall, Bath, BA1 6SX, 01225 427164, dave@bathampton.org, *Water:* 1.5 miles of Bristol Avon at Saltford, *Species:* Bream to 8lbs, Roach to 2lbs, Chub to 3lbs, *Permits:* Local fishing tackle shops, *Charges:* Adults £22, combined lady and gent £30, juniors £7, O.A.P £7. Registered disabled £7, Under 12's free. To year end 31/12/03. £3 day tickets available to Non-Members. must be purchased before fishing. *Season:* Standard river close season, *Methods:* Club byelaws apply.

Bristol & West Federation of Anglers
Contact: Hon Sec B Lloyd, 386 Speedwell Road, Kingswood, Bristol, BS15 1ES, 0117 9676030, brian.lloyd2@ukonline.co.uk, *Water:* Bristol and West waters are; Swineford to Keynsham, Jack Whites Cottage (Londonderry Farm) all right hand bank down stream, *Permits:* Open to affiliated clubs, including Bristol, Bath and Wilts amalgamation.

Bristol Avon
Contact: Abbey Angling, 61b High Street, Hanham, Bristol, BS15 3DQ, 0117 9677214, *Water:* Free stretch from Crews Hole Road - Chequers - Hanham mills, 2.5 miles approx, *Species:* All coarse fish, *Permits:* EA licence required, *Charges:* Free fishing (Further details contact Abbey Angling), *Season:* Closed season applies.

Bristol City Docks Angling Club
Contact: Bob Taylor, 27 Flaxpits Lane, Winterbourne, Bristol, BS36 1LA, 01454 773990, 07990 573831, bobtaylor@blueyonder.co.uk, *Water:* 3 miles on Bristol Avon from Chequers Weir to Netham. Feeder canal (Netham - docks), Bristol Docks system, *Species:* Skimmers, Bream, Roach, Dace, Chub, Pike, Eels, Carp, Tench and Perch, *Permits:* All Bristol tackle shops and Harbour Masters office, or from secretary above on 01454 773990 or 07790 573831, *Charges:* Season: Senior & 2 juniors under 12 £15, Seniors £12.50, Concessions, Disabled, Juniors, O.A.P's £6.50, Day tickets in advance: Seniors £2.50 + Concessions £1, Day tickets on the bank issued by Bailiff: Seniors £5, Juniors/Conc £2, *Season:* 1st April - March 31st inclusive, River - normal close season applies; Docks and Feeder Canal open all year, *Methods:* Docks: Pole and feeder. Pole & Waggler on Feeder Canal. All normal river tactics on the Avon. Daily update information from Tony on 0117 9517250.

Bristol PSV Club
Contact: Matt Coombs, Bristol, 01275 545245, matt@psvfishing.co.uk, *Water:* Well established club, fishing waters in Hereford, Gloucester, Bristol, Bath & Somerset. 25 matches a year. Meeting 1st Tuesday of every month in the Midland Spinner on Wick road, Kingswood, *Charges:* Membership £10 per year. Juniors welcome. Please contact Matt on number above or call in to the Midland Spinner.

Bristol, Bath & Wiltshire Amalgamated Anglers
Contact: Jeff Parker, 16 Lansdown View, Kingswood, Bristol, BS15 4AW, 0117 9672977, *Water:* Approx 80 miles Coarse Fishing on Bristol Avon & Somerset Rivers & Streams. Stillwaters at Lyneham, Calne, Malmesbury, Bath and Pawlett near Bridgwater. Trout only water on Cam Brook. Too much to list here, please contact the secretary for full details, *Species:* All coarse species, *Permits:* Full Membership available from the Secretary. Veterans over 70 years contact the secretary for details of discounted membership. Full members only may fish at Tockenham Reservoir, Burton Hill lake at Malmesbury & Shackells Lake. Day Tickets for all waters except Burton Hill & Tockenham are available at Tackle Shops. Limited night fishing, *Charges:* Adults £30 (discount for early purchase). Adult and child £35. Concessions £10. Night fishing full members £50 per season, *Methods:* No metal cans or glass bottles in possession, no fresh water fish as livebait, maximum 2 rods per angler, full rules on application.

Frys Match Group
Contact: Ray Cooper, 07811 256627, *Water:* 45 Pegs - 2 mile stretch single bank fishing, *Species:* Carp, Barbel, Bream, Roach, *Permits:* Membership available to all, please contact Ray, *Charges:* £10 season ticket. Under 16 fish for free if accompanied by adult, *Season:* E.A. Byelaws apply.

Avon Valley Country Park (River Avon)
Contact: Bath Rd, Keynsham, Bristol, BS31 1TP, 0117 9864929, info@avonvalleycountrypark.co.uk, *Water:* 1.5 miles on River Avon, *Species:* Tench & Coarse fish, *Permits:* From above, *Charges:* £4 Adult entrance to park (includes ticket to fish), £3 Child, £3.50 Senior Citizen, *Season:* Park open: Easter - 1st November 10am - 6pm. Current E.A. Byelaws apply on the river.

BRISTOL FROME

The Bristol Frome rises at Dodington and offers a fair standard of coarse fishing on the lower sections. The upper section contains limited stocks of Brown Trout, Roach and Perch. This tributary of the River Avon is culverted beneath Bristol and discharges into the Floating Harbour.

Frome Angling Association (River)
Contact: Gary Collinson, 94 Nunney Road, Frome, BA11 4LD, 01373 465214, *Water:* 12 miles River Frome - 10 acre lake, *Species:* River: Roach, Chub, Bream. Lake: Tench, Carp, Roach, Pike, *Permits:* Haines Angling, Christchurch Street West, Frome, *Charges:* £10 Senior, £5 Junior U/16, O.A.P's £5, Day tickets £2, *Season:* 16th June to March 14th, unless changes in legislation occur, *Methods:* No restrictions.

Farleigh Wood Fishery (River)
Contact: Wood Cottage, Tellisford, Bath, BA2 7RN, 01373 831495, bellagingell766@msn.com, *Water:* Brook with several pools plus 1 acre coarse fishing lake (see Stillwater Coarse, Bath), *Species:* River: Brown Trout to 2lb, *Charges:* Day ticket 2 fish £19, 1 fish £17, half a day 2 fish £15, Evening or sporting ticket £10, *Season:* EA season for river fishing, *Methods:* List of rules at fishery.

Frome Vale Angling Club
Contact: Nigel Vigus (Secretary), 32 Rock Lane, Stoke Gifford, Bristol, BS34 8PF, 01179 759710, nvigus@ukonline.co.uk, *Water:* 1 mile river Frome; half acre lake (Winterbourne), *Species:* Carp, Roach, Bream, Tench, Pike, Perch, Chub, *Permits:* As above, *Charges:* Per season: Seniors £15 - Juniors £7 - OAP's/ Disabled £5. Day tickets not available, *Season:* From Jun 16th - Mar 14th. Closed season Mar 15th - Jun 15th, *Methods:* Barbless hooks on all waters. Lakes: barbless hooks, no floating baits, no keepnets, hooks no larger than size 10, no cereal ground baits.

RIVER BOYD

The River Boyd rises just south of Dodington and joins the Bristol Avon at Bitton. In the middle and lower reaches coarse fish predominate. The upper reaches above Doynton contain Brown Trout.

BY BROOK

The Broadmead and Burton brooks together form the By Brook which flows through Castle Combe and is joined by several smaller streams before entering the River Avon at Bathford. Brown Trout predominate above the village of Box, mostly small in size but plentiful in number. At Box and below the fishery is mixed and Dace to 14oz and Roach of 2lb are not uncommon.

RIVER MARDEN

The River Marden is fed by springs rising from the downs above Cherhill and joins the river Avon upstream of Chippenham. Brown Trout occur naturally in the upper reaches. Downstream of Calne coarse fish predominate and weights of more than 30lb are regularly caught in matches. The Marden Barbel record stands at over 10lb.

SOMERSET FROME

The Somerset Frome is the main tributary of the Bristol Avon. It drains a large catchment area which is fed from the chalk around Warminster and limestone from the eastern end of the Mendips. There are numerous weirs and mills mostly disused. The tributaries above Frome provide ideal conditions for Brown Trout with fishing on the River Mells. The middle and lower reaches provide excellent coarse fishing.

Airsprung Angling Association (Frome)
Contact: Ian Stainer, 36 Downavon, Bradford-on-Avon, BA14 7SG, 01225 862683, *Water:* See also entry under Wiltshire, river fishing, Kennet & Avon Canal. River Frome at Stowford Farm (near Farleigh Hungerford), *Species:* Carp, Bream, Chub, Roach, Rudd, Dace, Tench, Perch, etc, *Permits:* Association Licence only (no day tickets on river), *Charges:* On application, *Season:* Subject to normal close season, *Methods:* Details from Association.

Avon & Tributaries Angling Association
Contact: Mr Miller (Secretary), 5 William St, Bath, BA2 4DE, *Water:* Somerset Frome, Cam, Wellow, Midford Brooks, *Species:* All Coarse species and Trout, *Permits:* No day tickets, guest ticket from individual members, *Season:* In rules, *Methods:* In rules.

MIDFORD BROOK

The Midford Brook runs through well wooded valleys with mostly mixed fishing on the lower reaches and Trout fishing in upper reaches. The largest Brown Trout recorded weighed 5lb 6oz.

KENNET AND AVON CANAL

There are some 58 kilometres of canal within the Bristol Avon catchment area which averages one metre in depth and thirteen metres in width. The Kennet & Avon Canal joins the River Avon at Bath with the River Kennet between Reading and Newbury. The canal was opened in 1810 to link the Severn Estuary with the Thames. The canal, now much restored, provides excellent fishing with Carp to 25lb, Tench to 5lb also Roach, Bream, Perch, Rudd, Pike and Gudgeon.

Bathampton Angling Association (Kennet & Avon Canal)
Contact: Dave Crookes, 25 Otago Terrace, Larkhall, Bath, BA1 6SX, 01225 427164, dave@bathampton.org, *Water:* 6.5 miles of Kennet and Avon canal. From Bath to Limpley Stoke hill, *Species:* Bream to 4lbs, Chub to 3.5lbs, Roach to 2lbs, Pike to 10lbs, Carp to 15lbs, Tench to 3lbs. Perch to 2.5lbs, *Permits:* Local fishing tackle shops, *Charges:* Adults £22, combined lady and gent £30, juniors £7, O.A.P £7. Registered disabled £7, Under 12's free. To year end 31/12/03. £3 day tickets available to non-members must be purchased before fishing, *Season:* Open all year, *Methods:* Club bye-laws apply.

BRUE

The River Brue is a Trout fishery from its source above Bruton to Lovington. From here to Glastonbury a number of weirs provide areas of deep water and coarse fish predominate, notably Chub and Roach, together with Bream, Dace and Pike. Similar species may be found between Glastonbury and Highbridge where the river is channelled across the Somerset Levels and connected with a number of drainage channels such as the Huntspill River and North Drain.

Glaston Manor Association
Contact: J. Ogden, 10 Dovecote Close, Farm Lane, Street, *Water:* Brue - approx. 15 miles both banks; 2/3 miles on Sheppey plus S. Drain from Catcott Bridge back to source. Also see entry in Street, Stillwater Coarse, Somerset, *Species:* Roach, Chub, Bream, Dace, Perch, Gudgeon, Pike, Tench and a few Carp, *Permits:* Thatchers Tackle, Wells. Street Angling, High St, Street, Somerset Tel: 01458 447830, *Charges:* Day ticket £4, Junior membership £6, Senior membership £18, OAP and disabled £9, *Season:* Current E.A. byelaws apply, *Methods:* No live bait permitted, full rules on day ticket.

Highbridge Angling Association
Contact: Mr C Brewer, 8 Willow Close, East Huntspill, Near Highbridge, TA9 3NX, 01278 786230, *Water:* Basin Bridge, East Huntspill, *Species:* Carp to 33lb, Pike to mid 20's, all other coarse species, *Permits:* Thyers Tackle, Highbridge - 01278 786934. Also available from other local tackle shops, *Charges:* Day tickets £3, 7 day ticket £10 or season ticket £18. Senior citizen £8, *Season:* March 15th - June 16th, *Methods:* No live baiting, full list with ticket.

Merry Farm Fishing
Contact: Mr.Peter Dearing, Merry Farm, Merry Lane, Basonbridge, TA9 3PS, 01278 783655, *Water:* 600 yards on the River Brue, *Species:* Pike 20lb plus, Bream 10lb, Tench 5lb, Chub, Carp, Roach 1.5lb, Gudgeon, Ruffe, Perch 4lb, *Permits:* Day tickets, *Charges:* £1 per day, *Season:* 16th June to 14th March, *Methods:* No restrictions.

CAM AND WELLOW BROOKS

The Cam and Wellow Brooks, rising on the north side of the Mendip Hills, flow through what was a mining area and now provide good quality Trout fishing controlled by local fishing associations.

Cameley Lakes (River Cam)
Contact: J. Harris, Hillcrest farm, Cameley, Temple Cloud, Nr Bristol, BS39 5AQ, 01761 452423, *Water:* Fishing on River Cam. See also entry under Stillwater Trout, Bristol, *Species:* Rainbow and Brown trout, 1.5lb - 5lb, *Permits:* Fishery car park, Cameley, Temple Cloud near Bristol, *Charges:* £20 - 4 fish limit (Day permit). £15 - 2 fish limit (Half day permit) 2002 prices, *Season:* 8am to sundown, *Methods:* Dry fly and Nymph fishing, no larger than 1 inch.

CHEW

The River Chew rises near Chewton Mendip and flows through the Bristol Waterworks Reservoirs at Litton and Chew Valley Lake. The river continues through Chew Magna, Stanton Drew, Publow, Woolard and Compton Dando to its confluence with the River Avon at Keynsham. A mixed fishery for most its length and is particularly good for Roach, Dace and Grayling below Pensford.

Bathampton Angling Association (River Chew)
Contact: Dave Crookes, 25 Otago Terrace, Larkhall, Bath, BA1 6SX, 01225 427164, dave@bathampton.org, *Water:* 1 mile of river Chew at Compton Dando, near Keynsham, *Species:* Roach, Chub, Grayling, Brown Trout, Rainbow Trout, Dace, Perch, *Permits:* Local fishing tackle shops, *Charges:* Adults £22, combined lady and gent £30, juniors £7, O.A.P £7. Registered disabled £7, Under 12's free. To year end 31/12/03. Members only, *Season:* Open all year. Fly only for trout from 15 March to 15 June inclusive , *Methods:* Club bye-laws apply.

Keynsham Angling Association
Contact: Mr K. N. Jerrom, 21 St Georges Road, Keynsham, Bristol, BS31 2HU, 01179 865193, *Water:* Stretches on the rivers Avon and Chew, *Species:* Mixed, *Charges:* Members only fishing. Membership details from secretary or Keynsham Pet & Garden Centre, tel: 01179 862366. Adult membership £12. Juniors, OAPs, disabled £4, *Season:* Current E.A. Byelaws apply, *Methods:* Details in members handbook. On rivers Chew and Avon there are no restrictions other than current E.A. Byelaws.

Knowle Angling Association
Contact: Keith Caddick, 41 Eastwood Crescent, Brislington, Bristol, BS4 4SR, 01179 857974, derek.ezekiel@adsweu.com, *Water:* 5 miles of upper and lower river Chew, 2 lakes - Publow and Ackers lake at Pensford. Plus fishing at Chew Magna reservoir (see Stillwater Trout, Bristol), *Charges:* £70 annual membership. New members pay extra £5 entrance fee, *Methods:* Fly only on upper Chew.

EXE & TRIBUTARIES

See detailed description under Devon.

Broford Fishing
Contact: P. Veale, Lance Nicholson Fishing, Tackle & Guns, 9 High Street, Dulverton, TA22 9HB, 01398 323409, lancenich@lancenich.f9.co.uk, *Water:* Approx 5 miles bank fishing on Little Exe, *Species:* Wild Brown Trout with occasional Salmon, *Permits:* As above, *Charges:* £10 per day - Trout. £25 per day - Salmon, *Season:* 15th March - 30th September, *Methods:* Fly Only for Trout. Any legal method for Salmon.

Dulverton Angling Association
Contact: P. Veale, Lance Nicholson Fishing, Tackle & Guns, 9 High Street, Dulverton, TA22 9HB, 01398 323409, lancenich@lancenich.f9.co.uk, *Water:* Approx. 5 miles bank on Exe & Haddeo. Membership open to all, *Species:* Brown Trout & Salmon, *Permits:* Adults £8 per day. Juniors 25p per day, *Charges:* Adults £10. Junior £1 (all juniors under 16 must be accompanied by an adult), *Season:* 15th March - 30th September, *Methods:* Any legal method.

Fly Fishing in Somerset (Little Exe)
Contact: Mr Robin Gurden, 3 Edbrooke Cottages, Winsford, Nr Minehead, TA24 7AE, 01643 851504, 07814 243991, complete.angling@virgin.net, *Water:* Upper Exe 2.5 miles, Barle 2 miles, *Species:* Wild Brown Trout, Salmon early and late season, *Season:* Mar 15th to Sept 30th, *Methods:* All waters fly only.

Lance Nicholson
Contact: 9 High Street, Dulverton, TA22 9HB, 01398 323409, lancenich@lancenich.f9.co.uk, *Water:* Approx 0.75 mile single bank on Exe above Exebridge. Approx 1 mile double bank on Barle at Dulverton, *Species:* Trout and occasional Salmon, *Permits:* As above, *Charges:* £10 Trout, £25 Salmon, *Season:* 15th Mar - 30th Sept, *Methods:* Any legal method.

Nick Hart Fly Fishing (Exe)
Contact: Nick Hart, Exford View, 1 Chapel St, Exford, Minehead, TA24 7PY, 01643 831101, 0797 1198559, nick@hartflyfishing.demon.co.uk, *Water:* 1.5 mls of Upper Exe, 3 miles Middle Exe (see also entries under Devon, Taw and Torridge), *Species:* Upper Exe: Trout to 1lb, Middle Exe: Salmon to double figures, *Permits:* From Nick Hart Fishing, *Charges:* Trout: £15/day, Salmon: £30/day, *Season:* Trout Season: 15th Mar - 30th Sept. Salmon Season: 14th Feb - 30th Sept, *Methods:* Upper Exe: Fly only, barbless hooks, compulsory catch & release - Middle Exe: Spin/fly fish year round.

ISLE

The River Isle rises near Wadeford and soon after its source is joined by a tributary from Chard Lake. Trout are found as far as Ilminster but below the town coarse fish predominate. The profile of the river is fairly natural though a number of shallow weirs provide increased depth in places. Species caught in the lower stretches include Chub, Dace and Roach.

Chard & District Angling Club
Contact: Mr Braunton, Planet Video & Angling, 19a High Street, Chard, TA20 1QF, 01460 64000, *Water:* Approx 3 miles on the river Isle. Also Chard Reservoir and Perry Street Pond, see entry under coarse fishery, *Species:* Dace, Roach, Chub, Perch, Bream, Gudgeon, *Permits:* Planet Video & Angling, 19a High Street, Chard, Somerset TA20 1QF. Tel: 01460 64000, *Charges:* Membership £15 per year, Juniors £8, OAP's & Conc. £10; includes coarse stillwater Perry Street Pond. No day tickets Perry Street or on river. *Season:* Closed season 14th Mar to 16th Jun on river.

Ilminster & District A.A
Contact: P. Lonton, Marshalsea, Cottage Corner, Ilton, Ilminster, 01460 52519, p.lonton@ntlworld.com, *Water:* Approx 6 miles on the river Isle, *Species:* Roach, Chub, Perch, Bream, Dace, *Permits:* Day tickets from Ilminster Warehouse. Membership details from the secretary. Annual membership tickets from Ilminster Warehouse, Yeovil Angling Centre, The Tackle Shack, Chard Angling, Enterprise Angling, Taunton, *Charges:* £16 annual membership. Day tickets £4. Junior £3, *Season:* Current E.A. Byelaws apply, *Methods:* Club rules apply.

Newton Abbot Fishing Association (River Isle)
Contact: Clive Smith (membership secretary), PO Box 1, Bovey Tracey, Newton Abbot, TQ13 9ZE, 01626 836661, newtonfishing@yahoo.com, *Water:* 1 mile stretch of the river Isle at Hambridge. Popular winter venue. See entry under Devon, Stillwater Coarse, Newton Abbot, *Species:* Pike, Roach, Rudd, Bream, Tench and Dace. Pike fishing can be frantic, *Season:* Rivers are controlled by the national close season for coarse fish.

KENN AND BLIND YEO

The New Blind Yeo is an artificial drainage channel which also carries some of the diverted water of the River Kenn. Both waters contain good Roach with Bream, Rudd, Carp, Perch, Tench and Pike.

Clevedon & District F.A.C
Contact: Mr Newton, 64 Clevedon Rd, Tickenham, Clevedon, BS21 6RD, 01275 856107, *Water:* 6 miles - Blind Yeo / River Kenn, *Species:* Roach, Bream, Rudd, Eels, Perch, Pike & Tench, *Permits:* NSAA Permit at all local tackle shops, *Charges:* Season - Seniors: £18, Juniors/OAP: £8; Weekly - £10; Daily - £3, *Season:* June 16th - March 14th inc, *Methods:* Waggler/ Stick, Pole, Ledger, no live baits, no coarse fish to be used as dead bait.

THE KINGS SEDGEMOOR DRAIN

The Kings Sedgemoor Drain is an artificial drainage channel dug c1790. As well as draining a large area of moor it also carries the diverted water of the River Cary and excess flood flows from the River Parrett. The KSD is a very well known coarse fishery and is used for both local and national match fishing competitions. Fish species present include Roach, Bream, Tench, Perch and Pike.

PARRETT

The River Parrett rises in West Dorset and there is some Trout fishing as far as Creedy Bridge upstream of the A303. Below this point a number of weirs and hatches result in deeper water and slower flows. The resulting coarse fishery contains a wide variety of species including Roach, Bream, Rudd, Chub, Dace, Carp, Crucian Carp and Pike. Similar species are found in the lowest freshwater section at Langport where the Rivers Isle and Yeo join the Parrett to form a wide deep river which becomes tidal below Oath Sluice.

Langport & District Angling Association
Contact: Den Barlow, Florissant, Northfield, Somerton, TA11 6SJ, 01458 272119, den@barlow65.fsnet.co.uk, *Water:* 5 miles on the river Parrett. Coombe Lake - 2.75 acres, no closed season, *Species:* All common coarse species except Barbel, *Permits:* Fosters Newsagency, Bow Street, Langport, *Charges:* Annual £11, junior £5, disabled/ OAP £5.50. Weekly £5. Senior day £3, junior day £1.50, *Season:* Closed season on river only. Membership from 16th Jun to 15th Jun inc. Night fishing permitted on river only from Langport A.A. controlled banks, *Methods:* Lake: Barbless hooks, No boilies, No Carp in keepnets.

Somerset Levels Association of Clubs
Contact: Newton Abbot Fishing Association, Clive Smith (Membership Secretary), PO Box 1, Bovey Tracey, Newton Abbot, TQ13 9ZE, 01626 836661, newtonfishing@yahoo.com, *Water:* See entry under Newton Abbot Fishing Association Devon, Stillwater Coarse. Rights to numerous parts of the Parret, Brue, Isle and other stretches of drain in the Langport area, *Species:* All coarse species.

Stoke Sub Hamdon & District A.A
Contact: Mr Derek Goad (Secretary), 2 Windsor Lane, Stoke-sub-Hamdon, (H.Q. Stoke Working Mens Club), TA14 6UE, 01935 824337, *Water:* Upper Stretches River Parrett approx 10km. Long Load Drain (Shared Water) also see entry under Stillwater Coarse, Yeovil, Bearley Lake, *Species:* Carp, Tench, Roach, Rudd, Bream, Perch, Dace, Chub, Pike, Eel, Gudgeon, Ruffe. Trout Fishing also available, *Permits:* Season permits only. Available from Stax Tackle, Montacute and Yeovil Angling Centre, Yeovil. Also available from secretary, *Charges:* Season tickets: Senior £11, Juniors/OAPs £6 (Bearley Lake). Juniors under 14 must be accompanied by an adult, *Season:* Trout 1st April - 31st October. Lake all year. Coarse (River & Drain) 16th June - 14th March, *Methods:* Trout: No maggot. River Coarse: No restrictions.

Tiverton & District Angling Club (River Parret)
Contact: Exe Valley Angling, 19 Westexe South, Tiverton, EX16 5DQ, 01884 242275, *Water:* Various stretches on several rivers in Somerset including Isle, Brue and North Drain. See also entry under stillwater coarse, Devon, Tiverton, *Permits:* Please ring Exe Valley for details. Also available from: Exeter Angling Centre, Enterprise Angling Taunton, Topp Tackle Taunton & Minnows Caravan Park - beside Grand Western Canal, *Charges:* Senior: Day £4, Annual £20. Conc: Junior & OAP Day £2.50, Annual £8, *Season:* Coarse: closed 15th March to 16th June. Trout: open from 15th March to 30th September. Salmon: open 14th February to 30th September.

TONE

The River Tone rises on the edge of Exmoor National Park and not far from its source it feeds into and out of Clatworthy reservoir. From here to Taunton there are some twenty miles of fast flowing Trout river, though Grayling, Dace and Roach appear near Taunton where weirs provide increased depth. Through the town and just below, Chub, Dace and Roach predominate but at Bathpool the river becomes wider, deeper and slower. Roach, Bream, Carp, Tench and Pike are the typical species in this stretch which continues to the tidal limit at New Bridge.

Taunton Angling Association (Tone)
Contact: Mr. J.Helyer, 40 Albemarle Road, Taunton, TA1 1BA, 01823 257559, jonhelyer@btinternet.com, *Water:* 6 miles on River Tone (See also entry under Taunton and Bridgwater Canal & Stillwater Coarse), *Species:* Roach 2lb, Pike 36lb, Dace 1lb, Bream 10lb, Tench 5lb, Perch 3lb, Carp 30lb, Grayling 2lb, Chub 5lb, *Permits:* Topp Tackle, Taunton, (01823) 282518. Enterprise Angling, Taunton (01823) 282623. Somerset Angling, Bridgwater (01278) 431777. Street Angling, Street (01458) 447830. Wellington Country Sports, Wellington (01823) 662120. Thyer's Tackle, Burnham-on-sea (01278) 786934. Yeovil Angling Centre, Yeovil (01935) 476777. Planet Video & Angling, Chard (01460) 64000. Exe Valley Angling, Tiverton (01884) 242275. Exeter Angling Centre, Exeter (01392) 436404. Thatcher's Pet & Tackle, Wells (01749) 673513. Weston Angling Centre, Weston-Super-Mare (01934) 631140, *Charges:* Season £25. Day tickets £5 senior, £2 junior, *Season:* Closed from 14th March to 16th June, *Methods:* All fish (including Pike and Eels) to be returned alive.

Wellington Angling Association
Contact: M Cave, 60 Sylvan Road, Wellington, TA1 8EH, 01823 661671, *Water:* Approx 2 miles on River Tone. Both banks from Nynhead weir to Wellington, *Species:* Brown Trout, *Permits:* Membership only, *Charges:* Joining fee £10, annual membership £12, *Season:* As E.A. season, *Methods:* No spinning.

WEST SEDGEMOOR DRAIN

This artificial channel was excavated in the 1940s on the lines of existing watercourses. Coarse fish species present include Bream, Roach, Tench and Carp.

Taunton Angling Association (W. Sedgemoor Drain)
Contact: Mr. J.Helyer, 40 Albemarle Road, Taunton, TA1 1BA, 01823 257559, jonhelyer@btinternet.com, *Water:* 2 miles of West Sedgemoor Drain, easy access for disabled anglers (also see entries under Stillwater Coarse), *Species:* Bream 7lb, Roach 2.5lb, Eels 2lb, Tench 7lb, Pike 29lb, Perch 2lb, Rudd 2lb, Carp 26lb, *Permits:* Topp Tackle, Taunton, (01823) 282518. Enterprise Angling, Taunton (01823) 282623. Somerset Angling, Bridgwater (01278) 431777. Street Angling, Street (01458) 447830. Wellington Country Sports, Wellington (01823) 662120. Thyer's Tackle, Burnham-on-sea (01278) 786934. Yeovil Angling Centre, Yeovil (01935) 476777. Planet Video & Angling, Chard (01460) 64000. Exe Valley Angling, Tiverton (01884) 242275. Exeter Angling Centre, Exeter (01392) 436404. Thatcher's Pet & Tackle, Wells (01749) 673513. Weston Angling Centre, Weston-Super-Mare (01934) 631140, *Charges:* Season £25. Day tickets £5 senior, £2 junior, *Season:* Closed from 14th March to 16th June, *Methods:* All fish (including Pike and Eels) to be returned alive.

YEO

The River Yeo rises near Sherborne and between here and Yeovil the river is a coarse fishery, though tributaries such as the River Wriggle have Brown Trout. Below Yeovil a number of weirs produce areas of deep water and the resulting fishery contains good Dace together with Roach, Chub, Bream and Pike.

Ilchester & District A.A
Contact: Mr B Bushell (Chairman), 1 Friars Close, Ilchester, Yeovil, BA22 8NU, *Water:* River Yeo above and below Ilchester, *Species:* Chub, Roach, Dace, Bream, Gudgeon, Tench and Carp, *Permits:* Tackle shops in Yeovil. Yeovil Angling Centre. Stax Tackle, Montacute. Ilchester Post Office. Newsagents, Ilchester, or from Club Chairman at above address, *Charges:* Season ticket £12. OAP/junior £6. Weekly ticket £5, *Season:* Open 16th June to 15th March, *Methods:* Current E.A. Byelaws apply. Club rules on ticket and fishery map.

Mudford Angling Club
Contact: Water: 3.5 miles double bank on river Yeo, *Species:* Chubb, Bream, Dace, Roach, *Charges:* Club membership available from Yeovil District Angling Centre: 01935 476777 and Stax Tackle at Montacute: 01935 822645.

N. Somerset Association of Anglers
Contact: Mr Newton, 64 Clevedon Rd, Tickenham, Clevedon, BS21 6RD, 01275 856107, *Water:* Blind Yeo, Kenn, Congresbury Yeo, Brue, Apex Lake, Newtown Ponds & Walrow Ponds, Tickenham Boundry Rhyne, North Drain (also see entry Stillwater, Coarse, Highbridge), *Species:* Roach, Bream, Eels, Perch, Rudd, Carp, Pike, Tench, *Permits:* NSAA Permits available at all local Tackle Shops, *Charges:* Season: Seniors £18. Juniors/OAP/ Disabled £8. Weekly: £10. Day £3, *Season:* June 16th - March 14th inclusive. Apex Lake & Newtown Ponds: June 1st - 28th February incl, *Methods:* Apex Lake and Newtown Ponds: Barbless hooks, No live or dead baits, no floating baits, min. breaking strain line 2.5lb.

Northover Manor Water
Contact: Ilchester, BA22 8LD, 01935 840447, northover@btconnect.com, *Water:* 50 yards single back fishing on the Yeo, *Species:* Roach, Bream and Carp, *Charges:* Please enquire at Reception, *Season:* E.A. Byelaws.

Yeovil & Sherborne Angling Association (Yeo)
Contact: Alex Murray, 2 Wisteria Close, Yeovil, BA21 2EE, 07818 098057, *Water:* 4 miles rivers, Sherborne Castle Lake & discounted tickets Viaduct Fishery, *Species:* Roach, Bream, Carp, *Permits:* Membership details from above & local tackle shops, *Charges:* No day tickets. River Club card £11, £2 off cost of day ticket at Viaduct.

SOMERSET Stillwater Coarse

BATH

Bath Anglers Association
Contact: Andy Smith, 68 Bloomfield Rise, Odd Down, Bath, BA2 2NB, 01225 834736, *Water:* Regular matches, open to all in region. Fishing amalgamation waters, *Charges:* Contact above, or Dave Bacon at Bacons Tackle - 01225 448850. Membership free, but must be member of Bristol, Bath & Wiltshire Angling Association. Adults & Children welcome.

Bathampton Angling Association
Contact: Dave Crookes, 25 Otago Terrace, Larkhall, Bath, BA1 6SX, 01225 427164, dave@bathampton.org, *Water:* Small pond at Weston village in Bath, *Species:* Carp to 10lbs, Roach to 1.5lbs, Bream to 2lbs, Hybrids to 1lb, Tench to 4lbs. *Permits:* Bacons Tackle Box, 83 Lower Bristol Road, Bath, *Charges:* Adults £22, combined lady and gent £30, juniors £7, O.A.P £7. Registered disabled £7, Under 12's free. To year end 31/12/03. Members only special day permits must be purchased in advance at £2 p/day, *Season:* Open all year, *Methods:* Special rules apply. Available from secretary, on website, from shop.

Bathampton Angling Association (Huntstrete Ponds)
Contact: Dave Crookes, 25 Otago Terrace, Larkhall, Bath, BA1 6SX, 01225 427164, dave@bathampton.org, *Water:* 3 lake complex at Hunstrete, near Pensford. Total 11 acres 120 pegs, *Species:* Bream to 8.5lbs, Chub to 2.5lbs, Roach to 2.5lbs, Pike to 22lbs, Carp to 28lbs, Tench to 9lbs, Perch to 2.5lbs, Crucians to 2lbs, Eels to 7lbs, *Permits:* Local fishing tackle shops (members only), *Charges:* Adults £22, combined lady and gent £30, juniors £7, O.A.P £7. Registered disabled £7, Under 12's free. To year end 31/12/03. Additional special day permit at £3 must be obtained before fishing, *Season:* Open all year fishing times vary according to time of year. No night fishing. *Methods:* Copies of rules available from secretary and tackle shops. Also displayed on notice boards at lakeside, and on website.

Bathampton Angling Association (Newton Park Pond)
Contact: Dave Crookes, 25 Otago Terrace, Larkhall, Bath, BA1 6SX, 01225 427164, dave@bathampton.org, *Water:* 2.5 acre lake at Newton park, near Bath, *Species:* Bream to 2.5lbs, Chub to 6lbs, Roach to 2lbs, Pike to 24lbs, Carp to 27lbs, *Permits:* Local fishing tackle shops (members only), *Charges:* Adults £22, combined lady and gent £30, juniors £7, O.A.P £7. Registered disabled £7, Under 12's free. To year end 31/12/03. Additional special day permit at £3 must be obtained before fishing. Members only, *Season:* Open all year fishing times vary according to time of year. No night fishing. *Methods:* Copies of rules available from secretary and tackle shops. Also displayed on notice boards at lakeside, and on website.

Farleigh Wood Fishery (Coarse)
Contact: Wood Cottage, Tellisford, Bath, BA2 7RN, 01373 831495, bellagingell766@msn.com, *Water:* 1 acre coarse fishing lake plus brook fishing (see entry River Frome, Bristol), *Species:* Carp to double figures, *Charges:* Price on application, *Season:* All year coarse fishing, *Methods:* List of rules at fishery.

Gurney Slade - Stockhill Ponds
Contact: Nitts Farm, Chilcompton, Radstock, Bath, BA3 4JQ, 01761 232271, *Water:* 2 ponds, *Species:* Carp, Tench, Perch, Roach, Rudd, Bream, *Permits:* Collect at Lakeside, *Charges:* £4 per day, £3 under 14, £3 evening ticket (after 4pm), *Season:* Open all year Dawn to Dusk, *Methods:* No night fishing, No tents. Barbless hooks only.

BRIDGWATER

Bridgwater Angling Association (Coarse Lakes)
Contact: Mr M Pople, 14 Edward Street, Bridgwater, TA6 5EU, 01278 422397, *Water:* See entry under Taunton and Bridgwater Canal. Various stillwaters. Stillwater fishing at Combwich, Walrow, Dunwear & Screech Owl.

Bridgwater Sports & Social Club
Contact: Duncan, Danny or Nick, Bath Road, Bridgwater, TA6 4PA, 01278 446215, *Water:* 3 large ponds, *Species:* Carp to 30lb, Crucian to 3lb, Bream to 4lb, Roach to 1.5lb, Perch to 4lb, Tench to 6.5lb, *Charges:* £25/person - private members fishing, *Season:* Normal open season, *Methods:* No night fishing.

Browns Pond
Contact: Phil Dodds, Off Taunton Rd (A38), Bridgwater, 01278 444145, doddphilelen@aol.com, *Water:* 2.5 acres, *Species:* Carp to 22lb, Tench to 5lb, Bream to 6lb, Perch to 2lb & Roach, *Charges:* On site. £2 per day, *Season:* Closed May, open June 1st - April 30th; dawn to dusk, *Methods:* No night fishing, barbless hooks only, no live bait, no Carp sacks.

Burton Springs Fishery (Coarse Lake)
Contact: Tony Evans, Lawson Farm, Burton, Nr Stogursey, Bridgwater, TA5 1QB, 01278 732135, burtonsprings@aol.co.uk, *Water:* Approx 2 acre lake, *Species:* Mirror, Common, Leather Carp, Ghost Carp to 20lb, Tench to 5 lb, Perch to 3.5lbs, *Permits:* Self Service at fishing lodge, *Charges:* £5 per day, 2 rods, *Season:* Open all year 8am - 9pm or dusk, *Methods:* Barbless hooks only, no nuts.

Durleigh Reservoir
Contact: Wessex Water, 0845 600 4600, *Water:* 80 acre reservoir, *Species:* Carp, Roach, Bream, Perch, Tench and Pike, *Permits:* Contact Ranger Paul Martin on 01278 424786, *Charges:* Day Ticket £5, Day Concession £3.50, Evening Ticket £3.50, Book of Tickets £40 for 10, *Season:* Open all year except Christmas day, Boxing day & New Years day.

Plum Lane Fishery
Contact: Julie, Plum Lane, Dunwear, Bridgwater, 01278 421625, *Water:* 1 acre pond, *Species:* Predominately Carp to 10lb plus Tench. Roach and Skimmers, *Permits:* On site, *Charges:* £5 per adult (2 rods). One child (up to 12 years) can fish with an adult free of charge, *Season:* Open all year, *Methods:* Barbless hooks only. No keepnets. Advice available on site.

Summerhayes Fishery
Contact: Mike, Somerset Bridge, Bridgwater, TA6 6LW, 01278 781565, 07703 115502, *Water:* Several lakes - totalling 6 acres, *Species:* Carp, Bream, Tench, Roach, Rudd, Perch, Ghost Carp, *Charges:* On bank £5 day, £3.50 Concessions. Disabled access, *Season:* Open all year dawn to dusk, *Methods:* Barbless hooks, no nuts. Maximum 2 rods.

Taunton Road Ponds
Contact: Phil Dodds, Off Taunton Rd (A38), Bridgwater, 01278 444145, doddphilelen@aol.com, *Water:* 3.5 acres, *Species:* Large carp to 32lb, Tench to 6lb, Bream to 13lb 6oz, Perch to 3lb, Rudd to 2lb, Skimmer Bream to 12oz & Roach to 8oz, *Charges:* On site, £2 per day, *Season:* Closed May, open June 1st - April 30th. Dawn to dusk, *Methods:* No night fishing, barbless hooks only, no live bait, no Carp in keepnets, no Carp sacks.

The Sedges
Contact: Pat & John, River Lane, Dunwear, Bridgwater, TA7 0AA, 01278 445221, *Water:* 2 lakes totalling 7 acres. New match lake for 2003, *Species:* Tench, Rudd, Roach, Bream, Chub, Carp to 32lb, *Charges:* On bank: £5 adult day, children accompanied by adult £4, *Season:* Open all year dawn to dusk, *Methods:* No keepnets in summer months, no carp sacks, barbless hooks, unhooking mats. Strictly no cat meat or nuts.

Trinity Waters
Contact: John Herring, Hopfield Fish Farms, Straight Drove, Chilton Trinity, Bridgwater, 01278 450880, 0772 0542141, johnandsue@trinitywaters.fsnet.co.uk, *Water:* Currently 3 lakes: 6.5 acres, 2 acres and 1 acre. *Species:* Rudd to 2lb. Roach to 2lb. Perch to 3lb. Tench to 6lb. Golden Tench to 5lb. Bream to 11lb. Mirror, Common to 20lb and Grass Carp to 12lb. Mirror and Common to 30lb in specimen lake, *Permits:* On site only, *Charges:* £5 per day, £7.50 for two rods. £3 juniors and concessions. Match rates on request, *Season:* Open all year dawn to dusk, *Methods:* Barbless hooks. No keepnets. No fixed rigs.

BRISTOL

Alcove Angling Club
Contact: Mr K.Davis (Membership Secretary), 6 Ashdene Ave, Upper Eastville, Bristol, BS5 6QH, 01179 025737, 07941 638680, alcove.a.c.bristol@blueyonder.co.uk, *Water:* 4 lakes in Bristol & South Glos, *Species:* Carp, Bream, Roach, Tench, Rudd, Pike, Perch, *Permits:* As above, *Charges:* Adult £40, OAP/Disabled £25, *Season:* No close season, *Methods:* As specified in membership card, Night fishing at Alcove Lido only.

Bagwood Lake
Contact: Woodland Golf Club, Trench Lane, Almondsbury, Bristol, BS32 4JZ, 01454 619319, woodlands@tracypark.com, *Water:* One coarse lake, *Species:* Carp, *Permits:* On site, pay in shop, *Charges:* £7 - 12 hour ticket. £13 - 24 hour ticket, *Season:* Open all year - night fishing by arrangement.

Bitterwell Lake
Contact: Mr C W Reid, The Chalet, Bitterwell Lake, Ram Hill,, Coalpit Heath, Bristol, BS36 2UF, 01454 778960, *Water:* 2.5 Acres, *Species:* Common, Mirror, Crucian Carp, Roach, Bream, Rudd, Perch, *Charges:* £4 -1 rod. £2 second rod, O.A.P.'s etc, Reg. disabled and arrivals after 4 pm, *Season:* Closed for spawning 4 - 6 weeks May - June, *Methods:* Barbless hooks size 8 max, no bolt rigs, no boilies, no nuts, hemp or groundbait.

Bristol, Bath & Wiltshire Amalgamated Anglers (Lakes)
Contact: Jeff Parker, 16 Lansdown View, Kingswood, Bristol, BS15 4AW, 0117 9672977, *Water:* See entry under Bristol Avon - Various stillwaters, too much to list here, please contact the secretary for full details; Stillwaters at Lyneham, Calne, Malmesbury, Bath and Pawlett near Bridgwater, *Species:* All coarse species, *Methods:* Maximum 2 rods, no metal cans or glass allowed on banks, no freshwater fish to be used as livebait. Full rules and maps available.

Carps AC
Contact: John Bennett, 30a Church Road, Hanham, Bristol, BS15 3AL, 0117 9601597, *Water:* Match orientated club (47 matches per year). Open to all in South West, fishing Carp lakes in the region, *Charges:* Contact John at number above. Seniors £10, OAP's £7.50, Disabled £7.50, Juniors £5.00, Ladies £5.00.

Cross Hands Angling Club
Contact: Bristol, 01179 9091421, 07713 258623, *Water:* The Crest lake - 30 pegs. Hunters lake at Clutton - 20 pegs. *Species:* Carp to 8lb, *Permits:* Members only - Limited membership available from above, junior section, *Season:* Open all year.

Duchess Pond
Contact: Wayne Tooker (Leaseholder), 0117 9372001, 07980 091286, *Water:* 2 acre pond, *Species:* Mixed fishery plus Carp to 28lb, *Permits:* Limited day tickets from Jarrats Garden Centre, Bitton - 01179 327659. Bristol Angling Centre - 01179 508723. Or direct from Wayne, *Charges:* £5 Adults, £2.50 under 16. £50 season ticket. £60 Parent & Child season ticket, *Season:* Open all year Dawn to Dusk. Night Fishing available to syndicate members only. Please enquire, *Methods:* Full rules displayed at Fishery.

Foresters Angling Club
Contact: Chris Gay, Bristol, 01179 095105, *Water:* Around 40 members meeting at Foresters Arms, Downend, Bristol every Sunday 8.30 onwards. Evening fishing matches throughout Westcountry every fortnight, *Charges:* £15 membership, pools money on the day, £15 inclusive. Juniors welcome, *Season:* If interested in starting fishing matches at a friendly club, please telephone Chris.

Ham Green Fisheries
Contact: Mr Hunt, Ham Green, Chapel Lane, Pill, 01275 849885, 07818 640227, *Water:* Two lakes. 1 acre 25 peg. 2 acre open bank, *Species:* 1 acre lake stocked with Carp, Roach, Rudd, Perch, Pike, Bream, Skimmers, Golden Tench and Golden Orfe. 2 acre lake all the above with Carp to 35lb, *Permits:* Mr Hunt, 21 Station Rd, Portishead, Bristol; also on lake side from Baliff. Veals Tackle Shop, 61 Old Market St, Bristol, *Charges:* £5 in advance from Veals Tackle or £7 on the bank, *Season:* No closed season. 7am to 8pm from 16 June to 13 October. 8am to 5pm from 1 November to 30 April. Night fishing strictly by arrangement, booking essential by telephone to Mr Hunt, *Methods:* No live bait, barbless hooks preferred, no keepnets for fish over 1lb, Carp sacks allowed.

King William IV Angling Association
Contact: Jerry Pocock, 86 Tower Road South, Warmley, Bristol, BS30 8BP, 01179 492974, 07761 799876, *Charges:* £3 joining fee. Juniors free of charge. Further details from Jerry, *Season:* Open to all in the area. Regular meetings and matches.

Kingswood Disabled Angling Club
Contact: Trebor, 0117 9641224, uktrebor@fsmail.net, *Water:* Bristol based Coarse fishing club meeting monthly. New members welcome. Must be registered disabled at local Social Services Office. Regular fishing trips and matches organised. Please phone for further information, *Charges:* £7.50 adults annual membership.

Mardon Angling Club
Contact: Mr Austin, 65 Grange Avenue, Hanham, Bristol, BS15 3PE, 0117 9839776, chrisjan5254@yahoo.co.uk, *Water:* Open to all. Regular monthly meetings, full match calendar, *Charges:* Please contact above. Charges £10 per annum, children under 16 free.

Paulton Lakes
Contact: John Wiles, Ruthin Villa, High Street, High Littleton, Bristol, BS39 5JD, 01761 472338, 07905 758149, john.wiles@virgin.net, *Water:* 2 lakes totalling 2.5 acres, *Species:* Carp 32lb, Tench 6lb, Roach 3lb plus, Grass Carp, Rudd, Chub 10lb, *Permits:* Day tickets available from A.M. Hobbs, Midsomer Norton. Tel: (01761) 413961and from Central Garage, Paulton, *Charges:* £6 per day ticket, *Season:* Open all year, dawn to dusk, *Methods:* Barbless hooks, no ground baiting, unhooking mats must be used.

Ridgeway & District AA
Contact: Steve Dumbleton, Bristol, 01179 603193, *Water:* Open to all. Match fishing every fortnight in Summer, less frequent in Winter months, *Charges:* Annual membership £8, Juniors welcome. Please telephone Steve on number above.

Royal British Legion Kingswood
Contact: Mr Lloyd, 386 Speedwell Road, Kingswood, Bristol, BS15 1ES, 0117 9676030, brian.lloyd2@ukonline.co.uk, *Water:* Open to all Royal British Legion members, regular matches.

Tan House Farm Lake
Contact: Mr & Mrs James, Tan House Farm, Yate, Bristol, BS37 7QL, 01454 228280, *Water:* Quarter mile lake, *Species:* Roach, Perch, Carp, Bream, Tench, Rudd, *Permits:* Day tickets from Farm House, *Charges:* Adult £3 per rod or £5 for 2 rods, Children & O.A.Ps £2, *Season:* Closed March 31st - May 23rd 2003, *Methods:* No Ground bait, dog & cat food, boilies, barbless hooks only.

BURNHAM-ON-SEA

Highbridge Angling Association
Contact: Mr C Brewer, 8 Willow Close, East Huntspill, Near Highbridge, TA9 3NX, 01278 786230, *Water:* Apex lake, Marine drive, Burnham-on-sea, *Species:* Mixed coarse fish. Carp to 20lb, Bream to 8lb, Roach to 3lb and Chub to 5lb, *Methods:* No night fishing.

CHARD

Chard & District Angling Club (Coarse Lakes)

Contact: Mr Braunton, Planet Video & Angling, 19a High Street, Chard, TA20 1QF, 01460 64000, *Water:* Perry Street Pond - 1.5 acres. Chard Reservoir - 48 acres. Also 3 miles on Isle see entry under associations, *Species:* Roach, Bream, Carp, Tench, Perch, Eels, Rudd, *Permits:* Planet Video & Angling, 19a High Street, Chard, Somerset TA20 1QF. Tel: 01460 64000.. Perry Street Ponds - members only, details from secretary, *Charges:* Chard reservoir £6 per day (£4 club members). Perry Street ponds members only, membership £15, *Season:* Open all year, *Methods:* Full list of rules from fishery notice board and membership book.

CHEDDAR

Cheddar Angling Club

Contact: Cheddar Angling Club, P.O. Box 1183, Cheddar, BS27 3LT, 01934 743959, *Water:* 200 acre Cheddar reservoir, *Species:* Pike, Perch, Tench, Roach, Eels, Carp, *Permits:* Permits are NOT available at the reservoir. Only from: Broadway House Caravan Park, Axbridge Road, Cheddar, Somerset. Bristol Angling Centre, 12-16 Doncaster Road, Southmead, Bristol. Thatchers Pet and Tackle, 18 Queen St, Wells. Veals Fishing Tackle, 61 Old Market St, Bristol. Thyers Fishing Tackle, Church St, Highbridge, *Charges:* Seniors season permit £40, Juniors season permit £20, Seniors day permit £5, Juniors day permit £3, *Season:* No closed season, *Methods:* No live baiting, Moderate ground baiting, No dead baiting 16th June - 30th September. No night fishing. Dawn to dusk only. Unhooking mats recommended. Rod limits: seniors maximum 3 rods, juniors one rod only.

Stone Yard Fisheries

Contact: Thatchers Angling, 18 Queen St, Wells, BA5 2DP, 01749 673513, *Water:* Small Ponds (15 Anglers) at Litton near Chewton Mendip, *Species:* Carp to approx 18lb, small Tench, *Permits:* Thatchers Angling 01749 673513. 5 tickets per day available from A.M. Hobbs Angling 01761 413961, *Charges:* Day £5 Senior, £2.50 Junior, *Season:* March 1st - October 31st, *Methods:* Barbless hooks only. No Boilies.

COLEFORD

Breach Valley Fishing

Contact: Lower Vobster, Coleford, Radstock, BA3 5LY, 01373 812352, *Water:* 2 ponds totalling 1.5 acres approx, *Species:* Carp 28.25lb, Roach, Tench, Perch and Bream, *Permits:* AM Hobbs Angling, Midsomer Norton, Bath, Tel: 01761 413961; Haines Angling, 47 Vallis Way, Frome, Tel: 01373 466406, *Charges:* Day tickets on bank, £6 per day, *Season:* Open June 14th - beginning March, dawn to dusk, *Methods:* No keepnets, no boilies, barbless hooks.

CONGRESBURY

Silver Springs Coarse Fishery

Contact: Liz Patch, Silver Street Lane, Congresbury, BS49 5EY, 01934 877073, liz-bar@silver-springs.freeserve.co.uk, *Water:* 4.5 acres, *Species:* Carp to mid twenties, Rudd, Roach to 3lbs, Tench, Chub and Bream, *Permits:* On site, *Charges:* £5 / £3.50 conc, *Season:* All year dawn till half hour before dusk, *Methods:* Barbless hooks.

CORFE

Taunton Angling Association (Wych Lodge Lake)

Contact: Mr. J.Helyer, 40 Albemarle Road, Taunton, TA1 1BA, 01823 257559, jonhelyer@btinternet.com, *Water:* Wych Lodge Lake, 5 acre large carp lake (also see entries under River & Canal Fishing), *Species:* Large Carp up to 25lb, Grass Carp 18lb, Roach, Rudd and Perch all to 2lb, *Permits:* Only from Topp Tackle, Taunton (restricted to 10 pegs). Please bring season ticket as proof of membership when purchasing day permit. Separate day ticket available for non season ticket holders, *Charges:* £3 per day. £6 for non season ticket holders, *Season:* Open all year, *Methods:* Barbless hooks, no Carp in keepnets, no lighting of fires, no litter.

CREWKERNE

Highlands Dairy Lake

Contact: J.Wyatt, Highlands Dairy Farm, Hewish, Nr Crewkerne, 01460 74180, *Water:* 2 x one acre lakes, *Species:* Carp, Tench, Rudd, Roach, Perch, *Permits:* At house, *Charges:* £4 per day including night fishing. £3 day ticket, *Season:* Open all year, *Methods:* No keepnets for Carp. Barbless hooks only.

Manor Farm

Contact: Mr A. Emery, Wayford, Nr Crewkerne, TA18 8QL, 01460 78865, 07767 620031, *Water:* 3 large ponds, *Species:* Carp - Mirror, Common and Ghost, Tench, Rudd, Gudgeon, Roach, Perch, Bream, Eels, *Permits:* As above, *Charges:* £5 per day, *Methods:* Barbless hooks.

Water Meadow Fishery

Contact: Mr. Pike, Pitt Farm, North Perrott, Crewkerne, TA18 7SX, 01460 72856, *Water:* 2 coarse lakes totalling approx 1.75 acres, *Species:* 16 different varieties of coarse fish, *Charges:* On site - £5 day. £3 morning/afternoon. £2 half day/ evening, *Season:* Open all year - dawn to dusk, *Methods:* No boilies or keepnets, barbless hooks only, ground baiting in moderation.

FROME

Edneys Fisheries

Contact: Richard Candy, Edneys Farm, Mells, Frome, BA11 3RE, 01373 812294, 07941 280075, *Water:* 2 lakes, *Species:* Carp to 30lb, Tench to 7lb, Roach, Rudd, Perch, Common, Mirror, Linear, Leather and Ghost Carp, *Charges:* Adults £5, Under 14 yrs £3. Night tickets available.

Frome Angling Association (Coarse Lake)

Contact: Gary Collinson, 94 Nunney Road, Frome, BA11 4LD, 01373 465214, *Water:* 10 acre lake. See entry under River Fishing - Bristol Frome.

Mells Pit Pond

Contact: Mr M.Coles, Lyndhurst, Station Road, Mells, Nr Frome, BA11 3RJ, 01373 812094, *Water:* 1 acre lake, *Species:* Various Carp, Rudd, Roach, Tench, Perch, *Permits:* Tickets issued at bankside, *Charges:* £5/day, season tickets £60, *Season:* March to November, *Methods:* Barbless hooks. No keepnets.

Parrots Paddock Farm

Contact: Mr. Baker, Wanstrow Rd, Nunney Catch, 01373 836505, 07931 273758, *Water:* 90yd x 75 yd pond, *Species:* Crayfish & Catfish, *Permits:* Please phone first, *Season:* Open all year, dawn to dusk, *Methods:* No night fishing, keepnets only for small fish, barbless hooks only, ground bait in moderation.

Shepards Lake

Contact: John Nicholls, Barrow Farm, Witham Friary, Frome, BA11 5HD, 01749 850313, *Water:* Half acre lake, *Species:* Carp, Perch and Tench, *Charges:* £4 adult. £3.50 children and OAPs, *Season:* February to September. Phone for details, *Methods:* No restrictions.

Witham Friary Lakes
Contact: Mr. Miles, Witham Hall Farm, Witham Friary, Nr Frome, BA11 5HB, 01373 836239, *Water:* Two lakes totalling approx. 2 acres, *Species:* Carp, Roach, Tench, Perch, Gudgeon, *Permits:* On site, *Charges:* £4 a day - £6 night ticket (dusk - 8 am), *Season:* All year, *Methods:* Barbless hooks only.

GLASTONBURY

Avalon Fisheries
Contact: Allan Tedder (Ted), 7 Coronation Road, Bridgwater, TA6 7DS, 01278 456429, 07855 825059, *Water:* 9 acre Match & Coarse lake approximately 70 pegs, *Species:* Carp to mid 20's, Tench 7.5lb, Bream 9lb 2oz, Perch 3lb, Roach, Rudd, *Permits:* Site office and on the bank. Mobile Phone 07855 825059, *Charges:* £5 Adult, £3 Junior / O.A.P. / Disabled, *Season:* No closed season - Open dawn to dusk, *Methods:* No floating or boilie baits, all nuts banned, barbless hooks, no night fishing.

HIGHBRIDGE

Emerald Pool Fishery
Contact: Mr Alan Wilkinson, Emerald Pool Fishery, Puriton Road, West Huntspill, Highbridge, TA9 3NL, 01278 794707, *Water:* 1.5 acre lake, plus 'Sapphire Lake' - new 20 peg disabled angler friendly pool for adults and juniors, *Species:* Bream, Golden Orfe, Roach, Rudd, Tench, Perch, Carp to low-mid 20's, Sturgeon to 4 feet long, Barbel 5lb, *Permits:* Enviroment Agency rod licence required on this water, *Season:* All year, *Methods:* Barbless hooks only, no Carp sacks, no peanuts or ground bait, all Sturgeon to be released immediately, no fish over 3lb to be retained at all.

Highbridge Angling Association
Contact: Mr C Brewer, 8 Willow Close, East Huntspill, Near Highbridge, TA9 3NX, 01278 786230, *Water:* 3 Lakes at Walrow, *Species:* Carp to mid 20's, Pike to mid 20's, Bream to 12lb, Tench to double figures and all other coarse species, *Permits:* Thyers Tackle, Highbridge - 01278 786934. Also available from other local tackle shops, *Charges:* Day tickets £3, 7 day ticket £10 or season ticket £18. Senior citizen £8. Night fishing £5 per night by prior arrangement only. Telephone Mr A Hardwidge - 01278 765941, *Season:* March 15th - June 16th close season.

N. Somerset Association of Anglers (Coarse Lakes)
Contact: Mr Newton, 64 Clevedon Rd, Tickenham, Clevedon, BS21 6RD, 01275 856107, *Water:* See also entry under Yeo. Apex lake: 6 acre lake, Newtown: 3 acre lake, Walrow ponds: 2 acre lake, 3 acre lake and 6 acre lake, *Species:* Apex: Carp to 18lbs, Bream to 7lb, Pike to 15lb, Roach, Rudd. Newtown: Carp to 24lb, Pike to 27lb, Bream 7lb, Roach, Rudd, Perch. Walrow: Carp to 26lb, Bream 11lb, Tench 10lb, Pike 24lb, Roach, Rudd, Perch, *Permits:* Local tackle shops, purchased in advance of fishing, *Charges:* £3 day, £10 week, £18 season, junior/ OAP/disabled £8, *Season:* Apex & Newtown Lakes 1 June - 28 Feb. (incl.), Walrow Pond 16 June - 14 March (incl.), *Methods:* Apex & Newtown Lakes: Barbless hooks, min. 2.5lb BS line, no live or dead bait, no floating bait.

KEYNSHAM

Avon Valley Country Park (Coarse Pond)
Contact: Bath Rd, Keynsham, Bristol, BS31 1TP, 0117 9864929, info@avonvalleycountrypark.co.uk, *Water:* Small Coarse pond, *Species:* Carp to 12lb, *Permits:* From above, *Charges:* £4 Adult entrance to park (includes ticket to fish), £3 Child, £3.50 Senior Citizen, *Season:* Park open: Easter - 1st November 10am-6pm, *Methods:* Barbless hooks only, no keepnets.

Keynsham Angling Association (Coarse Lake)
Contact: Mr K. N. Jerrom, 21 St Georges Road, Keynsham, Bristol, BS31 2HU, 01179 865193, *Water:* Century ponds 0.25 acres, see also entry under river Chew, *Species:* Mixed fishery, *Charges:* Day ticket for club members £2.50, *Season:* Open all year dawn to dusk. Closed alternate Sunday mornings until 1pm, *Methods:* Barbless hooks and no boilies.

KINGSTON SEYMOUR

Acorn Carp Fishery
Contact: Adrian and Bev Bartlett, Lampley Rd, Kingston Seymour, 01934 833760 or 834050 (lake), 07957 828721, *Water:* 3.5 acres of water full disabled access to every swim, *Species:* Specimen Carp from 10 to 36lbs, *Charges:* Day tickets 7am - 7pm £10. Night 7pm-7am £10. 24 hours £15. Weekly rates available.

Bullock Farm Fishing Lakes
Contact: Philip Simmons, Bullock Farm, Kingston Seymour, BS21 6XA, 01934 835020, bullockfarm@kingstonseymour1.freeserve.co.uk, *Water:* 4 Lakes totalling 4.75 acres, including specialist Carp lake, *Species:* Carp - Common, Mirror, Ghost, Crucian, Grass, Purple and Koi. Tench, Roach, Rudd, Chub, Bream, Skimmer Bream, Golden Orfe, Golden Tench, *Permits:* Only at lakeside, *Charges:* £5.00 day ticket, £3.00 O.A.P's / Under 14s / Disabled. Season tickets & Match rates available, *Season:* Open all year round Dawn - Dusk, *Methods:* No boilies, Barbless hooks, Fish friendly keepnets only, No dogs, under 14's to be accompanied by an adult, no loose-fed pellets, Common sense!

Plantations Lake
Contact: Mr or Mrs W.Travis, Middle Lane Farm, Middle Lane, Kingston Seymour, Clevedon, BS21 6XW, 01934 832325, watravis@plantations.freeserve.co.uk, *Water:* 0.75 acre Carp lake, 2.5 acre coarse lake, 1.75 acre match lake open, *Species:* 12 Species of coarse fish incl. Barbel, Crucian Carp. 3 Species of Carp in Carp lake, *Charges:* £5 Adult (£1 extra rod), £4.00 Juniors/O.A.P's/Disabled. Half days (from 2pm) available: adult £4, juniors/OAPs £2.50. Please enquire for membership details, *Season:* All year, *Methods:* No boilies, barbless hooks.

LANGPORT

Langport & Dist. Angling Association (Coarse Lake)
Contact: den@barlow65.fsnet.co.uk, *Water:* Coombe Lake - 2.75 acres. See entry under Parrett, *Species:* Carp to 30lb, Tench 6.5lb, Roach 1.5lb, Perch 2lb plus, Bream 7lb, Chub 4lb, *Permits:* See entry under Parrett, *Charges:* See entry under Parrett, *Season:* No closed season. No night fishing, *Methods:* Barbless hooks, no boilies, no Carp in keepnets.

Thorney Lakes
Contact: Richard or Ann England, Thorney Farm, Muchelney, Langport, TA10 0DW, 01458 250811, enquiries@thorneylakes.co.uk, *Water:* Two 2 acre lakes, *Species:* A selection of coarse fish including large Carp, *Permits:* On the bank, *Charges:* £5/day, £3/half day after 4 p.m, £3 for O.A.P.s & Children under 16, *Season:* 16th March - 31st January, *Methods:* Barbless hooks, no boilies, nuts or pulses, all nets to be dipped on site, no night fishing.

MARTOCK

Ash Ponds

Contact: Pat Rodford, Ash Ponds, Burrough Street, Ash, Marlock, 01935 823459, *Water:* Four 1 acre ponds, *Species:* Carp to 30lb, Tench to 6lb and Bream, *Permits:* On the bank, *Charges:* £3 for 12 hours, *Season:* No closed season.

SHEPTON MALLET

Bridge Farm Fishery

Contact: Jon Thorners, Bridge Farm Shop, Pylle, Shepton Mallet, BA4 6TA, 01749 830138, *Water:* 0.25 mile long x 30m wide lake, approx 3 acres, *Species:* Common Carp to 15lb, Roach, Rudd and other coarse fish, *Permits:* From farm shop on arrival, *Charges:* Adults £5, Juniors under 16 £2.50, *Season:* Open all year, dawn to dusk, *Methods:* Barbless hooks only, no keepnets, for Carp, no night fishing.

SOMERTON

Viaduct Fishery

Contact: Mr Steve Long, Viaduct Fishery, Cary Valley, Somerton, TA11 6LJ, 01458 274022, *Water:* Six Coarse Lakes including one specimen lake, *Species:* Mirror Carp 27lb, Crucian Carp, Common Carp 23lb, Perch 5lb, Roach 1.5lb, Bream 6lb, Tench 8lb and Golden Tench, Rudd, Ruffe, *Permits:* Fishery Shop or Pre-Payment Office; E.A. Rod licences available, *Charges:* Day ticket £5, Under 16 £4, Summer Evening ticket £3, Winter Half day ticket £3. £2 charge for second rod; Match bookings taken, *Season:* All year, *Methods:* All nets to be dipped, no nuts or boilies, barbless hooks size 10 max, no fixed rigs, no braid, fishing from pegs only.

STREET

Glaston Manor Association (Moorland Fishery)

Contact: J. Ogden, 10 Dovecote Close, Farm Lane, Street, *Water:* Moorland Fishery (stillwater), Meare, *Species:* Tench and a few Carp, *Permits:* Thatchers Tackle, Wells. Street Angling, High St, Street, Somerset Tel: 01458 447830, *Charges:* Day ticket £4, Junior membership £6, Senior membership £18, OAP and disabled £9, *Season:* Current E.A. byelaws apply, *Methods:* No live bait permitted, full rules on day ticket.

Godney Moor Ponds

Contact: Nick Hughes, Street Angling Centre, 160 High Street, Street, BA16 0NH, 01458 447830, *Water:* Approx 4 acres, *Species:* Coarse fish including Carp, *Permits:* Only from Street Angling Centre, *Charges:* £4 per day (All genders), *Season:* April to February inclusive. Sunrise to sunset only, *Methods:* No nuts, 2 rods max. Carp fishing in large pond only.

Taunton Angling Association (Walton Ponds)

Contact: Mr. J.Helyer, 40 Albemarle Road, Taunton, TA1 1BA, 01823 257559, jonhelyer@btinternet.com, *Water:* Walton Ponds, Two ponds (also see entries under River & Canal Fishing), *Species:* Carp 25lb, Tench 3lb, Roach 1lb, Rudd 1lb, Pike 22.5lb, *Permits:* Topp Tackle, Taunton, (01823) 282518. Enterprise Angling, Taunton (01823) 282623. Somerset Angling, Bridgwater (01278) 431777. Street Angling, Street (01458) 447830. Wellington Country Sports, Wellington (01823) 662120. Thyer's Tackle, Burnham-on-sea (01278) 786934. Yeovil Angling Centre, Yeovil (01935) 476777. Planet Video & Angling, Chard (01460) 64000. Exe Valley Angling, Tiverton (01884) 242275. Exeter Angling Centre, Exeter (01392) 436404. Thatcher's Pet & Tackle, Wells (01749) 673513. Weston Angling Centre, Weston-Super-Mare (01934) 631140, *Charges:* Season £25. Day tickets £5 senior, £2 junior, *Season:* Open all year, *Methods:* Barbless hooks, no Carp in keepnets.

TAUNTON

Follyfoot Farm

Contact: Rupert Preston, Follyfoot Farm, North Pertherton, TA6 6NW, 01278 662979, 07748 400904, rpreston@eurobell.co.uk, *Water:* Three acre Carp lake, *Species:* Mirror, Koi and Common to 30lb, *Permits:* On the bank - self service, *Charges:* £5 per rod, *Season:* Open all year dawn to dusk. Night fishing by prior arrangement only, *Methods:* No keepnets, barbless hooks only, no dogs or radios. Full rules at the fishery.

HBS Fishery

Contact: Mr Richard Bult, HBS Fishery, Adsborough, Near Taunton, TA7 0BZ, 01823 412389, richard.bult@farmline.com, *Water:* Two lakes of 2.5 acres and half an acre, *Species:* Match Lake: Roach, Rudd, Carp, Tench, Bream (Carp to 15lb). Specimen Lake: 43 Carp between 10lb and 28lb, *Permits:* Day and night tickets sold on the bank, *Charges:* Match Lake: £4 for 12 hours, £6 for 24 hours. Specimen Lake: £6 for 12 hours, £10 for 24 hours, *Season:* Open all year except a 1 month close season to allow fish to spawn, *Methods:* No nuts. Barbless hooks etc. Full rules at fishery.

Ilminster & District A.A. (Coarse Lake)

Contact: P. Lonton, Marshalsea, Cottage Corner, Ilton, Ilminster, 01460 52519, p.lonton@ntlworld.com, *Water:* Thurlebeare - 1.5 acres, *Species:* Carp 18lb, Bream 6lb, Roach 1.5lb, Perch 2.5lb, Tench 6lb - mixed fishery, *Permits:* Enterprise Angling, Taunton and Ilminster Warehouse. Membership details from the secretary. Annual membership tickets from Ilminster Warehouse, Yeovil Angling Centre, The Tackle Shack, Chard Angling, Enterprise Angling, Taunton, *Charges:* £16 annual membership. Day tickets £4. Junior £3, *Season:* Open all year.

Taunton Angling Association (King Stanley Pond)

Contact: Mr. J.Helyer, 40 Albemarle Road, Taunton, TA1 1BA, 01823 257559, jonhelyer@btinternet.com, *Water:* King Stanley Pond (also see entries under River & Canal Fishing), *Species:* Carp 20lb, Roach 1lb, Tench 3lb, Rudd 1lb, Perch 1lb, *Permits:* Topp Tackle, Taunton, (01823) 282518. Enterprise Angling, Taunton (01823) 282623. Somerset Angling, Bridgwater (01278) 431777. Street Angling, Street (01458) 447830. Wellington Country Sports, Wellington (01823) 662120. Thyer's Tackle, Burnham-on-sea (01278) 786934. Yeovil Angling Centre, Yeovil (01935) 476777. Planet Video & Angling, Chard (01460) 64000. Exe Valley Angling, Tiverton (01884) 242275. Exeter Angling Centre, Exeter (01392) 436404. Thatcher's Pet & Tackle, Wells (01749) 673513. Weston Angling Centre, Weston-Super-Mare (01934) 631140, *Charges:* Season £25. Day tickets £5 senior, £2 junior, *Season:* Open all year, *Methods:* Barbless hooks only. No Carp in keepnets.

Taunton Angling Association (Maunsell Ponds)
Contact: Mr. J.Helyer, 40 Albemarle Road, Taunton, TA1 1BA, 01823 257559, jonhelyer@btinternet.com, *Water:* Three Ponds together comprising Maunsell Ponds (also see entries under River & Canal Fishing), *Species:* Carp 21lb, Tench 5lb, Roach 1lb, Bream 3lb, Crucians 1lb, *Permits:* Topp Tackle, Taunton, (01823) 282518. Enterprise Angling, Taunton (01823) 282623. Somerset Angling, Bridgwater (01278) 431777. Street Angling, Street (01458) 447830. Wellington Country Sports, Wellington (01823) 662120. Thyer's Tackle, Burnham-on-sea (01278) 786934. Yeovil Angling Centre, Yeovil (01935) 476777. Planet Video & Angling, Chard (01460) 64000. Exe Valley Angling, Tiverton (01884) 242275. Exeter Angling Centre, Exeter (01392) 436404. Thatcher's Pet & Tackle, Wells (01749) 673513. Weston Angling Centre, Weston-Super-Mare (01934) 631140, *Charges:* Season £25. Day tickets £5 senior, £2 junior, *Season:* Open all year, *Methods:* Barbless hooks, no Carp in keepnets.

WEDMORE

Lands End Farm Fishery
Contact: Martin Duckett, Heath House, Wedmore, BS28 4UQ, 07977 545882, *Water:* Match lake and specimen lake, total 3 acres, *Species:* Carp to 22lb (Common, Mirror, Ghost, Crucian) Grass Carp to 17lb, Bream to 8lb, Tench and Roach 2lb, Rudd, Chub, Ide, Perch, Barbel, Golden Orfe to 4lb, *Permits:* From offfice on site, *Charges:* £5/day, £3 after 4pm, £4 juniors, £4 conc, *Season:* Open all year. 7am to dusk in the summer, *Methods:* Barbless hooks only, no keepnets, no dog biscuits, boilies or nuts.

WELLINGTON

Langford Lakes (coarse lakes)
Contact: Mr. Hendy, Middle Hill Farm, Langford Budville, Wellington, 01823 400476, langford.lakes@virgin.net, *Water:* 4 lakes, one Carp specimen lake, *Species:* Carp, Roach, Perch, Tench, Bream, *Charges:* Prices on application, *Season:* Open all year dawn to dusk, *Methods:* No keepnets allowed, children under 16 must be accompanied by fishing adult.

WELLS

Emborough Ponds
Contact: Thatchers Tackle, 18 Queen Street, Wells, BA5 2DP, 01749 673513, *Water:* 3.5 acre lake, *Species:* Carp to 25lb, Tench 8lb, small Roach, *Charges:* Limited membership, please enquire at Thatchers Tackle, *Season:* 1st March - 31st December.

WINTERBOURNE

Frome Vale Angling Club (Coarse Lake)
Contact: Nigel Vigus (Secretary), 32 Rock Lane, Stoke Gifford, Bristol, BS34 8PF, 01179 759710, nvigus@ukonline.co.uk, *Water:* Half acre lake at Winterbourne. See entry under Bristol Frome.

WIVELISCOMBE

Oxenleaze Farm Caravans & Coarse Fishery
Contact: Richard & Marion Rottenbury, Chipstable, Wiveliscombe, TA4 2QH, 01984 623427, enquiries@oxenleazefarm.co.uk, *Water:* 3 lakes 2 acres, *Species:* Carp 30lb, Tench 9lb, Roach 2lb 6oz, Rudd 2lb 3oz, Bream 8lb, *Permits:* At above address, *Charges:* £5/person/day (2 Rods max), Spectators 50p/person/day, *Season:* 1st April - 31st October, *Methods:* Barbless hooks, no ground bait.

YEOVIL

Ashmead Lakes
Contact: Steve Maynard, Stone Farm, Ash, Martock, TA12 6PB, 01935 823319, *Water:* 11 acres, *Species:* Mirror and Common Carp to over 30lb, *Charges:* Syndicate water. Please phone for details, *Season:* Closed January to mid February, *Methods:* No restrictions.

Stoke Sub Hamdon & District AA
Contact: Mr Derek Goad (Secretary), 2 Windsor Lane, Stoke Sub HAmdon, (H.Q. Stoke W.M. Club, TA14 6UE, 01935 824337, *Water:* Bearley Lake, see also entry under River Parrett, *Permits:* Season permits only. Available from Stax Tackle, Montacute and Yeovil Angling Centre, Yeovil. Also available from secretary, *Charges:* Season tickets: Senior £11, Juniors/OAPs £6 (Bearley Lake). Juniors under 14 must be accompanied by an adult, *Season:* Lake open all year, *Methods:* Lake, no boilies or nut baits (lake rules apply). No night fishing.

The Old Mill Fishery
Contact: Mike Maxwell, Tucking Mill Farm, Stoford, Yeovil, BA22 9TX, 01935 414771, roz_maxwell@hotmail.com, *Water:* Three 1.5 acre lakes plus fishing on a tributary of the river Yeo and a canal, *Species:* 21 different species of coarse fish. River contains Roach, Dace, Chub and Barbel, *Permits:* On the bank, *Charges:* Permit for lakes and river £5/day (£2.50 accompanied juniors under 16yrs). £2 evening ticket 5pm onwards in summer. Club bookings taken, *Season:* Open all year 7am to dusk, *Methods:* Barbless hooks only. Keepnets permitted in winter only. No keepnets between April and October. Keepnets allowed during organised matches.

Yeovil & Sherborne Angling Association (Coarse Lakes)
Contact: Alex Murray, 2 Wisteria Close, Yeovil, BA21 2EE, 07818 098057, *Water:* Sherborne Castle Lake & discounted tickets Viaduct Fishery. Also see River Yeo entry, *Species:* Roach, Bream, Carp, *Permits:* Membership details from above & local tackle shops, *Charges:* No day tickets. River Club card £11, £2 off cost of day ticket at Viaduct.

SOMERSET Stillwater Trout

BRIDGWATER

Burton Springs Fishery (Trout Lake)
Contact: Tony Evans, Lawson Farm, Burton, Nr Stogursey, Bridgwater, TA5 1QB, 01278 732135, burtonsprings@aol.co.uk, *Water:* Approx 2 acre lake, *Species:* Brown, Rainbow, Tiger & Blue Trout, *Permits:* Self service at fishing lodge, *Charges:* 4-fish ticket £25, 2-fish/ 5hr £18, sporting ticket £12 (catch & release permitted after limit), *Season:* Open all year 8am - 9pm or dusk, *Methods:* Barbless hooks only, only Rainbow Trout may be taken.

Hawkridge Reservoir
Contact: Wessex Water, 0845 600 4 600, *Water:* 32 acre reservoir, *Species:* Brown and Rainbow Trout, *Permits:* Gary Howe (Ranger) Tel: 01278 671840, *Charges:* Day Ticket £14, Season Ticket £320, Day Concession £12, Evening Ticket £8 (no concessions). Book of Tickets - £75 for 6 available only from the ranger. Concession book of tickets £65. Boat (rowing) per day per boat £12, Boat (evening) £6, *Season:* 19th March -12th November 2003.

BRISTOL

Blagdon Fly Fishers
Contact: Steve Taylor, 16 Kings Road, Wrington, BS40 5LW, *Water:* Small club. Limited membership. Club competitions, *Species:* Rainbow and Brown Trout, *Permits:* Bristol Water issue tickets, *Charges:* £5 per year, *Season:* March to end October, *Methods:* Fly fishing only.

Blagdon Lake
Contact: Bob Handford, Bristol Water Fisheries, Blagdon Lake, Park Lane, Blagdon, BS40 7UD, 01275 332339, bob.handford@bristolwater.co.uk, *Water:* 440 Acre Lake, *Species:* Rainbow Trout best 16lb 4oz, Brown Trout best 10lb 4oz, *Permits:* Woodford Lodge, Chew Valley Lake, Blagdon Lodge and Blagdon Lake, *Charges:* Day bank £15, O.A.P. £13, Junior £7.50, Evening Bank £11 - Day boat £22.50, O.A.P. £20.50, Junior £15.50, Afternoon £18.50, Evening £15 - Season £540, O.A.P. £340 (Valid at Chew and Barrows also), *Season:* 27 March - 30 Nov 2003, *Methods:* Fly fishing only.

Bristol Reservoir Flyfishers Ass.
Contact: Roger Stenner, 18 Stafford Place, Weston-Super-Mare, BS23 2QZ, 01934 417606, *Water:* Fishing on Bristol Waterworks reservoirs. Blagdon, Chew Valley and Barrows. Competitions organised from bank or boat. Tuition offered. Full winter programme of activities including: tackle auctions, fly tying sessions, beginners and improvers casting sessions, *Species:* Rainbow and Brown Trout, fly fishing for Pike, *Permits:* Day tickets direct from Bristol Water. Club does not sell day tickets, *Charges:* £3 joining fee. Annual membership £7.50 full members, £5 pensioners and registered disabled, joining fee £1 juniors - annual membership fee juniors free, *Season:* End March to end of October (extension of season on banks and at Barron Tanks), *Methods:* Fly fishing only.

Cameley Lakes
Contact: J. Harris, Hillcrest Farm, Cameley, Temple Cloud, BS18 5AQ, 01761 452423, *Water:* One 2.5 acre lake and three 1 acre lakes plus fishing on the river River Cam, *Species:* Rainbow Trout, Brown Trout 1 - 5lb, *Permits:* Car park, *Charges:* £20 incl VAT Day ticket 4 fish, £15 incl VAT Half Day ticket 2 fish (2002 prices), *Season:* Open all year - 8.00 till sundown, *Methods:* Fly fishing only. Hooks no larger than 1 inch.

Chew
Contact: Bob Handford, Bristol Water Fisheries, Woodford Lodge, Chew Stoke, Nr.Bristol, BS40 8XH, 01275 332339, bob.handford@bristolwater.co.uk, *Water:* 1,200 Acre lake, *Species:* Rainbow Trout to 14lb 6oz, Brown Trout to 13lb 3oz, *Permits:* Woodford Lodge, Chew Lake, *Charges:* Day bank £13, O.A.P. £11, Junior £6.50, Evening bank £10 - Day boat £28.50, O.A.P. £26, Junior £20, Afternoon £23, Evening £17.00 - Season £440, O.A.P. £285 (Valid at Barrows also), *Season:* 27 March - 30 November 2003, *Methods:* Fly fishing only.

Jacklands Trout Fishery
Contact: Mr H Waygood, Jacklands Bridge, Clevedon Road, Tickenham, Bristol, BS21 6SG, 01275 810697, *Water:* 1 acre lake, *Species:* Rainbow Trout from 1.5 - 12lbs, *Permits:* On site, *Charges:* Fish @ £1.90 per lb, *Season:* Open all year dawn to dusk, *Methods:* Fly only, no catch & release.

Knowle Angling Association
Contact: Keith Caddick, 41 Eastwood Crescent, Brislington, Bristol, BS4 4SR, 01179 857974, derek.ezekiel@adsweu.com, *Water:* 2 lakes - Publow and Ackers lake at Pensford. Plus fishing at Chew Magna reservoir, (also see entry in River Fishing, Chew), *Species:* Rainbow and Brown Trout up to 8lb. Restocking for 2003 season, *Charges:* £70 annual membership. New members pay extra £5 entrance fee, *Season:* Reservoir open 25th March - 31st December. Lakes open all year, *Methods:* Fly only on lakes and upper Chew.

Litton Lakes
Contact: Bob Handford, Bristol Water Fisheries, 01275 332339, bob.handford@bristolwater.co.uk, *Water:* 7 acre lake and 11 acre lake at Coley, Nr Chewton Mendip, *Species:* Brown & Rainbow Trout, *Permits:* Woodford Lodge, Chew Valley Lake, *Charges:* £100 permit for two rods, fishing both lakes exclusively, *Season:* Open all year, *Methods:* Fly fishing only.

The Barrows
Contact: Bob Handford, Bristol Water Fisheries, 01275 332339, bob.handford@bristolwater.co.uk, *Water:* Three lakes of 25 acres (No. 1) 40 acres (No. 2) 60 acres (No.3) at Barrow Gurney, Nr. Bristol, *Species:* Rainbow Trout (10lb 10oz) Brown Trout (9lb 1oz), *Permits:* Woodford Lodge, Chew Valley Lake, *Charges:* Day bank £10.50, O.A.P. £9, Junior £6, Evening bank £8.00, Season £330, O.A.P. £215, *Season:* 27th March - 30th November 2003, *Methods:* Fly fishing only.

CONGRESBURY

Silver Springs Trout Fishery
Contact: Liz Patch, Silver Street Lane, Congresbury, BS49 5EY, 01934 877073, liz-bar@silver-springs.freeserve.co.uk, *Water:* 2.5 acres, *Species:* Rainbow Trout, *Permits:* On site, *Charges:* 4 Fish £20 - 3 fish £17 - 2 fish £14 - O.A.P./ Under 16 £18, £15 & £12 respectively, *Season:* All year, *Methods:* Fly only.

DULVERTON

Exe Valley Fishery
Contact: Andrew Maund, Exebridge, Dulverton, TA22 9AY, 01398 323328, enquiries@exevalleyfishery.co.uk, *Water:* 3 Lakes fly only (2 + 1 + 3/4 acre lakes), 1 small lake any method half acre, *Species:* Rainbow Trout, *Permits:* Day Tickets, *Charges:* Day ticket £5.50 5 fish limit, plus £3.50 per kilo,rod hire £5, *Season:* All year, *Methods:* See above.

Fly Fishing in Somerset
Contact: R.M. Gurden, 3 Edbrooke Cottages, Winsford, Nr Minehead, TA24 7AE, 01643 851504, 07814 243991, complete.angling@virgin.net, *Water:* Small stillwater, *Species:* Rainbow Trout, *Charges:* By prior arrangement only, please contact above, *Season:* Open all year, Dawn to Dusk.

Wimbleball
Contact: South West Lakes Trust, 01837 871565, info@swlakestrust.org.uk, *Water:* Information Office Hours: 01398 371372, *Species:* Premier Rainbow Fishery - Boat & Bank (boats may be booked in advance: 01398-371372). Rod average for 2002: 3.5 fish/rod/day. Biggest fish: Rainbow 11lb 9oz, *Permits:* Self service at Hill Barn Farm, *Charges:* Full day £16.75, Season £390. Reduced day £13.50, Season £295, Child/ Wheelchair £3, Season £90. Evening Monday - Friday £13.50. Season Permits can be used on any Premier Fishery only. Boats £10 per day inc. 2 fish extra to bag limits, catch & release ticket (2 fish limit £16.75). 'Wheelie Boat' available for disabled anglers (must be booked at least 48 hrs in advance). This venue may be booked for competitions, *Season:* Opens 22nd Mar 2003 - 31st Oct, *Methods:* Fly fishing only. No child U.14 years may fish unless accompanied by an adult over 18.

TAUNTON

Hawkridge Fly Fishing Club
Contact: Mrs Sally Pizii, Tumbleweed Cottage, Curry Mallet, Nr. Taunton, TA3 6SR, 01823 480710, *Water:* Primarily fishing on Hawkridge Reservoir. Club meetings 8pm second Tuesday of the month at The Blake Arms, Bridgwater. Visiting speakers & monthly competitions in season. Club trips, fly tying and social evenings, *Species:* Rainbow and Brown Trout, *Permits:* From the fishing lodge at Hawkridge Reservoir, *Methods:* Fly fishing only. Boats available.

Otterhead Lakes
Contact: M.G. Woollen, Graylings, Frog Lane, Combe St. Nicholas, Chard, TA20 3NX, 01460 65977, *Water:* See main entry for Taunton Fly Fishing Club under River Axe, Devon, *Species:* Brown Trout, Grayling, *Permits:* None available, *Charges:* On application, *Methods:* Fly only.

WIVELISCOMBE

Clatworthy Fly Fishing Club
Contact: Mr F Yeandle, 51 Mountway Rd, Bishops Hull, Taunton, TA1 3LT, 01823 283959, *Water:* 130 acre Clatworthy reservoir on Exmoor, *Species:* Rainbow and Brown Trout, *Permits:* On site from Lodge, *Charges:* Day Ticket £14/5-fish limit, Conc. £12 OAP's. Evening Ticket £8. 6 Days £75, Conc. £65. Season £320/4-fish limit (only 4 visits/week allowed), no concession on season tickets. Boats £12/day, £6 evening, *Season:* Open 20th Mar -13th Oct, *Methods:* Fly fishing only.

Clatworthy Reservoir
Contact: Wessex Water, 0845 600 4 600, *Water:* 130 acre reservoir, *Species:* Rainbow and Brown Trout, *Permits:* Contact ranger Dave Pursey on 01984 624658, *Charges:* Day Ticket £14, Season Ticket £320, Day Concession £12, Evening Ticket £8 (no concessions). Book of Tickets - £75 for 6, available only from the ranger. Concession book of tickets £65. 'Wheelie' boat available for wheelchair users. Boat (rowing) per day per boat £12, Boat (evening) £6, *Season:* 19 March - 12 October 2003.

YEOVIL

Sutton Bingham Fly Fishers Association
Contact: Dave Stacey or Colin Greenham, 01935 423223/824714, *Water:* Hold regular competitions throughout the season. For members only. Tuition available. Fly tying classes held during the close season, *Charges:* New members always welcome. Adult and junior £3 per year.

Sutton Bingham Reservoir
Contact: Wessex Water, 0845 600 4 600, *Water:* 142 acre reservoir, *Species:* Rainbow and Brown Trout, *Permits:* Contact ranger Ivan Tinsley on 01935 872389. Advisable to book boats in advance, *Charges:* Day Ticket £14, Season Ticket £320, Day Concession £12, Evening Ticket £8 (no concessions). Book of Tickets - £75 for 6, available only from the ranger. Concession book of tickets £65. "Wheelie" boat available for wheelchair users. Boat (rowing) per day per boat £12, Boat (evening) £6, *Season:* 19th March - 12th October 2002.

WILTSHIRE River Fishing

AVON HAMPSHIRE

For detailed description of the Avon, see under Hampshire river fishing

Calne Angling Association
Contact: Miss JM Knowler, 123a London Road, Calne, 01249 812003, *Water:* River Avon, River Marden and a lake, *Species:* Barbel to 8lb, Pike to 8lb, Carp to 10lb, Bream to 6lb, Rudd to 8oz, Roach to 2.5lb; Wild Carp in lake, *Permits:* T.K.Tackle, *Charges:* Please enquire at T.K.Tackle, *Season:* River: June - March, Lake: open all year, *Methods:* No restrictions.

Salisbury & District Angling Club
Contact: Rick Polden - Secretary, 29a Castle Street, Salisbury, SP1 1TT, 01722 321164, sdacsec@onetel.net.uk, *Water:* Several Stretches on River Avon at Little Durnford, Amesbury, Ratfyn Farm & Countess Water. Also fishing on Dorset Stour, River Wylye, Nadder, Bourne & Ratfyn Lake at Amesbury.Premier stocked chalkstream fishing, *Species:* All species Coarse and Game. Carp to 30lbs plus, Tench to 5lbs, Roach to 2.5lbs, Chub to 6lbs plus, Barbel to 10lbs plus, Pike to 20lbs plus, *Permits:* Enquire via Secretary at sdacsec@onetel.net.uk or club address. Day ticket available for certain waters, *Charges:* Full or Associate Membership available. Details from the secretary.Waiting list for Game membership. Enquire for prices, *Season:* Lakes: 1st June - 31st March. Rivers: 16th June - 14th March - Coarse. 15th April - 15th October - Trout. 1st February - 30th September - Salmon, *Methods:* As per rules for each fishery.

Services Dry Fly Fishing Association
Contact: Major (Retd) CD Taylor - Hon Secretary, c/o G2 Sy,HQ 43 (Wessex) Brigade, Picton Barracks, Bulford Camp, Salisbury, SP4 9NY, 01980 672161, *Water:* 7 miles on River Avon from Bulford upstream to Fifield, *Species:* Brown Trout & Grayling, *Permits:* Fishing Restricted to Serving & Retired members of the Armed Forces. for membership details apply to Secretary, *Charges:* On application, *Season:* 1st May - 15th October. Grayling until 31st December, *Methods:* Only upstream fishing permitted, dry fly exclusively during May & dry fly/nymph thereafter.

Wroughton Angling Club
Contact: Mr T.L.Moulton, 70 Perry's Lane, Wroughton, Swindon, SN4 9AP, 01793 813155, *Water:* 1.25 miles Rivers Avon and Marden at Chippenham, Reservoir at Wroughton, *Species:* Roach, Perch, Bream, Pike, Barbel, Chub, Carp, Tench, *Permits:* Mr M. Shayler, 20 Saville Crescent, Wroughton, Swindon, Wilts, Tel: 01793 637313, *Charges:* £14 per season (day tickets £5 seniors), *Methods:* Restrictions - No Boilies, peanuts, particle baits, dog biscuits or nuts of any description.

AVON WILTSHIRE

Avon Springs Fishing Lake (River)
Contact: BJ Bawden, Recreation Road, Durrington, Salisbury, SP4 8HH, 01980 653557, 07774 801401, barrie@fishingfly.co.uk, *Water:* 1 mile Wiltshire Avon at Durrington, *Species:* Brown Trout and Grayling, *Charges:* £40 day ticket, *Methods:* Fly only.

Upavon Farm
Contact: Peter C Prince, No 3, The Old Tractor Yard, Rushall, Near Pewsey, SN9 6EN, 01980 630008, 07770 922544, chris.young16@btopenworld.com, *Water:* 0.75 miles on Hampshire Avon in Wiltshire, *Species:* Brown Trout, both stocked and Wild, up to 3lb avarage 1.5lb. Wild Grayling to 2lb average 1lb, *Permits:* Day, Season Permits, *Charges:* Day - £35 weekdays, £45 weekends and public holidays, *Season:* Brown Trout commences 15th April, ends 30th September. Grayling fishing thereafter, *Methods:* Catch and release, barbless hooks excepting annual season ticket holders.

Wiltshire Fishery Association
Contact: David Griffiths, 01747 871695, d.griffiths@freenet.co.uk, *Water:* Wessex Rivers Management. *Charges:* No day tickets available from association.

BRISTOL AVON

Malmesbury to Chippenham
Coarse fisheries predominate in this section, although Trout are stocked by fishing associations in some areas. Arguably one of the best fisheries in the country, this section contains a wide range of specimen fish. Local records include: Roach 3lb 2oz, Perch 3lb 3oz, Tench 8lb 5 1/2oz, Bream 8lb 8oz, Dace 1lb 2oz, Chub 7lb 10oz, Carp 20lb 8 1/4oz and Pike 33lb 3oz. Also many Barbel to 12lb have been reported.

Airsprung Angling Association (Bristol Avon)
Contact: Ian Stainer, 36 Downavon, Bradford-on-Avon, 01225 862683, *Water:* See also entry under Kennet & Avon Canal. Bristol Avon at Bradford on Avon, Pondfields, Staverton Meadows, and between Holt and Melksham, *Species:* Carp, Pike, Bream, Chub, Roach, Rudd, Dace, Tench, Perch, etc, *Permits:* Association Licence only (no day tickets on river), *Charges:* On application, *Season:* Subject to normal close season, *Methods:* Details from Association.

Avon Angling Club (Bristol Avon)
Contact: R.P. Edwards, 56 Addison Road, Melksham, SN12 8DR, 01225 705036, *Water:* 4 miles of Bristol Avon. see also entry under Kennet and Avon Canal, *Species:* Roach, Bream, Tench, Chub, Barbel, Perch, Pike, Eels, *Permits:* Robbs Tackle, Chippenham; Wiltshire Angling, Trowbridge or call 01225 705036, *Charges:* Day ticket £3. Full Licence £14. Junior/OAP Licence £5, *Season:* Current EA Byelaws apply, *Methods:* No blood worm or joker to be used.

Bradford-on-Avon & District A.A
Contact: c/o Wiltshire Angling, 5 Timbrell Street, Trowbridge, 01225 763835, *Water:* 7 miles River Avon at Staverton and Bradford-on-Avon. 2 miles river Frome at Langham Farm nr Tellisford. 5 miles Kennet & Avon Canal, *Species:* Barton Farm: Mainly quality Bream, big Chub, Roach, Tench & Dace. Nets of Bream in excess of 100lb. Canal: Mainly Tench, Bream with good Perch & Roach. Frome: large Bream, Chub, Tench. Quality Roach, Dace and Perch. Avon: Large Bream shoals, big Chub, Carp, Roach and Perch, *Permits:* Club licence and day/weekly permits from Wiltshire Angling (5 Timbrell St. Trowbridge, 01225-763835), Haines Angling, Frome. Season/ week/ day permits available from most tackle outlets in the area, *Charges:* Senior: season: £20 / week: £10 / day: £3 - Junior, OAP, disabled: season: £9 / week: £5 / day: £1.5 (2002 prices), *Season:* June 16th - March 14th inc. Canal open all year, *Methods:* Not more than 2 rods at any one time, no more than 4 mtrs apart. Keepnets allowed; Bloodworm allowed from October 31st. No livebaiting.

Chippenham Angling Club
Contact: Mr Duffield, 95 Malmesbury Road, Chippenham, SN15 1PY, 01249 655575, sw1/964952@aol.com, *Water:* 8 miles on River Avon. Carp lake at Corsham, *Species:* Barbel, Chub, Roach, Bream, Perch, Pike, Tench, *Permits:* Robs Tackle, Chippenham: 01249 659210, *Charges:* Please telephone for prices, *Season:* June 16th - March 14th, *Methods:* No boilies or keepnets on Carp lake.

Haydon Street Angling Society (Bristol Avon)
Contact: Mike Cottle, 01793 644748, *Water:* Bristol Avon at Dauntsey, Dodford Farm, *Species:* Mixed including Chub, Barbel and Roach, Tench, *Permits:* Members only. No day tickets, *Charges:* Full membership £30. Family membership (Husband, wife & two chldren) £30. Concessions £10, *Season:* Subject to statutory close season on rivers.

Swindon Isis Angling Club (Bristol Avon)
Contact: Water: Two miles of the Bristol Avon at Sutton Benger near Chippenham. See also entry under Thames, *Species:* Bream 9lb 9oz, Perch 4lb, Tench 8lb, Barbel 11lb, Pike 28lb, Roach 2lb 7oz and usual species, *Permits:* Tackle shops in Swindon, Chippenham, Cirencester and Calne, *Charges:* As per Thames entry, *Season:* From 16th June to 14th March, *Methods:* No bans.

KENNET AND AVON CANAL

There are some 58 kilometres of canal within the Bristol Avon catchment area which averages one metre in depth and thirteen metres in width. The Kennet & Avon Canal joins the River Avon at Bath with the River Kennet between Reading and Newbury. The canal was opened in 1810 to link the Severn Estuary with the Thames. The canal, now much restored, provides excellent fishing with Carp to 25lb, Tench to 5lb also Roach, Bream, Perch, Rudd, Pike and Gudgeon.

Airsprung Angling Association (Kennet & Avon)
Contact: Ian Stainer, 36 Downavon, Bradford-on-Avon, BA14 7SG, 01225 862683, *Water:* Two kilometres on Kennet and Avon Canal from Beehive Pub to Avoncliffe aquaduct at Bradford-on-Avon, *Species:* Carp, Bream, Chub, Roach, Rudd, Dace, Tench, Perch, etc, *Permits:* Wiltshire Angling, 01225-763835; West Tackle, Trowbridge, 01225 755472, *Charges:* Day ticket £2. Full licence price on application, *Season:* Open all year, *Methods:* No night fishing, No fishing on match days in pegged areas. No radios etc. No fishing within 25 metres of locks etc. No bloodworm or joker; be aware of overhead cables !

Avon Angling Club (Kennet and Avon)
Contact: R.P. Edwards, 56 Addison Road, Melksham, SN12 8DR, 01225 705036, *Water:* 1 mile of Kennet and Avon Canal. See also entry under Bristol Avon, *Species:* Bream, Tench, Roach, Carp, *Permits:* Wiltshire Angling, Trowbridge; Robbs Tackle, Chippenham or call 01225 705036, *Season:* All year.

Devizes A.A. (Kennet & Avon Canal)
Contact: T.W. Fell, 21 Cornwall Crescent, Devizes, SN10 5HG, 01380 725189, twfell@coopertyres.co.uk, *Water:* 15 miles from Semington to Pewsey, also 6.5 acre lake, *Species:* Carp 15 - 23lb, Roach, Tench, Pike to 26lb, Bream, *Permits:* Angling Centre, Snuff St, Devizes, Wiltshire. Tel: 01380 722350. Local tackle shops in Devizes, Melksham, Trowbridge, Chippenham, Calne, Swindon. Wiltshire Angling: 01225-763835, *Charges:* Adult £20 per season. Junior £7.50. Day tickets £3.50 (not sold on the bank). 14 day ticket £8, *Season:* E.A. byelaws apply, *Methods:* Anglers must be in possession of current Environment Agency rod licence.

Marlborough & District A.A
Contact: Mr.M.Ellis, Failte, Elcot Close, Marlborough, SN8 2BB, 01672 512922, *Water:* Kennet & Avon Canal (12 miles approx), *Species:* Roach, Perch, Pike, Tench, Bream, Carp, *Permits:* Mr M Ellis, 'Failte', Elcot Close, Marlborough, Wilts, SN8 2BB, *Charges:* Full membership £30 plus £5 joining fee, Junior up to 16 £5, Ladies £5, O.A.P's £5, *Season:* Open all year. Membership from 1st Jan - 31st Dec, *Methods:* No live baiting, no bloodworm or joker.

Pewsey & District Angling Association
Contact: Don Underwood, 51 Swan Meadow, Pewsey, SN9 5HP, 01672 562541, *Water:* 4 Miles Kennet & Avon canal, *Species:* Roach, Tench, Carp, Bream, Perch, Pike, *Permits:* The Wharf, Pewsey, *Charges:* Day tickets Senior £3 / Junior/OAP £2. Prices may change for 2002, *Season:* No closed season, *Methods:* Rod and line.

NADDER

The River Nadder rises near Tisbury draining the escarpment of the South Wiltshire Downs and Kimmeridge Clay of the Wardour Vale. The River Wylye joins the Nadder near Wilton before entering the main River Avon at Salisbury.
The Nadder is well known as a mixed fishery of exceptional quality; there is a diverse array of resident species including Chub, Roach, Dace, Bream, Pike, Perch, Brown Trout and Salmon. Much of the fishing is controlled by estates and syndicates although two angling clubs offer some access to the river.

Compton Chamberlayne Estate
Contact: Simon Cooper, Fishing Breaks, Walton House, 23 Compton Terrace, N1 2UN, 020 7359 8818, info@fishingbreaks.co.uk, *Water:* Four miles of double bank fishing, divided into 7 beats, *Species:* Brown and Rainbow Trout, *Permits:* By phone or e-mail from Fishing Breaks, *Charges:* £80 per person per day plus VAT - May 1st-14th & June 16th - September 30th. £90 per person per day plus VAT - May 15th - June 15th, *Season:* May to September, *Methods:* Dry fly and nymph only.

Tisbury Angling Club
Contact: Mr E.J.Stevens, Knapp Cottage, Fovant, Nr. Salisbury, SP3 5JW, 01722 714245, *Water:* 3 miles on River Nadder. 3.5 acre lake and 2.5 acre lake, *Species:* Roach, Chub, Dace, Pike, Bream, Perch, Carp, Brown Trout, *Permits:* £5 per day Guest tickets, *Charges:* Adult £4 joining fee and £24 per season. Juniors £7.50 per season. OAPs £12.50 per season. Seniors £5 per day (dawn to dusk) Juniors £3 per day (dawn to dusk). New members welcome, *Season:* 16th June to 14th March, *Methods:* General.

SEMINGTON BROOK

The Semington Brook is spring fed from Salisbury Plain and flows through a flat area to its confluence with the River Avon downstream of Melksham. In the upper reaches and in some of its tributaries Brown Trout predominate. Downstream of Bulkington coarse fish prevail with sizeable Bream, Chub, Roach, Dace and Perch.

STOUR

See description under Dorset, river fishing.

Stourhead (Western) Estate
Contact: Sonia Booth, Estate Office Gasper Mill, Stourton, Warminster, BA12 6PU, (01747) 840643, sonia@stourhead.com, *Water:* 10 ponds and lakes, largest 10 acres, on the headwaters of the Stour, *Species:* Wild Brown Trout, *Charges:* Season permit for fly fishing £100, no day tickets.

THAMES

Haydon Street Angling Society (Hannington)
Contact: Mike Cottle, 01793 644748, *Water:* Hannington: a prime stretch of the upper Thames, *Species:* Mixed including Chub to 6lb and Barbel to 12lb, *Permits:* Members only. No day tickets, *Charges:* Full membership £30. Family membership (Husband, wife & two chldren) £30. Concessions £10, *Season:* Subject to statutory close season on rivers.

Haydon Street Angling Society (Ingelsham)
Contact: Mike Cottle, 01793 644748, *Water:* Ingelsham: a prime stretch of the upper Thames, *Species:* Mixed including Chub, Bream and Roach, *Permits:* Members only. No day tickets, *Charges:* Full membership £30. Family membership (Husband, wife & two chldren) £30. Conc. £10, *Season:* Subject to statutory close season on rivers.

Swindon Isis Angling Club (Thames)
Contact: Peter Gilbert, 31 Havelock St, Swindon, SN1 1SD, 01793 535396, *Water:* 2 mile of river Thames at Water Eaton near Cricklade, Swindon, *Species:* Barbel 9lb, Chub 4.5lb, Roach 2lb, Bream 7lb, Perch 2lb, *Permits:* Tackle shops in Swindon, Chippenham, Cirencester and Calne, *Charges:* Club Permits: Senior £34.50. OAP and disabled £12. Juniors £8. The club permit contains two free day tickets and more day tickets can be obtained for £5 each; 1/2 year starts 1 November, £12 & £6 all others, *Season:* From 16th Jun to 14th Mar, *Methods:* No bans.

WYLYE

The River Wylye rises near Kingston Deverill and flows off chalk, draining the western reaches of Salisbury Plain. The river confluences with the River Nadder at Wilton near Salisbury, then joins the main River Avon which flows south to Christchurch.
This river is best described as a 'classic' chalk stream supporting predominantly Brown Trout; hence most fisheries here are managed for fly fishermen. The fishing is predominantly controlled by local syndicates and estates.

Boreham Mill
Contact: Simon Cooper, Fishing Breaks, Walton House, 23 Compton Terrace, N1 2UN, 020 7359 8818, info@fishingbreaks.co.uk, *Water:* Half mile of double bank fishing and Hatch pool south of Warminster, *Species:* Brown Trout, *Permits:* By phone or e-mail from Fishing Breaks, *Charges:* £65 plus VAT per day one person. £115 plus VAT per day 2 people, *Season:* May to Sep, *Methods:* Dry fly & Nymph only.

Langford Lakes (river Wylye)
Contact: Wiltshire Wildlife Trust, Duck Street, Steeple Langford, Salisbury, 01722 790770, wwtlangford@wiltshirewildlife.org, *Water:* Wylye - half mile, *Species:* Brown Trout, Grayling, *Charges:* £30 Trout, £20 Grayling per rod, *Season:* Apr 15th - Oct 14th Trout season. Oct 15th - Mar 14th Grayling season, *Methods:* Full details at Fishery.

Sutton Veny Estate
Contact: Mr & Mrs A.Walker, Eastleigh Farm, Bishopstrow, Warminster, BA12 7BE, 01985 212325, enquiries@chalkstream.co.uk, *Water:* 4 miles on River Wylye. 2 miles of only wild Trout, *Species:* Brown Trout and Grayling, *Charges:* £50/day plus VAT (no beats), Season tickets upon request. Sutton Veny Fishing Syndicate - details on request, *Season:* 15th April - 15th October, *Methods:* Dry fly and upstream nymph only. Catch and release on two miles.

Wilton Fly Fishing Club
Contact: Mr A Simmons, Keepers Cottage, Manor Farm Lane, Great Wishford, SP2 0PG, 01722 790231, 07866 343593, *Water:* Over 6 miles of chalkstream on the river Wylye (including carriers), *Species:* Wild Trout. Past record 7lb 2oz. Grayling to over 2lb, *Permits:* Season membership only via Secretary: Dr. J. McGill, Garden Croft, Beech Lawn, Epsom Road, Guildford, Surrey GU1 3PE. Tel: 01483 504201, *Charges:* Prices on application to secretary, *Season:* Trout 16th April to 15th October. Grayling 16th June to 14th March, *Methods:* Trout: Dry fly and upstream nymph only. Grayling: Dry fly and upstream nymph only in Trout season. Trotting also allowed from 15th October to 14th March.

WILTSHIRE Stillwater Coarse

CALNE

Blackland Lakes
Contact: J.or B. Walden, Blackland Lakes Holiday & Leisure Centre, Stockley Lane, Calne, SN11 0NQ, 01249 813672, fishing@blacklandlakes.co.uk, *Water:* One 1 acre, One 0.75 acre, *Species:* Carp to 33lb, Tench to 5lb, Roach to 4lb, Bream to 4lb, Perch to 4lb, *Charges:* 1 rod £8, extra rods £1, concessions OAP's and children, *Season:* Open all year, *Methods:* Barbless hooks, no ground bait, no large fish or Bream in keepnets.

Bowood Lake
Contact: Estate Office, Bowood, Calne, SN11 0LZ, 01249 812109, estateoffice@bowood.org, *Water:* 6 acre lake, *Species:* Coarse, *Charges:* Season only. £100 + VAT. Junior members £50 + VAT (under 16yrs), *Season:* June 2003 - March 2004, Dawn to Dusk.

CHIPPENHAM

Chippenham Angling Club (Coarse Lake)
Contact: Mr Duffield, 95 Malmesbury Road, Chippenham, SN15 1PY, 01249 655575, sw1/964952@aol.com, *Water:* See entry under Avon. Carp Lake at Corsham, *Permits:* Members only, no day tickets.

Ivy House Lakes & Fisheries
Contact: Jo, Ivyhouse Lakes, Grittenham, Chippenham, SN15 4JU, 01666 510368, 07748 144788, *Water:* 1 Acre & 6 Acre lakes, *Species:* Carp, Bream, Roach, Tench, Chub, Perch, *Permits:* On the bank day tickets, no night fishing, *Charges:* Day tickets £5 per day (1 rod). £3 Ladies O.A.Ps etc. Match booking £5, *Season:* All year, *Methods:* Boilies & tiger nuts banned, ground bait in moderation. No fixed feeders.

Sevington Lakes Fishery
Contact: Water: 2.5 acres in 2 lakes, *Species:* Mirror & Common Carp to 26lb, Crucians, Roach, Perch, Tench & Rudd.

Silverlands Lake
Contact: Mr & Mrs King, Wick Farm, Lacock, Chippenham, SN15 2LU, 01249 730244, 07720 509377, kingsilverlands2@btinternet.com, *Water:* One spring fed 2.5 acre lake, *Species:* Carp, Tench, Bream, Pike, *Permits:* Only from the fishery, *Charges:* Day/Night tickets £5, Season tickets 12 months - £100 Adult, £65 1/2 year. £8 - 24 hour ticket, *Season:* Open all year, *Methods:* No nuts, dogs to be kept on a lead at all times.

Wyatts Lake
Contact: L. Beale, Wyatts Lake Farm, Westbrook, Bromham, Nr Chippenham, SN15 2EB, 01380 859651, beale@totalise.co.uk, *Water:* 2 acre lake approx, *Species:* Mirror and Common Carp to 20lb, *Permits:* On site, *Charges:* £5 per person (unlimited rods), *Season:* Open all year 24 hours a day. Night fishing available, *Methods:* Good fishing practices required and expected.

DEVIZES

Devizes A.A. (Coarse Lake)

Contact: T.W. Fell, 21 Cornwall Crescent, Devizes, SN10 5HG, 01380 725189, twfell@coopertyres.co.uk, *Water:* New 6.5 acre lake. Crookwood Lake well stocked, *Permits:* Angling Centre, Snuff St, Devizes, Wiltshire. Tel: 01380 722350. Local tackle shops in Devizes, Melksham, Trowbridge, Chippenham, Calne, Swindon. Wiltshire Angling: 01225-763835, *Charges:* Please phone for details, *Methods:* Anglers must be in possession of current Environment Agency rod licence.

Lakeside Rendezvous

Contact: Phil & Sarah Gleed, Devizes Road, Rowde, Nr. Devizes, SN10 2LX, 01380 725447, enquiries@lakesiderendezvous.co.uk, *Water:* 2 acre lake, *Species:* Carp - 29lb 4oz, Bream, Roach, Perch, Rudd, Tench, *Charges:* Day tickets not available individually. Hire of whole lake is possible and by prior arrangement, can fit up to 20 anglers - £90 per day, *Season:* No closed season, *Methods:* Barbless hooks, no nuts. Keepnets permitted in competition only. All nets etc. must be dipped.

MALMESBURY

The Lower Moor Fishery (Coarse)

Contact: Geoff & Anne Raines, Lower Moor Farm, Oaksey, Malmesbury, SN16 9TW, 01666 860232, 07989 303768, lowermoorfarm@btinternet.com, *Water:* 7 acre coarse fishing lake (also see entry under Stillwater Trout, Malmesbury), *Species:* Carp, Pike, Perch, Tench, Mirror, *Permits:* From office adjacent to car park, *Charges:* £5/day, *Season:* We observe close season for coarse fishing, *Methods:* Barbless hooks.

MELKSHAM

Burbrooks Reservoir

Contact: A.J. Mortimer, 3 Talbot Close, Melksham, SN12 7JU, 01225 705062, 07946 400707, *Water:* 0.75 acre Lake between Melksham & Calne, and Devizes and Chippenham in the village of Bromham (New Road), *Species:* Mirror, Common & Crucian Carp, Bream, Tench, Roach, Perch, Gudgeon, Chub, *Permits:* Please contact Melksham Angling Centre, Melksham House, Melksham: 01225 793546, or the Spar Shop in Bromham Village: 01380 850337. Calne TK Tackle: 01249 812003. Robs Tackle, Chippenham: 01249 659210. Wilts Angling, Trowbridge: 01225 763835. West Tackle, Trowbridge: 01225 755472, *Charges:* £4.50 Adults. £2.50 Juniors and OAPs, *Season:* Open all year dawn to dusk, *Methods:* No night fishing, only one rod per person, no hooks above size 8.

MERE

Gillingham & District A A (Turners Paddock)

Contact: Simon Hebditch (Hon. Secretary), 30 Meadowcroft, New Road, Gillingham, SP8 4SR, 01747 825931, 07990 690613, ditch@ham5.fsnet.co.uk, *Water:* Turners Paddock at Stourhead Nr Mere (see also entry under river fishing Stour), *Species:* Tench 6lb, Bream 7lb, Carp 15lb, Roach 2lb, Rudd 2lb, Hybrids, Perch, Eels 6lb, *Permits:* Mr P Stone (Treasurer) The Timepiece, Newbury, Gillingham, Dorset, SP8 4HZ. Tel: 01747 823339. Mr J Candy, Todber Manor Fisheries Shop, Tel: 01258 820384. Mere Post Office, High Street, Mere, Wiltshire, *Charges:* £5 day ticket, £23 season ticket. £12 juniors and concessions. (probable charges for 2003), *Season:* June 16th to March 14th, *Methods:* No fish in keepnets for more than 6 hours. Leave no litter. Feeder best for Bream & Tench.

SALISBURY

Harnham Kingfishers

Contact: John Slader, 01794 884736, slader@john5.demon.co.uk, *Water:* Open to youngsters from 10 - 16. Regular meeting covering all elements of coarse fishing, including theory and pratical. Fishing locally at Witherington Farm Fishery, with matches and competitions, *Charges:* Nominal joining fee.

Longhouse Fishery

Contact: Tinca, The Longhouse, Teffont, Nr. Salisbury, SP3 5RS, *Water:* 3 x 0.25 acre pond; 0.75 acre lake; 15 pegs in total, all deep, *Species:* Common, Mirror, Ghost, Koi, Crucian Carp (23.6lb), Roach, Rudd (2.6lb), Perch (3.9lb), Tench (3lb), *Permits:* Lakeside only, *Charges:* £5/day, £6/night, £7/24hrs, *Season:* All year 24hrs/day, only 10 days closed for pheasant shoot (October - January), *Methods:* Only bans are no particles (pulses) other than hemp or corn.

Salisbury & District Angling Club (Coarse Lakes)

Contact: Rick Polden - Secretary, 29a Castle Street, Salisbury, SP1 1TT, 01722 321164, sdacsec@onetel.net.uk, *Water:* Peters Finger Lakes, Steeple Langford and Wellow Lakes. See entry under Avon Hampshire, *Species:* Carp, Tench, Bream, *Charges:* £55 per season. Concessions for Senior Citizens & Juniors, *Season:* 1st June - 31st March.

Tisbury Angling Club (Coarse Lakes)

Contact: Mr E.J.Stevens, Knapp Cottage, Fovant, Nr. Salisbury, SP3 5JW, 01722 714245, *Water:* See also entry under Nadder (3 mile stretch). Old Wardour Lake (3.5 acre), 2 miles south of Tisbury and Dinton Lake (2.5 acre), 2 miles north of Tisbury, *Species:* Roach, Chub, Dace, Bream, Perch, Crucian Carp, Carp, *Permits:* £5 p/day guest tickets, *Charges:* Adult £25 p/season, OAP £12.50, Juniors £7.50, *Season:* 16th June - 14th March.

Waldens Farm Fishery

Contact: David & Jackie Wateridge, Waldens Farm, Walden Estate, West Grimstead, Salisbury, SP5 3RJ, 01722 710480, 07766 451173, *Water:* 5 lakes for approx 7.5 acres, *Species:* All coarse fish. Specimen Pike Lake. Specimen Carp Lake. 27 peg match Lake for club or private hire, *Permits:* From the bank, *Charges:* Day (dawn to dusk) tickets Adult £6, Junior - O.A.P. £4, Evenings 5 p.m.on £3.50, Match peg fees £4. Night fishing by appointment only, *Season:* Open full 12 months, *Methods:* Barbless hooks, net dips to be used, limited groundbait, no boilies, nuts or cereals. Keepnets allowed.

Witherington Farm Fishing
Contact: Tony or Caroline Beeny, New Cottage, Witherington Farm, Downton, Salisbury, SP5 3QX, 01722 710088, *Water:* 3 Well stocked lakes. Plus new 93 peg match lake. Toilet facilities for disabled. All swims accessible to wheelchairs, *Species:* Carp, Tench, Roach, Bream, Rudd, Chub, Perch, *Permits:* From on-site Tackle shop, *Charges:* Full day £6, Half day £4, Full day Junior under 16 / Disabled / O.A.P. £4, *Season:* All year Dawn - Dusk, *Methods:* No boilies, barbless hooks, all nets to be dipped, no night fishing, keepnets only permitted on Match lake.

SWINDON

Haydon Street Angling Society (Telford Pit)
Contact: Mike Cottle, 01793 644748, *Water:* Telford Pit: a small private lake in central Swindon, *Species:* Mixed including Tench, Roach and Perch, *Permits:* Members only. No day tickets, *Charges:* Full membership £30. Family membership £30 (Husband, wife & 2 children). Concessions £10, *Season:* Subject to statutory close season on rivers.

TROWBRIDGE

Rood Ashton Lake
Contact: Marlene Pike, Home Farm, Rood Ashton, Trowbridge, BA14 6BG, 01380 870272, *Water:* 7 acre lake available for matches - please enquire for details, *Species:* Carp, Tench, Roach, *Permits:* Home Farm and Lake View, *Charges:* 6a.m.-6p.m. £5, O.A.P's / Juniors £4. 6p.m. - 11a.m. £4, O.A.P's / Juniors £3. Please enquire for match bookings, *Season:* Open all year, *Methods:* No keepnets (only competitions). No tin cans or boilies, Barbless hooks only. No nuts. No night fishing.

Tucking Mill
Contact: Wessex Water, 0845 600 4 600, *Water:* Free coarse fishing for disabled anglers from 16th June 2002 - 14th March 2003, *Species:* Roach, Chub, Tench and Large Carp, *Permits:* The site is regularly used by disabled angling clubs including Kingswood Disabled Angling Club. For more information please contact the club secretary Mr C Goodland, 58 Horthom Close, Patchway, Bristol BS34 5SE or Telephone 0117 975 4789, *Season:* 8am to sunset throughout the year except in the close season, *Methods:* No keepnets, barbless hooks.

WARMINSTER

Longleat Lakes & Shearwater
Contact: Nick Robbins, Longleat Estate Office, Longleat, Warminster, BA12 7NW, 01985 844496, 07889 625999, *Water:* Longleat 3 Lakes, Top lake Carp up to 32lb, Shearwater 37 acres, Carp up to 25lb. Longleat, 20 Carp over 20lb, *Species:* Carp, Roach, Bream, Tench, Perch, Rudd, *Permits:* From bailiff on the bank, *Charges:* Adult £6, Junior/OAP £3, *Season:* Upon request, *Methods:* No keepnets or carp sacks, no boilies except Longleat. No nuts, peas, beans on all lakes, no bolt rigs. Barbless hooks only.

Warminster & District Angling Club
Contact: c/o Steves Tackle, 3 Station Road, Warminster, 01985 214934, *Water:* Berkley Lake - 6 acres and Southleigh Lake at Crockerton - 2 acres, *Species:* Well stocked with all coarse fish, *Permits:* Club membership only. Details from Steves Tackle.

WESTBURY

Brokerswood Country Park
Contact: Mrs S.H.Capon, Brokerswood, Westbury, BA13 4EH, 01373 822238, woodland.park@virgin.net, *Water:* 5 Acre lake within 80 acre country park, *Species:* Carp, Roach, Tench, Perch, Dace, *Charges:* Adults £4.50, Children £3, *Season:* Closed Season 12th - 23rd May, *Methods:* Barbless hooks, no boilies, no keepnets.

Clivey Ponds
Contact: Mr Mike Mortimer, Lakeside, Clivey, Dilton Marsh, Westbury, BA13 4BA, 07970 411901, mporsche956@aol.com, *Water:* 1 acre lake, *Species:* Roach, Rudd, Bream to 2lb, Perch, Carp to 12lb, Crucians, Tench to 3lb and Gudgeon, *Permits:* On the bank or from Haines Angling Centre, 47 Vallis Way, Frome Tel: 01373 466406, *Charges:* £3/Day Ticket. Juniors OAPs etc. £2/day, *Season:* All year, *Methods:* Barbless Hooks only. No Groundbait.

Cuckoo's Rest Fishing Lakes
Contact: Barry & Eileen Flack, Fairwood Road, Dilton Marsh, Westbury, BA13 4EL, 01373 826792, *Water:* 1 x 4 acre lake & 1 x 2 acre lake, *Species:* Carp 23lbs, Perch 2lbs 14oz, Rudd 2lbs, Bream 2 - 4lbs, Tench 3lbs, Roach 2 - 3lbs, Chubb 2 - 3lbs, *Charges:* £4 a day, *Season:* All year Dawn to Dusk, *Methods:* Barbless hooks.

Eden Vale A.A
Contact: A.E.D. Lewis, Secretary, Station Road, Westbury, 01373 465491, *Water:* 5.25 acre lake, *Species:* Carp (Common to 15lb, Mirror to 10lb), Bream to 3lb, Roach to 1.5lb, Perch to 1lb, Rudd to 0.75lb, possible Pike to 15lb, *Permits:* Railway Inn opposite lake (max 8/day), Haines Angling, Badcox, Frome available from July 1st, Mon.-Fri. only, *Charges:* Day: £4 adult - £3 junior. Members (restricted to 15 mile radius of Westbury) at present £15 may increase in 2003. New Members £5 joining fee. Applications to Sec. with S.A.E, must be sponsored by two existing members, *Season:* Members only May 1st - March 15th, day tickets July 1st - March 15th, *Methods:* No fixed rigs, no keepnets before June 16th, no Carp or Tench in keepnets.

WILTSHIRE Stillwater Trout

CALNE

Calstone Fishery
Contact: Estate Office, Bowood, Calne, SN11 0LZ, 01249 812102, estateoffice@bowood.org, *Water:* 3/4 acre reservoir, *Species:* Trout (Brown & Rainbow), *Charges:* Season only, £175 + VAT per rod, *Season:* 9th April 2003 - 31st October 2003, Dawn to Dusk. *Methods:* Weekly bag limits - 2 brace. All brown returned. No catch & return of Rainbow after 15th September. First 2 Rainbow must be taken on each visit.

CHIPPENHAM

Pheasant Fly Fishers

Contact: Ian Breaker, 11 Walter Sutton Close, Curson Park, Calne, SN11 0RG, 01249 819068, r2.b2@virgin.net, *Water:* None - A fly fishing club where members fish local waters and go on organised trips further afield, *Permits:* Please contact us on the number above or phone Ricky Baptista on 01225 719175 for more details. Anglers are welcome to attend one of our regular meetings at the Pheasant Inn, Bath Road, Chippenham at 8pm on the first Tuesday of each month, *Charges:* Club membership fees £20.00, *Season:* Fly fishing trips are organised throughout the year.

DEVIZES

Mill Farm Trout Lakes

Contact: Bill Coleman, Mill Farm Trout Lakes, Worton, Devizes, SN10 5UW, 01380 813138, 07761 181369, *Water:* 2 Waters of 3.5 acres each, *Species:* Rainbow Trout. All triploids from 2lb to double figures, *Permits:* Great Cheverell Post Office. One mile from fishery and open on Sunday mornings, *Charges:* 5 Fish £26, 4 Fish £23, 3 Fish £18, 2 Fish £14, 1 Fish (2hrs before dusk only) £7, *Season:* All year, 7.30am to dusk. December and January 8am to dusk. Closed every Monday except Bank Holidays, *Methods:* Fly fishing only.

MALMESBURY

The Lower Moor Fishery (Trout)

Contact: Geoff & Anne Raines, Lower Moor Farm, Oaksey, Malmesbury, SN16 9TW, 01666 860232, 07989 303768, lowermoorfarm@btinternet.com, *Water:* 2 lakes, 34 acre Mallard lake, 8 acre Cottage lake (also see entry under Stillwater Coarse, Malmesbury), *Species:* Rainbow 13lb 4oz & Brown Trout 9lb 3oz, *Permits:* From office adjacent to car park, *Charges:* 4 Fish ticket £22, 2 Fish ticket £14, Junior 2 Fish ticket £12, *Season:* March 22nd - Jan 1st 2004, 8 a.m. to dusk, *Methods:* Mallard lake - any type of fly fishing, Cottage lake - nymph or dry fly on floating line.

PEWSEY

Manningford Trout Fishery

Contact: Dr Stewart Owen, Manningford Bohune, By Pewsey, SN9 6JR, 01980 630033, mail@barset.co.uk, *Water:* 4 acre lake fed by the Hampshire Avon, *Species:* Rainbow Trout to 18lb. Brown Trout to 10lb, *Permits:* From the Woodbridge Inn, 200yds from the lake, located on A345 between Pewsey and Upavon, *Charges:* Details from the fishery. 4 fish, 2 fish and junior tickets available, *Season:* Open all year from 8am to dusk, *Methods:* Fly fishing only.

SALISBURY

Avon Springs Fishing Lake (Stillwater)

Contact: BJ Bawden, Recreation Road, Durrington, Salisbury, SP4 8HH, 01980 653557, 07774 801401, barrie@fishingfly.co.uk, *Water:* One 4 acre lake, One 3 acre lake. One mile of upper Avon chalk stream left hand bank, *Species:* Brown Trout 17lb 9oz, Rainbow Trout 15lb 4oz (2002), *Permits:* EA fishing licences available on site, *Charges:* £35 per day, £25 junior. 1/2 day £28, junior £18, eve £18, *Season:* Open all year 8.30am to 8pm, *Methods:* Fly only no lures.

Chalke Valley Fly Fishery

Contact: Norman Barter, Vella House, Bishopstone, Salisbury, SP5 4AA, 01722 780471, 07778 769223, norman@chalkefish.fsnet.co.uk, *Water:* 2 lakes. 'Home' lake 1 acre and 'Marsh' lake 2/3 acre. Both spring fed. Maximum 4 anglers on each lake, *Species:* All Brown Trout Triploids, "Catch and Release", *Charges:* Booking requested. Wheelchair access for fishing. 8am - 12 noon £20, 12 - 4pm £15, 4pm - Dusk £25, *Season:* Open 15th April until 16th October - 8am till Dusk, *Methods:* Dry fly with barbless hooks.

If you would like a FREE entry in next years directory, or on our website www.gethooked.co.uk Please write with details to: PO Box 59, Bideford, Devon EX39 4YN Or Email us at: info@gethooked.co.uk If you cannot find the fishery you are looking for in the directory please check in the advertisers index.

Every care has been taken in compiling this directory and all information is believed correct at the time of printing. The publishers cannot however accept liability for any errors or ommisions.

Fishery rules may change throughout the year, if in any doubt always contact the owner.

GAME

COARSE

SEA

TACKLE

SERVICES

HOTELS

SELF CATERING

CAMPING

CARAVANS

BED & BREAKFAST

TUITION

Advertiser's Road Directions

GAME

1. Amherst Lodge
From the A35 Bridport to Honiton road, take the Hunter's Lodge turning onto the B3165 towards Lyme Regis. After 1.4 miles turn right down Cathole Lane. Keep to the right and you will come to Amherst. Tel: 01297 442773.

2. Angling 2000 (Game & Coarse)
Over 20 beats on the Tamar, Taw, Torridge & Camel. Please telephone 01566 784488.

3. Arundell Arms Hotel
Leave the A30 Dual Carriageway east of Launceston and follow signs for Lifton. The Arundell Arms is in the centre of the Village. Tel: 01566 784666.

4. Avon Springs
Please phone 01980 653557 or 07774 801401 for road directions.

5. Bake Lakes (Game & Coarse)
A38 to Trerulefoot. At roundabout (half way between Plymouth & Liskeard) take minor road to Bake. Turn right at T-junction, then take first left. Fishery is 200 yards on right. Tel: 01752 849027 or 0498 583836.

6. Blakewell Fishery
Take A39 from Barnstaple towards Lynton. 1.5 miles from Barnstaple turn left on to B3230 and follow signs to the fishery. Tel: 01271 344533.

7. Bridge House Hotel
The fishing is located just upstream of Oakford Bridge on the A396 approx. 15 miles from junction 27 on the M5. The Bridge House Hotel is in Bampton on the B3227 (A361 to Tiverton – A396 to Bampton). Please telephone 01398 331298.

8. Bristol Water Fisheries
a. Barrows. b. Blagdon. c. Chew. d. Litton. Bristol Water fisheries are well signposted from major roads. Tel: 01275 332339.

9. Cameley Lakes
Situated 10 miles between Bristol, Bath & Wells. Off A37.Tel: 01761 452423.

10. Clinton Arms
Take the Bideford to Torrington road (A386) and approx. 5.5 miles from Bideford there is a sign to Tarka Trail. Turn left and park outside the Puffing Billy. (Car park is council owned and free). Fishing is to the right, (with Puffing Billy behind you.) Maps available at the Clinton Arms. Tel: 01805 623279.

11. Coombe Mill
From Exeter take A30. After Launceston take A395 then A39 to Camelford. After Camelford turn left onto B3266 to Bodmin. After 3 miles turn left to St Breward and Coombe Mill. Fork right to Coombe Mill then next left to "Coombe" and Penrose Burden. Drive down the hill to Coombe Mill. Tel: 01208 850344.

12. Drakelands
From Exeter take the main road to Plympton. At Newnham Industrial Estate take the Cornwood Road to Hemerdon Village. Turn right past Miners Arms, the fishery is signposted 0.75 miles on the left. Tel: 01752 344691.

13. Drift Reservoir
Take A30 towards Lands End. In Drift village, turn right (signposted "Sancreed"). Reservoir car park is approx. 1/4 mile along this lane. Ticket sales enquiries please telephone 01736 363021 before travelling.

14. Eggesford Country Hotel
At Eggesford on the A377 midway between Exeter and Barnstaple. Tel: 01769 580345.

15. Environment Agency Fisheries
Watersmeet & Glenthorne Fisheries. Directions are supplied with permits.

16. Exe Valley Fishery
M5 exit 27 to Tiverton on A361. Take A396 towards Minehead at Black Cat Junction, continue on A396 towards Minehead, at Exebridge turn left at garage on B3222, over bridge at the Anchor Inn take first right to fishery. Tel: 01398 323328.

17. Fenwick Trout Fishery
From Bodmin take A389 toward Wadebridge, continue to village of Dunmere and turn immediate left off river Camel Bridge. Fishery is signposted. Tel: 01208 78296.

18. Flowers Farm Fly Fishery
Situated mid way Dorchester and Yeovil off A37. From Dorchester take A37, travel for approx. 7 miles look out for green dome on right, 0.5 mile turn right to Batcombe, 0.5 mile turn right at T junction marked to the Friary, take second left at fishing sign, then right at bottom of hill. The fishery is at the side of St Francis Friary. From Yeovil take A37 for approx. 6 miles, turn left at crossroads marked Batcombe, take 3rd left along top Batcombe Downs at fishing sign, right bottom of hill. Continue 0.5 mile to Fishery. Tel: 01300 341351.

19. Fly Fishing in Somerset
Please contact Robin Gurden on 01643 851504. Based in Winsford. Somerset. Exmoor.

20. Half Moon Hotel
Sheepwash lies 1 mile North of Highampton (A3072) between Hatherleigh & Holsworthy. Tel: 01409 231376.

21. Highbullen Hotel
Please telephone 01769 540561 for directions.

22. Higher Cownhayne Farm
Please phone for directions. 01297 552267.

23. Innis Inn & Fly Fishery
M5 to Exeter, A30 to roundabout west of Bodmin. A391 follow signs for Eden. Two miles from Eden, follow Innis Inn & camping signs to fishery. Tel: 01726 851162.

24. Lance Nicholson River Fishing
Permits & directions available from Lance Nicholson, 9 & 11 High Street, Dulverton, Somerset. Tel: 01398 323409 - Trout & Salmon fishing on the Exe, Barle & Haddeo.

25. Manningford Trout Fishery
On A345 midway between Pewsey & Upavon, next to the Woodbridge Inn. Phone 01980 630033 for more details.

26. Nick Hart Fly Fishing
Follow A358 out of Taunton, then the B3224 signposted to Exford. Tel: 01643 831101 or 07971 198559.

27. Prince Hall Hotel
From M5 - pass Exeter, then take A38 signposted Plymouth. Take second Ashburton turn-off, the B3357 signposted Two Bridges and Princetown. Hotel is situated one mile from this point on the left and one mile before Two Bridges Junction. From Plymouth - Take A386 to Yelverton, follow signs for Princetown, continue towards Two Bridges, turn right and stay on B3357. Hotel is one mile on the right. Tel: 01822 890403.

28. Rising Sun Inn
The Rising Sun Inn is on the A377 opposite T-junction with B3227 to South Molton Tel: 01769 560447.

29. Robert Jones Fly Fishing
Please telephone 070 20 90 20 90.

30. Rockbourne Trout Fishery
Please telephone 01725 518603 for directions.

31. Roddy Rae's Devon & UK Fly Fishing School

Please telephone 01647 24643 for directions.

32. South Hill - Gortleigh Fishing

Please telephone 01409 213291 for directions.

33. South West Lakes Trust (Game & Coarse)

a-Kennick, b-Siblyback, c-Wimbleball, d-Fernworthy, e-Colliford, f-Roadford, g-Burrator, h-Stithians, i-Crowdy, j-Wistlandpound, k-Meldon, l-Avon Dam, m-Venford. South West Lakes Trust fisheries are well signposted from major roads.

34. Southwood Fishery

From Barnstaple head for Bratton Fleming. Turn right at Bratton Cross, continue for approx 1/2 mile, turn left into fishery when you see our sign and continue down lane. Tel: 01271 343608 or 344919.

35. Sutton Veny Fishing

Please telephone 01985 212325.

36. Tavistock Trout Fishery

Entrance on A386 one mile from Tavistock. Tel: 01822 615441.

37. Tree Meadow Trout Fishery

Off B3302 Hayle to Helston. Tel: 01736 850899.

38. Two Bridges Hotel

Leave M5 southbound at Junction 31 and join A38 signposted Plymouth. After 18 miles take exit signposted B3357 Princetown/Two Bridges. After 11 miles the Hotel can be seen on left hand side at junction of the B3357 & B3212. Please telephone 01822 890581 for alternative Dartmoor route.

39. Upavon Farm Fishing

From centre of Upavon take the Salisbury road A345 & access to River is on the left within walking distance from village pub. Tel: 01980 630008.

40. Valley Springs

Half a mile from Cider Press, follow official tourist signs from Frogmore or Totnes Road. Tel: 01548 531574.

41. Wessex Water (Game & Coarse)

a Clatworthy. b Hawkridge. c Sutton Bingham. Please telephone 0845 600 4 600 for further details.

42. Wiscombe Park Fishery (Game & Coarse)

Leave A30 at Honiton, take A375 towards Sidmouth, turn left at the Hare and Hounds cross roads towards Seaton, after 3 miles turn left towards Blackbury Camp, fishery signposted on the left. Tel: 01404 871474.

Advertiser's Road Directions

COARSE

1. Acorn Carp Fishery

Lampley Road, Kingston Seymour. Please telephone 01934 833760/834050 or mobile 07957 828721.

2. Alcove Angling Club

Please telephone 0117 9025737 or 07941 638680 for directions.

3. Alder Hills & Fordingbridge Fishing

From Bournemouth: follow A35 (Poole Road), past Branksome Train Station. At double roundabouts go straight across then right onto the A3040 (Alder Road) keeping Home Base on your right. Continue for 1 mile straight across both sets of Traffic Lights. As road dips you pass Dorset Knob Pub & Save Petrol Station on right. Turn right immediately into Sharp road. Fishery can be accessed at bottom of road. Tel: 07939 514346.

4. Avallon Lodges

From Launceston B3254 towards Bude town turn left at Langdon Cross (just before the Countryman Pub) then next right signed Clubworthy. Avallon is 1.5 miles along this road, up a short drive on the left. Tel: 01502 500500.

5. Avalon Fisheries

Please telephone 01278 456429 or 07855 825059 for directions.

6. Badham Farm Holidays

A30 Liskeard turn off - Follow signs for St. Keyne. At St. Keyne take left hand turn just before church signed St Keyne Well & Badham. A38 at Dobwalls turn for Duloe & St. Keyne, then from St. Keyne as A30 route. Tel: 01579 343572.

7. Bickerton Farm Fishery

Please telephone 01548 511220 for road directions.

8. Bridgwater Sports & Social Club

Please telephone 01278 446215 for directions.

9. Bristol, Bath & Wiltshire Amalgamated Anglers

Please phone 0117 9672977.

10. Bullock Farm Lakes

From Junction 20, M5 follow B3133 for Yatton. Drive through village of Kenn, turn right for Kingston Seymour. Follow signs for Bullock Farm Fishing Lakes. Tel: 01934 835020.

11. Bush Lakes

Over Tamar Bridge, at Saltash roundabout turn right (A388). Continue 3 miles to Hatt, turn left onto Pillaton road. Continue for 1.5 miles up over 1st hill, turn left at red brick corner cottage by fishery sign. Tel: 01752 842148.

12. Christchurch Angling Club (Coarse & Game)

Please enquire at local Tackle Shops or telephone 01202 490014 or 07720 671706.

13. Clawford Vineyard

Take A388 from Holsworthy to Launceston. Turn left at crossroads in Clawton. After 2.5 miles turn left at T junction. Clawford is a further 0.6 miles on left. Tel: 01409 254177 or 07786 332332.

14. Cofton Country Holiday Park

From Junction 30, M5 Exeter, take A379 signed Dawlish. Park is on the left half mile after small harbour village of Cockwood. Tel: 01626 890111.

15. Coombe Fisheries

Leave the A386 (Plymouth to Tavistock road) at Yelverton and then follow signs to Buckland Abbey. The Fishery is signposted 100yds past the Abbey entrance on the left. Tel: 01822 616624 or 07899 958493.

16. Coombe Water Fisheries

Half a mile from Kingsbridge on road to Loddiswell, B3210. Tel: 01548 852038.

17. Coombelands Coarse Fishery

Only 15 mins. from junction 28 M5. Approx. 3.5 mls from Tiverton, .75 mls from Butterleigh on the Silverton Rd, 3.5 miles from Cullompton, 1 mile from Bunniford Cross on the Silverton Rd and 3 miles from Silverton on the Butterleigh Rd. Tel: 01884 32320.

18. Cranford Inn & Holiday Cottages

Please telephone 01805 624697 for directions.

19. Creedy Lakes

Travelling south down the M5 exit at junction 27. From Tiverton take the A3072 Exeter/Crediton road. At Bickleigh bear right towards Crediton. At Crediton town sign turn right. Follow blue and white fishery signs. Tel: 01363 772684.

20. Darts Farm

Leave M5 at junction 30. Follow signs to Exmouth (A376). After 2 miles follow brown tourist signs to Darts Farm Shopping Village. Tel: 01392 875587.

21. Diamond Farm
Fishing is on river Axe at Brean. Site can be found from M5 junction 22. Follow signs for Burnham-on-Sea, Brean. On reaching Brean turn right at junction for Lympsham and Weston Super Mare on the Weston road. Diamond Farm is approx half mile from junction on left hand side. Tel: 01278 751041/751263.

22. Dutson Water (Coarse & Game)
From A30 turn off at Launceston onto the A388 to Holsworthy road. Continue for 1.5 miles from town, passing Homeleigh Angling Centre on your right. The lake is at end of 30mph sign at Dutson on right hand side down a lane. Tel: 01566 776456.

23. East Moore Farm Fishery
Please telephone 01364 73276.

24. Edneys Fisheries
Please telephone 01373 812294 or mobile 07941 280075 for directions.

25. Elmfield Farm Coarse Fishery
From Launceston take the Egloskerry road found at the top of St.Stephens Hill. About 1 mile out of Egloskerry look for the Treburtle turn off to the right. Follow Fishing signs for 3 miles, signposted on the left. Tel: 01566 781243.

26. Emborough Ponds
Please contact Thatchers Pet & Tackle, 18 Queen Street, Wells, Somerset. Telephone 01749 673513.

27. Emerald Pool Fisheries
Off the A38 at West Huntspill, turn into Withy Road by the Crossways Inn. Take the next right Puriton Road. Travel for approx. 0.5 mile, over Huntspill river, take the next track on the left. Pool on right at top of track. Tel: 01278 794707 / 685304.

28. Escot Lake
Please telephone 01404 822188 for directions.

29. Exeter & District A.A.
Please telephone 07970 483913 or enquire in local Tackle Shops.

30. Follyfoot Farm Fisheries
We are on main A38, on the Taunton side of North Petherton. Entrance to lake in first layby on the right heading south. Tel: 01278 662979 or 07748 400904.

31. Glenleigh Farm Fishery
From St. Austell take A390 towards Truro, after approx. 3 miles second hand car garage on left, turn left to Sticker, follow road to top of hill, immediately before bus shelter turn left, past mobile homes park, over bypass to bottom of hill, car park on right. Tel: 01726 73154.

32. Godney Moor Ponds
Please telephone 01458 447830 for directions.

33. Gold Oak Fisheries
Hare Lane, Cranborne. Please telephone 01725 517275 for directions.

34. Goodiford Mill Fishery (Coarse & Game)
From Cullompton take the Honiton road, continue for over a mile past Horns Cross. Turn left at signpost for Wressing, Goodiford, Dead lane. Right at end of lane, fishery on left. Tel: 01884 266233.

35. HBS Fisheries
From J25 M5 come back through Bathpool on the A38. Pick up the A361 towards Glastonbury. At Durston Elms garage turn left. After one mile turn left again at crossroads, the fishery is half a mile on the right hand side. Tel: 01823 412389.

36. Hidden Valley Coarse Fishing
Easily found 4 miles west of Launceston, just off A395, 0.5 mile from Kennards House junction with A30. Follow Hidden Valley signs. Please note Hidden Valley can now be approached from new access road. Follow Hidden Valley signs. Tel: 01566 86463.

37. Highway Farm
On main A35 between Bridport and Chideock. Tel: 01308 424321.

38. Ivy House Lakes
From Swindon to Wooton Bassett, bottom of hill turn right down Whitehill Lane. Fishery is approx. 2 miles on the left hand side. Telephone 07748 144788.

39. Kingslake Fishing Holidays
From Exeter at end of M5 take A30 to Okehampton, in the centre of Okehampton at the lights, turn right onto A386 to Hatherleigh. At Hatherleigh (7 miles) take left onto A3072 Holsworthy/Bude. Travel 7 miles then turn left at sign 'Chilla 2 miles'. Kingslake is 0.75 mile along this road on left. Tel: 01409 231401.

40. Laburnum House
Please telephone 01278 781830 for directions.

41. Lakeside House
Take A30 towards Redruth from Launceston. Take bypass, passing McDonalds & follow road after roundabout to Redruth. Take B3285 turning right towards Perranporth. After aprox. 1 mile turn left into driveway signposted Oakridge Farm. Follow private farm drive and then turn right into Lakeside. Tel: 01872 572612.

42. Lakeside Rendezvous
Easily accessed off the A342 & is approximately a 20 minute drive from Chippenham exit off the M4 motorway. We are 1.5 hours from London. Nearest train station is Chippenham with direct links to Bristol & London. Tel: 01380 725447.

43. Lands End Fishery
From M5 junction 22, turn left at first roundabout, then first left and follow road to T junction, turn left signposted Wedmore, continue through village of Mark, then into Blackford where you turn right by the school signposted Heath House. Follow road to crossroads, turn right, then second right, fishery is at bottom of lane. Tel: 07977 545882.

44. Little Allers
From Exeter: Take Wrangaton Cross exit off A38, take 2nd road on left. From Plymouth: Take Ivybridge exit off A38. Go through Ivybridge to Wrangaton. Turn right and take 2nd road on left. Tel: 01364 72563.

45. Little Comfort Farm
From Junction 27 M5 take A361 to Barnstaple. Leave Barnstaple on A361 to Braunton, pass through Braunton still on A361 towards Ilfracombe. Pass through Knowle village on A361. After 2/3 mile turn right towards Halsinger at Heddon Mills Cross. Proceed 1.8 miles turning left at the 2nd crossroads, then left again after a short distance. Continue for one mile down winding lane over small bridge and take 2nd entrance into Little Comfort Farm. Tel: 01271 812414.

46. Longleat & Shearwater
From Warminster take 362 towards Frome, follow signs to Longleat. Further information from the bailiff, Nick Robbins on 01985 844496 or 07889 625999.

47. Lower Hollacombe Fishery
Please telephone 01363 84331 for directions.

48. Luccombes Fishery
From Exminster: Enter Exminster from Exeter on A379, pass the shops on right and Victory Hall on left, take first right into Days Pottels Lane, then next left into Towsington Lane, the fishery is situated approx. 0.5 mile on the left. Tel: 01392 832858.

49. Mangerton Valley Coarse Lake.
From Bridport take 3066 North for approx. two miles. Continue straight across mini roundabout, then turn immediately right. Look out for our sign after one mile. Tel: 01308 458482.

50. Meadowside Fishery
Located on A39, just south of the roundabout junction with B3274 at Winnards Perch, within the Cornish Birds of Prey Centre at St. Columb Major. Tel: 01637 880544.

51. Mellonwatts Mill Coarse Fishery
From St. Austell take A390 Truro road to end of Sticker bypass, then road signposted Tregoney and St. Mawes. Turn left after 1 mile for Mevagissey. Fishery 2nd farm on right. Tel: 01872 530808.

52. Middle Boswin Farm
Take Scorrier exit off the A30, follow signs to Helston (B3297) through Redruth. Take B3297 for approx. 5 miles passing Four Lanes, Nine Maidens, Burras and Farms Common. Turn Left at sign to Porkellis, follow for less than a mile. Turn left after White Bridge Weare 0.5 mile on left. Tel: 01209 860420.

53. Milemead Fisheries (Coarse & Game)
From Tavistock take B3362 (old A384) towards Launceston. Take turning left just outside Tavistock signposted Mill Hill. Entrance is 1 mile down lane on right. Tel: 01822 610888.

54. Millbrook Fishery
Approach Millbrook on B3247, follow brown Tourist Signs from Tregantle Fort. Tel: 01752 823210.

55. Millhayes Fishery
2 miles from junction 28 (M5) on the A373 towards Honiton turn left at Post Cross to Kentisbeare. 1 mile to village centre, turn right at Post Office and go down hill for 300yds, turn right at sign for Millhayes. Tel: 01884 266412.

56. Minnows Camping & Caravan Park
From the North or South exit M5 at junction 27 onto A361 signposted Tiverton. After about 600 yards take first exit signposted signposted Sampford Peverell. Turn right at next roundabout, cross bridge over A361. Straight across at next roundabout signposted Holcombe Rogus. Site is on left. From N. Devon on the A361 - go to end of A361 to junction 27 of the M5. Go all the way round and return back onto the A361. Then follow the above directions. Tel: 01884 821770.

57. Nance Lakes
From A30 take holiday route to St. Ives. Follow signs for holiday route for approx. 2 miles. Fishery is signposted on the left hand side. Tel: 01736 740348.

58. Nanteague Farm
We are situated on the main A30 between the Chiverton & Carland Cross roundabouts. From South on main A30 pass Zelah on dual carriageway and 2 miles further on through the hamlet of Marazanvose on the brow of the hill opposite Town & Country Nissan Garage you will find our entrance. Tel: 01872 540351.

59. New Barn Angling Centre
From Paignton bypass traffic lights, take the A385 to Totnes/Plymouth. Turn left after 2 miles into farm track signposted New Barn Angling Centre. From Totnes take the A385 to Paignton, turn right 200 yards past the Texaco garage into farm track signposted New Barn Angling Centre. Tel: 01803 553602.

60. New Forest Water Park
From Ringwood head towards Fordingbridge on A338. After 4 miles you will see signs on the left. Tel: 01425 656868.

61. Newberry Farm Fishing
On A399 western edge of Combe Martin village. Tel: 01271 882334.

62. Newcourt Ponds
Take junction 28 M5 into Cullompton town centre, follow B3181 towards Exeter for 2 miles. At Merry Harriers Inn turn left. After hump backed bridge turn right, at top of road turn right. Ponds 100yds on left. Tel: 01884 277326.

63. Newton Abbot Fishing Association
Please telephone 01626 331613/200198 for directions.

64. Northam Farm
Leave the M5 at junction 22. Follow signs to Burnham-on-Sea, Brean. Continue through Brean village and Northam Farm is on the right half a mile past Brean Leisure Park. Tel: 01278 751244.

65. Oakside Fishery
From Newquay take road to Quintrell Downs, at roundabout at Quintrell Downs take A3058, continue to Dairyland, first left, past Dairyland (signposted White Cross). Fishery is 1 mile down road on right hand side. Tel: 01637 871275.

66. Oaktree Carp Farm & Fishery
From Barnstaple take the A361 to Newtown. Left onto B3227 Bampton Road for 2.5 miles and left at fishery signpost. Down hill and entrance signposted on right. From M5 junction 27 take A361 to Newtown, then as above.T el: 01398 341568.

67. Osmington Mills
Approaching from Wareham on the A352 Dorchester road turn left at the A353 Weymouth junction. At the Osmington Mills sign opposite the Garage, turn left and follow the lane to Holiday Park. Approaching from Weymouth, follow the A353 Wareham road. Pass through Osmington and turn right at the sign for Osmington Mills. Follow lane to Holiday Park. Tel: 01305 832311.

68. Plantation Lakes
From Bristol - Weston-Super-Mare A370. Turn towards Yatton B3133 at Congresbury traffic lights. Go right through Yatton. Turn left towards Kingston Seymour. Just after the Bridge Inn. At village take middle lane. From M5 junction 20. Clevedon. Turn left at both roundabouts onto B3133 towards Yatton, after approx 3 miles turn right towards Kingston Seymour. At village take middle lane. Tel: 01934 832325.

69. Retallack Waters
Just off the A39 between Newquay and Wadebridge at Winnards Perch, signposted 'American Theme Park'. Tel: 01637 881160.

70. Ringwood & District A.A.
Please contact Tackle shops in Ringwood area or Telephone Caroline Groom on 01202 525615.

71. Rood Ashton Lake
Leave A350 heading through West Ashton Village. Take next left signed Rood Ashton, continue past East Town Farm, turn left. Home Farm is 0.5 mile on left, you will see a sign. Tel: 01380 870272.

72. Salmonhutch Fishery
A377 to Crediton, turn left after Shell Garage, follow road signed Tedburn St Mary for 1.5 miles, right at junction marked Uton, follow fishery signs. Tel: 01363 772749.

73. Silverlands Lake
From M4 Junction 17 take the A350 south (Chippenham bypass) continue for approx. 8 miles, still on the A350, you will be on the Laycock bypass. After passing a turn on the left for Lacock and on right for Whitehall Garden Centre, take the next turn on the right Folly Lane West, continue along this lane, under railway bridge to the No Through Road where you will see the sign for Wick Farm. Tel: 01249 730244.

74. Simpson Valley Fishery
1.5 miles from Holsworthy on main A3072 Holsworthy to Hatherleigh road. Tel: 01409 253593.

75 South Farm Holiday Cottages
Between the villages of Blackborough & Sheldon. Please telephone 01823 681078 for route.

76. South View Farm Fishery
From Bristol follow M5 onto A38. After 1.5 miles turn off into Kennford. Continue through village following Dunchideock signs until Shillingford signs are seen. Follow Shillingford signs. Entrance to fishery on left at sharp bend before village. From Plymouth turn left off A38 following Dunchideock until sign for Clapham is seen on right heading down the hill. At Clapham follow signs for Shillingford. From Exeter follow signs to Alphington then Shillingford St. George. Fishery on right after village. Tel: 01392 832278.

77. South West Lakes Angling Association
Please telephone 01884 256721 for directions.

78. South West Lakes Trust (Coarse & Game)
a-Slade. b-Jennetts. c-Darracott. d-Melbury. e-Trenchford. f-Upper Tamar. g-Squabmoor. h-Old Mill. i-Crafthole. j-Porth. k-Boscathnoe. l-Argal. m-Bussow. South West Lakes Trust fisheries are well signposted from major roads.

79. Spires Lakes
On the A3072 Holiday Route (HR) from Crediton.Turn right at Newlands Cross towards Sampford Courtney. Spires Lakes are on the left after approx. 0.5 mile. Tel: 01837 82499.

80. Stafford Moor Country Park
Clearly signposted on the A3124, 3 miles North of Winkleigh, 9 miles South of Torrington. Tel: 01805 804360.

81. Sunridge Fishing Lodge
Travelling west on A38, just after South Brent take slip road for National Shire Horse Centre, turn left, travel 2 miles to crossroads, turn right onto B3210, continue 3 miles to T junction, turn right onto A379 towards Plymouth, continue 2 miles to second cross roads (just before garage) and turn right. Travel 1 mile and you will find the lodge on left. Tel: 01752 880438.

82. Tan House Farm Lake
M4 exit Junction 18 onto A46 Stroud to Chipping Sodbury on to B4060 Wickwar. Continue until see Rangeworthy sign, turn left into Bury Hill Lane. Alternatively M5 to junction 14 to Wickwar to Choipping Sodbury B4060 for 1.5 miles. Take 3rd road on right to Rangeworthy and Bury Hill Lane. Tel: 01454 228280.

83. The Sedges
Please telephone 01278 445221 for directions.

84. Thorney Lakes
Directions from A303 to Muchelney. Turn off A303 dual carriageway signposted Martock Ash. Follow signs to Kingsbury Episcopi, at the T junction in village turn right, through the village of Thorney, over river bridge & disused railway. Lakes are on left. Tel: 01458 250811.

85. Town Parks Coarse Fishing Centre
From Paignton take the A385 towards Totnes. Look for signs to Town Parks, approx 2.5 miles on the right. Tel: 01803 523133 or 07973 433109.

86. Trencreek Farm Holiday Park
4 miles south west of St. Austell. On the A390 fork left on to the B3287. Trencreek is one mile on, on the left. Tel: 01726 882540.

87. Upham Farm Carp Ponds
From J30 on M5, take A3052 signposted Sidmouth. After approx 4 miles, after pasing White Horse Inn on right, sign to fishery will be seen on left. Turn left and after 700 yds fishery will be found on left hand side. Tel: 01395 232247.

88. Viaduct Coarse Fishery
From Yeovil take the A37 north towards Ilchester and then the B3151 to Somerton. Turn left onto the B3153 (Signposted Somerton) and go up hill to mini roundabout. Go straight over roundabout and take first right through housing estate to T-junction. Turn left and almost immediately first right onto track to fishery. Tel: 01458 274022.

89. Waldens Farm Fishery
Off the A36 Salisbury to Southampton road near Whaddon. Telephone for further details 01722 710480 or 07766 451173.

90. Warren Farm Holiday Park
Leave the M5 at junction 22 and follow the B3140 past Burnham on Sea to Berrow & Brean. We are situated 1.5 miles past Brean Leisure Park. Tel: 01278 751227.

91. Warren Park Farm
A31, just past Ringwood take B3081, about 1 mile fork right to Alderholt. On entering Alderholt turn left into Ringwood Road, as road bears right farm on the left. Tel: 01425 653340.

92. Week Farm
From Exeter bypass Okehampton, leave A30 dual carriageway at Sourton junction. At end of sliproad cross A386 at staggered crossroad (signposted Bridestowe). Week signpost on right after 1.5 miles (bottom of hill left 0.5 mile). Or, from Bridestowe village turn right towards Okehampton, pass garage on left & take next left, Week is 0.75 mile. Tel: 01837 861221.

93. Wessex Water (Game & Coarse)
a Clatworthy. b Hawkridge. c Sutton Bingham. Please telephone 0845 600 4 600 for further details.

94. West Pitt Farm Fishery
Junction 27 off M5, take Barnstaple signed dual way, almost immediately exit signed to Sampford Peverell. Right at mini roundabout, straight over second roundabout. Turn left signed to Whitnage, next right, then at Pitt Crossroads turn left. Fishery is a few 100 yds on left. Tel: 01884 820296.

95. White Acres Country Park
Please telephone 0845 458 0065.

96. Witherington Farm Lakes
2 miles out of Salisbury on A36 fork right as dual carriageway starts, then first right again after about 0.5 miles. Follow signs for Downton and Stanlynch. Witherington Farm is about 3 miles on the right. Tel: 01722 710021/710088.

97. Wood Farm Caravan Park
7 miles west of Bridport on A35, entrance off roundabout with A3052 (access to fishing through caravan park). Tel: 01297 560697.

98. Wooda Farm Park
From the A39 take the road signposted Poughill, Stampford Hill, continue 1 mile, through crossroad. Wooda Farm Park is 200 yds on the right. Tel: 01288 352069.

99. Wooda Lakes Holiday Homes
From M5 turn onto A30 towards Okehampton. After about 25 miles take turning for Holsworthy. On reaching Holsworthy turn right at Bude Road Garage signposted Chilsworthy. Follow road for about 4 miles then turn left at Youlden Moor crossroads. After 1.5 miles Wooda Lakes will be straight in front of you. Tel: 01409 241934.

100. Woolsbridge Manor Farm
Please telephone 01202 826369 for directions.